EARLY MESOPOTAMIA

EARLY

Montante Family Library
D'Youville College

MESOPOTAMIA

Society and economy at
the dawn of history

J.N. POSTGATE

Routledge
Taylor & Francis Group

LONDON AND NEW YORK

First published in 1992
by Routledge
11 New Fetter Lane, London EC4P 4EE

Reprinted in hardback and first published in paperback,
with revisions, in 1994 by Routledge

Simultaneously published in the USA and Canada
by Routledge
29 West 35th Street, New York, NY 10001

Reprinted in 1995, 1996, 1999, 2002, 2003(twice)

Routledge is an imprint of the Taylor & Francis Group

© 1992, 1994 J.N. Postgate

Typeset in 11/13pt Sabon Monophoto
Printed and bound by Bell & Bain Ltd., Glasgow

All rights reserved. No part of this book may
be reprinted or reproduced or utilised in any form
or by any electronic, mechanical, or other means,
now known or hereafter invented, including
photocopying and recording, or in any
information storage or retrieval system, without
permission in writing from the publishers.

British Library Cataloguing in Publication Data
Postgate, J. Nicholas
   Early Mesopotamia: society and economy at the dawn of history.
   I. Title
   935

Library of Congress Cataloguing in Publication Data

Postgate, J.N.
   Early Mesopotamia: society and economy at the dawn of history/Nicholas Postgate.
      p.   cm.
   Includes bibliographical references and index.
      1. Iraq–Civilisation–To 634. 2. Iraq–Economic conditions.
I. Title
DS73.1.P67   1992
935–dc20 91–33767

ISBN 0–415–00843–3 (hbk)
ISBN 0–415–11032–7 (pbk)

Printed on permanent paper in accordance with American Information Standards Organisation
(NISO) – 199x – proposed standard (revision of 239.48–1984)

DS 69.5
.P64
1994

This book is dedicated
to the people of Iraq.

JUN 10 2004

Contents

Texts

Figures

Preface and acknowledgements

The need for this book was brought home to me on my return to Cambridge in 1981 to succeed Margaret Munn-Rankin in the teaching of ancient Near Eastern history and archaeology. The archaeology of Mesopotamia had always formed part of the first-year course for all archaeology students, but there was no single book which exploited Mesopotamia's special advantage – the opportunity to combine documentary and archaeological evidence. The book therefore sets out to describe an early state in terms sufficiently broad for the general reader, but with enough detail to help the specialist and to convey the wealth of information still to be recovered. The result is more history than archaeology, but my intention has been to bring the two disciplines closer together, and this is reflected in the number of illustrations: there are far more of these than originally intended, but they imposed themselves on the text as it proceeded. Quotations from the cuneiform sources are treated in the same way as illustrations so as to unclutter the narrative. The translations have all been compared with the original text, although I have often borrowed them with few or no changes from the previous translator.

A glance at the bibliography will convince the reader that detailed study of ancient Mesopotamia requires a knowledge of German and French, but after each chapter I have recommended a few titles, mostly in English, which would serve to take the reader more deeply into the issues.

In writing this book my principal debt has been to Professor Marvin Powell, who read the majority of the text in draft, suggested improvements to style, substance and accessibility, and saved me from a number of serious howlers. I am very grateful to him for giving unstintingly of his time and his expertise.

Professor Peter Steinkeller advised and corrected me on points of detail in the translation of some of the texts, for which I am very grateful, as I am to Jean Bottéro, Tina Breckwoldt, Jean-Marie Durand, Peter Laslett and Roger Matthews for answering questions and supplying information.

I am greatly indebted to many colleagues who have freely offered help with illustrations, whether by supplying them or by giving permission to use them, or often both: to Professor R. McC. Adams, P. Amiet, Professor John Baines, Professor Dr R.-M. Boehmer, Dr A. Caubet, Dr Dominique Collon, David Connolly, Dr G. van Driel, Professor Jean-Marie Durand, Dr Uwe Finkbeiner, Dr Lamia al-Gailani, Dr L. Jakob-Rost, Professor Wolfgang Heimpel, Dr Bahijah Khalil Ismail, Dr Stefan Kroll, Professor Jørgen Laessøe, Professor Jean-Claude Margueron, Dr Roger Matthews, Helen McDonald, Dr Roger Moorey, Professor Raouf Munchaev, Professor Paolo Matthiae, Professor Hans Nissen, John Ray,

Dr Julian Reade, Miss Nancy Sandars, Dr U. Seidl, Professor Elizabeth Stone, Dr Geoffrey Summers, Dr Maurizio Tosi, Christopher Walker, Dr Trevor Watkins, Professor Dr G. Weisgerber. Thanks are also due to the museums that have permitted the use of their photographs: The British Museum, the Musée du Louvre, the Vorderasiatisches Museum in Berlin, the Oriental Institute Museum in Chicago, and the Iraq Museum, where special thanks go to Dr Sabah Jassim, Director, and to Dr Muayad Saeed Damerji, Director-General; also Cambridge University Library. I am very grateful to Tonia Sharlach for her help with the bibliography, to Andy Boyce for drawing Figure 3:7 and contributing to its interpretation, and to Elizabeth Postgate for help with drafting work. My thanks also go to the staff at Routledge: to Andrew Wheatcroft, and to Hilary Moor, Jill Rawnsley and Liz Paton for dealing very efficiently with a difficult manuscript. Finally, my thanks go to Trinity College, Cambridge, for support in various forms, including a grant towards the cost of gathering and reproducing the illustrations.

This book would not have been possible if I had not lived in Iraq. I would like to record my lasting gratitude to the modern inhabitants of Mesopotamia for their constant courtesy and hospitality, in homes and offices, in city and countryside, and in times good and bad.

Note to paperback edition: a few factual errors and misprints have been corrected, and some additional references added to the Notes and Further reading. My thanks to Bendt Alster, Rainer Boehmer, Tina Breckwoldt, Jerrold Cooper, Stephanie Dalley, Igor Mikhailovich Diakonoff and Dietz Edzard for pointing out mistakes and suggesting additions.

J.N. Postgate
1991, 1994

Note

In the transliteration of cuneiform texts certain conventions are used. The letter š is the equivalent of English sh; ṣ is the emphatic s encountered in Akkadian and other Semitic languages. In cases where the distinction is needed, **bold face** is used for Sumerian, *italics* for Akkadian words. Square brackets – [ ] – enclose portions of a text which are missing on the original but have been supplied in translation. When citing Sumerian I have dispensed with the diacritics used by specialists, except in a few cases where it seemed desirable to retain them.

The metrology of Mesopotamia is enormously complex, but in citing cuneiform documents some measures of weight, volume, etc. cannot be avoided. I have not adopted a rigid approach since (as explained in the Epilogue) there is no attempt to broach the quantitative aspects of the record. Nevertheless, the following list with approximate modern equivalences may be helpful to the reader. The tables are deliberately restricted to measurements used in the text; for the details of the complete systems see Powell 1989.

Length	1 stage	**danna**	*berum*	= 10.8 km	
	1 cubit	**kuš**	*ammatum*	= 0.5 m	
Area:	1	**bur**		= 6.48 ha	= 3 **eše**
	1	**eše**		= 2.16 ha	= 6 **iku**
	1	**iku**		= 0.36 ha	= 100 **sar**
	1	**sar**		= 36 sq.m	
Weight:	1 talent	**gun**	*biltum*	= 30 kg	= 60 minas
	1 mina	**mana**	*manum*	= 500 g	= 60 shekels
	1 shekel	**gin**	*šiqlum*	= 8 g	
Capacity:	1 bushel	**gur**		= 300/240 litres	= 5/4 **bariga**
	1	**bariga**		= 60 litres	= 6 **ban**
	1	**ban**		= 10 litres	= 10 **sila**
	1	**sila**	*qum*	= 1 litre	

Notes:

(1) The bushel in particular varied in the number of lesser units it contained, between different cities and dates; 300 **sila** is the norm from the Akkad Dynasty on.

(2) In some passages I have used the 'Sollberger convention' for this series, in which expressions such as 2.3.1 would refer to the 3 highest units in the series, thus: 2 **gur** 3 **bariga** 1 **ban**.

Prologue

The history of the western world begins in the Near East, in the Nile Valley and in Mesopotamia, the basin of the Tigris and Euphrates. Here two contemporary but strangely differing cultures served as the centres from which literate civilization radiated. Egypt, physically constrained within the narrow strip of the Nile Valley and isolated from western Asia, retained its highly idiosyncratic identity with little infusion from elsewhere, and did not export its language or script or other artistic forms, except upstream to Nubia. Mesopotamia was open along both flanks to intrusion from desert and mountain, and its cuneiform script was exported across thousands of miles and adapted to a great variety of languages. The record of the early stages of these two formative cultures also comes to us in different shapes: most of the early records surviving from Egypt are formal texts with a ceremonial or religious content, and much of our knowledge of their life comes from the superb detail of the tomb paintings. For Mesopotamia very little pictorial evidence has survived, but the durability of the clay tablet has given us enormous sheaves of written detail about the organization of early society.

A new account of the world's earliest urban civilization will always be needed, not least because the mass of documentary evidence is far from even a preliminary exploitation, and growing every year. Some explanation of the approach I have adopted may however be a good thing. Existing books on Mesopotamian history and civilization have usually been written by philologists working from the texts: they see the third and early second millennia as the first half of a 3000-year tradition of cuneiform culture in the Tigris–Euphrates basin, and indeed this is the case. I have deliberately taken a different course. First, I have stayed within the early period. There are various reasons for this. The documentary base is much richer at this time than later (although literary and religious texts are much rarer), both in numbers and in variety. We can therefore say much more in detail about the social and economic scene. Then, there is a major hiatus about 1500 BC, which to my mind divides the world of the ancient Near East decisively into two. The Old Babylonian world has deep roots in the third millennium BC: its documentary sources are mostly of a rather different nature from those of the third millennium, giving us more qualitative detail over a wider range of topics and less solid quantitative data, but time and again we find an assumption about the third millennium, extrapolated from the extra detail of the Old Babylonian period, is eventually vindicated by a contemporary reference. An understanding of early Mesopotamia is no more dependent on knowledge of the world after 1500 BC than fifth-century Athens requires a knowledge of the Byzantine Empire. Whereas the Kassite and Middle Assyrian kingdoms are the inheritors of the cultural traditions of Babylon, politically they belong to quite another order, well worthy of study in their own right but very different. Generalities can be made about the period 3000–1500 BC with some profit, but to attempt to generalize for the entire sweep of Mesopotamian civilization often reduces the statements to meaninglessness.

Chronologically, therefore, our subject is Mesopotamia from 3000 to 1500 BC. It is aggravating that no convenient term is available to refer to this period as a whole, but the phrase 'Early Mesopotamia' has been used by others before me, and will have to serve. Geographically, both South Mesopotamia, the alluvial Tigris and Euphrates plain, and North Mesopotamia, the lands between the Zagros, the Anatolian plateau and the Euphrates at Carchemish, are equal partners in the civilization of the third and second millennia. This book however concentrates on the south because it is only during the second millennium that the available documentary sources allow us to say much about the north. Further, the society and economy of the north are palpably different, and since my effort has been to give a coherent account of these aspects it is not helpful to jump about and include the occasional reference to the north where it happens to appear relevant. My apologies, therefore, to Subartu for seeming to ignore it, and let me stress here that this is not intended to diminish the importance of its contribution. That there is frequent reference to Mari and its amazing archives and discussion of Assur's merchant colonies in Turkey is only apparently an exception, since these two cities can be seen as outposts of the southern culture.

Most other general books about Mesopotamia are written by archaeologists for archaeologists. Some take us through prehistory, treating early historical Mesopotamia as the culmination of a process but not usually according it a detailed description in its own right; others are straightforward accounts of the archaeology, art and architecture. This book is designed to fill a void, by describing early Mesopotamia from the written sources, but in terms which will be useful to the archaeologist, whether a Mesopotamian specialist or from elsewhere. This means eschewing the traditional historical enumeration of kings and dynasties, and directing attention to those aspects of the culture which are most easily correlated with the archaeological evidence. There is a blatant proselytizing motive behind this. While the historian or anthropologist is usually willing to look back in time to an earlier world (and I hope they will find this account enlightening), the prehistorian all too often ignores what came later. Yet those who work with early administrative texts are continually aware that they contain detail on precisely those activities which can be reflected directly in the archaeological record. Mesopotamia should be able to offer archaeologists working in all comparable fields with a series of paradigms, in which the pure excavated record can be compared with documentary sources as a check on the deductions frequently made without such a cross-check. At present we are far from achieving this, because there are not enough specialists working with the cuneiform sources, and not enough archaeologists collecting evidence in the form required to enable such comparisons.

Concentration on the social and economic aspects of the society is therefore deliberate, and determined in good measure by the nature of the available documentation. It is in no way intended to belittle the importance of the less material aspects of the civilization, those reflected in 'literary' and 'religious' texts: in current archaeological usage, the 'symbolic' as opposed to the 'functional'. Although political ideology finds a place in chapter 16, I am conscious that my own specialization has left on one side much that should be said about the religion and the scribal world of early Mesopotamia. That would need a different book, not least because it would require constant reference to the cuneiform tradition after 1500 BC; for the present, A.L. Oppenheim's book, *Ancient Mesopotamia* (Chicago, 1964), covers much of this ground, but it is beyond question that more general study of the literature and religion of the early period by real specialists is desperately needed. Space has conspired with my own ignorance to confine my remarks on technical subjects like mathematics, music or astronomy to the minimum, but this should not be taken to imply that they are not important ingredients in Mesopotamian civilization. Some important topics, perhaps most notably taxation, have not been sufficiently studied by the specialists for me to have attempted even a provisional account. Others, like the origins of writing or foreign trade, seem to me to have attracted plenty of attention in recent years and I have kept my treatment of them brief for this reason. The astonishing wealth of detail from the palace archives of Mari is not perhaps exploited as much as it should be: but here again two recent books (Malamat 1989; Dalley 1984) afford an opportunity for the English reader to learn about some of the recent work.

Part I

Setting the scene

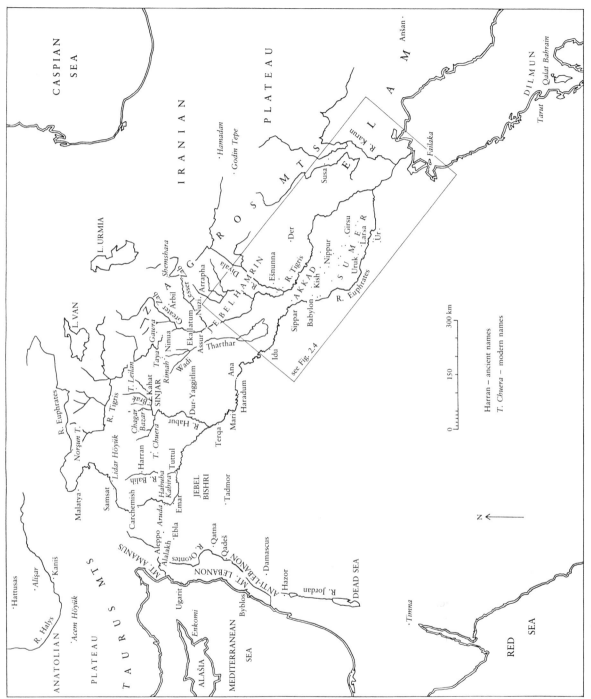

Figure 1:1 The Near East 3200–1600 BC

1

Mesopotamia: the land and the life

The name 'Mesopotamia', coined for a Roman province, is now used for the land between the rivers Tigris and Euphrates, and in many general books it features as the eastern horn of the 'fertile crescent'. The Mesopotamian heartland was a strip of land wrested by human vigilance from adverse climatic conditions. Its geography is essential to the understanding of its history: it defines the lifestyle of the agricultural community, and thereby of the city. It preordains the location of settlements and of the routes between them. Extremes of temperature and abrupt changes in landscape divide the area into very distinct environments, which can be blocked out on a map much more clearly than in most temperate parts of the world. The different zones favour or impose different lifestyles, which have often coincided with ethnic and political divisions and so have a direct impact on history. Sometimes it is the physical conformation of the country that has an obvious effect on its human geography: mountain ranges act as barriers to communication, plains enable it and rivers channel it. Major political units grow up in areas of easy communication, whether in the South or North Mesopotamian plain – Sumer, Babylon, Assyria – or on the Iranian or Anatolian plateaux – Elam, the Hittite Empire, Urartu; the intervening mountain ridges and valleys of the Taurus and Zagros, like so many mountainous areas in the world, foster local independence and discourage the rise of larger groupings, political, ethnic and linguistic. Here there were never major centres of cultural diffusion, and it was on the plains of North and South Mesopotamia that social and political developments were forged.

Our approach to Mesopotamia is that of many westerners before us, from Herodotus on, drawn by the reports of ancient cities in a fertile plain. Coming from the Mediterranean past Aleppo, the point of departure is a quay on the right bank of the Euphrates where it flows almost due south after leaving the Turkish mountains. Here at different times Zeugma (Birecik), Carchemish, Emar, and before history Habuba Kabira were the principal ports. As we float downstream, we leave behind us the agricultural lands which stretch almost unbroken from the Euphrates along the foot of the Turkish hills, and the river cuts its way through a dry plain on each side (Figure 1:2). Here and there along its course there is a village, or sometimes a small town, with orchards and crops flourishing on the alluvial soils left by the river and occasional side wadis in the bottom of the valley, but in the entire 700 km stretch the places of historical importance can be counted on the fingers of one hand: just below the junction with the Habur was the city of Terqa, already important

Figure 1:2 The Euphrates at Ana looking east. In the river, piers of a medieval bridge link the right bank to the island; on each side brown cliffs rise above the date palms, flanking the valley.

in the third millennium BC as recent excavations have shown, and another 80 km downstream, where the valley bottom opens out to a width of 15 km, lies Mari. Below this, the ancient island of Ana, now sadly under the waters of another dam, and Hit, where the bitumen bubbling up from underground was exploited long before Herodotus tells us that Nebuchadnezzar used it for the walls of Babylon.

The desert

Most of the landscape, if we disembark and scale the dusty cliffs each side, is empty, and, except in spring, brown. On the left is the Jazirah, which stretches to the Tigris and the fringes of cultivation south of Mosul, on the right the Syrian desert. Both are the ancestral home of the nomad. The desert, never uniform in character, encloses Mesopotamia on the west from the Euphrates bend down to the head of the Gulf, and is penetrated by only a few routes open to the traveller from outside, notably that taking off from Mari and making west to the oasis of Tadmor (classical Palmyra) on the road to Damascus. Until very recently it retained a fauna of its own with clear links to Africa: ostriches were hunted by the Assyrians, cheetahs were reported this century, and far down in the Arabian peninsula the hartebeest. The wild ass, or onager, is another casualty of modern times, but their herds were vividly described by travellers such as Xenophon and Layard.

Today's desert nomads are almost exclusively of Arab stock. Similar well-defined tribal groups were present round the fringes of settled lands as early as our records go, but one cannot assume that the modern lifestyle is of ancient origin. The bedu of the western romantic consciousness and Arab heroic tradition is a relative newcomer: as one penetrates deeper into the desert, pasturage becomes scanter and distances from well to well increase, making long-distance travel impossible without the camel, with its greater speed and endurance in desert conditions. As far as we know, before about 1000 BC the camel was not domesticated, and hence the 'archetypal' pure beduin lifestyle impossible.[1]

A great deal has been written in recent decades about nomadism in the ancient Near East, stimulated largely by the fascinating light cast by the documents from the palace at Mari, seat of a recently settled nomadic dynasty. As more detail is recovered it becomes increasingly clear that, although the contrast between 'the desert and the sown' was always vividly felt, they were never entirely independent of one another. Beduin often camp well within the limits of agricultural settlement today, finding grazing for their sheep. They act as shepherds for the urban landlord, or villagers who have larger flocks than they can graze in their own fields. The Arab tribes of the Jazirah do not roam aimlessly across the land, seeking grazing wherever they can find it, but have well-established summer and winter pastures, to which they move at the change of season every year along known routes, and there are often small settlements in the winter grounds where part of the tribe may stay and engage in agriculture (Figure 1:3). Grazing rights to different areas are agreed both within the tribe and with other tribes and any settled inhabitants of the areas in

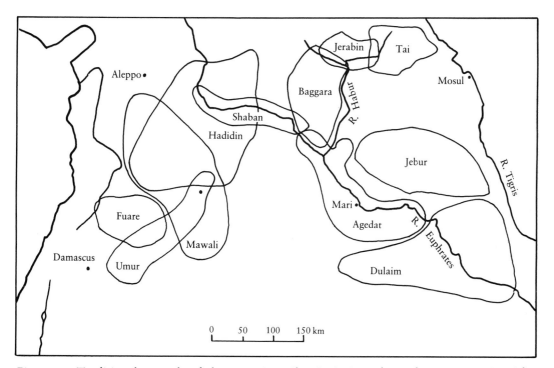

Figure 1:3 Traditional grounds of sheep-rearing tribes in Syria and North Mesopotamia. (After Wirth 1971, Karte 11)

question.[2] All the same, this is a fruitful ground for dissent, and the location of the summer grounds must have varied throughout history as climate or politics moved the southern fringes of settled agriculture closer to or further from the hills. Much of the political history of both South and North Mesopotamia revolves round the tensions between these different lifestyles, and we shall return to the role of the nomad below (chapter 4).

The southern plain and marshes

Eventually, after much meandering, the Euphrates enters the southern alluvial plain. The contrast with the lands to the north is intense, and is the direct consequence of the climate and the physical geography. Geologically, South Mesopotamia is of very recent origin – an alluvial deposit laid down by the two rivers (and their predecessors) in the deep trench formed between the Arabian shield to the west and the sharp folds of the Zagros mountains. The most obvious characteristic of this plain is its flatness. As much as 500 km north of the Gulf coastline, the general landscape is still less than 20 m above sea level, giving a gradient of 1:25000. This has various consequences. There is little to restrain a river which chooses to change its course, and in the space of a few years the natural landscape can change from barren sandy desert to marsh. It is very easy to direct water from the rivers on to the land, but much less easy to divert it and drain the land. The most conspicuous features of the landscape are the ancient sites, and the solid green blocks of palm-groves. Only the lowest of these are concealed by the long banks each side of ancient or modern canals. Although there can be much local variation, as we shall see later, the patterns repeat themselves time and again, and the landscape changes little overall.

Southwards the plain gives out where the rivers, united today at Qurnah into the Shatt al-Arab, lose much of their water into wide marshlands before reaching the open waters at the head of the Gulf. Here villages of reed houses perch on islands of vegetation (Figure 1:4). For mile upon mile one can slide through avenues of reeds which far overtop a man's

Figure 1:4 The marshes of the Tigris–Euphrates delta.

height, in a silence broken only by the calls of birds and the crashing of water buffalo in the thickets. Much romanticism has been lavished on the marsh dwellers of the south by European writers, attracted by their reed architecture and primeval lifestyle, as well as their extreme habitat with hidden ways through the reeds and the sense of penetrating a world apart. We have detailed accounts of their boats and houses, of their fishing and herding activities, and of their social customs. Life in the marshes is built round reeds and fish, with few concessions to the technical advances of civilization, so that it need have changed very little since neolithic times; but whether it is in fact an archaic survival or a much more recent adaptation to a marginal environment is another question. According to Salim, the usage of the marsh dwellers themselves confines the term Ma'dan to the buffalo breeders, and a good proportion of them are, or claim to be, descendants of beduin tribes.[3] Tradition also relates that many of the marsh dwellers are descended from escaped slaves from the time of the Zanj rebellion in the ninth century AD. In any case, since water buffalo were introduced to Iraq during the early Islamic period, it is deceptive to treat the 'marsh Arabs'' way of life as inherited unbroken from prehistoric times. As Salim's study makes clear, the establishment of stable political conditions tends to break down the isolation of the marsh dwellers, and in early Mesopotamia several of the principal cities were on the fringes of marsh or sea. True, we hear from Sennacherib about campaigns against Chaldaeans living 'in the middle of the marshes', but they must have taken up this life precisely during an absence of strong central authority. It would be wise, therefore, while accepting that the marsh dwellers of today may be living a life not unlike that of the earliest inhabitants of Ur or Eridu, not to assume that they represent an archaic survival.

The eastern flank

The marshes also stretch north for some 200 km along the east side of the Tigris as far as Amara, cutting Mesopotamia off from direct access to the neighbouring plain of Susiana, which was always an important centre of its own. To reach Susiana from Mesopotamia two routes were possible: a narrow and uncertain passage between the marshes and the Gulf to the south-east,[4] or the more normal route pushing north-east until the marshes give way to dry land and then turning to the south-east, skirting the flank of the Zagros, and during all our time span passing the city of Der. Precisely how far north this point was must have varied, and the nature of this route depended on the level of exploitation of the waters of the river Diyala: when this was actively pursued, irrigation from the left bank fingered out into the lands to the south-east, and enabled the growth of major cities such as Ešnunna (Tell Asmar) or Tell Agrab – sites which are now once again within the limits of cultivation but lay in high desert in the 1930s when the Oriental Insitute of Chicago began excavations there.

While the Diyala waters created a corridor between the north-eastern corner of the Mesopotamian plain and Susa and beyond, the river also served as a principal route for those travelling due east and even north as well. The eastern route is variously called the Silk Road or the Great Khorasan Road. After crossing the Iranian frontier it soon has to climb nearly 1,000 m in a spectacular pass called Tak-i Girreh to the plateau, leading through Kermanshah to northern Iran and on eastwards to the cities of Central Asia and finally China. The northern route unites travellers from Susiana with the even busier route from the Mesopotamian plain. From Baghdad, and before that from any of the great cities at the northern end of the plain, the road to Assyria did not head due north along the banks of the Tigris like the modern asphalt, but sought more hospitable terrain where villages were more frequent, supplies of food and water easier to come by, and there was less risk of marauders. This route, formalized by the Achaemenid kings as the Royal Road which ran from Susa to Sardis in western Turkey, meant following the Diyala upstream for some 180 km, until the abrupt rock wall of the Jebel Hamrin is reached. This outlying fold of the Zagros mountains runs in an amazingly straight and regular line for hundreds of kilometres. South of the Diyala breach it gradually loses height and dies out within about 25 km; but to the north it rises to over 300 m above the plain, and, although it is not high enough to feature on many maps, it is steep enough and rough enough to form a major barrier, with only a few crossing places (Figure 1:5).

Figure 1:5 The Jebel Hamrin: 'British transport crossing the Sakaltutan pass'. (From F.J. Moberly (ed.), *History of the Great War, based on official documents, vol. IV: The Campaign in Mesopotamia 1914–1918*, 1927, 94)

The range is not merely an obstacle to the traveller – it serves as an important natural and often political dividing line. Beyond it the alluvial plain and its familiar conditions are finished. Most of the terrain is far from flat, and, with increasing rainfall as one approaches the mountains, the countryside becomes greener. As a natural barrier, therefore, it separates the alluvium from the northern plains; as a political line it protects Sumer and

Akkad from the barbarous north and east. From early times the whole range, including the section called Jebel Makhul, south-west of Assur on the west bank of the Tigris, was known by the name of Mount Ebih: it features in Amorite personal names, and its symbolic value as the first outcrop of the mountains which fenced the eastern borders is expressed by the Sumerian myth of Inanna and Ebih, where it stands for unruly enemies in the hills.[5]

Before moving to the north, let us first follow the Diyala river further to the east, across sporadically cultivated rolling countryside, until we meet the first major Zagros ranges, and passing through them debouch on to the fertile plain of the Shahrizur in Iraqi Kurdistan. This is the largest of three intermontane plains nestled among the Zagros along the north-eastern borders of Iraq. The capital of the area today is the city of Sulaimaniyah, founded in 1781 as a summer station for the Pasha of Baghdad, but the centre of gravity has probably always been towards the south end in the region of Halabja.[6] Towards the north the plain is gradually hemmed in by the mountains, and finally reaches the left bank of the Lesser Zab which cuts through the range in deep chasms and was only traced to its source late in the nineteenth century. Upstream and on its right bank is the small Rania plain, now very largely under the waters of the Dokan dam but inevitably a natural and often political entity in antiquity, at least in the Old Babylonian period centred on the site of Tell Shemshara which has yielded archives of that date (Figure 1:6). And further north still is the plain of Rowanduz, only accessible by difficult mountain passes but large enough again to form a significant homogeneous area.

Today the mountain regions of modern Iraq are almost exclusively the preserve of a bewildering complex of Kurdish tribes, although towards Turkey there are still pockets of Aramaic-speaking villagers who retain Christianity and a fierce conviction of their Assyrian origins. There are a few towns, acting as centres for the different sectors, but most of the population are farmers, working fields in the valley bottoms or stepped in hard-won terraces up the hillsides on which their villages hug the slope. Often part of the village decamps in the summer months to take the sheep and goats up into the high country, living in tents or flimsy shacks. It seems probable that their traditional lifestyle is little changed from prehistory. Other Kurdish tribes, e.g. some of the Jaf, had an entirely different regime, being transhumant shepherds living exclusively in tents. Their summer pastures are high in the hills, previously across the Iranian frontier east of the Shahrizur, but in autumn they migrate westwards to the open plains and foothills beyond the mountain ranges.[7] The Kurdish language is Indo-Iranian, perhaps a descendant of Median, and as such probably entered the area during the late second or early first millennium BC. Before that the population of the Taurus and Zagros borders is mainly Hurrian speaking where we can identify them; but to the east in particular we have to reckon with other language groups including Gutians, Kassites and Elamites. What is clear from the accounts we possess is that, as in all mountain regions, the political scene was minutely fragmented; and the influence of the mountain tribes on the lowland political scene has never matched that of the nomad. Raids from the hills tended to be of short duration, and with the exception of the Kassites no mountain tribes succeeded in establishing themselves as the ruling dynasty of the plain before the Achaemenid empire.

In antiquity the slopes must often have been forested, but today there are only scattered

Figure 1:6 The plain of Dokan (or Rania): the Danish excavation camp, 1957. (Laessøe 1963, Plate 12a)

remnants left by the depredations of goats, charcoal burners, and other human activities. 'In favourable habitats the *Quercus* formations provide an almost closed forest of trees of medium height (5–10 m), especially in relatively inaccessible mountain districts remote from villages and trade routes' (Guest 1966, 73). In the eighth century BC, Sargon of Assyria passed through the Zagros on to the Iranian plateau, and in his letter to Assur, the national god, reported that 'I passed between Mt Nikippa and Mt Upa, high mountains clothed with all kinds of trees, ... over which shade is spread like a cedar-forest, and on whose paths the traveller does not see the rays of the sun'.[8]

The northern plains and the jazirah

The Assyrian kings were much impressed by the mountains which fringed their land, and Sargon's son tells us how, when campaigning in the modern Cudi Dağ, which tradition identifies as the Ark's final resting place, he 'leapt from rock to rock like an ibex, and then sat on a rock and had a cold drink'. The awe with which these absolute despots describe their mountaineering exploits reflects their lowland background, the wide open spaces of northern Iraq, which stretch westward across North Syria to the Euphrates. On the map, these northern plains look just as flat as the southern, but this is deceptive. For one thing, there are minor ridges of hills which, however low, form significant natural divisions of the landscape, 'rugged ranges, scored deeply by ravines, and except for goat-tracks crossed by no regular paths ...' (Mason 1944, 79). Two examples may serve: the jebel behind Kerkuk to its east (Kani Dolman Dagh) divides the Zab–Diyala block longitudinally, much like the Hamrin itself further to the south-west, and so decrees that most routes run parallel to the range on one side or the other, or confines them to certain crossing places where the terrain is easier. Similarly on the other side of the Tigris routes are aligned with the Jebel Sheikh Ibrahim, which merges eventually into the imposing hump of the Jebel Sinjar. It too is a low range, but it is a fault with a steep broken escarpment on its south-western face, and to scale it involves scrambling and discomfort, and the regular routes will always have passed parallel to it to the south or north. Where there is a convenient crossing place there will usually be a settlement of some importance, of which Tell Afar, ancient name unknown, and Kerkuk, ancient Arrapha, are good examples.

Even apart from these minor ranges, the general terrain is far from flat (Figure 1:7). Much of it is broken limestone country, with 'shallow valleys between low, smooth hills, often with rock outcrops near their summits' (Dorrell 1972, 69), only occasionally cut through by deep seasonal wadis. In places there are patches of good soils forming miniature alluvial plains; one example of this is south of the Jebel Sinjar: Soviet archaeologists working in the region have used the term 'valley' to refer to this environment, but the English word is deceptive, since the strip of well-cultivated land south of the hills is transected by the wadis making their way southwards to join the Wadi Tharthar, and is bounded on the south only by the transition to broken limestone country.

In contrast with the south, the rolling configuration of the land does not permit cross-country canals except as enormous engineering projects – such as the Assyrian and Sassanian kings, and modern governments, have created – and agriculture is therefore dependent for its water on rain. While the settled plains are delimited to north and east by the foothills of the Zagros and Taurus, their southern and eastern borders are therefore defined by the limit of adequate rainfall. This runs in an arc parallel to the mountains, from the Euphrates at the latitude of Aleppo, close to the Jebel Sinjar, and then curving to the south-east across the Tigris above Assur to cross the Diyala near the Jebel Hamrin. The exact location of the limit varies considerably both from year to year and with the modern authorities writing about it. Geographers link places receiving equal amounts of rainfall with contour lines known as isohyets, and different writers may choose slightly differing definitions. According to Wirth, a successful barley crop can be achieved with

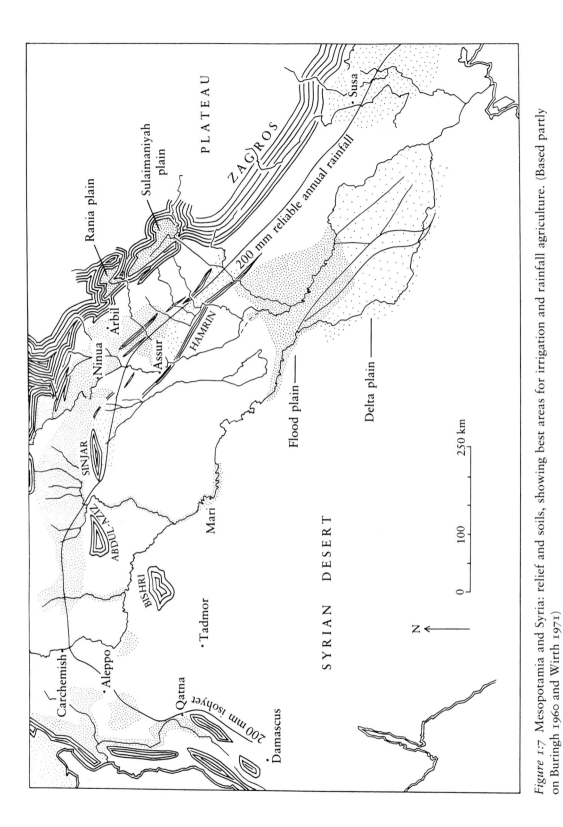

Figure 1:7 Mesopotamia and Syria: relief and soils, showing best areas for irrigation and rainfall agriculture. (Based partly on Buringh 1960 and Wirth 1971)

200 mm of fairly consistent winter rainfall, and wheat with 250 mm; orchards and summer crops need to be north of the 400 mm isohyet.[9] It is not sufficient, though, to draw the annual rainfall averaged over a number of years onto the map and assume that agriculture is possible above the resulting 200 or 250 mm isohyet: for a continuous settled existence the farmer requires a locality which can *depend* on adequate rainfall in at least three years out of five, and this generally corresponds to an annual average of about 300 mm. Because the change in rainfall on these flat plains is much more gradual than in the hills and mountains, this means that the effective limit of settlement is well to the north and east of the 200 or 250 mm isohyets. Hence the southern limit of agriculture, and thus of settlement, must always have been a tattered fringe giving onto the semi-desert between Tigris and Euphrates and, east of the Tigris, between the Zabs and the Diyala.[10]

Today there are no substantial settlements in the Jazirah south of the Sinjar range, and yet any visitor can, like Layard in the 1840s, count 'above one hundred mounds, throwing their dark and lengthening shadows across the plain' (Figure 1:8).[11] These include a chain

Figure 1:8 Ancient mounds in the jazirah between the Tigris and Sinjar: view south from the modern citadel at Tell Afar. (Photo: courtesy David Connolly)

of major second and third millennium sites, of which Tell al-Rimah is the only one excavated, and some of which were the capitals of small independent polities, proving that in antiquity the area supported a considerable population. At least two major factors may help to explain the difference between modern and ancient conditions, one social, the other climatic. Clearly a slight reduction or increase in the average annual rainfall would shift the limit of viable agriculture. Unfortunately, evidence for climatic fluctuation of this kind is lacking for Mesopotamia proper, and although it does exist for surrounding areas, it is not precise enough to help in this context, because even a slight shift in precipitation has a major effect in terms of horizontal extent (Figure 1:7). It has often been suggested that tree-cover was better in prehistoric times, that the oak and terebinth scrub still visible on the Jebel Sinjar would have been widely spread across the currently treeless plains to north and south of the hills as well, but this is not supported by any hard evidence as yet. Traces of water courses near Tell al-Rimah suggest that there may have been better water resources within historical times. Wadis, running from the slopes of the Jebel Sinjar, today cut into the plain and make their way to join the Wadi Tharthar; perhaps in earlier years these were more reliable, and could even have been diverted into local canal systems, or perhaps there were springs of sub-surface waters which are now depleted.

Life on the alluvial plains

In order to understand the nature of Sumerian civilization, we must now look more closely at the southern plains. The land of Sumer and Akkad forms a well-defined unit not merely because it occupies the southern alluvium, but because an urban lifestyle there requires a very specific subsistence strategy. Despite the natural vegetation which provides grazing in the steppe and thickets along the rivers, rainfall here is quite unreliable and inadequate to support agriculture. On the other hand, the soils of the alluvium are deep, and the flatness of the landscape enables an ordered system of fields and canals bringing water to them. Throughout history whenever South Mesopotamia has fostered a flourishing society this has been centred round an efficient agricultural regime, dependent on the controlled exploitation of the rivers. The limits of the potentially homogeneous area can be easily defined, since they are the limits of the alluvial soils accessible to canal or lift irrigation. Along the south-western flank are the rocky scarps which herald the edge of the desert west of modern Kerbela and Nejef. On the south the plain is hemmed in by the marshes at the head of the Gulf, in which the two rivers almost lose themselves before they reach the sea. Eastwards the southern reaches of the Tigris are also separated by marshes from Susiana (modern Khuzistan), while further north there are drier lands which can be irrigated from the left bank of the Diyala, and so form a north-eastern lobe of the settled plains. Northwards the limits are imposed by the geology: above Ramadi to the west and Baquba on the east the alluvial soils come to an end except in a narrow strip along the river beds, and hence there are no major settlements north of this point away from the rivers until we reach the North Mesopotamian plains. This enumeration shows how the lands of Sumer and Akkad are boxed in by natural frontiers on all sides, and explains how their inhabitants were linked by a common lifestyle even when politically they may have been quite disunified.

Thousands of years of human interference prevent us from knowing what that plain may have been like in its pristine condition, but it was certainly never a homogeneous environment. Although apparently flat to the eye, it is nowhere entirely so. Any water course, natural or controlled, will gradually build up a shallow bank or levée, to the extent that in time the rivers and canals flow above the level of the surrounding land, which is divided by their banks into basins imperceptible to the eye, but critical to the flow of water. To quote H.T. Wright, 'When ... man-made factors compound the varied natural situation on the surface of the Euphrates geosyncline, then the physical environment becomes so complex that it defies detailed interpretation.'[12]

Under natural conditions, as the two rivers make their way through the alluvial plain they would tend to meander and to burst their banks in flood. Neither of these habits is convenient to the farmer, and from prehistoric times efforts would have been made to contain the flood water and discourage meandering and minor shifts in the course by building up earth banks. When the river does get out of control there is a serious risk that it may change its course drastically. This has certainly happened several times in the last few thousand years: below Kut there are at least three Tigris channels – the modern channel which may be of relatively recent origin, the modern Shatt al-Gharraf (now a man-controlled canal, but very likely on the line of an earlier natural bed), and the Dujail, on which the medieval city of Wasit stood, now abandoned. Above Kut the Tigris has probably not shifted substantially in historical times, although the Diyala has certainly shifted eastward at least once, but at least four major Euphrates channels are known at different dates, diverging from each other up at the top end of the alluvium above ancient Sippar.

How the landscape appears is directly affected by the level of human intervention. Under 'natural' conditions the mud-flats and levées of the major rivers could support a dense tangle of vegetation, including willows, poplars and liquorice, the domain of wild boar, big cats, and other wild animals like the Mesopotamian deer, now almost extinct. As the fresh ground water of the river tails off and saline conditions increase in the less well-drained areas, this poplar and willow maquis thins out, and very little survives along the rivers in South Iraq today; but dense tamarisk thickets, which are more salt tolerant, can spring up wherever water is sufficient and the land is not wanted by man or his herds.

Out beyond the tails of the canals, cultivation ceases abruptly and, except where there are shifting belts of sand dunes, the raw surface of the land is exposed (Figure 1:9). Between the Tigris and Euphrates and any canals taken off their banks, there is to this day a broad strip of desert not reached by any water, as barren as any landscape outside the alluvial plain, home to hyenas, jackals, eagles, lions, gazelle, and in antiquity no doubt the onager. Today, as for thousands of years, this does not mean a pristine surface: as the watercourses have moved, so has human activity. Alongside the canals, river beds and meanders and levées, are the scars of ancient cities and villages, and massive boundary walls, all eroded by wind and water or shrouded in silt and sand (Figure 1:10). This is a palimpsest of human history on the plains, and with skill and patience it may be read, with the help of aerial photographs, maps and surface survey (Text 1:1).[13]

Where no escape for the waters is available they will of course collect and marshes rapidly form. The most extensive marshes are in the south of the country, but they are not only there. An extensive marsh was formed this century at the tail-end of the Musayeb canal, while the site of Nippur, now sandwiched between the irrigated regime of the Shatt al-Daghghara and the sand dunes, was in the 1880s accessible only by boat. Although the marshes obviously preclude agriculture, and today's water buffaloes were not there in antiquity, they were still a rich resource, teeming with fish, marsh birds and turtles, and

Figure 1:9 South Mesopotamia in the late nineteenth century AD. (Section from the map of W.B.

Figure 1:10 View from the ziggurrat at Nippur, looking across the excavated walls to the sand dunes of the central desert.

Text 1:1 Layard on southern Mesopotamia in the nineteenth century AD
The plains between Khan-i-Zad and the Euphrates are covered with a perfect network of ancient canals and watercourses; but 'a drought is upon the waters of Babylon, and they were dried'. Their lofty embankments, stretching on every side in long lines until they are lost in the hazy distance, or magnified by the mirage into mountains, still defy the hand of time, and seem rather the work of nature than of man. The face of the country, too, is dotted with mounds and shapeless heaps, the remains of ancient towns and villages.

(Layard 1853, 479)

supporting the different species of reed which are used to this day, for architecture, furniture and containers.

Comparison of north and south

Thus the agricultural conditions of settled life in north and south are fundamentally different: the southern farmer needed constant vigilance to control and exploit the irrigation system, and cultivation was necessarily confined to cells fed by each river or canal, separated in many cases from the next by desert grazing. In the north no such discontinuities were necessary, and indeed common sense dictates that the band of cultivation spreads uniformly out into the desert on the line of the diminishing rainfall contour. Beyond this, in the lands between the two blocks the great majority of land is uncultivated: not only the Jazirah to the west of the Tigris, but also the flat lands south-west of the Jebel Hamrin are out of reach of irrigation and too dry to be worth trying to farm.

This has isolated the two main centres of Mesopotamia from one another, restricting cultural, political and military contact between north and south to two or three routes which offered the necessary access to water and a measure of security. At times there was some continuity of settlement along the Zagros foothills through Kerkuk (ancient Arrapha) down to the Diyala behind the Jebel Hamrin, and it was here that the principal overland trade routes ran. Otherwise the only links are afforded by the alluvial strips along the two river valleys. Here the soil is rich, and can be watered by hand from the river or by canals taking off from further upstream and running along the foot of the cliffs. These 'river oases' formed tentacles of the southern culture reaching up to the north: Mari on the Euphrates and Assur on the Tigris were outposts of Sumer and Akkad. They are both placed where the river bed widens out and there is enough good land to support a considerable settlement, but their importance undoubtedly also derives from their control of the traffic passing up and down the rivers.

Nevertheless, in the times we are concerned with the two major areas shared a common lifestyle based on agricultural subsistence and the sedentary urban environment it enabled. They grew the same or similar staple crops, and lived the stationary life of the farmer. They sowed, harvested and threshed their wheat and barley, and any farming village will have had its flocks of sheep and goats, which are often the form in which capital can be stored and wealth measured. For many centuries north and south were also linked through the medium of the Akkadian language, bridging the Hurrian and Sumerian speakers. And equally they shared common enemies, the tribes of mountain and desert.

The climatic question

Our description so far has reflected conditions as they are today, or at best in the accounts of fairly recent travellers. It is unlikely that they are unchanged over the last four or five thousand years, but it is easy to say this and less easy to identify the differences. Change in the environment may be due to a variety of natural causes or to human interference, and there is evidence for both. Changes in sea level are detectable in the Gulf, changes of temperature are reflected in glacial deposits in the mountains, vegetation cover at different dates is reflected in pollen records from lakes, and the behaviour of rivers can be traced in the geomorphology of the foothills. Although all outside the alluvial plain itself, these separate strands can be woven together to suggest some of the changes which may have affected conditions there.

Observations of the advance or retreat of glaciers show that as expected the Near East was very much colder during the last Ice Age (Würm), summer temperatures being some 6–7°C below today's, but that a global warming to some 1–2°C above present levels also affected the Near East in the period roughly 5000–2000 BC.[14] Changes in temperature can affect the environment in various ways. The relatively cold and dry conditions of the Ice Age resulted in a steppe vegetation dominated by plants such as goosefoot and wormwood (Chenopodiaceae and Artemisiaceae). The warming released water from the polar caps to raise sea level and increase rainfall. Vegetation responds differently in different zones to the changes in humidity resulting from the combination of temperature and precipitation: thus the tree line could move higher up the mountains in warmer periods, but also spread into the steppe because of the higher rainfall; and indeed pollen evidence suggests that the oak forests in the Zagros and Van regions did expand between about 8500–3500 BC and 4400–1400 BC respectively. A similar expansion is observable in north-western Syria even earlier (8000–6000 BC), but increased forest cover in the north and east might be offset by a reduction in oak and other trees in Palestine, perhaps resulting from increased aridity in that area. As a whole, the evidence does not suggest that any major climatic shift has taken place since the Ice Age, the present pattern of forest and steppe being established by about 2000 BC, but as the pollen record comes down closer to our own time we begin to detect the impact of human activity.[15]

This shows up partly as the spread of cultivated species, such as vine and olive, but also in the disappearance of forest cover. The oak forest must have fallen prey to goats, fuel gathering and clearance of fields for agriculture. Forests in the higher hills included other species and already in the third millennium rulers of South Mesopotamia chronicle their acquisition of timber from distant parts, especially the mountains of Syria and Lebanon. Assyrian kings regularly marched to Lebanon or the Amanus to find the beams to span their temples, but these royal expeditions in themselves can hardly have had a lasting effect. Nevertheless it is significant that the Mesopotamians are obliged to search so far afield for good timber, and it does suggest that the nearer hills were not heavily forested. After considering Rich's descriptions of the Shahrizur, Guest comments that 'it is clear ... that the condition of the oak forests in Sulaimaniya province ... was not so very different in 1820 from what it is today. The deforestation of the route Chemchemal–Sulaimaniya must have been completed well before 1820.'[16] On his campaign in the Zagros, Sargon speaks of 'mountains whose vegetation – karšu and ṣumlalu – smelled good', presumably human activity was already preventing the vegetation from reaching its natural forest climax here. It is not clear whether the northern plains would ever become heavily forested if permitted, and evidence from relict populations and equally dry areas of Jordan suggests that without human intervention the northern plains would be a savannah, with extensive small trees especially terebinth. Further south, in the dry steppe, there is evidence that dense thickets could thrive.[17] How far back does this relatively treeless condition go? Xenophon's description of the northern plains suggests that it was little different in his time, and campaign accounts of the Assyrian kings in the first millennium make special mention of areas of dense scrub, suggesting that it was exceptional then. The goat is often held to blame for this degradation, but some of the blame must be given to charcoal burners and the commercial exploitation of the timber in response to the demand in the cities, described vividly by C.J. Rich in 1836.[18]

The vegetation shifts are probably the most conspicuous effect of change in most of the region, but for the south the regime of the rivers is more critical. During the last Ice Age, sea level throughout the world dropped by some 130 m, leaving the bed of the Gulf as dry land (c. 20,000–15,000 BP). How fast and how full the rivers were not only affected their ease of exploitation, but also in the long term affected their own behaviour. A river's speed is directly affected by its gradient, and as it flows slower it drops more silt and tends to meander more. Along stream beds in the foothills it can be seen that periods of incision, when the stream was cutting through the surrounding land, alternated with periods of alluviation. As water level in the Gulf rose, the rivers ceased to deposit silts along their upper reaches, cutting their beds deeper in the foothills, but presumably flowed slower in the plains and brought alluvial deposits there and into the Gulf itself.

Changes in sea level can be observed in the Gulf reflected in fossil shorelines, although the tectonic instability of the Gulf makes it hard to be certain of the general applicability of local variations; but, because the two opposing shores are relatively steep, its east and west limits have not shifted significantly since the Ice Age. At the head of the Gulf, however, the position is quite different. Exactly where the sea gave way to land in antiquity has been a major problem for many years, because the land is so flat that even a small change in the level of the sea could have a dramatic effect on the shoreline. The naivete of the old idea that the Euphrates and Tigris have simply been pushing out their alluvial fan year by year and so moving the head of the Gulf imperceptibly southwards was exposed by the famous article of Lees and Falcon (1952). Among other points, they demonstrated that the rivers in fact deposit the majority of their silt before they enter the marshy lands in the south, that there is clear evidence for tectonic movement, with subsidence and uplift, within the last 10,000 years, and that field systems of Islamic date at the head of the Gulf are now beneath the sea. They therefore suggested that the deposition of silt at the mouth of the Shatt al-Arab has been balanced by geological subsidence, and that the head of the Gulf has not really shifted significantly during the Holocene.

As geological research has continued, further complications have emerged. Their paper does not take much account of the effect on the alluviation process of the changes in sea level in the Gulf and in the river regimes, and some drillings in the bed of the Gulf have led Nützel to suggest that the old concept of the sea reaching at least as far north as Ur and Lagaš may in fact be valid, especially as there is evidence that the Gulf was over 2 m higher around 5000 years ago.[19] Others are unconvinced, and the interplay of variables is so complex that no consensus is likely to be reached without further research in the field directly aimed at answering these questions. It is however generally agreed that in the period between 5000 and 3000 BC the region experienced its highest temperatures and the highest sea level. It is obviously tempting to seek some causal connection between these natural conditions and the rapid rise of urban society at this time. Nissen concentrates on the proposed change in the southern landscape, accepting on the basis of Nützel's data that around 4000 BC most of the south of Sumer was a marsh, capable of sustaining a fishing and fowling population but not agriculture. He supposes that a relatively sudden drying of this area was accompanied by a large-scale colonization by farming communities. This remains a possibility but requires improved scientific evidence; and in any case whether or not the land was under water is not the only question. The temperature rise would have meant greater precipitation – enabling settled life further south on the northern plains and in particular in the Zab–Diyala block (but not of course on the alluvial plain), higher river levels – presumably making autumn irrigation easier but spring control of the rivers not necessarily more difficult because there was less snow and glacier melt,[20] and movement of tropical weather patterns further north up the Gulf – making much of Arabia a less hostile environment than it is today.

The uncertainty is frustrating because, without a more accurate understanding of the natural constraints and conditions, we are not able to judge the relative importance of environmental changes in the changes in society attested in the archaeological and historical record during the Uruk period, now to be described.

Further reading

An invaluable general account of Iraq and neighbouring Near Eastern countries is given by the British Admiralty Handbooks, e.g. Mason 1944. Guest 1966 has a fundamental description of the vegetative and climatic zones of Iraq, and Wirth 1971 is invaluable for Syria. Life in the southern marshes is described by Salim 1962, as well as by W. Thesiger in his book *The Marsh Arabs*, 1964. For the Iraqi Zagros, Edmonds 1957 is invaluable.

Accounts of the Mesopotamian environment written by archaeologists are to be found in Adams 1981, Wright 1969 and, for the North, D. Oates 1968. For a vivid picture of the land in pre-modern times the books of A.H. Layard remain unchallenged.

2
Cities and dynasties

Traditional histories of Mesopotamia are obliged by the nature of their sources to recount the rise and fall of dynasties – from Amurath to Amurath. Although we are deliberately eschewing the recitation of lists, the alternation of strong centralized political control with periods of turmoil is so characteristic of Mesopotamian history that the events recorded in royal inscriptions cannot be simply ignored: documentary and archaeological sources cluster in the periods of peace, and the recurrent effects on the social institutions we are describing are too evident to be missed. Changes may be the direct consequence of political acts, or more indirectly of economic conditions or of the expansion or contraction of geographical horizons. Even the more subtle changes, such as the apparent shift towards private from institutional enterprise, or the gradual separation of cities from their hinterlands, can be related more convincingly to particular political situations than to some long-term yeast. It would be dangerous to deny that some underlying trends may have

Years BC

5000–4000	Halaf/Ubaid	
4000–3200	Uruk	} Protoliterate period
3200–3000	Jemdet Nasr	
3000–2750	Early Dynastic I	
2750–2600	Early Dynastic II	} Pre-Sargonic period
2600–2350	Early Dynastic III	
2350–2150	Dynasty of Akkad	
	(Gutian interregnum)	
2150–2000	3rd Dynasty of Ur	
	(Amorite interregnum)	
2000–1800	Isin–Larsa Dynasties	
1800–1600	1st Dynasty of Babylon	} Old Babylonian period
	(Kassite interregnum)	

Figure 2:1 Outline of archaeological and historical periods.

been at work within the Mesopotamian urban society independently of, or indeed in spite of, the potent extraneous influences imposed by dynastic ambitions and disasters, but they are hard to detect behind these much more dramatic oscillations. The similarities between one period of prosperity and another, one 'Dark Age' or Zwischenzeit and another, seem more than their differences (see chapter 16).

Origins

The first serious encounter with Mesopotamian prehistory came with Sir Leonard Woolley's work on the mound of Tell al-Ubaid a few kilometres north of the city of Ur, on which a small Sumerian shrine had been built in the third millennium BC. The period recognized by the painted pottery found here, and in the deepest levels of the city of Ur itself, was called the Ubaid period and taken to represent the earliest settlement in the south. Since then many other sites of the Ubaid period have been identified on the surface, and deep soundings at Eridu, and recently at the site of Tell Oueili next to Larsa, all at the southern end of the plain, have exposed earlier phases of the Ubaid culture. Whereas on the North Mesopotamian plains settled agricultural life reaches back thousands of years earlier, in the south we have yet to locate any archaeological remains earlier than the Ubaid.[21] At present it is impossible to say why with any certainty: one view is that, in Nissen's words, 'the land which, because of the high water level in the Gulf or the quantity of water in the rivers, was mostly uninhabitable, would initially have offered only a few isolated opportunities for settlement, but became available for more extended occupation from the moment the waters began to recede'.[22] This may well be part of the picture, but as we have just seen, more work is needed to establish the timing of the archaeological sequence in relation to the environmental conditions, and the extent of early settlement is difficult to determine because the fifth and sixth millennium land surface has been shrouded by alluvium in some parts of the plain. The evidence at Eridu does however suggest that a shift towards a more agricultural lifestyle was under way during the earlier Ubaid phases, with hunting and fishing implements prominent in the early levels, and agricultural tools such as sickles coming in somewhat later.[23] On this basis it seems acceptable at present to consider the early Ubaid – say about 5000 BC – as the time of the first permanent agricultural settlements in the land.

Naturally, this raises the question of who were the 'Ubaid people', and where they came from. The divergent answers offered by distinguished scholars to this question over the years show how dangerous it is to misuse prehistoric archaeological data in this way. Statements such as 'these changes, and particularly the abandonment of the earlier stamp seal, are radical enough to betray the intrusion of a forceful and heterogeneous ethnic group',[24] or 'not long after the establishment of the first settlement by the Iranian immigrants, the Semites probably infiltrated into Southern Mesopotamia both as peaceful immigrants and as warlike conquerors ...',[25] go beyond what can reasonably be deduced from the archaeological evidence available. At the root of much of this speculation lies the urge to come closer to the Sumerians by tracing their origin. For one reason or another, there has been a temptation to assume that they entered Mesopotamia from outside –

usually from the east – and therefore to search the archaeological record for signs of an invasion or at least of a cultural shift. Some have suggested that they 'arrived' at the end of the Uruk period, some at the end of the Ubaid, others that they were the earliest settlers of all. Arguments based on the supposed traces of an earlier language in the place names and vocabulary passed down to us through the cuneiform texts have not achieved general acceptance. On the other hand, looking at the later history of Mesopotamia, with the known incursions of Gutians and Kassites from the east, and different groups of Semitic nomads from the west, it would be rash to deny that a Sumerian-speaking group could have slipped in to the land without leaving much trace in the artefactual record. Much more significant, though even less easy to assess, is the presence and cultural dominance of the Sumerian language, since the same historical examples show how rare it is for an intrusive ethnic group to impose its own language on an existing population: in historical times only Aramaic and Arabic have achieved this.

This is not the place in which to pursue this theme further, even though it is an important unknown in the factors which converted a flourishing but by no means exceptional agricultural society into the world's first urban civilization. Most of the significant developments involved in that transformation seem to have taken place in the Uruk period which follows the Ubaid: monumental architecture, public art, specialization and standardization of industrial production, the invention of writing and greatly expanded trading horizons. We are not yet in a position to say how, or why, or even perhaps where these changes occurred, because virtually nothing of the early Uruk period has yet been excavated in South Mesopotamia. The mapping of sites in southern Iraq and Susiana has suggested significant shifts in the patterns of settlement but, without better stratified excavated sequences to set alongside these, it is not possible to assess the interplay of cultural and social developments with population trends and settlement patterns.

One thing however seems clear, that there was not some sudden cataclysmic break with what had gone before. The continuity with the Ubaid culture is epitomized in the famous sequence of temples at Eridu, enlarged time and again through the centuries; the latest surviving remnants of the temple's platform are in fact from the Uruk period, although the plan of the building itself is lost. More recently excavations deep below the Anu ziggurat at Uruk itself have shown that the Uruk period temple on its platform was also built over the site of an Ubaid period temple, giving us another clear instance of continuity of worship in one place (Figure 2:2). No doubt the same picture would be repeated at other sites, such as Ur, Tello (Girsu) or Nippur, could archaeology probe deep enough into the mounds. It is fair to conclude that the major cities of the Uruk period are in part at least an indigenous development.

With a suddenness which may be partially the consequence of the poverty of archaeological excavation, the artistic output of the late Uruk opens up another sort of evidence in the shape of figurative art. On the cylinder seals, which make their appearance in Eanna VI, there are scenes, whether narrative or symbolic, which demand an explanation in historical terms. Bound captives kneel, or enemies are smitten, and a ruler is identified by his characteristic hat and skirt (Figure 2:3). He also features on a carved boulder shooting lions,[26] and the vases carved in relief from the temple quarter at Uruk show an offering

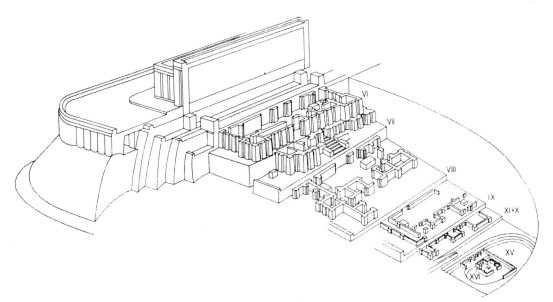

Figure 2:2 The Temple at Eridu. Reconstruction showing the development from the earliest Ubaid level (*c.* 5000 BC) to the Uruk period temple (*c.* 3000 BC). Levels VI–XVI were built one immediately above the other, but have been shown offset here. (After Heinrich and Seidl 1982, Abb. 60)

procession in which he stands at the shoulder of the goddess (Figure 6:1). From Uruk, and from Susa, there are also seals and their impressions showing the pursuit of crafts and communal activities which bespeak a level of social order; but we still lack the critical written sources to allow us to push our identifications further in this direction.

Figure 2:3 Scene from cylinder seal impressions found at Uruk. (After Brandes 1979, Tafel 3)

The Early Dynastic period

Cities and temples

If events in the Uruk period remain, for the present, prehistoric, Mesopotamia undeniably enters history in the Early Dynastic period, as archaeologists now generally call the 700 years or so which separate the Uruk from the Dynasty of Akkad. However, even if we wished to, the sources will not permit us to offer a detailed account of events, and to describe this period in traditional historical terms it is easiest to sketch in a general outline by looking at two later documents which convey a very clear image of the fabric of early Sumer as seen by its inheritors: the Temple Hymns and the Sumerian King List.

The literary compilation called the Sumerian Temple Hymns is known to us from the output of scribes working in schools of the Old Babylonian period, around 1800 BC, but the text itself states that its author is Enheduana, daughter of Sargon of Akkad and priestess of Nanna, the moon-god at Ur. Although there are some obvious later additions, like the hymn to the deified Ur III King Šulgi, this is generally accepted as an original composition of the Akkad period. The poem is a collection of short individual addresses to all the major sanctuaries of the southern plain. Each one describes the temple and then its deity in figurative language which must be full of allusions now mostly lost to us (see Text 2:1).

> **Text 2:1** Temple Hymn No. 21 to the Temple of Bau in Urukug (= Lagaš)
> Urukug, shrine which causes the seed to come forth, belonging to the holy An, called
>   by a good name,
> Within you is the river of ordeal which vindicates the just man,
> House of widespread counsel, storehouse which eternally possesses silver and lapis lazuli,
> Etarsirsir, from which decision and **me**'s come forth, where the 'man' greets (the goddess),
> Your princess, the merciful princess of the land, the mother of all lands,
> The lady, the great healer of the dark-headed, who determines the destiny of her city,
> The first-born daughter of the holy An, the maid, mother Bau,
> Has, O house Urukug, placed the house upon your . . ., has taken her place upon your
>   dais.
> 8 (lines). The house of Bau in Urukug.
>
> (After Sjöberg and Bergmann 1969, 32–3)

There are forty-two hymns in all, referring to about thirty-five different cities, since some are represented by more than one temple. The cities range from Ur, Eridu and Lagaš on the fringes of the Gulf to Kazallu and Marad in the north-west, Sippar in the north, and Ešnunna and Der to the north-east (Figure 2:4). They thus cover the southern alluvial plain (though not all its traditional centres), but do not extend beyond its confines (e.g. to Mari or Assur on the Euphrates and Tigris). Pre-Sargonic texts found at Abu Salabikh show that the genre of temple hymns was already known two centuries before Enheduana, and they epitomize the ideology according to which the land was composed of individual equal-ranking city-states, each with its principal deity and sanctuary. This ideal is fundamental to the Sumerians' accounts of their land, whether in myth and legend or in contemporary political statements, and it is interesting that – for whatever purpose – it is here set out by the daughter of Sargon himself, the archetypal conqueror! The reality is reflected in the archaeological record: both excavation and surface survey substantiate the picture of a fairly uniform class of major population centres distributed widely across the southern plain, with strong local identities expressed in their allegiance to a city god and their pride in the temple.

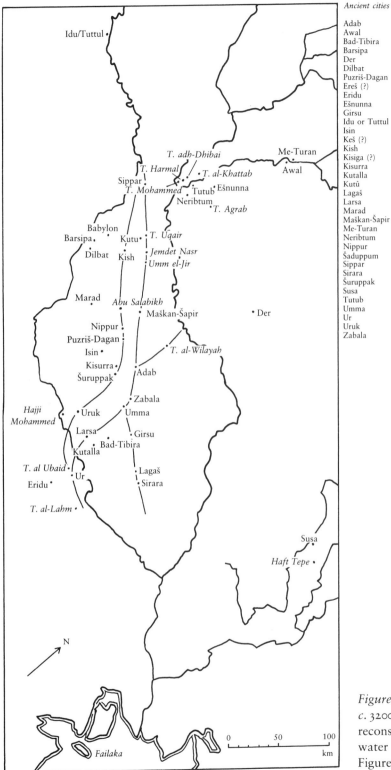

Ancient cities	Modern sites
Adab	T. Bismayah
Awal	T. as-Suleimeh
Bad-Tibira	T. al-Mada'in
Barsipa	Birs Nimrud
Der	T. Aqar (Badra)
Dilbat	T. Dlehem
Puzriš-Dagan	T. Drehem
Ereš (?)	Abu Salabikh
Eridu	Abu Shahrein
Ešnunna	T. Asmar
Girsu	Tello
Idu or Tuttul	Hit
Isin	Ishan al-Bahriyat
Keš (?)	T. al-Wilayah
Kish	T. Ingharra + T. Uheimir
Kisiga (?)	T. al-Lahm
Kisurra	Abu Hatab
Kutalla	T. Sifr
Kutû	T. Ibrahim
Lagaš	Al-Hiba
Larsa	Senkereh
Marad	Wannat es-Sa'dun
Maškan-Šapir	T. Abu Duwari
Me-Turan	T. Haddad
Neribtum	Ishchali
Nippur	Nuffar
Šaduppum	T. Harmal
Sippar	Abu Habba + T. ed-Der
Sirara	Zurghul
Šuruppak	T. Fara
Susa	Shush
Tutub	Khafajah
Umma	T. Jokha
Ur	T. al-Muqayyar
Uruk	Warka
Zabala	T. Ibzeikh

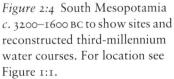

Figure 2:4 South Mesopotamia
c. 3200–1600 BC to show sites and
reconstructed third-millennium
water courses. For location see
Figure 1:1.

Rulers and dynasties

The other work is universally known today as the 'Sumerian King List', but in antiquity it was called, after its first line, 'When kingship came down from heaven'. In the form known to us it was probably compiled shortly after the downfall of the Ur III Dynasty. It lists kings with their lengths of reign, dynasty by dynasty, winding up with the well-known rulers of Ur III and their successors at Isin. The premiss on which the text is constructed is that only one city at a time was the seat of the 'kingship' (**nam-lugal**): as we shall see, the Sumerian word **lugal**, meaning literally 'big man', was not the usual title of the ruler of a city(-state), and as the King List follows the shift of power from one dynasty to another it comments 'City A was smitten with weapons [or: destroyed], its kingship was taken to City B' (Text 2.2). In other words, it presents a formulaic view of politics in the third millennium BC, whereby the rulers of some of the city-states (and those listed after the Flood are only Kish, Uruk, Ur, Adab, Akšak and finally Isin, inside The Land, plus Mari, Awan and Hamazi from outside) exercised a more or less transitory hegemony over some or all of the others, known as 'kingship'.

> **Text 2:2** The Sumerian King List: last two kings of 1st Dynasty of Kish
> En-mebaragesi, the one who carried away as spoil the weapons of the land of Elam, became king and reigned 900 years; Akka, son of En-mebaragesi, reigned 625 years.
>
> 23 kings reigned its 24,510 years, 3 months, and $3\frac{1}{2}$ days. Kish was smitten with weapons; its kingship was carried to Eanna [= Uruk].
>
> (After Jacobsen 1939, 82–5)

It has often been pointed out that this composition is far from a dispassionate chronicle of events. It begins with an entirely fanciful antediluvian section devoted to the cities of Eridu, Badtibira, Sippar, Larak and Šuruppak and their legendary rulers with reigns of marvellous length, but beyond this there are omissions and biases which reflect partly the inadequacy of whatever sources may have been available to the original compilers, and partly their political motivation for undertaking it in the first place. Moreover, it is obvious to even the most cursory reader that the format of a list of kings is inadequate to convey the real complexity of events in the Early Dynastic period. Despite all these difficulties, we cannot merely leave the King List out of consideration. In part this is because Mesopotamian historians, whether they admit it or not, are influenced by this propaganda document of nearly 4000 years ago; in part because it can be checked in places with independent contemporary documents which show that there is genuine historical tradition incorporated within it. Hence, if the King List speaks of the hegemony of foreign powers like Mari, or Awan and Hamazi somewhere to the east, we cannot dismiss this as mere legend, but have to give it the benefit of the doubt even if there are no contemporary records of such a domination.[27]

Broadly, other sources tend to confirm the importance attached by the King List to the four cities of Kish, Ur, Uruk and Adab during the age before Sargon of Akkad. Ur's fame centres round its wealth as revealed by Sir Leonard Woolley's excavation of the temple and royal cemetery in the 1920s and 1930s. The contemporary expedition to Kish revealed two Early Dynastic buildings which remain the earliest secular palaces in the archaeological record (cf. Figures 2:5 and 7:2). Although these are probably no older than the ED III period, there are other indicators that Kish exercised significant hegemony before this time, as implied by the King List, which lists Kish as the first holder of the 'kingship' after the Flood. One of the poems in the 'Uruk Cycle' of legends concerns a confrontation between Kish, under King Akka, and Uruk under Gilgamesh: although the honours, naturally, go to Uruk, it is clear that at the start of the poem the city had acknowledged the hegemony of Kish.[28] Purists will argue, with good reason, that this poem is not a historical document; perhaps more convincing is the curious fact that 'King of Kish' was a title adopted by members of other dynasties to constitute a claim of paramount hegemony. The first two Akkad Dynasty kings called themselves 'King of Kish' rather than 'Akkad'; and the same applies to Me-salim, of whom more shortly. Kish too can boast the earliest 'royal inscription' of all. The father of Gilgamesh's opponent Akka was, according to the King List, En-mebaragesi. From Khafajah in the Diyala region north-east of Babylonia a small fragment of marble vase bears part of his name, similar to another – unprovenanced – which has his name and the title 'King of Kish' (Figure 2:6). The significance is not only

Figure 2:5 War scene, shell inlay on slate, found in the audience hall of Palace A at Kish. (S. Langdon, *Excavations at Kish* I, 1924, Plate XXXVI.1)

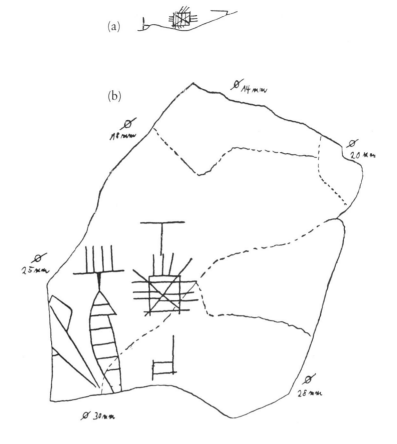

Figure 2:6 Earliest royal inscriptions: two stone bowl sherds bearing the name of (En-)Mebaragesi: (a) excavated by the Chicago expedition at Khafajah; (b) purchased on the antiquities market, but probably also from Khafajah. (b) Reads: 'Me-barage-si, King of Kish.' (a) Kh.III.35, after Jacobsen in Delougaz 1940, 147; (b) IM 30590, Edzard 1959.

the attestation of his historicity, but the location of the find: for later parallels strongly suggest that for him to have dedicated a bowl at a Khafajah temple implied that the city acknowledged his hegemony.

The best parallel for this perhaps comes from another man who claimed the title 'King of Kish' – but does not feature in the King List at all. Me-salim's name is found on stone offering bowls from the city temple of Adab, excavated, with more enthusiasm than science, by Banks at the site of Bismaya in the early years of the twentieth century.[29] They also mention the name of the local city ruler or '**ensi**', and it is clear that there is a two-tier political hierarchy with Me-salim as the overlord. One can propose this with greater confidence because exactly this relationship is attested with the southern city-state of Lagaš: here the local ruler (**ensi**) is Lugal-šag-engur, Me-salim is again the **lugal**, and their names are on a stone macehead decorated with lions (see Figure 2:7).

Figure 2:7 Macehead of Me-salim. The inscription reads 'Me-salim, King of Kish, builder of the temple of Ningirsu, set this up for Ningirsu. Lugal-šag-engur was the **ensi** of Lagaš.' (AO 2349 A. Photo: Musée du Louvre/AO)

That his role was not purely nominal follows from an inscription from a later Lagaš ruler, Enmetena, who tells us that 'Enlil fixed the frontier between Ningirsu and Šara [the city-gods of Lagaš and Umma respectively]. Me-salim, King of Kish, on the order of Ištaran, measured it and put up a stele'.[30] All this is entirely in accord with Me-salim's assumption of the title 'King of Kish' – but why, in that case, does he not figure in the King List? The answer seems to be in two parts: first, he is not himself from Kish, but assumed that title once he had achieved a hegemony, and, second, his home city was not acknowledged by the King List. The only clue to his home city is afforded by his association with the god Ištaran, which suggests, without proving, that he may have hailed from Der, on the road to Susa. The points we should perhaps stress here are that he provides a good example from contemporary sources of a superordinate tier of kingship, just as it is portrayed by the King List, and that despite this he does not himself feature there.

The selectivity exemplified by this omission of one of the few historical figures that emerge from the mists of the Pre-Sargonic period is even more striking with the King List's silence on the subject of Lagaš itself. Admittedly our view is biased because it is from

Lagaš (and more specifically from the capital city of Girsu [= Tello]) that by far the longest and most numerous historical inscriptions derive. Nevertheless, there is no doubt that Lagaš did play a leading role in the politics of Sumer from time to time, as one would expect from its size and cultural distinction: some of its kings adopted the title of **lugal**, and Eanatum mentions that he defeated Kish, Akšak, Mari, Elam and Subartu (North Mesopotamia), which led him to claim the title of 'King of Kish' (though who knows for how long!). We know that its rulers corresponded on terms of equality with the ruling house of Adab, and from the time of Ur-Nanše to the end of his dynasty – some 150 years – there is no sign in our sources of any external domination.[31]

Although the authentic sources confirm the general picture of a number of rival cities with changing fortunes and claims to hegemony, neither they nor the King List itself enable us to reconstruct the course of events in any detail. It is irrelevant to accuse the King List of omitting things when we don't know why it was compiled and from what sources. Let us turn, therefore, to the less explicitly political evidence provided by documents written at the time without any intention of conveying that kind of information.

Cultural and commercial union

In the 'Seal Impression Strata' outside the walls of the main temple of Ur, Woolley found deep deposits of debris, which must have been thrown out from its ovens and storerooms. For the excavator the most noticeable component of this rubbish was the large number of clay sealings, from goods, jars or doors, bearing the imprints of seals of ED I date. Among these is a small group known as the 'city seals' because the design consists of a number of symbols each of which must represent one of the city-states (see Figure 2:8). The symbols are composed of a schematic altar base plus the symbol or totem associated with the city god: altar + snake, altar + bird, etc. Some of these cannot yet be identified with their cities, but others are well known to us because they later become the standard cuneiform signs for the cities in question: altar + sun = Larsa, altar + doorpost = Zabala, etc.[32] Ur has given us the majority of such sealings, but earlier examples are now attested at Jemdet Nasr, both on a sealing and on tablets, and two Early Dynastic sealings come from Uruk itself.[33]

What are the implications of these seals? Application of a seal is an act implying responsibility or authority, and the mere existence of a seal which includes the symbols of different cities implies some form of co-operation. This was recognized by Th. Jacobsen in an influential article in 1957, when he described the sealings as 'most easily understood as used for sealing deliveries from a common fund of goods, created for a common purpose by individual contributions from the cities collectively sealing'.[34] This agreed well with his broader conception of Early Dynastic Sumer as constituting a league of city-states, collaborating in the economic sphere and therefore, to some extent, in politics as well.[35]

Inter-city co-operation in a military sphere was demonstrated by Jacobsen from the administrative texts found at the central Sumerian city of Šuruppak by the German expedition to Fara. These list workers or soldiers in hundreds, from cities such as Nippur, Adab, Umma, Lagaš and Uruk, but in the nature of such documents we can only guess at

(a) A group of symbols from one seal impression (ED I levels at Ur). (Drawing: courtesy R.J. Matthews)

(b) Selected symbols from various seals:
(1) Eridu? (2) Larsa (3) 'snake' (4) 'bird' (5) Ur
(6) Der? (7) Keš. (After Legrain 1936)

1 2 3 4 5 6 7

(c) Egyptian Pre-Dynastic city symbols on a palette. (Baines 1989, 474)

Figure 2:8 Symbols of cities from Sumer and, for comparison, from Egypt at about the same time.

the political reality behind these arrangements. One Fara document also hints at peacetime relations between the different cities, with a list of lands held by Adab, Umma and Lagaš.[36] A similar situation is suggested by an Abu Salabikh land allocation text which mentions an **ensi** probably from Uruk, while at the central city of Zabala at the end of the Early Dynastic period the temple lands included allotments to the rulers (**ensi**) of Nippur and Adab.[37]

It is only to be expected that close links were maintained between the different cities on the alluvial plain. For the import of luxuries and staples they were often dependent on one another for safe passage of the goods, and the paramount importance of controlling the river regime imposed some form of collaboration between one settlement and another. In other places and times common economic or political interests have often led to leagues of one kind or another, Delphic or Hanseatic. In later times Nippur played a central role in the ideology of Sumer: those who achieved political control of the land were seen by official ideology as having been given the kingship by Enlil, the leading god, with his shrine at Nippur. How Nippur came to play this role remains obscure: Jacobsen suggests that in the ED I period 'Nippur was originally the meeting place to which the citizens of the Sumerian cities assembled to elect common leaders'.[38] Undeniably, as we shall shortly see, effective domination of Nippur was seen as conferring legitimacy of a kind on a supra-local hegemony, but it is hard to avoid the conclusion that Nippur's principal qualification was its location at the centre of the plain, and there does not appear to be any reason for supposing that in the early days of the 'league' the collaboration included the selection of leaders, rather than the formation of mutually agreed arrangements on an equal footing, as with the Amphictyonic league which met at Delphi and Thermopylae.

There was also undoubtedly a sense of belonging to a common cultural entity. In comparable instances, such as Classical Greece, the 'koine' could be more or less defined in terms of language. As we shall see shortly, both Sumerian and Akkadian were spoken in South Mesopotamia, and the concept of 'The Land' (**kalam**) seems to have included the entire alluvial plain. The common consciousness shows, for example, when a peace treaty was concluded between Lagaš and Umma: the oath-taking to solemnify the agreement was attended by a curious ritual of smearing ointment on the eyes of doves and despatching them to the principal Sumerian divinities: Enlil at Nippur, Ninhursag at Keš, Enki at Eridu, Nanna at Ur and Utu at Larsa. In this way the participants were obviously bringing the treaty to the notice of these gods, who would act as witnesses to it, which meant in human terms that it was brought before the consciousness of the other city-states in Sumer.

At the very end of the Early Dynastic, in the third year of the last independent ruler of Lagaš, UruKAgina, we happen to know that his wife sent an extensive offering of different kinds of fish to Nippur.[39] This is obviously some move in the complex diplomatic game of the time, and underlines the potential role of a religious centre in the realm of secular politics. This comes out much more clearly in an almost contemporary inscription found on a great number of stone bowls excavated at the central shrine of Enlil by the Philadelphia expedition in the 1890s. Its presentation of the ideology surrounding the events is so precise as to make it worth quoting in full (Text 2:3). Here, at its most explicit, is the formal ideology of Sumerian politics: Lugal-zagesi, who originated from Umma, tells us that as a result of his military or political prowess he has achieved the domination of Sumer, expressed as being given the Kingship of the Land by Enlil; hence his dedication of these bowls to him at Nippur.

We know very little more of the events which led to Lugal-zagesi's rise; he seems to claim to have marched from the Gulf to the Mediterranean. He mentions only a few of the traditional cities of The Land, and we are unable to assess the significance of the omissions: were they not, at the time of the inscription, under his control, or is the list very selective? One city he does not mention is Lagaš, where ironically his activity is best attested, in the shape of a sack of temples in the countryside which was the subject of a lamentation condemning him and exonerating UruKAgina, the **ensi** of Lagaš at the time (Text 6:4, p. 119).

To conclude, the evidence of contemporary inscriptions agrees with later traditions in painting a picture of Early Dynastic South Mesopotamia. There were a number, perhaps thirty individual city-states with strong local individualities symbolized by their city gods and their main shrines. These cities shared a consciousness of belonging to 'The Land', with Nippur and the Temple of Enlil there acting as the symbolic centre. There is evidence of considerable interaction, both peaceful political and economic co-operation, and military confrontation leading to the domination of one polity over another, but there is no evidence that there was significant interference with the internal affairs of one city by another.

Text 2:3 Vase inscription of Lugal-zagesi

When to Lugal-zagesi – King of Uruk, King of the Land, priest of An, 'prophet' of Nisaba, son of Bubu (Governor of Umma, 'prophet' of Nisaba), looked on favourably by An, king of countries, the Chief Governor of Enlil, granted wisdom by Enki, chosen by Utu, High Vizier of Sin, General of Utu, provider for Inanna, son born of Nisaba and suckled on the milk of Ninhursag, man of Mes-sanga-unuga, *brought up* by Ningirim the lady of Uruk, and High Steward of the gods – Enlil, king of countries had given the Kingship of the Land, made the Land obedient to him, thrown all countries at his feet, and subjected them to him from sunrise to sunset, – at that time he made his way from the Lower Sea, via the Tigris and Euphrates, to the Upper Sea, and Enlil had allowed none to oppose him from sunrise to sunset. Under him all countries lay (contented) in their meadows, and the Land rejoiced. The shrines of Sumer, the Governors of all countries and the region of Uruk *decreed* the role of ruler for him. At that time Uruk spent the days in celebrations, Ur raised its head to heaven like a bull, Larsa the city beloved of Utu rejoiced, Umma the city beloved of Šara raised high its horn, the region of Zabala cried out like a ewe reunited with its lamb, and (the city) KI.AN raised its neck to the sky.

Lugal-zagesi, King of Uruk, King of the Land, ... made great offerings at Nippur to Enlil his king, and libated sweet water to him.

If Enlil, King of all countries, would say a prayer for me to An, the father who loves him, and add life to my life, then will the country lie (contented) in its meadows under me, then surely will mankind spread abroad like grass, the udder of heaven will operate properly, the Land will experience comfort under me. May (the gods) not revoke the favourable destiny they have decreed for me, may I forever be shepherd....

For his life he dedicated this to Enlil, the king who loves him.

(See Cooper 1986, 94–5, for another translation and bibliography)

'Sumerian' and 'Akkadian'

I have used the term 'The Land' to refer to South Mesopotamia, partly to follow contemporary usage and partly to avoid using more specific terms, since, unlike the monolithic structure of ancient Egypt, these are constantly shifting and confusing. With the advent of the Dynasty of Akkad we cannot defer any longer dealing with the languages spoken and the various names for the country. After that dynasty the rulers of South Mesopotamia called themselves 'King of Sumer and Akkad', and from these toponyms the two major languages of third-millennium Mesopotamia are named 'Sumerian' and 'Akkadian' by both the Mesopotamians themselves and modern scholars. In view of the languages' ethnic, social and political correlates, it is essential to understand the implications of each term. Let us begin with Sumerian. It is only known as a living language from South Mesopotamia in the third millennium BC,[40] but in cuneiform schools it survived until the first century BC as a scholastic exercise like medieval Latin. Thanks to this, we have bilingual vocabularies or dictionaries and texts with Akkadian translations, from which we can understand a good deal of the original Sumerian inscriptions which have come down to us. Nevertheless, the further back one goes in time, writing is more pictographic and less explicit, to the degree that with the very earliest Uruk period texts we can only guess (albeit confidently) that the language being recorded is Sumerian (see chapter 3). Added to this is the problem that Sumerian has no known relations (despite the best efforts of the optimistic) so that neither its grammatical structure nor its vocabulary can be reconstructed by reference to any previously known language.

Fortunately the same does not apply to Akkadian (see Figure 2:9). This term is derived directly from the name of the capital city founded by Sargon at the beginning of the Dynasty of Akkad. Our use of it today follows the example of those who spoke it, the Babylonians of the second and first millennia BC, and it covers the dialects spoken in both Babylonia (South Mesopotamia) and Assyria (North Mesopotamia) for most of this period until they were gradually ousted by Aramaic in the first millennium BC. We can first discern these two major dialects only after the collapse of the Ur III empire, when Old Babylonian becomes the lingua franca of most of South and much of North Mesopotamia, and Old Assyrian emerges as the dialect peculiar to the city of Assur. Since the incoming population at that date was Amorite, speaking an entirely different Semitic language, the Babylonian and Assyrian speakers must already have been settled in Mesopotamia, but it is at present impossible to determine the exact relationship of these younger dialects to that used by the kings of Akkad and their scribes, generally known as Old Akkadian. What is clear is that it retained some features found in other Semitic languages (e.g. in morphology, such as a freely formed dual, or in phonology, such as the 'ayin or a separate phoneme corresponding to the interdental th) which did not survive in later Akkadian, perhaps under the influence of Sumerian.[41]

Obviously Akkadian too did not suddenly come into existence with the founding of a new city. In the last two decades it has become clear that a Semitic language akin to Akkadian was widely spread in the settled societies of the early third millennium. Previously the best hint of this came from the names of the legendary kings of the 1st Dynasty of Kish, several of which were clearly Semitic; but the King List does not have the authenticity of a contemporary document, and it was a considerable surprise to scholars when in 1965 Robert Biggs announced that a good proportion of the scribes who had written the early Sumerian literary tablets found in excavations at Abu Salabikh, not far north of Nippur, bore Semitic names. It subsequently emerged that they also used some Semitic words when writing administrative documents, such as the numbers '100' (*mi-at*) and '1000' (*li-im*), and words for 'and' (*u*) and 'in' (*in*). This made it clear that there was a Semitic element in the population which was well integrated in the life of the cities, at least in the northern region, not a mere rabble of nomadic tribes on the fringes of civilization.[42]

The second surprise was even bigger: in 1976 an Italian expedition working in northern Syria, at an impressive walled site called Tell Mardikh not far south of Aleppo, discovered the palace archives of a kingdom of the mid-third millennium. The town was called Ebla, and the archives were on cuneiform tablets baked hard by the conflagration which had

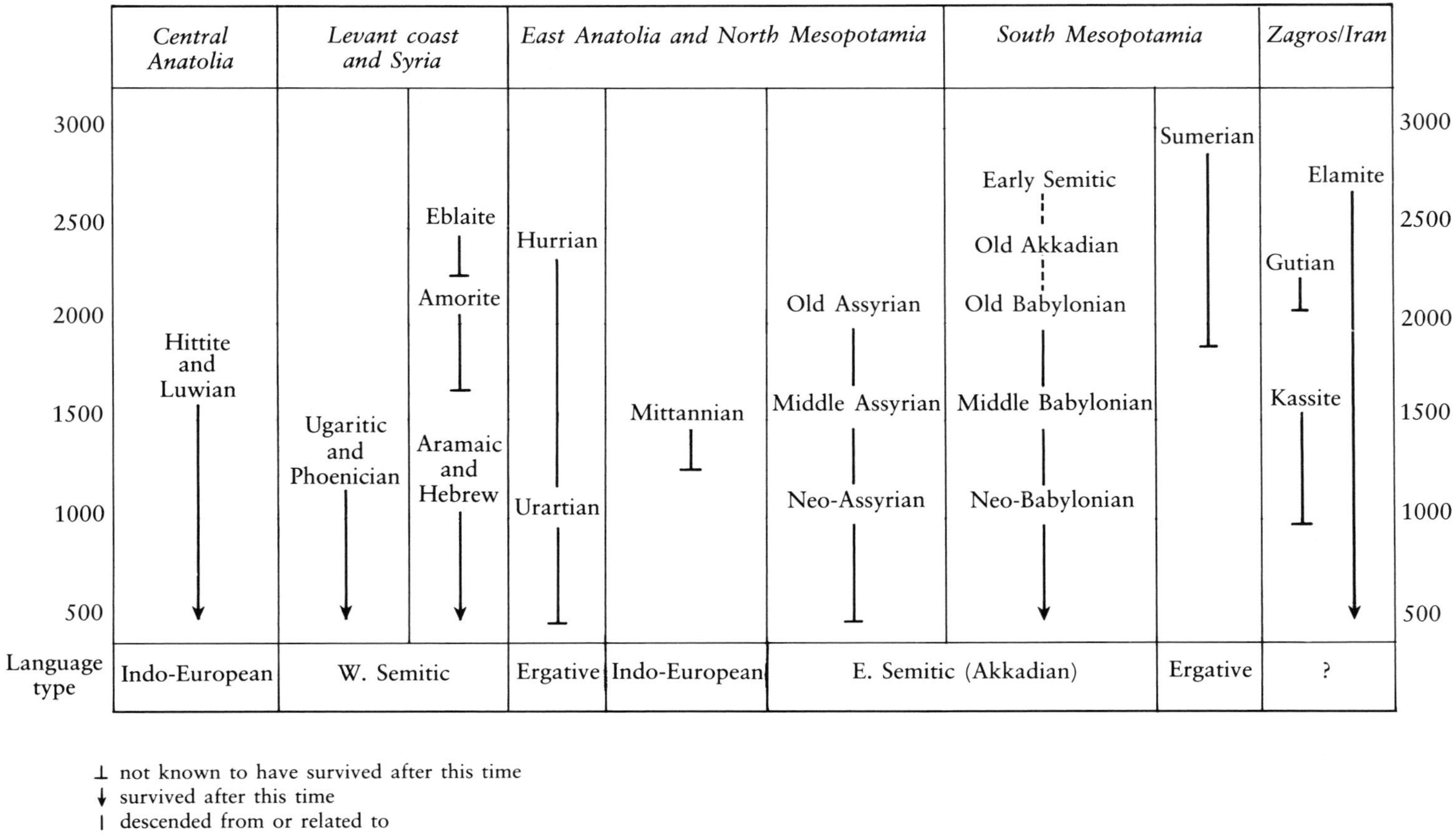

Figure 2:9 Chart of the principal languages of the ancient Near East with their geographical base and genetic relationships.

⊥ not known to have survived after this time
→ survived after this time
| descended from or related to

	Central Anatolia	Levant coast and Syria	East Anatolia and North Mesopotamia	South Mesopotamia	Zagros/Iran
3000				Sumerian	Elamite
2500		Eblaite	Hurrian	Early Semitic	Gutian
2000	Hittite and Luwian	Amorite / Ugaritic and Phoenician		Old Akkadian / Old Babylonian / Old Assyrian	Kassite
1500			Mittannian	Middle Babylonian / Middle Assyrian	
1000		Aramaic and Hebrew	Urartian	Neo-Babylonian / Neo-Assyrian	
500					
Language type	Indo-European	W. Semitic	Ergative / Indo-European / E. Semitic (Akkadian)	Ergative / E. Semitic (Akkadian)	?

destroyed the palace (see Figure 3:8, p. 59). The exact date of this disaster remains to be determined, but most of the tablets are probably contemporary with the closing years of the Early Dynastic period in Mesopotamia. Among them were scholastic or literary texts already known in fragmentary state from the Sumerian archives of Fara (Šuruppak) or Abu Salabikh, but the majority were administrative documents, written in a mixture of Sumerian and a Semitic dialect provisionally known as Eblaite. As time has passed, close similarities have been observed between the early Semitic of Mesopotamia and Eblaite, and also of Mari, on the Euphrates route between the two. In fact, it becomes clear that there were close cultural and linguistic links between Ebla, North Mesopotamia, Mari and the region of Kish as far south as Abu Salabikh.[43] How these links came into being is beyond our knowledge and my remit, but analogous patterns can be observed in later times, as a result of the establishment of Amorite, Aramaean and Arab dynasties in the Near East, whereby close links were maintained between new dynasties controlling the old settled lands from southern Syria, across North Mesopotamia and down to South Iraq.

However the situation arose, it is clear that the Akkadians (in the strict sense) were not the first Semitic dynasty to rule part of The Land, and a significant proportion of the people of the northern part of the alluvial plain probably spoke a Semitic language – how significant must await more evidence from Kish or a similar site. We don't at present have enough of that language to be sure whether it could be considered a direct ancestor of Old Akkadian, or is the same or nearly the same as the languages of Ebla and Mari, so that for the present the cautious nomenclature of Robert Biggs' 'early Semitic' is probably the best to adopt, while recognizing that a close connection between some or all of these is entirely possible.[44]

'Sumer' and 'Akkad'

Enheduana's Temple Hymn addressing the Temple of Enlil at Nippur says 'on your right and left are Sumer and Akkad'. This reflects a long-lasting tradition that north is 'left' and south 'right',[45] but the terms translated 'Sumer' and 'Akkad' are very enigmatic: in translation we use the Akkadian words, but in Sumerian they are **ki-en-gi** and **ki-uri**. 'Akkad', or rather 'the land of Akkad' (*māt akkadîm*) is straightforward, as it is simply named after Sargon's new capital at a site somewhere in the northern alluvial plain still to be identified; but it follows that we do not know what this part of the land was called before Sargon. The Sumerian term is **ki-uri**; **ki** means 'region', but **uri** remains an enigma, and the term is not yet attested before the reign of Sargon.[46] 'Sumer', or rather 'the land of Sumer', is first attested even later, in an Akkadian inscription of Sargon's successor Rimuš. The derivation of the term is quite obscure. 'Sumer' in Sumerian is **ki-en-gi(r)**, likely to mean 'land (of) Sumerian tongue'.[47] The word itself is used regularly in the Akkadian Dynasty to refer to part of the southern alluvium, and crops up sporadically in texts as early as the beginning of ED III, in contexts which are generally consistent with that part of The Land south of Nippur.

If this analysis is correct, the broad implication is that there was a significant divide between a predominantly Sumerian-speaking south and a predominantly(?)

Lagaš Dynasty	2550 Ur-Nanše
	Akurgal
	Eanatum
	Enanatum I
	2450 Enmetena
	Enanatum II
	Enentarzi
	Lugalanda
	2380 UruKAgina

	Conquest by Lugal-zagesi
	2350 Conquest by Sargon
Akkad Dynasty	2371 Sargon
	2315 Rimuš
	2306 Maništušu
	2291 Naram-Sin
	2254 Šar-kali-šarri

2230 Gutian interregnum

Gudea's dynasty at Lagaš

	Conquest by Ur
Ur III Dynasty	2113 Ur-Nammu
	2095 Šulgi
	2047 Amar-Suen
	2038 Šu-Sin
	2029 Ibbi-Sin

Conquest by Amorites/Elamites

Isin	*Larsa*	*Babylon*	*Mari*
	2025 Naplanum		
2017 Išbi-Erra		1894 Sumu-abum	
1934 Lipit-Ištar		1880 Sumu-la-el	
1861 Enlil-bani		1844 Sabium	Yaggit-Lim
	1834 Warad-Sin	1830 Apil-Sin	Samsi-Addu
	1822 Rim-Sin I	1812 Sin-muballiṭ	Išme-Dagan Yahdun-Lim
1816 Damiq-ilišu		1792 Hammurapi	Yasmah-Addu
		1749 Samsu-iluna	Zimri-Lim
1794 Conquest by Larsa	1763 Conquest by Babylon	1711 Abi-ešuh	1759 Conquest by Babylon
		1683 Ammi-ditana	
		1646 Ammi-ṣaduqa	
		1625 Samsu-ditana	
		1595 Conquest by Mursilis	

NB All dates are approximate, many dynasties and rulers omitted!

Figure 2:10 Principal Mesopotamian dynasties and rulers, 2350–1595 BC. (Dates after *Cambridge Ancient History*)

Semitic/Akkadian-speaking north, centred round Kish. In detail it is difficult to assess differences between the two regions, since very little of our documentation refers to the northern area, but the political aspect of the antithesis is crystallized in the story of Gilgamesh, hero of Sumerian Uruk, and his resistance to the imperial ambitions of Akka of Kish, and it throws another light on the episode of Me-salim, with his Semitic name and interference in southern affairs. We should not conclude that the north–south opposition was caused by a linguistic or ethnic difference, since it is clear that speakers of the two languages were peacefully integrated in both regions.[48] It does throw a different light on the Akkad episode however, to which we now turn.

The Dynasty of Akkad

The fame of Sargon of Akkad, which survives in omens and epics as far afield as Hattusas and El-Amarna, is that of a conqueror. The scanty contemporary documentation we have for him and his dynasty substantiates their military accomplishments and ideology, but also reveals the other side of the coin and underlines the superficiality of their territorial achievements. Both the literary tradition and the dynasty's own inscriptions – mostly copied by antiquarian Old Babylonian scribes from monuments erected at Nippur – show a wide geographical horizon. Ships from down the Gulf and beyond docked at the quays of Akkad, and the armies of Akkad cross the sea to Magan (= Oman), campaign through northern Mesopotamia into Syria, and penetrate on to the Iranian and Anatolian plateaux. The question to be asked in each case is: was it a lightning raid, yielding fame and booty but little else, or an effective annexation of territory? Administrative tablets of the Akkad Dynasty have been excavated quite far afield, at Susa, Gasur (= later Nuzi in the Zab–Diyala block) and Tell Brak in the Habur triangle. Evidently for a period the kings did establish their own administration at these ancient centres.

In the south too Sargon introduced a new level of central intervention. After his initial defeat of Lugal-zagesi he reports that he razed the walls of his capital Uruk, and the other principal cities of Ur, Lagaš and Umma, and installed 'sons of Akkad' as governors, giving them the title of **ensi** and hence displacing the traditional local civilian hierarchy. They must have been accompanied by some kind of administrative cadre and some military support. Indeed the Akkadian period sees the introduction of the Akkadian language in administrative documents even from the southern, Sumerian, cities, and some of these record the presence of troops with Akkadian names, evidently garrisoned there (e.g. at Girsu and even Susa). The political aspect of the hegemony was not neglected: documents are now dated with the formulae of the Akkad king (Text 2:4),[49] and legal oaths are by the king's life. Akkad Dynasty tablets adopt new formats, and a 'chancery' script of great

Text 2:4 Akkad Dynasty year-names
(a) The year when Sargon went to Simurrum.
(b) The year when Naram-Sin conquered … and Abullat, and felled cedars in Mt Lebanon.
(c) The year following the year when Šar-kali-šarri went down to Sumer for the first time.

(After Westenholz 1975, 115, and 1987, 203)

regularity and formality is introduced. In an attempt to engage with the traditional religious ideology, Sargon's daughter, and after her Naram-Sin's, were installed as high-priestesses of the moon-god Nanna at Ur, with the names Enheduana and Enmenana. The drive for a standardized central system is perhaps expressed most dramatically in the reform of the metrology. Previously each city had its own systems of weights and measures, which must have been almost as much of a headache for their contemporaries as they are to modern scholars. Probably in the reign of Naram-Sin the measures of length, area, dry and liquid capacity, and probably also weight were integrated into a single logical system which remained the standard for a thousand years and more.[50]

These changes did not come in without resistance. Sargon's inscriptions make it clear that he viewed himself as freeing the north from southern domination, in the shape of Lugal-zagesi. He records that a large number of men (5,400) took their daily meal before him at Akkad. Military leaders through time have needed land to reward their followers, and clear written evidence survives that the Akkad kings overrode local property status quo to find somewhere for their men: one of the most revealing documents of the time is the Obelisk of Maništušu (Figure 5:5, p. 94), on which large areas of land owned by extended families in the northern plain are purchased by the king, under what compulsion is not made explicit, while in the fully Sumerian south confiscations and purchases of large estates are also recorded.[51] With this sort of interference from an upstart dynasty, rebellion was to be expected, especially after his death: Rimuš faced revolt by a king of Ur, and **ensis** at Lagaš, Zabala, Adab and Umma. Naram-Sin records a massive revolt, remembered in later tradition as 'when the four edges of the world rebelled against him', involving nine major battles and most of the Mesopotamian cities. However, he did re-establish Akkad's control, and for a while at least it enjoyed a golden age (see Text 4:4, p. 78).

Later tradition saw Naram-Sin as presiding over the demise of the dynasty, but in fact we know that his successor Šar-kali-šarri retained the throne for a good quarter century, even if the foreign conquests dropped away. As with the closing years of the other dynasties, there is evidence of infiltration of the land by foreign tribes, in this case the Guti, who came from the Zagros hills and are described by the Sumerian King List as 'the horde of Gutium'. Apart from a couple of anxious letters reporting their marauding, we have no documentary sources for this time, nor would we expect them, since orderly bureaucracy is one of the first things to go when the times are out of joint. The disruption was no doubt greatest in the northern part of the plain, and before long Lagaš was experiencing a Sumerian 'renaissance' under Gudea and his dynasty; unfortunately we have no way at present of guessing whether or not there was an overlap with the end of the Akkad dynasty. Freedom from the Gutians was eventually achieved by a certain Utu-hegal, ruler of Uruk, who has left us an account of a decisive campaign in which he drove them from The Land.

The 3rd Dynasty of Ur

Once the scourge of the Gutians had been dissipated, no doubt other ancient centres as well as Lagaš nursed aspirations of independence, but if they were successful it was not to last. Seven years after the defeat of Tirigan, Utu-hegal died and domination passed to

Ur-Nammu, once probably one of his governors, but now the founder of the 3rd Dynasty of Ur. The course of conquest is not known, and need not have been specially arduous, but by the end of his reign he had established control of most, if not all, of Sumer and Akkad, adopting for the first time the title 'King of Ki-engi and Ki-uri'. Under his son Šulgi, who ruled for forty-eight years and is the central figure of the dynasty, the area directly administered by Ur was extended into the eastern fringes of The Land as far as Susa and Assur, but although he adopted the title used by Naram-Sin, 'king of the four rims [of the world]', the sheer extent of the Akkadian empire was not equalled. There are very few historical texts from his reign or either of his two sons, Amar-Suen and Šu-Sin, but the year-names reveal a stick and carrot policy towards the troublesome lands of the north and north-east, repeated campaigns alternating with alliances cemented by international marriages (see Text 2:5).

Text 2:5 Ur III year-name
Year the king's daughter married the **ensi** of Anšan.

(Ungnad 1938, 141, No. 49)

Among modern scholars the Ur III Dynasty is synonymous with one thing: the corpus of thousands upon thousands of administrative documents now scattered through museums and private collections large and small across the world. They were illicitly excavated between 1880 and 1920 in three of the cities of Sumer, Tello (ancient Girsu), Tell Jokha (= Umma) and Drehem (= Puzriš-Dagan, a satellite of Nippur). Official excavations have also turned up lesser numbers at sites like Ur, Nippur itself, and Ešnunna. Over 25,000 of these texts have been published, many more remain in museums, and it is obvious that under the soil of South Iraq there must be comparable archives at other provincial centres. These tablets are the concrete output of a massive programme of bureaucratic control undertaken under Šulgi. Adulatory hymns to the monarch preserved in the school curriculum refer to his introduction of a system of messengers and road stations.[52] He eased administration, and perhaps also commerce, by standardizing weights and measures and introducing a new calendar, and following the Akkadian precedent he installed his own nominees in the traditional role of **ensi**, converting the ancient independent cities into provincial capitals. We shall have much more to say about the contents of these Ur III archives, which convey detailed information about all sorts of unexpected aspects of the society; for now let us simply note that the enormous bureaucratic exercise required a hierarchy of government officials, among whom orders were transmitted and responsibilities meticulously recorded in writing. Indeed when the death of a single sheep appears three times in the government archives, it is hard to believe that the bureaucratic ideal had not become an encumbrance which ultimately contributed to the state's inability to respond to internal and external threats.

Whatever the cause, the downfall of the Ur III Dynasty was as absolute as that of Akkad, only in this case we can observe the process in greater detail. The later years of the dynasty saw an increase of pressure from the Amorite nomads outside the confines of the settled lands. Already the thirty-fifth year of Šulgi was named after the construction of a wall, and its purpose is made clear by another wall after which Šu-Sin named his fourth year

'The year Šu-Sin, king of Ur, built the Amorite Wall [called] "Muriq-Tidnim" ["Fender-off of Tidnum"]'.[53] References in later documents make it probable that this line stretched for more than 200 km across the northern limits of the irrigated plain, from the Euphrates above Sippar to the far side of the Tigris in the region of Baghdad, but it has not been located on the ground.[54] Evidently the wall, and a campaign in which Šu-Sin claims to have defeated the Amorites ('the land of Amurru'; see Text 4:8, p. 84), were essentially defensive measures to keep the nomads out of the settled territories.

Bureaucrats do not record the exceptional, and in the administrative documents contact with the Amorites is generally limited to peaceful intercourse with individuals, whether envoys from outside or immigrants in search of employment. However, some correspondence between a harrassed Ibbi-Sin and his governors was preserved for us because it was included in the curriculum of the schools, and among these letters are some referring to the Amorite threat. He writes to the governor of Isin for supplies of grain to be sent downstream to the capital, and hears back that the boats are not available and that the Amorites have invaded the land and captured forts. The capital's desperate need for these supplies to stave off famine is reflected in administrative texts from Ur, giving vivid evidence of serious inflation, prices of staples such as barley, fish and oil rising sixty-, twenty-four- and fivefold respectively. At the same time the lists of offerings to the Nanna Temple give a clue to the diminishing geographical control of the dynasty, and the process of disintegration is also illustrated by the disposition of the surviving administrative documents: if the latest occurrence of Ur III tablets is plotted at different sites, it becomes clear that during Ibbi-Sin's reign the reach of Ur was rapidly contracting. Texts at Ešnunna cease after his second year, at Susa after his third, and at Lagaš, Umma and Nippur after the fifth, sixth and seventh years in turn.[55]

Disintegration and reintegration

Later tradition lays responsibility for the final defeat of the Ur Dynasty on an invasion from the east, and indeed for a brief period there was an Elamite garrison in the capital, but the inheritors of power were the Amorites. The exact course of events is never likely to be known, but within half a century of the fall of Ur, Sumer and Akkad were divided into numerous small states, most of which had an Amorite ruling house. The period is often referred to as the 'Isin–Larsa' period, and Isin was one of the first cities to establish itself as an independent state, under Išbi-Erra, the very governor with whom Ibbi-Sin had been corresponding. Indeed, documents at Isin begin to be dated by his independent year-names well before the last years of Ibbi-Sin. Similarly other cities would have been taken over by local dynasties as Ibbi-Sin's power waned and his ability to enforce his rule and protect his subjects dwindled.

The Isin Dynasty at least presented itself as the inheritor of the Ur III mantle, and Išbi-Erra records that he ousted the Elamite garrison from the ravaged capital. For two centuries or so in their formal guise the successor states were very much in the shadow of Ur III. Details of political events are very scanty, and a good deal of our information comes from year-names: these betray the concern of the monarchs with cultic events such as the

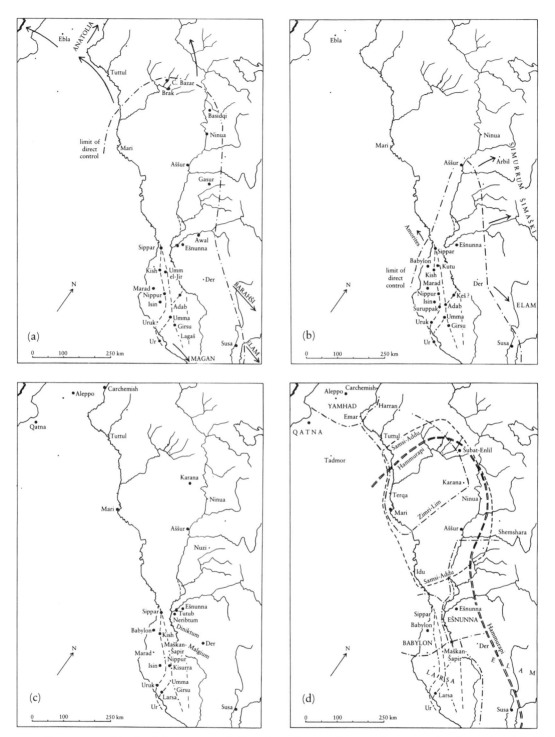

Figure 2:11 Territorial extents and direction of campaigns under successive dynasties. (a) Akkad Dynasty. Sites marked with a large dot have yielded textual evidence of direct Akkadian control. (b) Ur III Dynasty. Sites marked with a large dot known to have been seat of a governor. (c) Isin–Larsa period (*c.* 2000–1800 BC). Sites marked with a large dot known to have been capitals of independent polities. (d) Age of Hammurapi (*c.* 1800–1750 BC), showing approximate maximal limits of direct territorial control. Sites marked with a large dot functioned as capital cities at some time.

dedication of new divine statues or temple furnishings, with the installation of priests, and with the maintenance of the irrigation system and other public works – all very much in the image of the traditional Mesopotamian ruler (see Text 6:2, p. 118). While most of the dynasties in question were of recent Amorite stock and proud of it, their position required that they subscribed to the traditional metaphors of power. For most official purposes Sumerian continued in use, although less formal correspondence and a lively literature show that the Old Babylonian dialect of Akkadian was now the principal language of South Mesopotamia. Similarly the kings of the Isin–Larsa period aped their predecessors by assuming divinity, and a genre of Sumerian royal hymns in praise of different monarchs underlines the search for some kind of legitimacy (see chapter 14). It could not be founded on political inheritance from Ur, for that line was extirpated and the city never again served as a political capital. Recourse was therefore had to the metaphor of Enlil and Nippur, from the last time when the land was divided between equal-ranking city-states.

Not all was continuity. For one thing some of the ancient cities were dying on their feet, and new ones being founded. Ancient Sumerian centres, like Šuruppak, Keš and Ereš were probably more or less moribund and do not seem to have survived the collapse of the Ur III empire. Others were moving in that direction: Old Babylonian texts have been found at Lagaš (= Al-Hiba), Girsu (= Tello) and Adab, but these places are scarcely mentioned in the contemporary political record, and the archaeological evidence for their occupation in Old Babylonian times is scanty.[56] The centre of gravity of The Land was moving inexorably northward. Most of the local dynasties were installed in erstwhile Ur III provincial capitals, but within these separate states other towns gain in importance, like Maškan-šapir, and Dilbat and Borsippa. Behind the political events shifts in the irrigation system were probably responsible for this change: at least the Euphrates moved to a western channel, and despite major projects during the dynasties of Larsa and Babylon much land seems to have fallen out of cultivation.[57]

The world outside

The push and pull of competing dynasties within South Mesopotamia involved a complex network of alliances – not only within Sumer and Akkad, but to the outside world: the importance of Elam is only beginning to be appreciated, and it is significant that the dynasty of Rim-Sin at Larsa had its origins there, to judge from the Elamite name of Kudur-mabuk.[58] The Amorite houses had close links with tribes further north and west, thus for instance the name of Yamutbalum, a district within the kingdom of Larsa itself, crops up again as a tribal group on the upper Habur.[59] The complexity and breadth of the pattern only became apparent with the publication of the amazing diplomatic archives from the palace at Mari (Text 2:6). Here we find that alliances stretch from Elam and the small states bordering it right through northern Mesopotamia to Aleppo in northern and Qatna in central Syria. By the time of the Mari archives, the political dust in the south had settled somewhat and the pattern was clearer: Larsa had annexed its old rival Isin and controlled the southern half, Babylon had emerged as the strongest state in the region of

Akkad, and on its north-eastern flank was the third strong kingdom, centred at Ešnunna. Further north the position was more complex, and requires a separate description.

Text 2:6 Letter to Zimri-Lim, King of Mari

... and with reference to my lord's message to the kings that they should come for the sacrifice to Ištar, I have gathered the kings at Sarmaneh, and made a statement to them as follows: 'There is no king who is strong on his own: Hammurapi of Babylon has a following of 10 or 15 kings, Rim-Sin of Larsa the same, Ibal-pi-El of Ešnunna the same, Amut-pi-El of Qatna the same, and Yarim-Lim of Yamhad has a following of 20 kings ...

(After Dossin 1938a, 114)

The North

With the startling exception of Ebla, we have no substantial historical sources for northern Mesopotamia before the end of the Ur III Dynasty. With the new millennium this changes. Pride of place goes to the two huge archives excavated at Mari and Kaneš, but considerable bodies of tablets have been found in several widely scattered places (Figure 2:12). In some degree this may be a result of chance, but not entirely: political and commercial horizons did recede. The new dynasties in the south were more closely related to those in power elsewhere: while many of the minor city-states of North Mesopotamia remained in the hands of Hurrian princes, as many were now under Amorite rule, and further west the major powers were Amorite dynasts – Aleppo (Yamhad) and Qatna in particular.[60] The geographical scale of events can be illustrated by the fact that at one point the King of Aleppo kept a fleet of boats on the Tigris at Diniktum (near Baghdad) to assist his fellow Amorite sheikhs in their resistance to aggression from Elam (Text 13:6 below). Contact between these 'brothers' was likely to be maintained in any case, but it was ensured because of the fragmented nature of the political scene: where Larsa, Isin, Ešnunna and Babylon vied for supremacy, or at least to maintain their status, alliances were inevitable, and outside South Mesopotamia proper the constellation of minor powers led to immensely complex patterns of alliance and opposition (Text 2:7).

Text 2:7 Letter from Samsi-Addu to Kuwari of Šušarra

Say to Kuwari: Thus says Šamši-Adad. You have of course heard of the hostile behaviour of the Ahazaean Yašub-Adad. Earlier he followed the people from Šimurrum; he then left the people of Šimurrum and followed the Turukkaeans; he then left the Turukkaeans and followed the tribe of Ya'ilanum; then he left Ya'ilanum and followed me; now he has left me and gone with the ruler of Kakmum; and to all these kings he has sworn an oath. From the time when he entered into alliance with these kings, less than three years have passed. When he entered into alliance with me he swore an oath before me in the temple of the god Adad at Arrapha, and in the town of A'innum on the banks of the River Zab he again swore an oath before me, and I swore an oath before him ...

(After Laessøe 1963, 147–8)

This network does not seem to have stretched over the Taurus into Anatolia. The archives of a colony of merchants based at Assur, discovered in the commercial suburb of

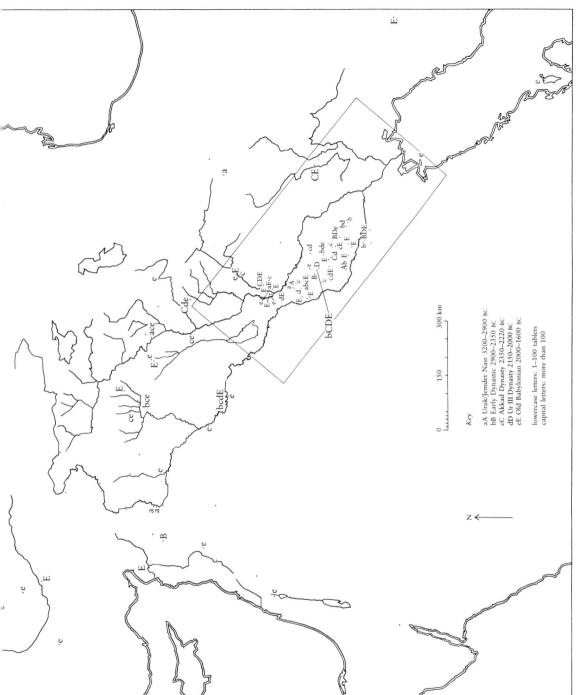

Figure 2:12 Principal cuneiform archives discovered, 3200–1500 BC.

the city of Kaneš (modern Kültepe in central Turkey), reveal a patchwork of local dynasties on the Anatolian plateau, but no sign that they were involved in the power politics of Syria and Mesopotamia. The Assur merchants, whose activities are described in chapter 11, reached their own agreements with the local kings (and queens), but avoided politics as far as possible. Their home city of Assur was not one of the major powers of the day, and it is highly misleading to speak of 'Assyria' at this date, since their ambitions seem to have been exclusively commercial, not territorial. Few contemporary documents are known from Assur itself, but the Kültepe archives give us echoes of a small self-contained community, its ruler constrained by strong merchant houses and a city assembly which kept tight financial and legal control of its distant colony. Like the earlier population of Mari, the people of Assur spoke Akkadian, although a different dialect not known from elsewhere.[61]

Figure 2:13 Statue from the royal suite in the south-west corner of the palace at Mari: 'Iddin-ilum, Governor of Mari, dedicated his statue to Inanna. Whoever destroys this inscription, may Inanna abolish his line.' (Photo: Mission Archéologique de Mari. Courtesy J.-Cl. Margueron)

Like Mari too, Assur fell to the ambitions of an Amorite sheikh, in this case Samsi-Addu (or in Akkadian, Šamši-Adad). He is often referred to as a king of Assyria by modern writers, but it would be better to say that one of his titles was 'Governor of Assur'. The best guess at present is that his father initially established his sedentary base at Terqa, on the Euphrates above Mari, but was dislodged by another Amorite usurper, Yaggit-Lim, who installed his dynasty at Mari itself.[62] Via Babylon, Samsi-Addu took a town called Ekallatum on the middle Tigris from the control of Ešnunna, and then went on to usurp the throne of Assur, to move into the Upper Habur region where he established his capital at a city he renamed 'Enlil's Residence' (Šubat-Enlil; now Tell Leilan), and finally to exact vengeance on Yaggit-Lim's son by turning him out of Mari.

Samsi-Addu appointed his son, Yasmah-Addu, as king of Mari and another son, Išme-Dagan, to cover his eastern flank from Ekallatum. The Mari archives included correspondence between him and his son, but most of the documents date from after his death when Yasmah-Addu had been thrown out by Zimri-Lim, aided by the King of Aleppo, whose daughter he had married. Although bitter enemies, the two families had much in common, as the latest Amorite houses to find a foothold in the traditional urban scene, and to adopt many of the ways of the settled lands including the bureaucratic paraphernalia of a capital city, with officials and scribes writing in the Old Babylonian dialect which is used by the ruling houses as far west as Qatna and deep into the Zagros at Shemshara.[63]

The last two centuries

Ironically, we owe our detailed knowledge of the archives at Mari to the palace's destruction by Hammurapi of Babylon, whose soldiers left the tablets lying in various rooms, along with some of the labels they had written identifying the baskets into which they had sorted them. This was in Hammurapi's thirty-second regnal year. Although previously an ally of Zimri-Lim, it seems as though Hammurapi, having in his thirtieth year annexed the south of The Land by his defeat of Rim-Sin, and defeated Ešnunna in his thirty-first year, determined to make a clean sweep. His stele lists proudly the ancient centres of civilization, north and south, which the gods had entrusted to his rule: including Assur, Mari and an ancient Hurrian centre, Ninua, the later capital of Assyria. This political success was not just another of the swings of the political pendulum, but represents a turning point. Even if more by default than otherwise, Babylon takes on the role of the single capital of the south: only the 1st Dynasty of Babylon remains as a dynastic line, and despite a murmur of resistance from Larsa, the only contenders for power in the future would be outsiders: the Sea-Land Dynasty, the Kassites and, still later, the new nomadic stock of the Aramaeans and Chaldaeans.

This can hardly be laid to the credit of the military prowess of Hammurapi's successors. Ešnunna has vanished from the scene, Mari was dead, and Babylon's control reached no further than the Habur. Across the Euphrates the kings of Aleppo were left almost unchallenged, and were perhaps the first formally to adopt the title Great King, ushering in an era of power politics which involved the Mitannians, the Hittites and the Egyptians, and is most vividly illustrated by the Amarna archive, and falls outside our scope. New light may soon be thrown on this time by the archives of Tell Leilan, Samsi-Addu's one time capital, which reportedly include treaties and other texts revealing the eastward advance of the Aleppo Dynasty at this time, but this need not have brought them into conflict with Babylon, since the horizon of South Mesopotamia seems to contract rapidly, here and in the south. No texts are known from the southern cities like Ur, Uruk and Larsa after Samsu-iluna's tenth year; at Nippur and Isin the writ of Babylon was still acknowledged as late as Samsu-iluna 29, but thereafter documents disappear here too. This documentary hiatus is mirrored archaeologically as well. Careful observation at Nippur has identified a distinct break between the late Old Babylonian and early Kassite layers, confirming observations made more summarily at Ur and elsewhere. To all appearances people not only stopped writing documents at Nippur, Larsa and the other southern cities, but actually moved away from there.[64] No doubt the new holders of power – perhaps the kings of the Sea-Land Dynasty – attracted some of the southern population to them, as their adoption of consciously Sumerian throne-names suggests, but this can only be speculation.

The simple fact is that the kingdom of Babylon ceased to control Nippur or anywhere to its south. Urban and rural life appears to continue peacefully, though with occasional economic distress, at the major northern sites – Sippar, Babylon, Kish, Borsippa and Dilbat in particular. However, the southern cities did not lose all their identity, since – unlike the third-millennium Sumerian centres mentioned above – they are all re-occupied under the Kassite kings. The exact details of the passage of power from Hammurapi's dynasty to the Kassite line are lost. Like the Gutians, the Kassites were almost certainly from the Zagros, and spoke a language without known affinities. They are already in evidence early in the reign of Samsu-iluna, who records a clash with them, but it is only in the final century of the 1st Dynasty of Babylon that we find them on the fringes of the urban world, in encampments on the middle Euphrates or acting as migrant workers or mercenaries in the vicinity of Babylon.[65] Their role resembles that of the Amorites at the end of the Ur III Dynasty, and similarly it was not in fact they, but the quite unexpected appearance of a raiding force under the Hittite king Mursilis, that delivered the coup de grâce. At this point the documentary record ceases abruptly, and when the curtain rises again – after an interval of unknown length – it reveals a very different world.

Further reading

The detail of political events is recounted by the authors of the *Cambridge Ancient History* (CAH), vols 1 and 2. For a more summary version see also W.W. Hallo and W.K. Simpson, *The Ancient Near East: A history* (Harcourt Brace Jovanovich 1971), or J. Bottéro, D.O. Edzard, A. Falkenstein and J. Vercoutter, *The Near East; The early civilizations* (Weidenfeld & Nicolson 1967). Algaze 1989 is an attempt to give the Uruk period a 'historical' dimension, necessarily speculative. For my account of conditions in the Early Dynastic period I am much influenced by Jacobsen, especially Jacobsen 1957. The chapter on the Old Assyrian period in the *Cambridge Ancient History* is entirely outdated by Larsen 1976.

3
The written record

Any attempt to define civilization will at some stage include writing. Obviously the ability to convey information through time and space is a major enabling factor in the organization of a society, and writing, which was probably invented in Mesopotamia, therefore deserves to be studied in its own right. Here, though, my reason for considering it first is not so much its intrinsic importance, but because the written record is the channel through which most of our information about Mesopotamia reaches us. It is therefore important before looking at other aspects of the civilization to appreciate the nature of the writing system, and its applications. Only then are we briefed to know what may have been recorded, and what not, and what parts of that record we should hope or expect to recover.

At the same time, we have to consider the effects of writing on society. It is not merely a mirror of human behaviour but an active ingredient in the system. It can bridge time, space and social distance. Information can be committed to clay for the future, whether as a public record of past events or to satisfy an accounting system. Across space it provides a way of conveying complex messages for political or commercial purposes, while the possibility of creating a mutually agreed record of a transaction gives the opportunity of regulating and hence enhancing economic relationships between different sectors of society.

Origins of writing

Writing is not the only means of recording, nor the earliest. The Incas (and no doubt their predecessors) managed to store their imperial data on devices made of string. String, wooden tallies and other perishable substances are of course lost to us, although occasional references in texts suggest that they may have existed (Text 3:1), and the mention of a 'loom' in lexical lists among scribal devices hints at an abacus.[66] Archaeologists have also recovered suggestive clay tokens from Ubaid period and earlier sites, and a single rare find from the fringes of literate society at fifteenth-century Nuzi illustrates the survival of

---

Text 3:1 From the Debate between the Sheep and the Grain
Every day an account of you (the sheep) is made,
The tally sticks are planted in the ground;
Your shepherd tells the owner, how many ewes and how many little lambs,
How many goats and how many little kids there are.

(After Civil 1969, 168; see now *ASJ* 9 (1987) 25)

non-inscriptional recording devices;[67] but throughout the time span with which we are concerned there is no doubt that any data of importance would have been entrusted to writing, rather than some survival of earlier devices.

The earliest writing in Mesopotamia, and perhaps in the world, is on clay tablets found in the Eanna Temple complex at Uruk. Until recently it claimed this distinction merely by the negative argument that we know of no earlier version; but in the last two decades the case has been strengthened as a number of scholars have shown that in Mesopotamia during the Uruk period recording practices were in use which are very likely to have led directly into the Eanna IV writing tradition. The pieces of this reconstruction have partly been available for some time, and partly emerged during excavations in the 1970s as far apart as Habuba Kabira on the Euphrates bend and Godin Tepe on the Iranian plateau. Although the chronological sequence is not attested stratigraphically, but is reconstructed logically from the evidence, it will be simplest to present it in stages.[68]

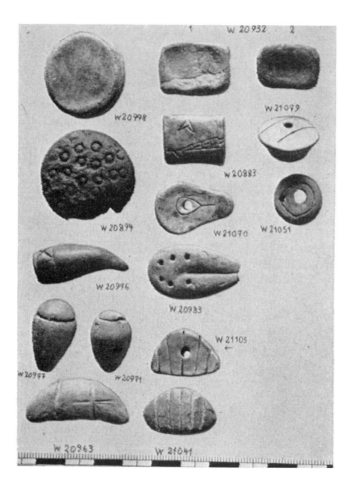

Figure 3:1 Clay tokens from Uruk. (W. 20987,27, Lenzen 1966, Tafel 19b)

Stage 1: 'Bulla with tokens'

At Uruk, but also in particular at Susa, there have been found hollow clay 'balls', usually known as 'bullae' because they bear seal impressions all over their surface. When found intact, these balls contained a variety of little clay tokens (Figure 3:1). Some of these suspiciously resemble the signs for 1, 10 and 60 in the later sexagesimal Mesopotamian numeral system, and others (not all found in association with bullae) are obviously animals or other recognizable commodities.

Stage 2: 'Bulla with tokens and impressed numerals' (Figure 3:2)

Some of these bullae also have impressions in the outer surface, made after the seal-rollings, and in one case, at least, these marks correspond with numeral tokens contained within the bulla.

Figure 3:2 Sealed bulla and tokens from inside. Susa. (P. Amiet, *Glyptique susienne*, Paris 1972, Planche 68, no 539)

Stage 3: 'Tablets'

Logically the next stage in the process was the realization that the information protected so elaborately by the sealed clay sphere could be conveyed equally securely simply by means of marks impressed on the exterior and also authenticated by sealing, because once the clay had dried both marks and sealing were immutable. There are two varieties of tablet, which differ more in their geographical than their chronological distribution:

Stage 3a: 'Numeral tablets'
Roughly rectangular clay 'tablets' impressed with numerals, found at sites as far afield as Habuba Kabira and Godin Tepe, both within the influence of the Uruk culture as their pottery and other artefacts testify (Figure 3:3).

Figure 3:3 Uruk-period tablet from Jebel Aruda, Syria, with numerical notations, *c.* 3200 BC. (Photo: courtesy G. van Driel. Cf. Figure 4 in Kraus FS, 1982, 20)

Stage 3b: 'Tablets with signs'
Here, in addition to numerals, 'signs' are written on the clay. These are the Eanna IV tablets, and the critical point is that some of the signs can be confidently identified with clay tokens used in Stage 1. As yet this earliest phase of real writing is attested only at Uruk; it is possible, indeed probable, that it will be found on other Mesopotamian sites, and isolated pictograms occur in Iran (Algaze 1989, 580).

A system of recording which involves numerals and commodities, and authentication by means of sealing wet clay, is thus seen in the stages of conversion into the earliest known cuneiform script, strongly suggesting that the idea of writing was invented here. Once the idea caught on it was rapidly elaborated into a full-blown system. At least 2000 signs have been listed in the Eanna IV tablets, and only very few of these can be traced to an original three-dimensional token, but the majority are recognizably pictographic (Figure 3:4), and it is easy to envisage how the repertoire of signs was built up. While considerable licence as to the exact shape of the signs remains, already in this earliest phase the scribes had begun to draw up lists of signs, and shortly after, in the Eanna III phase, the variability is much reduced, while the tablets found at Jemdet Nasr and Uqair have the same signs and sign-forms, showing that there was an accepted corpus of signs throughout South Mesopotamia.[69]

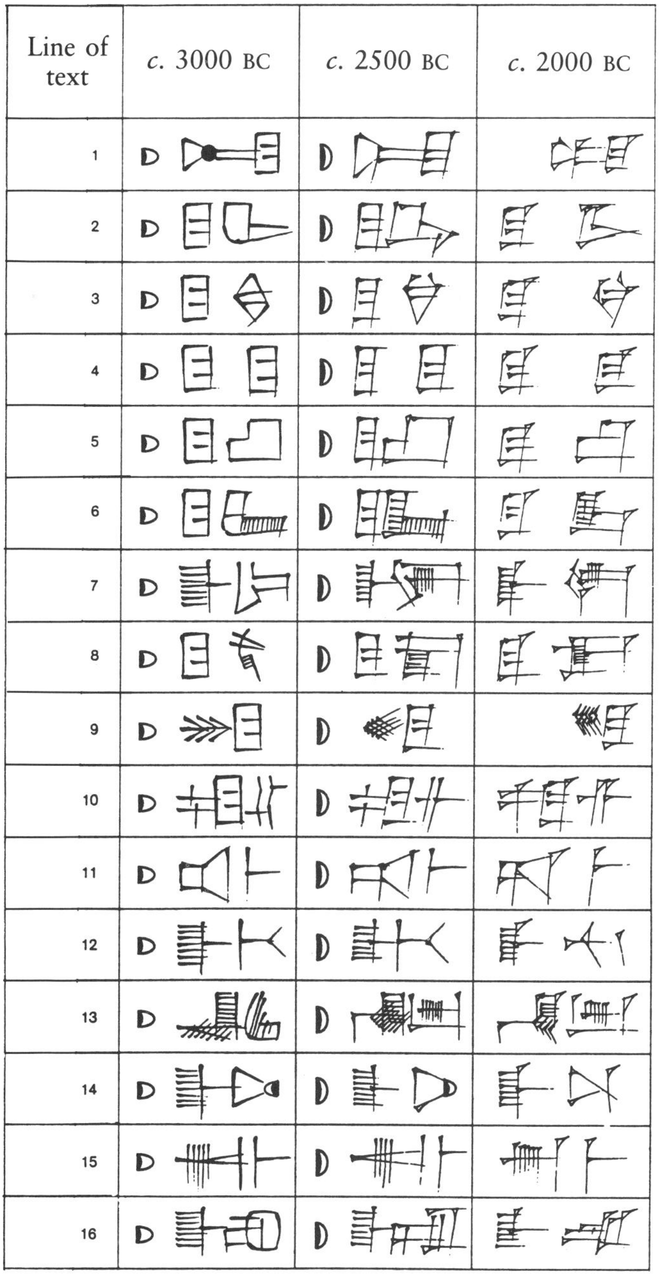

Line of text	c. 3000 BC	c. 2500 BC	c. 2000 BC
1			
2			
3			
4			
5			
6			
7			
8			
9			
10			
11			
12			
13			
14			
15			
16			

Figure 3:4 Development of cuneiform signs: the opening lines of the 'Professions List' at three stages of the script. (After Damerow *et al.* 1988, 83. Courtesy H.J. Nissen)

Writing emerged elsewhere in the Old World at about the same time. In Iran the Proto-Elamite script succeeds the Mesopotamian pictographic system and was clearly influenced by it. In Pakistan and India the Indus civilization also developed its own script, probably rather later and stimulated by the Mesopotamian or Elamite example. In Pre-Dynastic Egypt traces of Mesopotamian influence suggest that the idea (though not the form) of writing may have reached there from our area too. Perhaps most telling is the fact that, although writing begins in Egypt at almost the same time, it lacks the elaborate precursors of bullae and tokens attested for Mesopotamia. Instead we find, just before the emergence of the hieroglyphic script, objects displaying clear Mesopotamian influence, including cylinder seals, whose appearance in the late Uruk had coincided with that of the sealed bullae; and most recently excavations at Buto in the Nile delta have reportedly revealed Uruk-style pottery and cone mosaics.[70]

Text 3:2 Episode from 'Enmerkar and the Lord of Aratta'
The High Priest of Kulaba formed some clay and wrote words on it as if on a tablet –
In those days words written on clay tablets did not exist,
But now, with the sun's rising, so it was!
The High Priest of Kulaba wrote words as if on a tablet, and so it was!

(After Cooper and Heimpel 1983, 82)

The tablets (Figure 3:5)

Once created, the clay tablet was central to the cuneiform writing tradition; cuneiform signs could be written on other materials, but the script was developed for writing on soft damp clay and the tablet remained unchallenged, although its size and shape varied widely. Clay has various valuable qualities. Not trivial in the history of writing is its universal availability and ease of preparation, by comparison with papyrus or leather, for instance. People write more readily when they are not using up a valuable resource. Clay also has advantages for us today. Later, many of the tablets in the libraries of the Assyrian kings were baked to the consistency of well-fired pottery, but even unbaked tablets harden up in the dry heat and may survive in the ground indefinitely. Unwanted tablets were of no intrinsic value and were simply discarded or even used as floor packing, where they await the archaeologist.

For the scribes themselves the use of this material naturally had disadvantages as well. Compared to later materials, tablets are bulky. Long texts in cuneiform have to be written on a number of tablets, and already in the ED III period tablets as large as 40 cm square are in use for administrative and literary purposes (Figure 3:6). A large clay tablet cannot be readily held in one hand for any length of time – one Ur III account in the British Museum weighs 6.8 kg[71] – and sometimes two people may have been needed, one to write and the other to hold and turn the tablet (cf. Figure 3:7). For long documents in later times state administrations turned to hinged wooden boards with wax filling, which were lighter and less bulky, but more expensive and less secure. So far, there is no evidence that these were introduced before the end of the Old Babylonian period, and this is undoubtedly one

Figure 3:5 Cuneiform tablets. (a) Jemdet Nasr period tablet, *c.* 3000 BC. Oriented in original alignment. A list of offerings? Note 'Day 1', 'Day 2' and 'Day 3' at the left side of the top three registers. (BM 116730. Photo: courtesy Trustees of the British Museum) (b) Administrative list of prebend fields. Abu Salabikh, *c.* 2450 BC; original alignment (Biggs and Postgate 1978, IAS 518) (c) Letter from Aleppo, found at Mari, quoted as Text 13:6. (Photo: Martin Sauvage, UPR 193, CNRS)

Figure 3:6
Administrative list of textiles from the Palace at Ebla, *c.* 2350 BC. Cf. Figure 3:8. (E. Sollberger, *Archivi Reali di Ebla Testi* 8, 1986, Plate VI, No. 523. Photo: courtesy P. Matthiae)

reason why the detailed accounts of third-millennium institutions have come down to us in greater numbers than those from later.[72]

Since the reed must sink into the surface, tablets can only be inscribed when their clay is of the right consistency. How to keep the clay from drying out in the Mesopotamian summers must have been a crucial part of the scribal training. We know nothing of the technical details of how it was selected and prepared, or of how it was stored and kept at

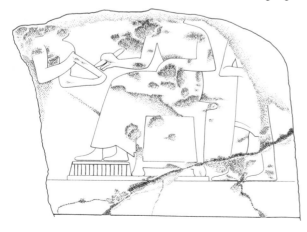

Figure 3:7 Scene from a Neo-Sumerian stele, *c.* 2100 BC. The scribe's stool is on a low platform, the tablet is held by an assistant who seems to be bending forward from the waist. The details of the hand and stylus are hard to discern. (Drawing by A. Boyce after D. Opitz, AfO 6, 1930–1, 63–4; also illustrated in W. Orthmann, *Der Alte Orient*, 1985, Propyläen Kunstgeschichte, Band 18, Tafel 118)

the right consistency while the tablet was actually being written. With big tablets especially one can clearly see the depth of the wedges and ease of the script diminishing as the scribe reaches the end and the clay is beginning to harden up. Corrections could be made as the text was being written, by squashing the clay flat and perhaps damping it slightly, but, once the clay is dry, additions are impossible, unless they are scratched in.[73] This means that, once written, the tablet is an immutable document, which had consequences both convenient and inconvenient. As we shall see, it made them very suitable to use as legal documents, or as final records of administration, but they were no good for any sort of running record. It is probable that this is another reason for the use of waxed writing boards, since they could take additions. There is an interesting contrast with contemporary Egypt where the papyri could be added to at any time, entries could be made in red or black ink, and large documents posed no problem, as they could simply be rolled up.

Tablets were kept in various ways. The palace archives at Ebla were stacked on shelves and found as they had fallen when the archive room was burnt (Figure 3:8). Huge numbers of archival tablets were found by licit and illicit excavators in the late nineteenth century, at sites like Sippar and Drehem, but few if any details were recorded. The Ur III archives at Tello were found by de Sarzec in long archive rooms, but nothing was recorded of the

Figure 3:8 The archive room at Ebla in the course of excavation. Tablets had fallen from their wooden shelves when the room was burnt. (Courtesy P. Matthiae)

order in which they had been stored. In Neo-Babylonian and Neo-Assyrian temples large pigeonholes were built of brick and plaster against the walls of an archive room or library.[74] For smaller groups of tablets it was common to store them in chests made of wood, or more often stiff reed (cf. Text 3:3). All that survives of these are clay labels with a description of the contents. Many are known from Pre-Sargonic and Ur III times, and the excavators of the palace at Mari found labels which had been attached to tablet-chests into which the correspondence of the two previous rulers of Mari had been filed by Hammurapi's conquering administration.[75] Pottery containers were also used, and the accounts and correspondence of the merchants of Assur are still being found at Kültepe in their sealed jars.

Text 3:3 Letter to Zimri-Lim of Mari from his queen
Tell my lord, thus speaks Šiptu, your handmaid. The palace is well. My lord had written as follows: 'I am now sending Yassur-Addu to you. Send along with him some responsible officials and have them take out the tablets from the places he indicates. Those tablets are to be deposited with you until my arrival.' Now in accordance with what my lord wrote, I sent Mukannišum, Šubnalu and (a third man) with that man, and Yassur-Addu indicated to the officials one room in the workshop under Etel-pi-šarrim's supervision, and they opened the door of the room which he indicated, which was sealed with the seal of Igmilum of the secretariat, and took out two baskets of tablets, the baskets sealed with the seal of Etel-pi-šarrim. With their sealings those baskets are deposited with me until my lord's arrival, and I have sealed the door of the room which they opened with my seal.

(After Sasson 1972, 58)

Sealing and envelopes

The realization that once an impression in wet clay hardened it could not be altered long predates the invention of writing in the Near East. Stamp seals are known from at least the Ubaid period, and sealed lumps of clay, such as some from Arpachiyah, prove that they were used in this way. In the later historical periods, the second and first millennia BC, the combination of written text conveying information and a sealing to authenticate and protect was basic to legal documentation, perhaps not least because even the illiterate could use their seal to participate in the creation of a valid document. Curiously enough, it took a long time for this practice, which survives in legal contexts to the present day, to be institutionalized, and even then practices differed widely in place and time.

Although the earliest tablets inherited the practice of sealing from the bullae which preceded them, this died out during the beginning of the Early Dynastic period. The seals continued in use, but not on tablets: they are found rolled out on lumps of clay used to seal doors, jars and merchandise, occasionally even rolled into the wet clay of a pot before it was fired, but it was not until just before the Akkadian Dynasty that we find seals used on inscribed documents again. The earliest instances are not on tablets, but on clay sealings from a wooden peg which had been driven into a wall to symbolize the sale of a house (Figure 3:9).[76] Doors had been sealed in this way for centuries, and these are therefore more inscribed sealings than sealed inscriptions. The seal probably belonged to the city herald: the text states that he was present to authenticate the proceedings, and other early documents were sealed by a judicial authority, not by one of the parties to the transaction. It was only gradually that the later regular practice was established by which the seller, or the person incurring a liability, impressed the seal (or its substitute, a finger-nail or garment hem; see chapter 15 and note 524).

At about the same time the first envelopes appear, the earliest example coming from the Bau Temple archive just before the Akkad Dynasty.[77] Literary tradition suggesting that they were invented by, or at the time of, Sargon, is thus not far out (Text 3:4).[78] An

Text 3:4 Episode from the 'Sumerian Sargon Legend'
In those days, writing on tablets did exist, but clay envelopes did not exist.
King Ur-Zababa wrote a tablet for Sargon, creature of the gods, which would cause his own death,
And dispatched it to Lugal-zagesi in Uruk.

(After Cooper and Heimpel 1983, 77)

Figure 3:9 Clay sealing formed round a wooden peg and inscribed with the text of a house sale. Girsu, in the state of Lagaš, *c.* 2350 BC. Note the seal impression at the base. (A. 13240; = Allotte de la Fuÿe 1912, No. 33. Photo: Musée du Louvre/AO)

Figure 3:10 Old Babylonian legal document from Sippar: inner tablet with four seals and identifying notes, outer envelope with seals. (Tablet: BM 92649a, copy CT 8 47 = Kohler and Ungnad 1909–23, No. 375; Envelope: BM 80140. Photo: courtesy Trustees of the British Museum)

envelope was simply a thin layer of clay formed round the tablet so that it looks like a fatter version of itself (Figure 3:10). It had two uses: to conceal the contents of the tablet, especially the wording of a letter,[79] and to protect the contents from damage, in which case the text on the tablet can be repeated on the envelope. This repetition is a legal measure against forgery, and like the practice of sealing has a long legacy through classical antiquity and the medieval world to the present day, giving us terms like 'letters patent' and 'diploma' (see chapter 15).[80]

The stylus and the wedge

In the 3000 years of the cuneiform script it changed continuously as it moved through time and space and served different purposes. It went through periods of standardization, resulting from a strong central political authority, and periods of diffraction, when central control evaporated and permitted local peculiarities to develop into traditions of their own. Even if we had the space to trace these processes in detail, it would not be possible because of the patchy quality of our sources. Instead, we may observe some general processes which operate throughout the period between the Uruk and the end of the Old Babylonian period.

Cuneiform (= 'wedge-shaped') writing was so named in AD 1700 after the triangular shape of the straight strokes of which the signs were composed in Babylonian and Assyrian times. In Eanna IV the sign forms were as pictographic as Egyptian or Chinese characters, but a continuous process of adaptation has left most signs in the standard form of the script unrecognizably distant from their originals (Figure 3:11). The priority of the impressed clay

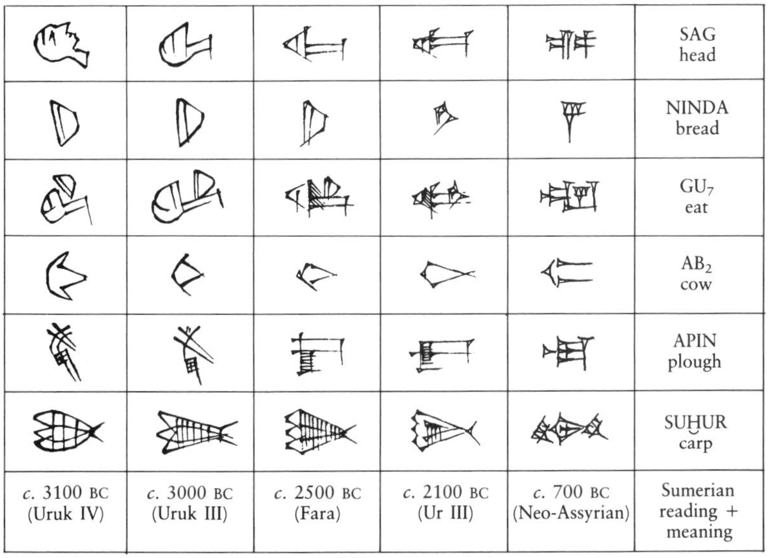

c. 3100 BC (Uruk IV)	c. 3000 BC (Uruk III)	c. 2500 BC (Fara)	c. 2100 BC (Ur III)	c. 700 BC (Neo-Assyrian)	Sumerian reading + meaning
					SAG head
					NINDA bread
					GU₇ eat
					AB₂ cow
					APIN plough
					SUḪUR carp

Figure 3:11 Development of cuneiform sign forms. (After Damerow *et al.* 1988, 84, with Neo-Assyrian sign forms added)

tablet as the medium of the script is epitomized by the choice of the scribes' patron: when a scribe had completed copying a literary text he signed off with the phrase 'Praise to Nisaba', because Nisaba, goddess of cereals, was also the patroness of the scribal craft through the reed they used to write with. In the Akkad period, inscriptions on stone or metal begin to reproduce the characteristic wedge-shape of the stylus on clay. Already in the Uruk period the curving free-hand sign forms, drawn with a sharp point in the damp clay, are being formalized into a number of single strokes with a clear, slightly curved head and tapering tail. These gradually become shallower and wider and give the characteristic triangular impressions made by the sharp end of a tool cut from a reed. From the beginning, numerical signs were made by using the round ends of two different sizes of stylus.

Another change, which it is very difficult to date, is in the direction of the script. Modern cuneiform scholars treat the script as though it ran from left to right in long horizontal lines, and the same applied to ancient times, at least after the Old Babylonian period. However, when we go back to the time when the signs are still recognizably objects, it is clear that they need to be rotated 90° to make sense, so that pots and people are standing upright. This meant that a text began at the top right-hand corner of the surface and was written in vertical columns, like Chinese today. This direction of the script was certainly still formally correct in the reign of Hammurapi, since it is used for his stele, but in everyday use it may well have changed to the left–right horizontal style much earlier.[81]

Simplification

As time progressed, the practicalities of how the tablet and stylus were held led the scribes to favour some directions of wedge over others: vertical wedges almost always have their 'heads' at the top, horizontals have their 'heads' on the left. By the Akkadian period only very few wedges have their heads below or to the right, and in cursive Old Babylonian virtually none, leaving only three or four kinds of wedge from which every sign could be composed: this reflects the fact that the scribes would only need to turn the tablet or stylus through an angle of 90°. At the same time, other simplifications of the sign repertoire took place. There was an incentive to reduce the complexity of individual signs. When they were essentially pictographic, nothing was easier than to draw, for instance, a jar with a substance inside it, the resulting combination becoming a separate sign. Later the scribes found it more convenient to place the two components side by side thus reducing the number of these complex signs, and the Uruk repertoire of 2000 signs was reduced to well below 1000 by Old Babylonian times, of which only a small proportion were in frequent use, as we shall see. These changes to individual signs are associated with innovations in the disposition of the script on the tablet, and indeed the shape of the tablets themselves. While in the later Early Dynastic period the signs are still arranged in narrow boxes in columns, the Akkadian scribes introduced the 'line', with the signs placed one after the other from left to right (Figure 3:5, p. 57). The adoption of a strict linear sequence, the successor to which is before your eyes on this page, also tended to standardize the signs and encourage them to conform to an even height.

Use of script

In some degree these changes in the outward appearance of the tablet reflect changes in how the script conveyed the language. It is easy to see that in its early, pictographic stage the script was not well adapted to represent the morphemes which distinguish the details of tense, mood, person, case and number in the spoken language. Even in the early literary texts of Fara and Abu Salabikh only a few of these 'grammatical elements' are shown. We should not be misled into thinking that the language was less developed at this date: the idea that writing could have a one-to-one correspondence to language was still to come, and we should see the signs only as 'mnemonics' to be interpreted by those who were already familiar with the text.[82] One reason for the slow development was of course the difficulty of making pictographs of abstract concepts such as grammatical elements. Gradually, just as in other pristine scripts from China to central America, the solution to this was found by creating signs which conveyed not meaning but sound. Words which sounded alike could be written with the same sign. Thus the Sumerian for 'to give' is **sum**; they did not have a pictograph for it, and used the sign for 'garlic', also **sum** (though not necessarily pronounced identically). This is sometimes described as a rebus ('by means of things') writing, and the punning element can be technically called paronomasia.[83] As they built up a repertoire of 'syllabic' signs, the scribes found themselves more and more able to fit the script to the language, and as time passes more and more of the grammatical elements are indicated. This of course increased the number of signs needed to convey a given statement, but improved the accuracy and versatility of the script. Undoubtedly one factor influencing this development was the nature of the Akkadian language. Sumerian, being an agglutinative language, which conveys grammatical information by prefixing or suffixing elements on to a mostly unchanging, and often mono-syllabic 'root', was particularly well suited to a pictographic script. Akkadian, on the other hand, like other

	Sumerian	Akkadian	
Verbal base	sum	NDN = nadānum	'to give'
Imperative	/sum . a . b/ sum - ma - ab 	/idin/ i - di - in 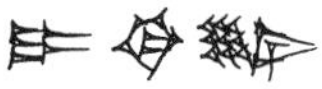	'give (it)'
Past tense	/mu . na . b . sum/ mu - na - ab - sum 	/iddin . šum/ id - di - iš - šum 	'he gave to him'
Precative	/ḫe . b . sum . e/ ḫé - íb - sum - mu 	/liddin/ li - id - di - in 	'let him give'

Figure 3:12 Comparison of graphic rendering of verbal forms in Sumerian and Akkadian.

Semitic languages, conveys much of its grammatical information by internal modifications of a triconsonantal 'root' or skeleton (see Figure 3:12). Hence one could convey the essential nouns and verbs in each language by means of the same pictographs; but to give detailed grammatical information Sumerian need only add syllabic signs to the front or back of the root, which is impossible for Akkadian. There must, therefore, have been a very strong incentive on the part of those writing Akkadian (and its predecessors and relatives) to move towards a syllabic system.

By the Old Babylonian period, when Sumerian was dying as a spoken language, the cuneiform script may be said to have three kinds of sign use: syllabic, in which the sign represents a syllable, ideographic or logographic, where the sign stands for a word or idea, and determinative, where the sign acts as a classifier, telling the reader what sort of word is following. Thus the sign *an* may be used to convey a syllable with the sound /an/, to represent the entire words for 'heaven' or 'god', whether in Akkadian or Sumerian, or to stand before the names of gods, when it would not be pronounced, and so should be seen as a purely graphic device to assist in the reading of the text. Quite a few signs can be used in all three ways, and only the context will tell us which is intended. Worse than this, because of the way the script developed, the same sign may be used for various different words (though these are usually related in meaning), or for different syllables. The consequence for the student beginning in cuneiform is bewildering, but in practice at any one time and place it cannot have been as bad as it seems today. In the early second millennium, legal documents and various literary texts were still written in Sumerian, which retained the largely logographic system with a sign representing a word rather than a syllable; but when the scribes used their vernacular Akkadian, as they did when writing letters and Akkadian literature, the script was mostly used syllabically, allowing a much smaller repertoire of signs. The nearest approach to a purely syllabic script was achieved by the Old Assyrian scribes, who got by with about 70 signs, with only the occasional logogram (e.g. for 'silver'). We can see here a pragmatic approach which dispensed with the clutter of scribal training still prevalent in the south, and concentrated on the straightforward communication which their commercial undertakings required.

Writing and society

Just as it took time for a fluent writing system to be developed, so also society, on this first occasion, took its time discovering the various ways in which writing could be put to use. Only over the course of centuries do we find that it expands to fulfil all the functions we tend to associate with writing in our society. Figure 3:13 illustrates this very crudely, and deserves some explanation. Although we cannot 'read' the earliest Uruk tablets, we can identify most of their signs. One category can be read, in a sense, because they are sign lists (known to cuneiformists as lexical texts) which were still being copied well into the third millennium, when the script is better known.[84] However the majority are obviously administrative documents concerned with the movement of commodities. Since they were found within the precincts of the Eanna complex, it is usually supposed that they belong

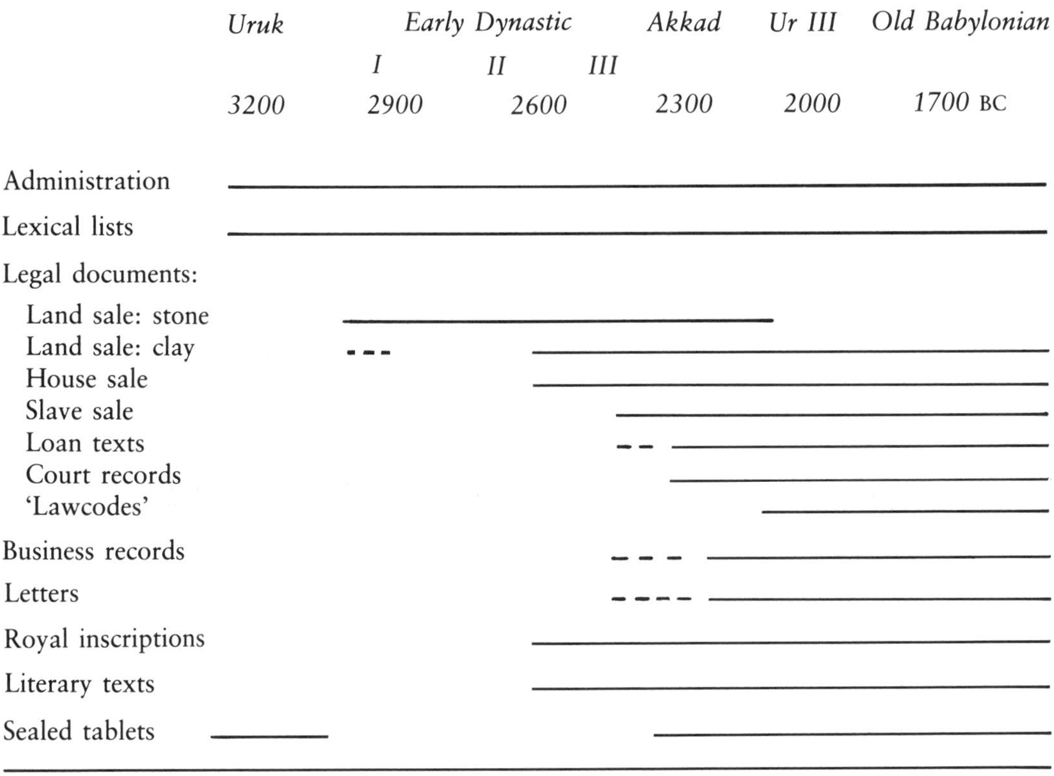

	Uruk	Early Dynastic			Akkad	Ur III	Old Babylonian
		I	II	III			
	3200	2900	2600		2300	2000	1700 BC
Administration	——
Lexical lists	——
Legal documents:							
Land sale: stone		—————————————				
Land sale: clay	- - -		———————————————————
House sale			———————————————————
Slave sale				—————————————
Loan texts			- - —————————————
Court records			———————————
'Lawcodes'				—————
Business records			- - - - ———————————————
Letters			- - - - - ———————————————
Royal inscriptions		———————————————————————
Literary texts		———————————————————————
Sealed tablets	———————		———————————————————

Figure 3:13 Applications of writing in Mesopotamia through time.

to the temple's administration, and this remains the likeliest explanation. The same may well apply to the few documents found at the ancient shrine of Tell Uqair, but at Jemdet Nasr there is at present no way of judging the nature of the building in which the tablets were found.

Outside a temple context the only evidence for writing comes from the Stage 3a 'numeral tablets' found, for instance, at Jebel Aruda and Habuba Kabira in Syria. Here one may reasonably speculate that they are records from commercial activities which need not (although they could well) have been associated with a temple. Arguments from silence are particularly perilous when considering the Uruk period in Mesopotamia, as so few sites have been excavated; but *at present* there is no reason to think that writing had extended beyond the confines of large institutions, or been used for anything other than the recording of their economic activities.

The same applies to clay tablets from the excavations at Ur, which came from the massive rubbish tips of the Nanna Temple, and are of an exclusively utilitarian character. However, at about this time, ED I, we begin to have a new application showing up, telegraphic texts carved on to stone with details of the purchase of land (Figures 3:14; 15:2). These earliest legal documents, sometimes known as archaic *kudurru*, unfortunately have no good archaeological context, and because of the depth at which ED I levels lie on most excavated sites we have virtually nothing else from this time, although one cannot doubt that writing had continued in use. The next big change is illustrated for us by two large bodies of tablets, one from Fara (ancient Šuruppak), where the German excavators in 1903 found various archives in different parts of the city, and the other from Abu Salabikh (ancient name uncertain), a small town not far north of Nippur, where a large

Figure 3:14 Early real estate sale documents: the 'Blau Monuments'. Dimensions: 'chisel' 17.8 cm; 'rubber' 15.9 cm. (Photos: courtesy Trustees of the British Museum)

library and some administrative texts were found in the 1960s by an American team. The administrative texts are, as one might expect, more sophisticated than the earlier ones, and sometimes are very big, but it is on the 'library texts' that attention focuses, because here for the first time we can recognize not only lexical lists, but what Sumerologists rather flatteringly call 'literary' compositions. They include magical incantations, hymns to temples, myths about the gods, and 'wisdom' literature in the shape of a series of aphorisms conveyed to his son by Ziusudra, the 'Babylonian Noah'.[85]

At this stage, about 2500 BC, the writing is still more 'mnemonic' than plenary, and we can usually only 'read' these texts because we have versions of them from the Old Babylonian schools of more than 500 years later. From the intervening times very scanty fragments of similar texts from Akkadian and Ur III times are enough to show that the literary tradition was continuous, but the chances of archaeological survival have meant that the voluminous written material of those dynasties is almost entirely from administrative archives. There are some signs of change detectable: correspondence becomes normal, generally from one official to another; and 'public' compositions (like royal inscriptions) become longer and more informative. In the legal sphere the written document takes on fresh roles: formal records of court proceedings are kept from the Akkad Dynasty on, and the practice of sealing tablets gives them a more significant role to play, and a bilateral validity which they had hitherto lacked (see chapter 15).

At this time too are found the first architect's house-plans and rudimentary field surveys, a reminder that the authors of the texts would have been scribes with training in a variety of skills (Figure 3:15; see also Figures 6:8, 12:3 below). It is generally assumed that the

Figure 3:15 Old Babylonian tablet with geometrical problems. (BM 15285 – see Thureau-Dangin, RA 19, 1922, 149. Photo: courtesy Trustees of the British Museum)

temples played an important role in employing and educating scribes, but the evidence for this is very circumstantial. In the old Babylonian period it is certain that schools (é.dub.ba.a) were attached to some palaces (Larsa, Mari, etc.), but it is difficult to assess how widely scribal education may have been found outside the major institutions even in the Old Babylonian period when our evidence is best.[86] Most of Sumerian literature comes from houses of this period in the scribal quarter at Nippur, but the texts are mostly the same as those written by contemporary scribes at Ur, showing that there was a fairly uniform traditional syllabus. The texts they copied include a class of Sumerian 'literary' texts portraying life in an educational establishment, often with a humorous twist. From such accounts we learn of fierce headmasters, patronizing senior pupils and beginners sent off to school from home, and of a syllabus which included mathematics, field surveying and legal and accounting practices (Text 3:5).

Text 3:5 Excerpt from a scene of school life
I will write some tablets: the tablet (of measures) from 1 **gur** of barley up to 600 **gur**; the tablet (of weights) from 1 shekel up to 10 minas of silver. I . . . a man with a marriage contract. I can choose the partnership agreement for 1 certified talent. Sales of houses, of fields, of slaves male and female, silver guarantees, field rental contracts, contracts for planting palm-groves, . . ., even tablets of adoption contracts [lit. 'of children found at the well-side'] – I know how to write all that.

(After Civil 1985, 72, lines 40–8)

Literacy surely reached its peak in Old Babylonian times, when writing permeated society more thoroughly than at any time until the introduction of the alphabet, both in the variety of roles it played and, one suspects, in the number of people who could read and write. We may guess that most members of the merchant houses of Assur, male and female, were literate; but this is in a severely commercial context. We cannot judge how much ordinary people could read and write, and how scribes were integrated into society, since the sources make few explicit statements, and some of the issues have not been seriously tackled by cuneiform experts. King Šulgi claimed to be able to write, with some pride, but we have no idea, for instance, whether this may have been among Hammurapi's accomplishments. We do know that sons might follow their fathers in the scribal craft, and that some women were scribes.[87] In the south at least, letters from this time may be written from one member of a family to another about trivial domestic matters, and frequently these are exclusively agricultural, reflecting the fact that cuneiform tablets have been found in small towns in rural districts. Perhaps the clearest indication comes from the widespread use of labels or tags (Figure 3:16). Clay lumps formed round string were attached to tablet containers, or even cows; some with dates and names were presumably hung round the neck or wrist of harvesters, brick-yard workers and craftsmen as a record of attendance. This means that the immediate supervisors of menial labour, even if they could not write themselves, had a scribe with them on the job, and that the effects of writing had reached to the most mundane levels of society.[88]

There is a contrast here with other parts of the ancient Near East to which the practice

Figure 3:16 Clay label, probably from a basket. The cuneiform note says merely 'Basket of aromatic plants'. Dimensions: 7.8 × 5.5 cm. (BM 122179, CT 50 No. 84. Photo: courtesy Trustees of the British Museum)

of cuneiform writing spread: the archives at Ebla are clear proof that the system had been adopted by palace administrators far beyond the limits of the South Mesopotamian plain, but at present it seems that this borrowing was part of a package, encapsulated within the palace itself, and that it did not spread further throughout society. Similarly the Old Assyrian writing tradition, best known to us from the voluminous archives of their merchants in central Anatolia, does not seem to have left any lasting traces there, a sign of the self-contained nature of their business. These instances of the restriction of the cuneiform scribal skills to a specific function within one sector of a society warn us not to assume that literacy was as deeply or uniformly embedded in earlier societies as it is in ours. The specificity of use of different writing systems may help to provide an explanation, later in the second millennium, for the regular use of Akkadian legal and diplomatic documents in the palaces of the Levant at just the time when the first alphabetic scripts were being created in the same region – no doubt with different purposes and quite possibly in a different social milieu.

Further reading

For a recent short introduction to cuneiform see Walker 1987 (now republished as a chapter in J.T. Hooker, C.B.F. Walker and W.V. Davies *et al.*, *Reading the Past*, London 1990, 15–73); see also Edzard 1976–80b (in German). Two valuable collections of articles on writing in different early civilizations are in *World Archaeology* 17 (1986) and *Visible Language* 15/iv (1981); see also Christin 1982 (in French and unfortunately out of print). A comprehensive survey of early recording technology is promised from the pen of D. Schmandt-Besserat in the near future, and a detailed but non-specialist description of early cuneiform is to be found in Nissen *et al.* 1990 (German). On literacy in the ancient Near East see Larsen 1989; for a collection of articles on seals and sealing practice see Gibson and Biggs 1977.

Part II

The institutions

4
City and countryside

While its true singularity may lie deeper in the complexity of social organization, the two most striking characteristics of early Mesopotamia are its literacy and its urbanization. Just as we need to appreciate the nature of the written record to use its messages, we must be aware that all our documentary and archaeological evidence derives from the city, and so be conscious of the inherent biases which result from this. Perhaps we would in any case have chosen to approach Mesopotamian civilization through its cities, since it is there that everything most special to it is concentrated, but in fact we have no choice. Although we have some insights into the rural scene, this is only by courtesy of documents which were themselves generated within the city. It is only those aspects of the countryside with which the city-dweller was involved that the texts will illumine, and at present the only archaeological evidence is the distribution of settlements. Fortunately there was a very close relationship between the early cities and their hinterland, so that the texts are more informative than we might expect. The links fall into legal relationships, the contractual bonds between landlord and tenant, palace and dependant, recruiting officer and recruit, and the political movements exposed by state correspondence from Mari and elsewhere, from which great shafts of light have transformed our picture of the nomads in the ancient Near East.

Defining a city

Usually the first question asked about an ancient city is how big it was. A simple answer to this is to quote the size of the ancient mounds, and, although this simplicity conceals a host of technical and procedural problems, at one level it has a certain validity. Archaeological surveys can distinguish a hierarchy of settlement size even before the Uruk period, and Adams' work in particular shows that during the fourth millennium a separate class of larger settlement – or 'city' – can be differentiated from the smaller sites or 'villages' (Figure 4:1). It must be stressed that the transition from one settlement class to another may be drawn at different points on the absolute scale in different periods, since the classification depends not on absolute size, but on the relative position within a hierarchy. If our classes have any significance, they will correspond to the function of the settlement within that hierarchy. We have already seen how the ceremonial role of the city as the home of the central shrine of a district follows from the literary compositions of Early Dynastic times, and this gives us a solid criterion on which to isolate a class of major settlement, recognized as such by the people of the time (chapter 2). We can also assume

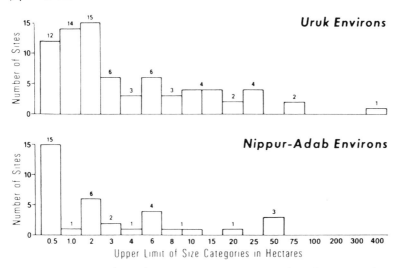

Figure 4:1 Bar graph to show ED I site areas in South and in Central area. (Adams 1981, 84)

with confidence that most of these also functioned as economic and political centres, and that their functional differences from other settlements should be detectable in the archaeological record.

The outward form

The range of city size is well illustrated in the Early Dynastic period by the cases of Uruk and Abu Salabikh (Figures 4:2a and 4:2b). At the beginning of the Epic of Gilgamesh we are exhorted to admire the size of his city Uruk, in particular the wall he built round it (Text 4:1), and indeed at Uruk the city wall dates to the ED period and is 9 km in length,

---

Text 4:1 Epic of Gilgamesh: the listener invited to admire the city of Uruk

See if its wall is not (as straight) as the (architect's) string,

Inspect its . . . wall, the likes of which no-one can equal;

Touch the threshold-stone – it dates from ancient times.

Approach the Eanna Temple, the dwelling of Ištar,

such as no later king or man will ever equal.

Go up on the wall and walk around,

Examine its foundation, inspect its brickwork thoroughly.

Is not its masonry of baked brick,

did not the Seven Sages themselves lay out its plans?

One square mile city, one square mile palm groves, one square mile brick-pits, (and) the . . . of the Ištar Temple:

3 square miles and the . . . of Uruk it encloses.

(From Tablets I and XI: cf. Dalley 1989, 50, 120)

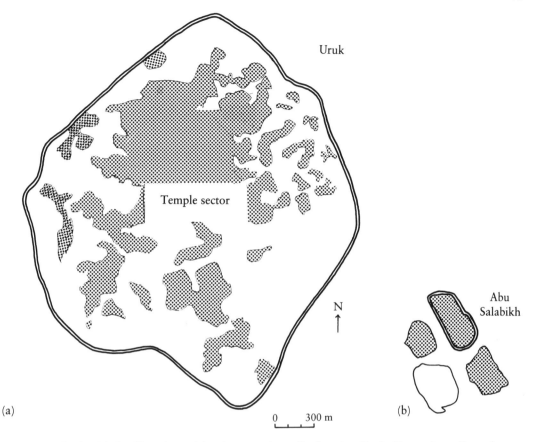

Figure 4:2 Early third-millennium cities, large and small: showing Early Dynastic walls and areas of occupation (shaded). (a) Uruk (*c.* 400 ha). (b) Abu Salabikh (*c.* 20 ha).

enclosing 400 ha, by any standards a city; at Abu Salabikh the Main Mound is encircled by a wall only 1.3 km long, and the area within it is scarcely more than 10 hectares, no more than a village in many societies. These are the extremes, but there are good reasons to consider them both cities. One such reason is the wall itself. If the city's religious identity is expressed in the temple, its fortification walls represent its political identity (see Figure 13:2 below). Even at small sites these walls may be several metres thick, and the effort of their construction is sufficient sign of their collective importance (see Text 4:2).

Text 4:2 Samsu-iluna boasts of rebuilding the wall of Kish
At that time Samsu-iluna the strong with the force of his troops built the city of Kish, dug its moat, surrounded it with a marsh, established its foundations like a mountain with large amounts of earth, had its bricks moulded and made its wall. Within a single year he raised its head above the previous level.

(After Sollberger and Kupper 1971, 225)

Walled settlements are not, of course, a novelty of the urban age, but the walls of our cities are both practical and symbolic. Rulers celebrate their construction of a new wall, and when a city is taken in war it is standard policy to 'demolish' its fortifications (Text 4:3). In practice, a city wall will tend to be too small or too big. Several of the Early

Text 4:3 Inscription of Rimuš

Rimuš, King of Kish, defeated Ur and Umma in a battle and killed 8040 men. He took 5460 prisoners and captured Kaku, the King of Ur. He also captured Kikuid, the **ensi** of Lagaš, and conquered their cities and destroyed their ramparts.

(After Sollberger and Kupper 1971, 102)

Dynastic cities found themselves confined on the ancient mounds by the limitations of the city wall, within which the occupation levels had risen well above the surrounding countryside. At Ur, for instance, it is clear that the ancient, Early Dynastic, walls were seriously constraining inhabitants in the Old Babylonian period. Two obvious solutions can be adopted: to sacrifice security and build suburbs outside the walls, and/or to abandon the old wall line and enclose a much larger space: at Old Babylonian Sippar we have a city wall, reconstructed by Samsu-iluna, but the texts refer regularly to at least one suburb, named Sippar-Amnanum after an Amorite tribe and no doubt originating in encampments outside the walls.[89] There is no archaeological or textual evidence to suggest it was ever walled in. The city plan of Ešnunna shows the second option: a densely built tell in the north-west corner represents the original Early Dynastic city, and in places the line of the old wall can be guessed, enclosing it; but during the late third and early second millennium the city burst its bounds, and was swallowed up in a new enclosure of post-Ur III date of several times the area (Figure 4:3).

While some of this expansion may reflect a growth in the resident population, other factors must be involved. Major changes visible to archaeologists almost always derived from deliberate public acts, out of phase with purely demographic trends controlling the expansion or contraction of population and settlement. One obvious reason is political: new rulers from outside, without their own residences at the city, can hardly have constructed huge new administrative buildings within the tight-packed old city, and, indeed, the large structures at the centre of the redrawn enclosure at Ešnunna are the governors' or kings' palaces. Further, in a capital city, accommodation for the officials and visitors from other centres will have been needed, and the increase in economic activity will inevitably draw in commercial interests. The recently identified city of Maškan-šapir was probably expanded greatly to fulfil its role as a government centre for the north of the kingdom of Larsa.[90] The extreme case of this, the construction of an entire new capital, familiar in later contexts from Khorsabad through Chang-an and Samarra to Islamabad, is rare at our time and the only instance is perhaps the city of Akkad, which has yet to be discovered.

Within the gates

We can hardly hope to recreate the true nature of city life in early Mesopotamia, although literary texts convey a sense of the busy hum of men (Text 4:4). One necessary step is to

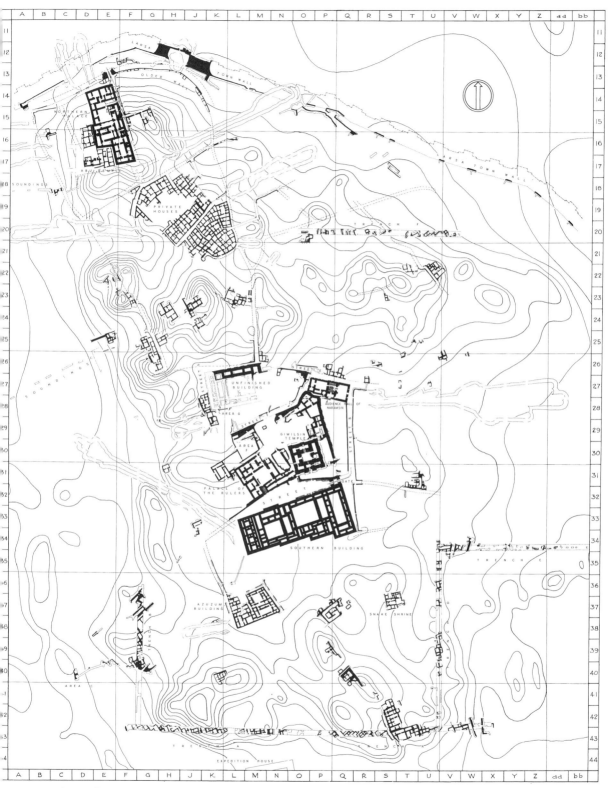

Figure 4:3 Ešnunna: the old city occupies the north-west quarter of this plan where the contours are highest. The monumental buildings in the centre, and the massive city wall along the northern edge are from the dynasties of Akkad, Ur III and Ešnunna itself (2300–1800 BC) (Delougaz, Hill and Lloyd 1967, Plate 23). Courtesy the Oriental Institute of the University of Chicago)

Text 4:4 Curse on Akkad: the city in its hey-day
So that the warehouses would be provisioned,
That dwellings would be founded in that city,
That its people would eat splendid food,
That its people would drink splendid beverages,
That those bathed (for holidays) would rejoice in the courtyards,
That the people would throng the places of celebration,
That acquaintances would dine together,
That foreigners would cruise about like unusual birds in the sky,
That (even) Marhaši would be re-entered on the (tribute) rolls,
That monkeys, mighty elephants, water buffalo, exotic animals,
Would jostle each other in the public squares ...
Holy Inanna did not sleep.

(Cooper 1983a, 50–1)

establish the degree of variability within the walls, and to determine the use of space within each house. Both texts and archaeology can contribute, and neither will be adequate in isolation. For obvious reasons, complete cities, unlike palaces and temples, have not been excavated. At present we can only pick and choose our examples from different times and places. There are no general rules: while the central shrine remained at the heart of the city, the growth and decline of each city depended on its particular economic and political roles. All one can say with safety is that it is a great mistake to conceive of the average Mesopotamian city as an unbroken expanse of homogeneous housing neatly filling the space within the city walls and clustered round a central temple or palace. At Uruk the redrawing of the line of the city wall may well have taken place a thousand years before the expansion of Ešnunna, and it seems that the residential quarters never filled the huge space enclosed (perhaps reflected in its sobriquet of 'Uruk the sheep-fold'). Moreover, the later Epic of Gilgamesh – poetry though it is – tells us that the wall enclosed date plantations and perhaps brick-pits as well as the houses and shrines (Text 4:1).

Nothing illustrates better our ignorance about the structure of an early Mesopotamian city than the question of craft quarters. The assumption that members of the same craft may have shared the same part of a city is not supported by any hard evidence. It is a natural assumption, however, based on the two premises that craft skills would have been passed down from father to son, and that families tended to stay close. To some degree it is perhaps supported by the evidence from Old Babylonian Ur, where merchants seem to have occupied the south-east part of the city, while some members of the temple personnel lived close to one another just south of the main temple, and from contemporary Nippur, where the huge libraries of Sumerian literary texts excavated by the nineteenth-century American expedition came from a scribal quarter of the city. Perhaps it is not surprising that other craft quarters have not been recognized, since trade, religion and schools would naturally attract the greatest concentration of tablets and incidence of literacy. In default of written sources, archaeological evidence may come to our aid here: huge expanses of the site at Warka are covered in vitrified clinker, presumably from pottery production;

and the surface remains also show there were areas specializing in the working of semi-precious stones and shells.[91] Even in a small town like Abu Salabikh, surface distribution of clinker, confirmed by excavation, shows that there was a concentration of pottery production at the north end of the settlement, within the city wall.[92] Their scale alone does not necessarily allow us to deduce that these concentrations represent craft activity dependent on the major institutions, such as the temple or palace, since it would be quite in accord with more recent cities for members of one craft to be clustered together even in the private sector.

Equally as uncertain as craft quarters is the problem of where commerce was transacted in the ancient Mesopotamian city. Modern Near Eastern towns have extensive suqs, comprising narrow covered lanes lined each side by small single-room shops or by larger establishments with doorways leading through to a central courtyard. As in medieval Europe, both craftsmen and merchants tend to keep together according to their wares and products. Economic historians have been arguing for years, since the writings of Polanyi in the 1950s, as to whether or not there were 'markets' in ancient Near Eastern cities, and we do not at present have unequivocal evidence to answer this: we have no archaeological example of a market-place (this would be difficult to identify, in any case), but it would be perfectly possible to have a market without the kind of forum that western perceptions tend to expect. Words do exist in both Akkadian and Sumerian which seem to refer to relatively open spaces, such as *rebītum* 'a square' in Akkadian, equated with the Sumerian **sila dagala**, literally 'wide street'.[93] However, there is nothing in the texts to suggest that these spaces were used for commerce, or that they housed the assembly, which may rather have met in the courtyard of the city's main temple. More evidence exists for the city 'gate' as a public space, presumably an open area just within the wall.[94] Shops may have existed, e.g. in Old Babylonian Sippar, but we find no mention of commercial areas like 'the street of the cloth-merchants', for instance, and the very existence of retail trade of this kind remains controversial.[95] We do know, of course, of the 'quay' (*kārum*). This began no doubt simply as the place where goods were unloaded at the city harbour, but by Old Babylonian times had become the society of merchants in a city, who formed a guild. It is likely enough that, if they had an office or base (e.g. the *bīt kārim*), it would have been close to a harbour, but neither the texts nor the archaeology show that this formed part of a commercial quarter (see chapter 11).

The population

The size of a city's population is arguably a more significant statistic than the area it occupies. Statements in the texts do not help us here, either because they are so vague that we cannot tell to what they are really referring, or because they relate only to one sector of society, such as a military force or temple personnel, from which we have no way of extrapolating to a whole city. Although we may reasonably hope that further detailed investigation of the Ur III archives will in due course provide clues, our best approach at present seems to be from the archaeological evidence. Not that this is simple either. Even if we know a city's spatial extent, it will tell us the size of its population only if we have an idea of the density and homogeneity of occupation. As we have just seen, these are largely unknowns, and quite likely to vary widely from city to city.

In the absence of any other criterion, the problem has been approached by Adams and others by adopting a figure of between 100 and 400 persons per hectare, derived principally from statistics for more recent Near Eastern towns.[96] Quite possibly our cities do mostly fall within this range, but the procedure is unsatisfactory on two counts – in its method, since the use of later statistics begins from an assumption we should be setting out to prove, and in its results, since the range is wider than is useful. The only other approach has to be from the other end of the archaeological spectrum, observing the size and internal organization of individual buildings and their density in different areas of the site. This immediately confronts us with a lot of tough old archaeological chestnuts to crack. Did the houses have one or two storeys? How can we decide whether rooms were used for living, storage, reception and ceremony, cooking and food preparation, industrial activities? What was the residential pattern of contemporary society? Some of these questions have at least a partial answer in the documentary sources (see chapter 5), although we have hardly begun to exploit them to this end, but others must remain within the archaeologists' domain. A start has been made on some of them in the Early Dynastic at Abu Salabikh, where we are accumulating evidence for the density and variability of occupation, the size of houses and of their component rooms and courtyards, and, through quantitative micro-archaeological observation, for the activities in each space, both inside and outside the houses.[97] If, for the sake of argument, we estimate 5 souls per house and 40 houses per hectare, since the city wall enclosed about 10 ha, the old city would have had a population of 2000; with 10 persons per house this would rise to 4000. Another approach would be to allow a figure of 10 sq. m roofed space per person (taken from world-wide ethnographic observations),[98] but this cannot be applied uniformly since larger houses may be expected to have devoted more space to storage. Furthermore, it would not do to forget that there was another part of the city of almost equal size outside the walls to the south. Nevertheless, with due regard paid to sample size and location, the block by block approach to reconstructing the city and its population does seem to offer the best hope of answering the questions of population size and density.

City institutions

1: Assembly

For a city to function as an entity, it required some central direction which could be independent of the source of political power. At Šuruppak in the Early Dynastic period we hear of plough animals belonging to 'the city', and public administration seems to have been distributed among buildings in different parts of the city, suggesting that the more powerful families may have assumed a role in local government.[99] One of the most influential contributions to Mesopotamian history was made by Thorkild Jacobsen in two articles dealing with 'primitive democracy'.[100] Pulling threads together from disparate sources, he put together a case for the importance of democratic institutions in the Early

Dynastic period, which retains its conviction today. The city assembly (**ukkin**/*puhrum*) was the forum for popular debate and decision: Jacobsen shows that in the myths of later times the gods are portrayed in their Assembly as reaching political and military decisions by consensus. The model for these has to go back to the early years when the city was itself the state, and the short Sumerian epic of Gilgamesh and Akka portrays decisions at Early Dynastic Uruk being made in the light of the (sometimes conflicting) advice of both the elders and the young men of the city. This dual system survived at least into Old Babylonian times, when we read of 'the city and the elders', though only as a law-court (see chapter 15), since the seat of power has moved elsewhere, to the palace. It is virtually only at Assur that we still see the Assembly, or rather the elders acting on its behalf, take an active role in the political as opposed to the legal affairs of the city.[101]

Even in judicial affairs we know very little about the Assembly: we are never told where it met, perhaps in the courtyard of the main temple. The members were no doubt the citizens, the 'sons' of the city, but nothing has come down to us as to how one qualified and whether 'dual citizenship' was possible. In the light of the Uruk cycle epics, and by analogy with similar institutions, it may be that there was an 'upper house' or 'executive council' of city elders, and the proceedings in the Assembly were controlled by one or more designated officials.[102] These may well have been responsible for the non-judicial administration of the municipality also, but we hear virtually nothing about them, and there is little doubt that the duties of the Assembly were largely devolved to the local councils just to be described, and its powers long since usurped by the ruler, whether local or from outside.

2: The ward

Quite how different parts of a city were differentiated is one of the outstanding problems, solutions to which are unlikely to surface in the textual sources. Help could well come from archaeological work, but little has yet been done. We may expect the city layout itself to reveal spatial divisions or differentiation within the city, which would correspond to residential groupings or various activities or lifestyles. The degree to which these residential or occupational differences, with at least theoretically recoverable archaeological correlates, will have coincided with agnatic, or at least kin-based, groupings within the population, hardly detectable archaeologically, must vary in time and place. In Old Babylonian times cities were divided administratively into separate 'wards' or 'neighbourhoods', represented by the heads of household ('elders') and a mayor (*rabiānum*), perhaps consciously modelled on the administration of villages.[103] The word for these wards in Akkadian is *bābtum*, closely related to the word for a gate (*bābum*) and it is natural to assume that the divisions were at least originally related to the different city gates. A fascinating document from Ešnunna lists Amorites 'living in the city' according to their wards (Text 4:5). The wards are named after the first man listed in each group. There are seven, nine and ten men listed in the three wards, which could reflect the number of Amorite families. This gives a minimum of say thirty to forty people in a ward, but,

Text 4:5 From an administrative list found at Ešnunna
1 – son of Milki-la-El
1 – Ugazum
1 – Šalanum
1 – Mut-kabid
1 – son of Iblinum
1 – son of Palusum
1 – son of Ilan[um]
1 – brother of Zama[ra]num
1 – Uda[ma], his brother(?)
1 – son of E[. . .]
[Total] 10 – city-ward (*bābtum*) of Milki-la-El.
Total 26 Amorites, 'nobles' (*ellūtum*).

[After listing three reserves (**dah-hu**) the text concludes:]
(Grand) total: 29 Amorites residing in the city. Control of Lu-šalim. [Date]

(After Gelb 1968, 40–1)

given the purely Amorite nature of the names, we cannot rule out the existence of numbers of non- or pre-Amorite families within the same residential grouping.[104]

There must always have been a tension between the institutions of municipal government on the one hand, and kin-based divisions in society on the other. On the whole, we would expect an archaeologically detectable – hence topographical – division to coincide most closely with the administrative wards, in view of their presumed spatial integrity. At the beginning of the Early Dynastic period, when cities were perhaps re-establishing themselves after a period of abandonment, there is evidence that settlements were composed of large open enclosures surrounded by massive mud-brick walls and separated by narrow lanes, which no doubt corresponded to social, probably kin-based, groupings (see Figure 5:4, p. 92). In the course of time it is likely that pressure on space wore down the physical barriers, and urban intercourse the social barriers, but the outlines of both probably remained drawn in much the same place. Nevertheless we are not yet in a position to draw together the archaeological and the textual evidence. The *bābtum* as an 'urban village' does not seem likely to have begun life merely as the residence of a single extended family; both the social group and the actual enclosures would need to be bigger. This is illustrated by a recent study of two excavated housing areas at Nippur which might be considered as 'neighbourhoods', but seem much too small to constitute a ward or *bābtum* since otherwise the Old Babylonian city would have comprised hundreds of *bābtum*.[105]

Agnatic groupings

Was there then a social grouping larger than the family? In the case of recently settled nomadic populations, this will obviously have been the tribe, in whatever form it took before settlement, but there is also evidence, in the form of scattered references, to clans or tribes within the long-established urban communities of the third millennium. When

Gudea inaugurated the E-ninnu temple at Girsu, he called up labour from three groups called **im-ru-a**, each of which was represented by a symbolic standard (**šu-nir**), and named after a major deity: Ningirsu 'the king smiting the foreign land', Nanše, 'the pure bow of the ship', and Inanna 'the rosette'. While literary texts sometimes refer to clans, and their expansion, they are very rarely mentioned in administrative documents.[106] Once a clan holding of land is referred to in a legal text from the Ur III period;[107] and in an Early Dynastic text from Šuruppak a laconic note records 539 boys from 7 clans (**im-ru**), showing that they must have been composed of several families each.[108] The question is whether the greater occurrence of clan affiliation in the earlier period is the result of a real change, or simply that the documentation is increasingly refined to specifically legal points, shedding the non-legal (though perhaps still socially relevant) aspects of the situation.

The countryside

Every city had its hinterland, which looked to it as a political centre and with which, as we shall see in chapters 8 and 9, it maintained an intimate symbiosis. It was responsible for the administration of the countryside as much as of the city. The Pre-Sargonic Girsu archives are largely concerned with rural matters, and we have already noted that the city of Šuruppak in the Early Dynastic period administered its own plough teams. Adams has shown how at this time the cities tended to concentrate the population at the expense of the scatter of small settlements present in earlier times. Nevertheless, at different periods villages were founded and flourished, and in the Old Babylonian period especially we can see that although politically dependent on the local city – whether it was sovereign or reduced to a provincial capital – each village undertook the administration of its own territory. Villages were called *ālum* just as larger towns, and in fact we hear more of the smaller rural settlements acting as an official body than we do of the cities. In the Code of Hammurapi (CH §23) it is stipulated that the *ālum* should take responsibility for crimes committed within its territory, and the village's role in local government appears clearly in Old Babylonian correspondence (see Text 4:6; chapter 15). It was the elders and the

> **Text 4:6** From an Old Babylonian letter
> The village (*ālum*) has given me 10 **iku** [= 3.6 ha] of land, the holding of a soldier who campaigned with me and whose 'hearth is extinguished' [i.e. who has no heir].
> (See Bayliss 1973, 120)

mayor (*rabiānum*) who represented the village, probably setting the pattern which was adopted in the city wards. Apart from administering the law, the principal matters for communal decision will have been the organization of water rights, fallow and other agricultural affairs within the village boundaries.[109]

The desert and the nomad

On the fringes and in the interstices of settlement are the nomads, who maintained a much less stable and less easy relationship with the settled population. There were surely mountain tribes with a transhumant lifestyle like recent Kurdish groups, but they would not have been forced into interaction with the settled plains by the climatic imperatives which bring the bedu north seeking grazing in the summer, and their intrusions on the Mesopotamian scene, such as the Gutian incursion, tend to have only a transient effect.[110] By contrast, the lifestyle of the desert nomads meant that they were ever present, and there is no doubt that their tents were perceived as a menace by the city dwellers (Text 4:7).[111]

Text 4:7 Descriptions of the Amorite
(a) A tent dweller ... wind and rain, ..., who digs up truffles from the hills, but does not know how to kneel; who eats raw meat; who has no house during the days of his life, and is not buried on the day of his death.
(Myth of the wedding of Amurru: after Buccellati 1966, 92)

(b) Since that time the Amorites, a ravaging people, with the instincts of a beast, ... the sheepfolds like wolves; a people which does not know grain ...
(Inscription of Šu-Sin: after Civil 1967a, 31)

Although recent studies have emphasized that they were economically dependent on the sedentary sector, engaging in 'enclosed nomadism', they could not be controlled like other members of the state, since they were not tied to a time or a place.[112] First and foremost they were shepherds. This meant that they ranged far in search of grazing, and in times of friendly relations the villagers and townsfolk might employ the nomad to tend their sheep, or agree to let him graze their young fields in exchange for some benefit. The Amorites were also breeders of donkeys (Text 4:8), which were used by farmers and soldiers as draught animals, and were no doubt sold to merchants for their caravans.[113] They could also engage in trade in their own right, and at times the routes between Mesopotamia and the west, especially that taking off from the Mari region to reach Syria via the oasis of Tadmor (classical Palmyra), were in the hands of the desert tribes.[114] Their role here was no doubt largely to provide the animals and local expertise to enable the journey to take place: but the recent example of the Slubba, a non-bedu tribe, renowned hunters living rather like tinkers, with metal-working and other less material skills such as star-gazing and primitive medicine, shows that other subsistence strategies were possible.[115]

Text 4:8 Animals received by the Ur III administration
6 male donkeys
1 female donkey
booty of the land of Amurru
from Lu-Nanna, under Etum the courier.
1 goat – Hunhalbida
2 grain-fed female goats – Ṣilluš-Dagan,
contribution.
Naša took delivery.
[Date:] 20/3/Šulgi 48.
(Lieberman 1968–9, 53)

Text 4:9 Prayer accompanying a funerary offering to Ammi-ṣaduqa's ancestors and predecessors

Arammadara : Tubtiyamuta : Yamquzzuhalamma : Heana : Namzu : Ditanu : Zummabu : Namhu : Amnanu : Yahrurum : Iptiyamuta : Buhazum : Sumalika : Ašmadu : Abiyamuta : Abiditan : [3 broken names] : Sumu-abum : Sumu-la-El : Sabium : Apil-Sin : Sin-muballit : Hammu-rapi : Samsu-iluna : Abi-ešuh : Ammi-ditana : Dynasty of the Amurru people : Dynasty of the Heana people : Dynasty of Gutium : any dynasty which is not written in this tablet : and any soldier who fell in the service of his lord : the King's sons : the King's daughters : all people from the rising of the sun to the setting of the sun, who have no-one to care for them or intercede for them, come and eat this, and drink this, and bless Ammi-ṣaduqa the son of Ammi-ditana, King of Babylon.

(After Finkelstein 1966b, 96–7)

However much the details have been modified in recent years, it remains the case that the desert population seems to renew itself from time to time with fresh, but always Semitic, tribal stock: the Arabs were preceded by the Aramaeans (emerging around 1400 BC), and they by the Amorites (first recorded giving trouble in the later third millennium). Lacking a permanent territorial base, such groups are always identified by their tribes, and tribal affiliation is central to the social context of the nomad, who lays great weight on his patrilineal descent. The ancestral tradition may not be as accurate as we might expect, both ancient texts and modern parallels indicate, but it is an important social and political perception, reflected in semi-legendary lists of ancestors and the use of Amorite names by Hammurapi's dynasty to its very end (Text 4:9).[116] The nomenclature of nomadic groups is always confusing and shifting. In the early second millennium the Amorites were sometimes divided into 'Sons of the North', who included the important Hanaeans, and 'Sons of the South', but they were more alike than different (Text 4:10).[117] The affinities

Text 4:10 From a letter to Zimri-Lim

If indeed they come to the banks of the Euphrates, is it not like beads in a necklace, distinguished because one is white and one is black? Thus they say: This village is Bin-Šimal ('Sons of the Left = North'), this village is Bin-Yamina ('Sons of the Right = South') – is it not like the flood-waters of a river in which the upper confronts the lower?

(Durand 1991)

between the different groups which usurped political power from the borders of Palestine right through Syria to Babylon undoubtedly affected the interaction between different parts of the Near East in much the same way as under the newly formed Aramaean states in the first, or perhaps at the time of the Kish, Mari and Ebla axis of the mid-third millennium. Yahdun-Lim's account of his march to the Mediterranean reveals the nature of Amorite power in those days, each 'king' being associated with both a city, such as Tuttul, and a 'land' (*mātum*) which bears a tribal name like Amnanum and evidently refers to his less sedentary Amorite subjects (Text 4:11). Similarly, in a famous letter, Zimri-Lim is described as ruling both the sedentary Akkadian population of Mari and the Hanaeans of his own Amorite origins (Text 4:12).

Text 4:11 From inscribed bricks of Yahdun-Lim in the Šamaš Temple at Mari
In that same year, La'um king of (the city of) Samanum and the land of Ubrabu, Bahlu-kulim king of (the city of) Tuttul and the land of Amnanum, and Ayalum king of (the city of) Abattum and of the land of Rabbum – these kings became hostile to him (Yahdun-Lim) and the troops of Sumu-Epuh of the land of Yamhad came to their aid, and these forces of *tur-mi-im* gathered together against him in (the city of) Samanum. By force of arms he bound these three kings of *tur-mi-im*, and killed their troops and the troops of their allies, accomplished their defeat and made a pile of their corpses. He destroyed their ramparts and turned (the cities) into ruin mounds.

(Dossin 1955, col. iii.3–27; cf. Malamat 1989, 42)

Text 4:12 From a letter to Zimri-Lim from his Governor at Terqa
Let my lord give dignity to his kingship. If you are King of the Hanaeans, and secondly you are King of the Akkadian(s), then my lord should not ride on horses. My lord should ride on a carriage and mules, and so give his kingship dignity.

(Kupper 1954, No. 76, 19–25)

The political upheavals which brought the Amorites on to the scene at the end of the third millennium probably occasioned a widespread abandonment of rural settlements, comparable to that associated with the arrival of the Aramaeans a thousand years later. Yet in time each of the nomadic groups is either absorbed into other populations or becomes sedentary itself. Thus in Mesopotamia the Amorites are integrated so completely into society that no trace of them survives the fall of the 1st Dynasty of Babylon. It was traditional to see this process as a succession of waves, with tribes moving from a state of complete nomadic barbarism to settled life. However, this is certainly an over-simplification, and various intermediate stages may be surmised from ethnographic parallels and observed in the cuneiform sources. Even a largely mobile group could have its sedentary sector. It cannot be accidental that both Amorites and Aramaeans are recorded as having a base at the Jebel Bishri, between the Euphrates and the major oasis of Tadmor (Palmyra): in the later second millennium there were villages here, and an Amorite connection with the mountain is found back into the third millennium.[118]

Nearer to urban civilization, along the Euphrates and Habur rivers, a process of gradual assimilation to sedentary society is revealed by Mari letters: part of the tribe, part perhaps even of a single village, may fix its winter residence and cultivate fields round a settlement, while another part continues to take the flocks further north in the summer in search of grazing (Text 4:10).[119] As with such regimes in other places and times, the annual migration may follow recognized routes to recognized encampments (*nawûm*), where the grazing rights were defined in relation to other nomads and the settled population. Nevertheless, the demarcation will not have been as precise as that of sedentary farmers, and there must have been plentiful occasion for dispute. In times of stability some of the desert nomads even turn up in the employment of the urban sector, usually either in undemanding roles such as door-keepers, or in service as mercenaries. The Ur III texts show that some

Amorites were integrated into sedentary life, especially in the south at Lagaš and Umma, while those mentioned in Isin and the Nippur region further north and west are engaged in miscellaneous casual jobs. Late in the Old Babylonian period we find encampments of Kassites, both on the Euphrates towards Mari and receiving beer rations from the urban administration in Sippar, very likely acting for the time being as mercenaries for the state (see chapter 13).[120] It has always proved politic for a state to secure the continued attachment of its fighting men by finding plots of land for them, and no doubt this was another frequent route towards settled life.

Further reading

Little of a general nature has been written about urban and rural life: two Old Babylonian cities have been studied from different viewpoints by Harris 1975 (Sippar) and Stone 1987 (Nippur), and a study of Ur in the Old Babylonian period is expected from M. van de Mieroop. For the phenomenon of urbanization, with specific reference to settlement distribution and size, Adams 1981 is basic. On nomadic lifestyles in Mesopotamia two basic works are Kupper 1957 (in French) and Buccellati 1966. The doctoral dissertation of Luke 1965 is also important. For an anthropological approach see Kamp and Yoffee 1980 and, world-wide, Khazanov 1984.

5

Household and family

In recent years historians have applied a new rigour to the study of family and household structure, and although our documentary sources in Mesopotamia lack (with rare exceptions) the details of family size, of age and life expectancy, and of change through time that are needed for serious demographic research, they need to be approached in the light of this experience. The distinction between a family and a household is fundamental. While the family is composed of members related by blood or marriage, with limits which are inevitably vague, a household may be defined as a 'co-resident domestic group' (Laslett 1972, 24), whose limits at any time should be more or less precise. For government administrators and archaeologists alike the household is a much easier concept to cope with, while the family, whose members may have links of varying tenacity and proximity, is much less accessible. It is traditional to borrow from anthropology the terms 'nuclear' and 'extended' family, but they must not be allowed to suggest an inappropriately rigid dual polarity. Intermediate forms always exist, and over time the same family or household can move from one such type to another. A household composed of a single 'conjugal family unit' may be called 'simple', one with more than one conjugal family unit is conveniently called a 'multiple household'; where the simple household is enlarged by the addition of an extra generation the term 'expanded family household' is less ambiguous than some.[121] An 'extended family' refers to 'all relatives in habitual contact with a person, irrespective of whether they live with him' (Laslett 1972, 29–30). Thus one can perfectly well have an 'extended family' composed of 'simple households'. That members of such a family do not live together need not diminish its social significance, which operates most evidently in the realm of land tenure and marriage custom; for the archaeologist, however, it does diminish the opportunities of detecting the existence of extended families and their role in society. Fortunately in Mesopotamia the documentary sources come to our aid here.

The household and its members

The materials of an ancient Mesopotamian house were those still in use today: mud brick, mud plaster, mud and poplar roofs, wooden doors and door-frames, all naturally available round the city, but the architecture betrays a craftsmanlike concern for quality, with thick, well-constructed walls and carefully laid floor and wall plaster. In the Old Babylonian period extra sophistication takes the form of baked brick for the lower parts of the walls, which tend to suffer from rising damp (Figure 5:1), but the only imported materials are

Figure 5:1 'No. 3, Gay Street': Old Babylonian courtyard house at Ur during Woolley's excavations. Note how the walls have about 12 courses of baked brick with mud-brick superstructure. (Woolley and Mallowan 1976, Plate 23a. Photo: courtesy Trustees of the British Museum)

bitumen, probably from Hit, and lime plaster (cf. Text 12:5, p. 233). None of these materials, except perhaps the beams and doors, is particularly expensive, and the value of a house resides in its site. Mesopotamian houses of the third millennium were often large and well planned, round a square courtyard (Figures 5:2; 5:3).[122] Like a settlement, too, the bigger the house or household, the more clearly differentiated and easier to identify are its activities. One can often distinguish between reception rooms, kitchen and courtyard, and regular fireplaces and water installations. Other usages, such as storage or animal stables, are more difficult to detect but improved archaeological techniques and observation promise to answer some of these questions.[123]

The principal change through time concerns the size of the city house: the sample is still inadequate, but whereas several 'town houses' at Fara and Abu Salabikh exceed 400 sq. m in surface area, the average size of the Old Babylonian houses at Ur, for instance, is under 100 sq. m. The reasons for this are not apparent: the pressure of space in a closely settled and thriving city could be a factor, but the relative frequency of sale documents referring to waste plots suggests that this was not the only reason. It could be thought that the increased stratification of society was responsible, with wealth and power shifting

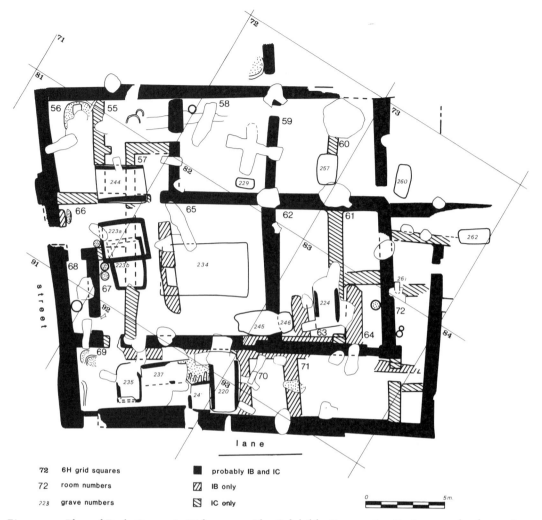

Figure 5:2 Plan of Early Dynastic III house at Abu Salabikh. Rooms 67, 68, 69 were the domestic wing, 70–72, 62 the main reception rooms. (Postgate 1990a)

away from the traditional urban families to the palace sector, or that long-term economic trends had led to an impoverishment of the urban population,[124] but since the raw materials for a perfectly respectable house were not expensive it is not obvious that such trends would have this effect on house size. Hence it is tempting to see the differences as reflecting a shift in the residential structure of society, involving changes in the size and/or complexity of households. In theory, archaeology could help us here: just as the city plan is more apt to betray the existence of city wards than of clans, so the house plan correlates with the household rather than the family. In practice, we are still a long way from being able to tell the number of occupants of a house or the level of their co-operative activities, despite new techniques, so that we are obliged at present to turn to the documents once more.

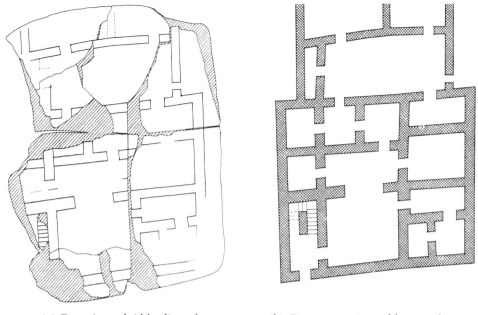

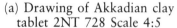

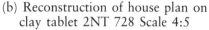

(a) Drawing of Akkadian clay
tablet 2NT 728 Scale 4:5

(b) Reconstruction of house plan on
clay tablet 2NT 728 Scale 4:5

Figure 5:3 Plan of house on an Akkad-period tablet from Nippur, with modern reconstruction. (After McCown and Haines 1967, Plate 52. Courtesy the Oriental Institute of the University of Chicago)

The problem of correlating household and family in the textual sources was expressed by Gelb: 'The question is to what extent do the coparcenary rights of extended-family groupings to field and house coincide with a common residence either in one house or in a compound of neighboring houses' (1979, 71). For various reasons co-resident 'multiple' or 'extended family households' are more a feature of rural than of urban life.[125] Whether or not a family remains co-resident has much to do with external conditions: within the city the finite availability of space combined with existing property rights forces an expanding family apart, while it is much easier for a large group to stay together in the countryside. Nevertheless, it is critical to appreciate that the dissolution of co-residence and the consequential division of rights in urban property does not necessarily undermine the theoretical or practical role of the extended family in the areas of marriage and land tenure.

The layout of a housing quarter built at Abu Salabikh at the very beginning of the Early Dynastic period (Figure 5:4) is very suggestive of a stage when the city was composed of self-contained enclosures which could well have housed co-resident extended families. In the textual sources, evidence for residential practices in the third millennium is very scarce,[126] but the frequent assumption that kin-based residential grouping was more usual in the earlier cities does take some support from house sales at Fara in the early ED III period, where relatives seem also to be neighbours.[127] There is some evidence for patrilinear

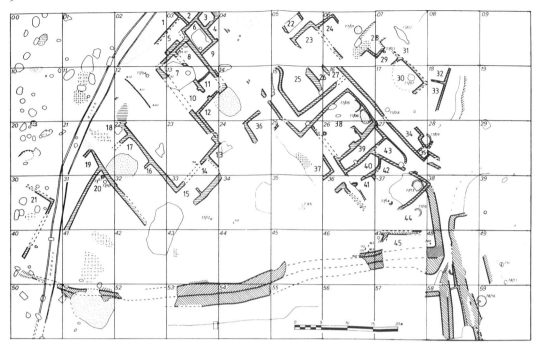

Figure 5:4 House walls and lengths of double and triple enclosure walls on the Early Dynastic I mound at Abu Salabikh, *c.* 2900 BC. (Postgate 1983, Figure 354)

descent in the third millennium,[128] but we are better informed in Old Babylonian times, when the normal residential unit was clearly patrilinear and patrilocal, and the male line of descent was a principal ingredient in society. Men are identified by their father's name (as in Russia and the Near East today). To have a son and heir was of great importance: it gave you someone to support you in your old age, and to appease your spirit after your death (Text 5:1). A childless couple could resort to various expedients – adoption was a well-recognized legal act, or the husband could choose to recognize the children of one of his slave-girls (Text 5:2).[129] The wife too could protect herself from divorce by supplying a slave-girl of her own by whom the man could have children, who would then be treated as her own (see p. 105).

Text 5:1 Curse from an inscription of Rimuš
Whosoever erases the name of Rimuš, King of Kish, and puts his name on the statue of Rimuš, saying 'It is my statue' – may Enlil the owner of this statue, and Šamaš tear out his stock and remove his offspring. Let them not give him male (issue) to appear before his god.

(After Sollberger and Kupper 1971, 103)

Sons and daughters lived in the father's house until they left for another household, either founding their own or marrying into another.[130] A recently published text from Kish gives a clear picture of residential conditions in a north Babylonian city (Text 5:3): using

Text 5:2 Adoption contract

Yahatti-Il is the son of Hillalum and of Alittum. He shall share their good times and their bad times. If Hillalum his father and Alittum his mother say to Yahatti-Il their son 'You are not our son', they shall forfeit house and property. If Yahatti-Il says to Hillalum his father and Alittum his mother 'You are not my father. You are not my mother', they shall shave him and sell him for silver. Even if Hillalum and Alittum have many sons, Yahatti-Il is the heir, and shall receive two shares from the estate of Hillalum his father; his younger brothers shall take shares brother like brother. A claimant who raises a claim against him infringes the taboo of Šamaš, Itur-Mer (god of Mari), Samsi-Addu and Yasmah-Addu, and shall pay $3\frac{1}{3}$ minas of silver, (penalty in) a lawsuit involving a life. 18 witnesses. Date.

(Boyer 1958, No. 1)

Text 5:3 Excerpts from a distribution list

90 litres – Puzur-Ištar, son of Dazuzum
30 litres – Yadidatum, his wife
30 litres – Ahassunu, bride
House of Puzur-Ištar

30 litres – Ištar-gamelat, his wife
20 litres – Ahassunu, his daughter
20 litres – Ikuppi-Adad, his son
15 litres – Šamaš-andulli, his son
House of Išme-Adad

30 litres – Humusi, his wife
20 litres – Ibbi-Adad, his son
20 litres – Tabni-Ištar, his daughter
15 litres – Rabi-sillašu, his son
20 litres – Munawwirtum, his slave-woman
10 litres – Ad-mat-ili, her son
House of Sin-išmeni

90 litres – Dadanum son of Laliya
30 litres – Arwia, his wife
20 litres – Ahati-waqrat, his/her slave-woman
20 litres – Appan-il, his/her son
20 litres – Humusi, his/her sister
House of Dadanum

(Donbaz and Yoffee 1986, 58–9, Sections D, G, H and K)

historian's terminology, most of the households are either 'simple' – a married couple with offspring – or 'expanded' – a simple household 'with the addition of one or more relatives other than offspring': there are sisters, evidently unmarried, mothers, presumably widowed, and brothers, perhaps still minors. What we do not find are 'multiple family households', comprising 'two or more conjugal family units connected by kinship or marriage'. It is true that the household may also include a slave-girl, with her children, but in these particular instances there are no male slaves, and she must be considered as a concubine, and hence a member of a single 'triangular' conjugal family unit.

The extended family and land ownership

Although the dissolution of a residential bond may well follow as a settlement matures, this does not necessarily imply that the role of the extended family itself was also weakened. It is often assumed that the more archaic the society, the stronger the role of 'extended families', and among Mesopotamian historians there is a considerable body of opinion which attributes a much more active role to the extended family in the early third millennium than later, in the Old Babylonian period. This revolves round evidence for the joint ownership of land. The surge of interest in this subject dates to the pioneering work of I.M. Diakonoff, who demonstrated from the earliest land sale documents that the relatives of the seller were present not only as witnesses to the transaction, but also as recipients of payments from the purchaser. In some cases sales are made by brothers or

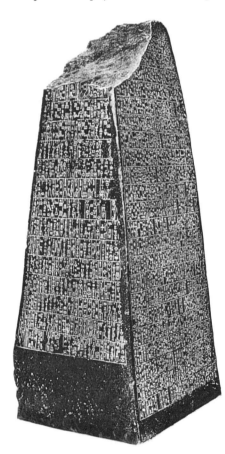

Figure 5:5 The Obelisk of Maništušu: record of land purchases in central South Mesopotamia. (MDP I, 1900, Planche IX, opposite p. 142)

other relatives jointly.[131] The most extreme case of this is the Obelisk of Maništušu (Figure 5:5; Text 5:4), recording fields in the north-western part of The Land, purchased by the second king of the Akkad Dynasty from four extensive groups of land-owners, mostly related: the owners ('lords') of the field are distinguished from those with a less direct claim on the property, called 'brother-lords of the field' (to use Gelb's term).[132] Working, as we are, on the fringes of history, it is difficult to exclude the possibility that the land-owning pattern in the Akkad region is of relatively recent date and reflects tribal conditions similar to those after the Kassite take-over, but a similar pattern seems to be attested for the Lagaš region as well. As in rural communities the world over, there are strong practical incentives not to divide the land but to cultivate it jointly: in particular, the equal division of agricultural land between successive generations of brothers can lead to an impossible degree of fragmentation. Small size is not helped by the complications of alternating fallow (so that a viable holding has to be in two separate areas), and of access to irrigation water, which also is bound up in the title to land.[133] Two strategies are available: to reduce the even-handedness of the division, thus leaving a larger share in the hands of the eldest son, or not to divide at all, making the exploitation of the land communal. Given the tangible advantages of joint cultivation (see chapter 9), it is not surprising that families held together.

> **Text 5:4** Excerpt from the Obelisk of Maništušu (Figure 5:5)
> Ilum-aha, son of Ilulu, the 'colonel'
> Watrum, son of Lamusa, of the steward
> Ayar-ilum, son of Pu-balum, the shepherd
> Sin-alšu, son of Ayar-ilum, of Pu-balum
> UD-IŠ (and) Zuzu, 2 sons of Ištup-Sin, grandsons of Irrara
> Ama-Sin, son of Gazualum, of Ilulu
> Ilu-asu, son of Aši-qurud
> Pu-Dagan, son of Allala
> Warassuni, son of Mesi-ilum
> Total, 10 men, brother-owners of the field.
>
> Grand total 17 men, 'grandsons' of Mezizi
> 821 **iku** of land,
> its price 2736.2.4 bushels of barley,
> its value 1 shekel silver per 1 bushel,
> its silver 45 minas 36⅔ shekels of silver –
> price of the field, 7 minas minus 9½ shekels silver –
> additional payment of the field.
> 1 *šuganu* overlaid with silver, its weight 15 shekels silver;
> (Scheil 1900, translation with assistance of P. Steinkeller)

For some unexplained reason no documents recording sale of land are preserved from the Ur III period, and later too in South Babylonia field sales are very rare, so that Diakonoff can write that 'sale of land was apparently prohibited throughout the Kingdom of Larsam (and before that, throughout the Kingdom of Ur)'.[134] In the absence of sale documents it is difficult to know how patterns of land ownership were affected by the upheavals at the end of the Akkad and Ur III Dynasties, but field-leases do seem to confirm the importance of the extended family at Old Babylonian Ur, revealing the joint ownership of leased fields in a group of texts where 'the average group of holders consisted of no less than 8 men enjoying full property rights' (Diakonoff 1985, 48). Inheritance texts from Nippur attest at least one case where the division of a city plot between brothers was defined in writing, but only carried out on the ground a generation later.[135] This contrasts strongly with – but does not directly contradict – the opinion of a distinguished legal historian of ancient Mesopotamia, who denies the importance of the extended family in the Old Babylonian sources: 'property left undivided, or the fact that the members of the family inherited houses which were adjacent, does not, therefore, imply any cooperation or interdependence in economic activities' (Leemans 1986, 18).

Differences of opinion as radical as this revolve not around disputed details within the documentation, but around its context within society. The sources contain biases, and different approaches will recognize these differently and attempt to compensate in different ways. In this case the problem derives from the nature of the legal documents and what they record. Both the law, in so far as it is concerned with property rights and liability, and government bureaucracy prefer to deal with individuals, rather than an amorphous and dispersed extended grouping. The government prefers to see land in one identifiable person's ownership; and even in the Fara period the legal document was usually able to specify a single principal owner. That other members of the family no longer feature in documents of the Old Babylonian period does not necessarily reflect a diminution of their role: it may simply be that in law the receipt of the sale price by the single legally recognized owner was all that the documentation required. No distribution of gifts is recorded, but it is perfectly possible that, as in the earlier period, social conventions meant that members of the extended family were involved and did still receive gifts. On the other hand, it would be difficult to disprove the opposite view that it is precisely on the occasion of a land sale that, to conform with legal requirements, we see the resuscitation of family links which are otherwise little more than a vestigial archaism.

Property and succession

Fathers and sons

As we have seen, urban conditions are much less favourable to joint property ownership, and elaborate inheritance documents from Old Babylonian times make it clear that, in the city at least, property rights were usually vested in the simple family unit. After the death of a household head it would be considered normal for the brothers to divide the estate between them. We have fascinating documents listing the division of paternal estates between the heirs (Text 5:5). Everything non-perishable could be included: land, house, furniture, animals and slaves, but also temple offices ('prebends', see chapter 6), debts and *ilkum*-duties.[136] The underlying principle is the patrilinear system in which property was

Text 5:5 From the division of paternal estate between four brothers (Šallurum, Apiyatum, Ziyatum and Lugatum) at Old Babylonian Nippur

$\frac{5}{6}$ **sar** of built house, beside the house of his share; $\frac{1}{2}$ **iku** 20 **sar** 'marra' field, neighbouring (his) share; 1 shrine-table; 3 sheep; 3 bushels of dry bitumen in place of the preferential share in oxen; $\frac{1}{2}$ shekel of silver, one-tenth of the Great Gate – (all this) the preferential share of the status of elder brother.

1 **sar** 5 **gin** built house, share of his father; 1 **sar** waste ground beside the house of Lugatum; $1\frac{1}{2}$ **iku** 30 **sar** 'marra' field, neighbouring Igmilum the butcher; 1 ox (called) Minam-epuš-ilum; 1 cow (called) Taribatum; 8 sheep; one-quarter of the prebend of the Great Gate; 1 waggon, unfinished; $1\frac{1}{2}$ shekels of silver, bequest(?); 1 potter's [or: pottery?] grindstone, handle attached; 1 wooden door, the gate of the sanctuary; 1 wicker door, the gate of the cella – (all this) the share of Šallurum, the elder brother.

$1\frac{1}{2}$ **sar** built house (in respect of 10 **gin** of built house Apiyatum has compensated Lugatum with 1 shekel 20 grains of silver) beside the house of Sin-lidiš the leather-worker; $1\frac{1}{2}$ **iku**, upper field, neighbouring Ir-Nanna; 1 **iku** 'ganda' field, neighbouring Ziyatum; 1 cow (called) Ili-dumqi; 1 cow (called) Ištar-rimti-ili; 8 sheep; one-quarter of the prebend of the Great Gate; 1 waggon, old (he has compensated Lugatum in respect of the waggon with 1 shekel of silver); 1 basalt grindstone, handle attached; 3 palm-rib (doors) inside the house of his share – (all this) the share of Apiyatum.

1 **sar** 16 **gin** built house, beside the temple of Lugalbanda; 1 **sar** waste ground beside the house of Šallurum (because house-area was not equal to house-area he has compensated the brothers with 4 bushels of grain and a ladder); $1\frac{1}{2}$ **iku** 'marra' field ... etc. etc.

The heirs of Imgua of their free-will divided by lot and swore by the name of the king not to raise claims against one another in future.

(After Prang 1976, 3–7)

divided between the sons, or, rather, each surviving male line, because the male offspring of a dead brother would also inherit: hence the protracted efforts of the wicked uncles to cast slurs on the paternity of a baby born posthumously (Text 5:6).

There were two major modifications of the general rule that all the sons inherited equal shares. The head of the household was entitled to make separate gifts during his lifetime which were not accounted in the division of the estate (although this may well not have extended to land). This was particularly relevant to the provision made for daughters. A father was expected to provide each daughter with an appropriate dowry, and if this had not been done before his death, the sons were obliged to set aside part of the estate to this end (Text 5:7). Unless the girl died or left her husband's family without sons, this property was lost to the patrimonial estate, her sons representing a living investment in another patrimonial group. Cross-cousin marriage is not well attested, although it would not be easy to detect in our sources. Equally, in those cases where a girl went to be a priestess, the brothers had to provide her with support; on her death they expected to recover such property, but this was evidently a controversial issue leading to much litigation, since some

Text 5:6 An excerpt from a lawsuit about disputed paternity

Ninurta-ra'im-zerim the son of Enlil-bani petitioned the officials and judges of Nippur, (saying) 'Enlil-bani my father, the son of Ahi-šagiš, died while I was placed inside my mother Sin-nada. Before my birth Habannatum, my father's mother, informed Luga the herdsman and Sin-gamil the judge, and fetched the midwife, who delivered me. After I grew up, in year 20 of Samsu-iluna ... [his uncles attempt to question his paternity ...]. The officials and the judges examined their case, and read the previous tablet of the oath, and questioned their witnesses.... They ordered that (the divine emblem) Udbanuilla should take up residence, that the witnesses who knew the filiation of Ninurta-ra'im-zerim should make a declaration on oath, and that the matter should be returned to the Assembly. Udbanuilla took up residence in the Gate of the Heroes' Hill, and Lipit-Enlil, son of Nabi-Enlil, stated: 'When Enlil-bani, son of Ahi-šagiš, left Ninurta-ra'im-zerim his son inside Sin-nada his wife, ... [break] ... Ninurta-ra'im-zerim is indeed the progeny of Enlil-bani, until he was born Habannatum guarded her, and he is indeed the progeny of Enlil-bani.' Ummi-waqrat, the wife of Iddin-Ninšubur and Šat-Sin the priestess, daughter of Sin-išmeani, declared: 'When Sin-nada gave birth to Ninurta-ra'im-zerim the son of Enlil-bani, Habannatum her mother-in-law notified Luga the herdsman and Sin-gamil the judge, and they sent a soldier, and the midwife of Habannatum delivered her. Until she gave birth they guarded her. We know that Ninurta-ra'im-zerim is the progeny of Enlil-bani'.... [Further witnesses add:] '... Habannatum brought a midwife, a soldier, and Luga the chief herdsman and Sin-gamil the judge. She had guarded her and when Ninurta-ra'im-zerim was born they took him in a reed-basket and brought him to the house of Sin-gamil the judge' ...

(cf. Leichty 1989)

Text 5:7 From a letter from a *nadītum* priestess at Sippar

(I swear) by my lady, with my hands clasped, until recently I had not heard the wording of my tablet, and indeed up till now my tablet was deposited with my ... Since my father went to his fate, my brothers have not given me the dowry on the tablet. Now the word is – let us speak frankly – that a *nadītum* whose brothers do not maintain her may give her inheritance where she will. I will appeal to the judges.

(After Wilcke 1982, 448)

of the *nadītum* ladies preferred to hand their property down to adopted daughters (see below, chapter 6).[137]

The other modification differs from city to city according to local custom. A variety of devices was used to favour the eldest son: he might be allocated two of the shares instead of one, he might get an agreed extra proportion of the total estate, sometimes at least 10 per cent, and he might be entitled to choose his share, the others being allocated by the drawing of lots.[138] As far as real estate was concerned, the disposal of buildings in the city posed problems for the bereaved brothers rather different from land. After the death of the father it was normal, though not invariable, for the patrimony to be physically divided and for at least the married brothers to establish independent households if they had not already done so. The eldest son may have had certain privileges and duties: at Nippur, for instance, it seems that temple offices were normally passed down to him,[139] and he would normally have first claim on the family house; if big enough, it was sometimes divided to accommodate some of the brothers separately, with consequent alterations to room use and means of access. Many of the apparent house-sale documents of Old Babylonian times are merely 'paper transactions' transferring the ownership of very small areas of 'built house' so as to compensate one heir for a difference in size in the part of the house he inherited, a difference enforced by the practicalities of the architecture (see Text 5:5). Often, though, the house would be too small to divide, and being bounded by other properties on each side would have no room for enlargement. Here residence in simple households may be the practical consequence of crowded urban conditions, and was probably the norm.

One reason why the eldest son would normally inherit the family house may have been connected with his duties, since in some places and periods the building housed beneath it the ancestral tombs. From, at latest, Early Dynastic times until well into the Old Babylonian period it was common practice to bury the dead within the four walls of the house, although separate cemeteries might also exist both inside and outside the city.[140] The reform texts of UruKAgina tell us that burial ceremonies were attended by a priest – whose exorbitant charges he was curbing – and texts and archaeology attest to the range of household and luxury items accompanying the deceased to the underworld. Almost nothing is known of how a grave would have been marked,[141] but we do know that it was common practice to make libations over the ancestor's grave, at intervals no doubt prescribed by tradition – a tradition which is reflected in the universal celebration of memorial ceremonies at prescribed intervals after a death in the Near East today. In this ceremony, known as a **kisega**/*kispum*, water was poured over the grave and food offerings placed there, while prayers were spoken naming the dead.[142] Both in textual sources and in the Royal Cemetery of Ur there is considerable evidence for the practical aspects of such libations, especially terracotta pipes designed to channel the liquids.[143] The importance of this in conserving the patrilineal identity and self-consciousness of the group shows in the inclusion of a list of ancestors in the prayers (Text 5:8). Such a ceremony was attended by Samsi-Addu at his father's tomb in Terqa, and as one might expect royal houses were especially assiduous in carrying out such rites: kings and high officials were involved in arranging the commissariat for a public *kispum* which took place during the month of Abum.[144] Although the duties of the chief heir are only explicitly described for us in texts from outside the Mesopotamian heartland (at Susa, and, in the later second millennium, from Nuzi), the duty of the eldest son to carry out these rituals, and thus represent the line, is implicit in inheritance documents from Nippur where the eldest son regularly receives in his pre-emptive share the 'offering-table of the shrine'.[145]

Evidence for a shrine in the family house is absent from before the Ur III period, but in an Old Babylonian inheritance division of a Larsa household the eldest son receives 'a share, together with the shrine',[146] and houses at Ur had separate rooms apparently designed as shrines, associated with the baked brick family vault. More commonly, as in the kingdom of Ešunnna or at Nippur, the function of the shrine was performed by one of the reception rooms. There was usually a small rectangular pedestal in one corner of

Text 5:8 An Old Babylonian libation prayer

Sin, you are god of heaven and earth. In the morning I am pouring water to you for the family of Sin-nasir son of Ipqu-Annunitum.

Release the family of Sin-nasir son of Ipqu-Annunitum, that they may eat his bread and drink his water:

Išme-Ea son of Šamaš-nasir, his wife and his family.
Iltani, *nadītum* of Šamaš, his daughter.
Sin-nasir, son of Išme-Ea,
Ku-Aya, *nadītum* of Šamaš, his daughter.

[etc., ending up with:]

Ipqu-Annunitum, son of Ipqu-Aya, Belessunu, his wife.

(After Wilcke 1983)

Figure 5:6 'No. 1, Boundary Street': altars in each corner of a domestic shrine at Old Babylonian Ur. Between them the pottery bowls probably represent funerary offerings over the graves beneath. (Woolley and Mallowan 1976, Plate 43B. Photo: courtesy Trustees of the British Museum)

the room, often associated with a hearth or chimney (Figure 5:6). Standing about waist high, it resembles the solid altar blocks of temple shrines, and its religious nature is made explicit by the decoration of recessed niches imitating temple architecture, often with the ends of the roof-beams indicated just below the 'roof' or top.[147] Presumably these altars were designed for the cult of the personal god of the household head, or the god of the family (although the offering vessels found in one case at Ur raise an ambiguity, since they could also be seen as *kispum* offerings over the family tombs). Unfortunately the Old Babylonian and earlier sources are mute about this intimate side of the religion, and nothing is known of private cults of this sort, or of the religious thought behind them, except for passing references to personal deities in conventional greetings found in letters and elsewhere. Individuals certainly had personal gods of their own, such as Eanatum and Šulutula, Gudea and Ningišzida. On the other hand, we know that kin-based groups also had their own gods (and goddesses), whose worship was as much a statement of identity with a social group as the worship of a city god.[148]

Wives and daughters

As in most places at most times, marriage in early Mesopotamia was a link between families, or larger groups, as much as between individuals. Just as the daughters of Šulgi might be sent to be brides of his tougher opponents in the eastern mountains, so considerations of local power and prestige must have dictated the choice of a husband or

Text 5:9 Excerpt from the accounting of a marriage transaction between a Larsa family and an Ur family

His mother came to Ur and they brought for her 1 sheep, worth $1\frac{1}{2}$ shekels silver, 1 second-class beer and 1 measure of barley-flour.

His mother … ed in the Enki Gate, and they brought for her 20 litres of bread, 40 litres of beer and 1 offering sheep worth 1 shekel silver.

On the day they bathed, 1 measure of beer for the feast.

On the day she left, 20 litres of bread, second-class beer, and 1 offering sheep worth 1 shekel silver.

On the day he entered my house, 1 sheep worth 2 shekels silver was slaughtered, 1 measure of barley flour was baked, 2 second-class beers were poured.

He was entering my house for 4 months and his daily commons were 10 litres of bread, 20 litres of beer, 1 second-class beer. Over 4 months: 4 bushels of bread, 8 bushels of beer, 60 second-class beer; 10 litres fine oil worth 10 shekels, 10 litres sesame-oil worth 1 shekel, his ointment. . . .

(After Greengus 1966, 56–7)

bride in many marriages between ordinary families. It is difficult for us to reconstruct these relationships because there is little call for them to be mentioned in the legal documents, which are only drawn up in order to define property rights between the two parties or in cases of dispute or difficulty. Hence we are lucky to have a unique text from Ur which is not a legal document but a memorandum recording the expenditures incurred by the father of a bride in the course of the negotiations which led up to the marriage of his daughter with a member of a family from Larsa (Text 5:9). That it involves both families as much as the two individuals emerges very clearly. Gifts, payments or expenditures are noted over a span of at least four months. It is not easy to be certain why or at what stage some of the transactions took place, but the text gives us a context for bald statements in other sources, such as the various kinds of gift mentioned in lexical texts, including 'sheep contribution of the in-laws' and 'sheep contribution of the women',[149] or mentions of a feast (*kirrum*) in the laws and letters.

While customs no doubt varied through time and space, we can distinguish at least four stages in the marriage process:

1 betrothal or engagement;
2 reinforcing exchanges or payments
  a by the groom's side (= *terhatum* and *kirrum*)
  b by the bride's side (e.g. **níg.dé.a** = *biblum*);[150]
3 the physical move of the girl to the father-in-law's house;
4 establishment of co-habitation with husband.

There are various reasons for the protracted nature of these proceedings: after an agreement has been reached, it will inevitably take time to make the practical arrangements for the final ceremonies of the wedding, and, since relatively large amounts of wealth are involved, it may well take time to gather the resources. Further, in some cases the girl, and even the groom, may not be old enough for the full form of marriage to be realized. Some of the possible complications emerge from the legal documents and laws. The documents are concerned with property rights: where property is concerned, disputes will follow, and the laws are mostly devoted to rulings on difficult issues. One of these, which occurs in the earliest code and is repeated later, is the legal definition of marriage: in the eyes of the law it is the 'contract' (**inim-kešda**/*riksatum*) which constitutes the condition of marriage, but this is also coupled with the 'feast' (*kirrum*; Text 5:10).[151]

Text 5:10 The Ešnunna 'Law code', §§27–8

If a man took the daughter of a man without asking her father and her mother, and has not held a feast and made a contract for her father and her mother – even if she lives in his house for a full year, she is not a wife. If he did hold a feast and make a contract for her father and her mother, and took her, she is a wife: the day she is caught in the embrace of (another) man, she shall die, she shall not live.

(After Yaron 1969, 32)

Unfortunately the laws do not give any definition of these terms, so that we have to work this out for ourselves. Legal scholars long considered that the contract must have been in writing, but Greengus has demonstrated that it was an oral agreement, solemnized in ways which must have extended back before written documents: these no doubt included formal or symbolic actions, and also a prescribed form of words (as indeed does marriage in most modern societies to this day). Clear evidence for symbolic acts on concluding a contract, whether for a marriage or something else, is lacking. Documents from the Ur III period show that betrothal involved an oath in the name of the king (**mu lugal**), but this need only have been the regular way of formalizing any oral agreement, rather than peculiar to marriage. One form of words connected with marriage can be reconstructed fairly confidently: legalizing a divorce requires the spoken formulae 'You are not my husband', 'You are not my wife' – and these form the annulment of words quoted in a wedding scene from a magical text: 'I will fill your lap with silver and gold: You are my wife, I am your husband.'[152]

However, these words pass between the bride and groom, and are hardly the 'contract' of which the laws speak, which was between the two families, usually represented by the fathers. What the groom's family seems to be securing by the agreement and associated payment (*terhatum*, in OB times usually a substantial sum in silver, but earlier in naturalia[153]) is the right to the girl. A long debate has flourished among legal historians as to whether this was 'Kaufehe' (purchase marriage), but since the bride money was often returned at the conclusion of the wedding process it was more like a cautionary down-payment or earnest of good faith.[154] The next step varies. She may continue to live in her father's house, and especially when young this may have been normal, or she could move to her father-in-law's house and live there.[155] This practice is well attested in legal contexts, and 'brides' (*kallatum*/**egia**) are listed in the household census from Kish (Text 5:3). The bride will come with her dowry, sometimes perhaps stored up for her for years.[156] In later Old Babylonian times a typical document made out at this stage will list the dowry, will specify that the bride's father 'sent it and her into the house of A, her father-in-law, for B, his son'. At the end, there is sometimes added a cautious note defining the payment to be made in the event of a divorce. This did not necessarily mean that the marriage was at once consummated, since there are clear indications that a period could elapse before this happened,[157] and indeed that the agreement did not necessarily prescribe marriage to one person in particular, merely to a member of the family. This is symptomatic of the fact that she is marrying into a patrilinear group, not to an individual.

Where, on the other hand, the girl remained in her parental home, the groom – whose rights had long since been agreed – is said to 'call on the house of his father-in-law', and the consummation of the marriage process begins.[158] Undoubtedly this would have been accompanied by traditional ceremonies. There is some evidence that in this case the bridegroom would come with his male accompaniment (*susapinnu*), and sometimes they would remain in the father-in-law's house for a while. Not surprisingly, a bed played a role at this stage: we know from terracotta models that Babylonian beds were well constructed pieces of furniture, and both the models and the royal hymns make it clear that they were the right place for making love (Figure 5:7). That they feature in dowry lists is only to be expected, but in Ur III times we find occasional references to 'erecting

Figure 5:7 Terracotta figurine. Models of beds are frequent in the later third and early second millennium BC, often with detailed representation of the construction of the bed. Examples like this complete with human occupants are probably more common than the rarity of published examples might suggest. (BM 115719. Photo: courtesy Trustees of the British Museum)

the bed' in the context of one of the diplomatic marriages, and a later marriage document writes of 'when they lay on their bed'.[159]

Since the law codes and legal contracts are usually concerned with property rights, they have less to tell us about the human side of the marriage bond. Despite earlier speculation by legal historians, the virginity of the bride is of concern: at the conclusion of one marriage contract the husband is said to have 'loosed the dress-pin of her virginity', and in a case where a bride's virginity was disputed the courts were prepared if necessary to call on the expertise of female witnesses to give testimony in such a matter.[160] This can also be attributed to the paramount desire of the family to ensure that it is its own male line which will be perpetuated, and is of course matched by the expectation that the wife, or the living-in bride, will behave respectably and remain within the family's vision.[161] On the other hand, she is not simply a chattel held in common by the entire family: the laws make it clear that strong taboos on incest existed. This emerges very clearly from CH §§155–6: if a father-in-law 'knew' a bride brought to his house for one of his sons, the law requires a fine of half a mina of silver and the girl is released. If, on the other hand, his son had already co-habited with her, incest had been committed and the father is sentenced to drowning. The same emphatic prohibition of incest is present in other sections of the code.[162]

Separation

Although both in law and in custom the women of ancient Mesopotamia seem to have been treated more equally than in many more recent societies, that they had no full equality emerges very clearly from the divorce provisions preserved in the lexical compilation *ana ittišu*: 'If a wife rejects her husband and says "You are not my husband", they shall cast her into the river. If a husband says to his wife "You are not my wife", he shall pay $\frac{1}{2}$ mina of silver.' In later Old Babylonian times marriage contracts often include provisions referring, rather pessimistically in our eyes, to the event of a divorce: just as *ana ittišu* suggests, if the woman denies her marriage she is condemned to death, by a variety of grisly means like drowning or throwing off a tower, or to be sold into slavery. True, these are conditions imposed by a contract, to which she, or at least her family, was a party, but the contrast with denial of the contract by the man remains just as stark, since the document may prescribe the sum of silver to be paid as compensation, which is usually less than 1 mina of silver. Divorce initiated by the husband was accompanied by a symbolic act of cutting the hem of the wife's robe, which may be connected with the practice of knotting the original bride-payment up in it.[163]

Despite these hard conditions, the reality may not have been as bad as it sounds. It seems that divorce was not acceptable without grave cause, and the social stigma attached to an unreasonable divorce shows through in the communal opinion: 'Is a lady who has lived in your father's house, and whose married status is known to your ward, to leave just like that? Give her the equivalent of what she brought with her' (CT 45, 86). The commonest grave causes were alleged misbehaviour by the wife, or a childless marriage. Once again one must remember that marriage is a bond between families, and the purpose of marriage within each family is to secure sons to perpetuate the male line. This did not however mean that an infertile marriage automatically subjected the wife to the indignity of divorce, because law and custom permitted her to provide sons for the family by supplying a slave-girl to substitute for her and bear her children, a solution long familiar from the story of Sarah and Hagar in the Bible. Any sons of this union were then treated in all respects as her own: 'the sons are her sons', and when the law says 'she has not enabled him to have sons' (CH §163), it has in mind both the more normal and this surrogate motherhood. The same principle applied in the case of a *nadītum*, who could marry but could not co-habit with her husband (Text 5:11).[164] Not surprisingly, there is some evidence that the conditions of divorce were radically affected by whether or not the

Text 5:11 The Code of Hammurapi, §§144–5

If a man married a *nadītum*, and that *nadītum* has given a slave-girl to her husband and (so) produced sons, and that man decides to marry a concubine, they shall not consent to that man, he shall not marry the concubine.

If a man married a *nadītum* and she has not got sons for him, and he decides to marry a concubine, that man may marry the concubine: he may bring her into his house, but she shall not be made the equal of the *nadītum*.

wife had had sons, for if she had she was thereby linked to the patrilinear family whether the parties concerned wished it or not. If not, it was a matter of indifference to the husband's family whether she returned to her father's house or went elsewhere.[165]

Women outside the patrilinear household

By the nature of legal documents, we learn little about those women (and indeed men) who fell outside the framework of the patrilinear household. Widows, like orphans, were the defenceless of society who qualified for the charity of the righteous ruler. If a rejected wife or a widow did not return to her father's household, she might 'go after the man of her heart', and we read, for instance, of a lady 'who upped and left her in-law's house'. Prostitutes existed, and were associated with the public spaces of the city. Whether the 'ale-wives', like the philosopher of the Epic of Gilgamesh, who were clearly an institution of city life, were respectable married women or not, our sources do not disclose. Unquestionably, as we shall see, some of the orphans and illegitimate children ended up in the temples, boys as well as girls; but this did not necessarily protect them from exploitation, since it is possible that the practice of temple prostitution, reported more than a thousand years later by Herodotus in rather lurid terms, was already current in Old Babylonian times.[166]

Polygamy

The sparse available evidence from both the second and third millennia confirms the predominance of one man, one wife.[167] A man could not, with rare exceptions, have more than one formally recognized wife at a time. This is not usually stated explicitly, but both the law codes and accounts of court proceedings confirm it. The exceptions known to us are where the first wife has been incapacitated through illness, when Hammurapi's Code permits the husband to take a second wife (CH §148); and complicated cases to do with priestesses, who were probably not co-resident in the patrilinear household, and where the second wife may have been her sister.[168] A complete anomaly – if we have not misunderstood the Sumerian – is UruKAgina's inclusion of the practice of polyandry among one of the social abuses he reformed. On the other hand, it is clear that slave-girls might be treated as concubines, whether they were supplied by the wife or – perhaps more often – belonged to the man (CH §§170–4). The law codes permit, but do not require, the children of such a union to inherit from the paternal estate, and this leads us to consider the status of slaves within the household more generally.

Domestic slaves

While the Kish household list (Text 5:3) includes only female slaves, there is no doubt that male slaves could also be resident members of a household. 'One or more slaves are found in all partitions of sizeable estates', but only occasionally do we find as many as ten male and ten female, or fourteen male and six female slaves in a single household.[169] They are

Text 5:12 Old Babylonian letter

Say to my sister, Etirum says: ... About the slave on which I gave you instructions – Ibi might come and let that slave out without asking me. Put a halter on that slave, and put the copper band which I left for you on him. Call on Beletum, the barmaid of Ibi and say: 'The slave is entrusted to you until Etirum comes. The slave must not go out of the gate. Keep an eye on him, and don't let him get upset.'

(Kraus 1964, No. 39)

listed like other property in inheritance divisions, and frequently sold. Their children belonged to their owners, and a house-born slave was specified as such (*wilid bītim*). Fresh blood came in from abroad, either as a result of war and plunder, or through commerce.[170] In the Old Babylonian period slaves from the mountain fringes of Mesopotamia were popular, and some merchants specialized in the slave trade. Naturally some slaves attempted to escape, and the law codes show that the loss of a slave would be announced by the public herald, and that citizens had an obligation to turn a runaway in. However, unless a slave was liable to flight or violence he (or she!) was not usually constrained. Chains are occasionally mentioned (see Text 5:12), and a slave marking, called an *apputtum* and perhaps no more than a distinctive hair-do, was normal.

Text 5:13 The Code of Hammurapi, §§226–7

If a barber has shaved away a slave's *apputtum* without the consent of the slave's owner, they shall cut off that barber's hand.

If a man has forced a barber, and he has shaved away the *apputtum* of a slave who is not his own, they shall kill that man and impale him in his doorway. The barber who shaved him unwittingly shall take an oath and be released.

The manumission or freeing of slaves is well attested already in the Ur III documents (often because it is being contested in court). As CH §§226–7 make clear, this would be accompanied by the removal of the slave mark by a barber (Text 5:13), and this is doubtless why manumission was formally known as 'clearing the forehead' (Text 5:14). Children of a freed slave are themselves usually free, and the law codes are concerned with nice legal points to do with the offspring of a free person and a slave, and with property rights as between children of fully free and mixed marriages. In all these cases it is generally assumed (although rarely stated by the sources) that we are talking of chattel slaves, not debt slaves who might also, albeit temporarily, be resident in the household. They too were freed, whether on payment of their debt or as a consequence of its annulment, and the sources

Text 5:14 An Old Babylonian letter

Say to Lipit-Ištar and Lu-Bau, Ahum says: Sumu-abum has set Buttatum free [lit.: 'has cleared his forehead with Buttatum']. No-one should make any claim on him, his wife or his sons. He has entered the city of Umma, and no-one shall ... him. His forehead is clear, and I shall hold you responsible for non-[compliance(?)].

(Frankena 1966, No. 122)

tell us nothing about the possibilities for them to maintain a family while serving their term (see chapter 10).[171]

Further reading

The two most pertinent archaeological studies of housing quarters in early cities are Henrickson 1981 and Stone 1987. For the house itself, see E. Heinrich, 'Haus', in *Reallexikon der Assyriologie* IV, 176–220 (in German). See Gelb 1979 for family structure, and Diakonoff 1974 on early systems of land ownership. The monumental work on early land sale documents initiated by Gelb has now been brought to fruition by Steinkeller and Whiting (Gelb *et al.* 1991). There is no satisfactory recent survey of domestic slavery, despite a number of articles on the subject by Gelb (see notes). For the details of inheritance and marriage law see particularly Landsberger 1968, Kraus 1969a and b, and Wilcke 1985 (all in German). Also R. Westbrook, *Old Babylonian Marriage Law* (*AfO* Beiheft 23; Horn 1988).

6
The temple

Until the 1950s the government of the early city was almost universally characterized as a 'theocracy', and cuneiform scholars wrote of the 'temple-city'. Claims were even made that at Lagaš (in truth, the only place for which adequate evidence survived) the temple owned all the land and employed the entire population: 'The gods, as representatives of the tribe and clans, own the farm land created by social labour ... The tribal territory of Lagash, for example, appears divided into the estates of some twenty deities, eminent domain over them all being perhaps retained by the chief god of the city or tribe' (Gordon Childe, What happened in history, rev. edn, Harmondsworth, 1954, 94). This extreme view is now discredited. We cannot any longer maintain that because the temple collected commodities and distributed them to its dependants the entire economy operated through 'redistribution', or that the priests controlled all agricultural production and commercial activity. Nevertheless, we must not overcompensate, and so underrate the importance of the temple's role. In a sense it represents the communal identity of each city: it symbolizes it, but it also concentrates wealth and offers services to the community which are far more critical to the growth of an urban civilization than the exploitative strategy of the palace, similar though the two institutions often appear in practice. It is right, therefore, that we should treat the temple first.

The temple building

As we have already seen in chapter 2, the 'city sealings' of the Early Dynastic I period use symbols for different cities which subsequently become the cuneiform writings of their names. The symbol is composed of the picture of an altar, which became the cuneiform sign for a shrine, and the identifying emblem of the city, such as 'sun' for Larsa (Figure 2:8 above). This gives unequivocal expression of the essential role of the temple within the settlement, one which is expressed in words by the series of Temple Hymns (see above, p. 26). In the flatness of the South Mesopotamian plain there were no natural features which might mark out any place as specially numinous – the only holy sites were those which had been hallowed by long use as the focus of a community's identity. We need now to look at the temple itself and how it functioned. It is easy to see why it is the temples that have often attracted the attention of archaeologists at the expense of the rest of the city. They usually occupy a central position within the ancient site, often raised high, and in them were concentrated the kind of high-quality artefacts which delight the discoverer and encapsulate the culture. While there is archaeological evidence for religion in the neolithic of the Near East, the place of communal worship or temple is first attested in a deep sounding at Eridu, and then only as a small hut which is identified as such simply from the fact that it is the first of a series which eventually emerges with unmistakable features (Figure 2:2): niched decoration, an 'altar', and in one level of the building a mass of blackened fish bones from the offerings. A shallow platform becomes a major feature shortly after Level IX (late Ubaid), and in the Uruk period a high platform was built and repeatedly extended by adding a skin of masonry which also no doubt raised the top. In the course of the third millennium, architects converted this organic growth into the well-

Figure 6:1 The Warka Vase. Worshippers bear the fruits of the temple's flocks and fields to the goddess in whose shrine they are stored in the top register. (Photo: courtesy of Hirmer Fotoarchiv)

known stepped towers we now call ziggurrats after the Akkadian word. There is little need to connect these structures with the Egyptian pyramids (and no justification for positing a Mayan connection!): the similarities can be adequately accounted for by the exigencies of primitive architectural technology.

For the building on the summit we have to turn to other sites, especially Uruk and Uqair. At Uruk a similar sequence has been identified in recent years, with small Ubaid

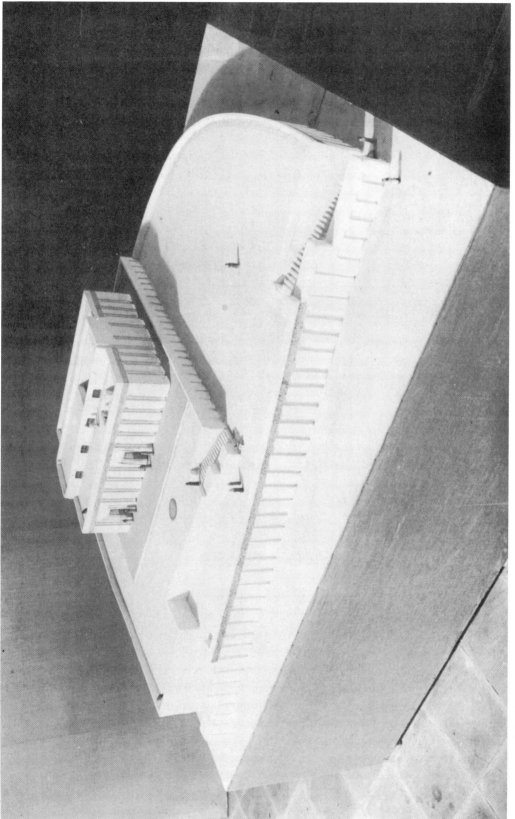

Figure 6.2 Model reconstruction of the Uruk-period temple at Uqair. (Lloyd and Safar 1943, Plate XIV)

temples being built over by the foundations of the later platforms, with the difference that the top of the platform still survives from the late Uruk. The temple standing here has the same characteristics as the late Ubaid ones: a tripartite plan, niched walls, an 'altar'. The walls of the building and the edges of the terrace had been ornamented in various ways, including clay cones and 'bottles' built into the façades, and the temple itself is known as the 'White Temple' because it had been liberally plastered with lime. At Uqair, also an important site in the Ubaid period, there was an irregular platform, not yet a ziggurat, and again a small temple of standard tripartite plan on the top, differing only in its polychrome wall-paintings, which include a pair of seated leopards (Figures 6:2 and 6:3).

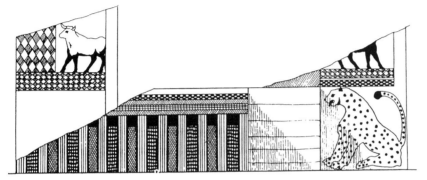

Figure 6:3 Painted walls of the Uruk temple at Uqair. Most of the geometric decoration imitates the coloured mosaics known from contemporary shrines at Uruk itself. (Sandars in P.R.S. Moorey, ed., *The Origins of Civilization: Wolfson College Lectures 1978*, Oxford, 1979, Figure 41)

In the Uruk period the city of Uruk itself is probably the largest settlement in the entire world, and to the east of the 'White Temple', the traditional shrine on its platform, there is the huge 'Eanna' complex of ceremonial buildings, commensurate with the size of the city. Within the walled precinct of some 400 × 200 m there are several separate shrines, and other buildings which from their size and the wealth of their ornamentation must have served a public function (Figures 6:4 and 6:5). There were frequent rebuildings. The excavated levels date from the end of the Uruk period, with the exception of the strange rambling pisé structure known as the 'Stampflehmgebäude', which probably represents the foundations of the residential sector of Eanna in Early Dynastic times.[172] Its super-structure and any later incarnations were totally removed some 2500 years later under Sargon II of Assyria, and the earlier phases have as yet hardly been touched.

Although unique in scale, Uruk was not an isolated phenomenon. The temples at Eridu and Uqair had the same elaborate decoration, and are placed on a massive terrace. Such decoration, and monumental architecture, represent a significant input of communal resources, and the example of Early Dynastic Khafajah, where there were several temples of different sizes, confirms what one would expect, that not every shrine received such treatment. The difference naturally reflects each temple's 'constituency', and Old Baby-lonian texts occasionally mention small chapels, sometimes even the gift of an individual.[173] We can only speculate about the social order responsible for the enlargement and

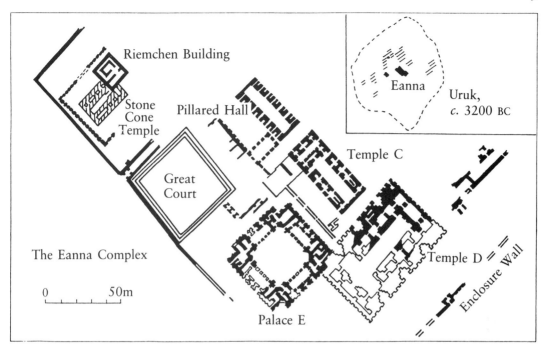

Figure 6:4 Part of the Eanna Temple enclosure at Uruk, Level IV B, *c.* 3200 BC. (After Nissen in Damerow *et al.* 1988, 79)

Figure 6:5 Terracotta wall decoration from Uruk. (Photo: Vorderasiatisches Museum, Berlin, VA 13354)

beautification of the Eanna complex, but during the third millennium, as some temples found themselves the symbolic focus not only of the city and its hinterland but also of an entire state, the self-esteem of the state, and especially of its rulers, dictated a concentration of communal effort. Huge rebuilding projects were undertaken, bigger and better ziggurrats built. Most 'royal inscriptions' in fact commemorate the construction (or at least the renovation) of temples, seen as one of the duties of the ruler on behalf of the populace. Kings and **ensi**s are proud to commemorate their major projects, recording their piety and their pride in writing and sometimes in images (Figure 6:6), and the search for the best

Figure 6:6 Ur-Nanše of Lagaš and his family: limestone door plaque commemorating temple construction. Such plaques were fixed to the wall to secure the wooden peg to which doors were fastened. (de Sarzec 1884–1912, Planche 2 bis)

materials for the gods' house is mirrored in the Enmerkar story, composed in the late third millennium, with its echoes of elite exchanges between heads of state (Text 6:1).

The buildings in the sacred enclosure did not necessarily constitute the entire establishment. As Jacobsen (1946) has best portrayed, the temple was seen as the god's 'house' or perhaps better 'estate', and was run along the lines of a secular institution. Like other households it might have property in more than one place and engage in a variety of productive and commercial activities. Our most complete picture of a Mesopotamian temple comes from the archives of the second-ranking temple at Girsu in the state of Lagaš, just before it fell under Akkadian rule. The 1600 or so tablets known to scholars at present must have lain buried untouched in the archive rooms of the Bau Temple until local antiquities robbers raided the French excavations at Tello in the late nineteenth century. The sad result is that the tablets are scattered, in large batches or by ones and twos, in museums and private collections across the world. It is a sign of the paucity of Sumerologists

Text 6:1 Enmerkar and the Lord of Aratta (legendary city on the Iranian plateau): Enmerkar
        beseeches Inanna to help him beautify her temple

Enmerkar, the son of Utu,
To his sister, the lady benefactress of desires,
To holy Inanna made a plea:
'O my sister, for Uruk may Aratta
Fashion artfully gold and silver on my behalf,
Let them cut the pure lapis lazuli from the lumps,
The brightness of pure lapis lazuli . . . .,
In Uruk a holy 'mountain' let them lavishly decorate.
The house 'descending from heaven', your place of worship,
The shrine Eanna, let Aratta build,
Of the holy Gipar, your abode,
Its interior let Aratta artfully fashion. . .'

(Cohen 1973, 113–14)

that studies of the archive as a whole mainly date to the 1920s, since when many significant advances have been made in understanding the language, and the accepted opinion that the temples were the state has been drastically revised. Nevertheless, the range of the temple's economic activities recorded in the texts remains unchanged: cultivation of cereals, vegetables and fruit trees, including the control of irrigation waters; management of flocks of sheep and goats and herds of cows and equids; fishing in fresh and salt water; manufacture of textiles, leather and wooden items, metalwork and stone; promotion of trading links with foreign lands.

Evidently such activities required, at the least, storerooms and granaries, and workshops. In some cases, like the immense Bagara at the city of Lagaš, there may have been room for these establishments within the temple enclosure, but more often there can have been no space for major expansion in the crowded vicinity of the old shrine, and they were doubtless dispersed, some within the city, others in the countryside.[174] The Sin Temple at Khafajah in the Old Babylonian period certainly stored the grain from its fields in different villages, and issues were made from them on the authority of the central shrine.[175] Most of the craft activity was probably destined to furnish the temple's own needs, but textile production in particular was a highly organized commercial undertaking. At Ešnunna the so-called 'North Palace' seems likely to have been largely devoted to a weaving establishment in the Early Dynastic III and Akkadian periods, attached to the Abu Temple (Figure 6:7). The Old Babylonian temple at Neribtum (Ishchali) was also engaged in textile production, and presumably controlled a specialized workforce, though there is nowhere within the excavated plan of the temple which could have accommodated them.[176] The need to use and dispose of large amounts of water probably ensured that activities like washing and fulling were usually away from the centre of a city. As in most things, the extreme must have been reached in the Ur III period when one temple workshop, at Guabba in the southern edges of Lagaš, employed 6000 workers, mostly women and

Figure 6:7 The 'North Palace' at Tell Asmar (= Ešnunna), probably the dependencies of the Abu Temple. This Akkadian phase of the building had a less massive Early Dynastic forerunner. (Delougaz, Hill and Lloyd 1967, Plate 37. Courtesy the Oriental Institute of the University of Chicago)

children.[177] Even though this is more of a palace undertaking behind a temple façade, it does build on an existing tradition.

The temple's religious activities

The focus of activity was of course the divine sanctuary itself, with functions sometimes differentiated into two rooms, the larger known as the 'seat' or 'residence', and a subsidiary room identified as the *papahum* on architects' plans (Figure 6:8).[178] The main sanctuary had a raised block at the centre of its back wall, which was probably itself the 'seat' (Figure 6:9). Firm evidence for how it was used is very hard to come by, but the assumption that

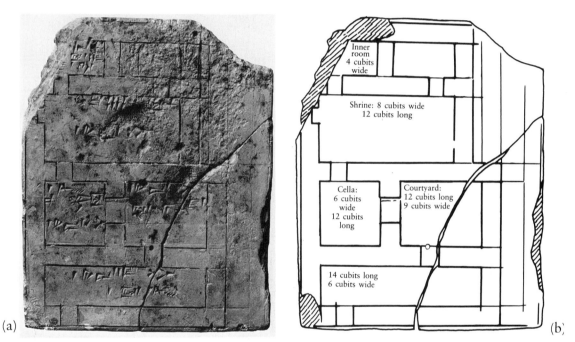

(a)

(b)

Figure 6:8 Architect's plan of a Neo-Sumerian temple, *c.* 2100 BC. (AO 338, Thureau-Dangin RTC 145. Photo: Musée du Louvre/AO)

it served as the emplacement for a statue of the god is probably correct. One reason to think this is that on cylinder seals and similar scenes the god is shown as a human figure seated on a block which clearly resembles those found by the archaeologists: they have the same rebated niche decoration, and they often stand on a low brick dais which runs under the god's feet as well (cf. Figure 14:1). However, it is not clear how literally this scene can be taken: it is a metaphor, since the deities are said to 'sit' in their city or temple, which is the same word as to 'dwell' (*wašābum*/**tuš**), and both the iconography of seals and the architecture mirror this verbal metaphor. Unfortunately excavation has not recovered any divine statues which certainly fulfilled this purpose, but that does not mean they did not exist. There are sound reasons why they would not be found in position: they would have been made of the most precious materials (gold, silver and lapis lazuli) which aroused the cupidity of despoilers of the temple, and since gold and silver were probably not available in such quantities that a figure of any size could have been cast solid, they usually had a perishable wooden core. An over-life-size golden ear from the Šamaš Temple at Mari very likely derives from one such composite cult image.

Happily the written sources offer some confirmation of this rather tenuous archaeological argument. We can form some idea of the nature of the divine figures from references to their manufacture and repair. Creating a divine figure must always have been a solemn ceremonial task for the temple workshops; often the ruler undertook this as part of his duties, and years were named after the fabrication of a statue or its induction into its seat (see Texts 6:2a and 2b). Rituals for the 'opening of the mouth' of such statues are known already in the third millennium.[179] The statue would have been created anew only in exceptional cases, and the year-names also include mention of ancillary items (Text 6:2c). The texts do not usually describe the divine statue so that we can know its size and posture. Some at least were seated, to judge from the mention of thrones (Text 6:2d). The date formulae of the Ešnunna kings also mention Tišpak's golden robe (*tēdiqum*), his ring (GIL) and his 'exalted axe' (Spycket 1968, 91). Sometimes a god was represented by a symbol, erected on a standard.[180]

Text 6:2 Four Isin–Larsa period year dates
(a) The year in which Išme-Dagan installed the copper statue of Ninurta for the Ešumeša on its high dais.

(b) Year in which the gods Numušda, Namrat, and Lugal-apiak were created and introduced to the city of Kazallu.

(c) The year in which Ipiq-Adad introduced the pair of silver daises to the House of Tišpak.

(d) The year in which Ibalpiel made the throne of Tišpak of ivory and gold appliqué.
(After Spycket 1968, 77–8 and 91)

The gods and goddesses were envisaged as of human shape, and were dressed and adorned like their models in the best finery the community could afford. With the passing of years they accumulated more robes, jewellery and other paraphernalia than they could wear at one time, and the strongrooms began to fill up. An inventory of the storeroom of a small Ištar Temple at the Old Babylonian town of Lagaba gives an idea of the range of items (Text 6:3), and similar lists come from as far west as Qatna on the Orontes in Syria. What one might have found in one of the larger temples is hinted at by an inventory of the temple of Nisaba at Ereš in the Ur III period, which included 217 cylinder seals, 290 carnelian beads, various garments, a tablet-box and a throne-cloth.[181] Like the gold and ivory statue of Athene in which much of Athens' wealth was invested, this accumulation

Text 6:3 Inventory of the treasure of Ištar of Lagaba

2 gold rings; 1 gold vulva; 19 gold flowers(?); 2 gold rods [branches?]; 2 gold dress-pins; 2 silver ear-rings; 1 … of carnelian; 4 cones; 6 cylinder seals; 2 stamp seals; 1 chain of electrum(?); 6 ivory pins; 1 large ring of carnelian; 2 fleeced skirts; 3 linen robes; 6 woven head-bands; 4 … head-bands; 5 head-dresses(?); 1 cover; 3 bronze cups; [x] lamps; all this, the amounts written down, deposited in the chest is the old equipment.

4 gold flowers; 8 silver vulvae; 1 silver mother(?); 2 stamp seals; 3 cylinder seals; 2 bronze cups; 3 robes; 6 woven head-bands; 2 … head-bands – the new addition to the chest. 2 head-dresses(?); 2 loin-cloths – this is the clothing of Inanna … excluding that in the chest.

Authority of Awil-Ištar. Ahum-waqar and Šamaš-gamil, who were appointed to the temple of Išar-kidišu.

[Date]

(After Leemans 1952, 1–2)

of precious goods can be seen as a form of capital reserve for the community – whether or not it was ever actually realized – and the violation of a sanctuary and plunder of its wealth accordingly constituted an economic as well as an ideological disaster (Text 6:4).

Text 6:4 From the lament for the sacking of the temples of Lagaš

The leader of Umma … sacked the Bagara temple and looted its precious metals and lapis lazuli; he set fire to the Dugru temple and looted its precious metals and lapis lazuli; he sacked the Abzu'eg; he set fire to the temple of Gatumdug, looted its precious metals and lapis lazuli, and destroyed its statuary; he set fire to the shrine Eanna of Inanna, looted its precious metals and lapis lazuli and destroyed its statuary … In the fields of Ningirsu, whichever were cultivated, he destroyed the barley. The leader of Umma, having sacked Lagaš, has committed a sin against Ningirsu. The hand which he has raised against him will be cut off! It is not a sin of UruKAgina, king of Girsu! may Nisaba, the goddess of Lugal-zagesi, ruler of Umma, make him bear the sin!

(After Cooper 1986, 78–9)

Supplying the gods' table

Being made in the image of humans, Mesopotamian gods needed regular meals, and sometimes they had visitors and laid on a special spread. In general, both art and literature are very coy about the mundane details of how offerings were placed before the gods, but a broad outline can be recovered from the vivid imagery of the Gilgamesh epic (Text 6:5) and the explicit statement of the 'Warka Vase', where offerings of food, clothing and jewellery are brought to the goddess on her dais by the temple staff (Figure 6:1). In the Pre-Sargonic period both texts and archaeological discoveries show that the meals were still being served to the gods in stone bowls, and to judge from later practices these were placed in the sanctuary on 'tables', twice a day, in the morning and evening. In later Mesopotamia the offerings were certainly on separate 'tables' (*paššūrum*), but it is unknown whether these were in use in the third and early second millennium shrines, or the food

Text 6:5 Ut-napištim makes offerings after the retreat of the Flood
I offered incense in front of the mountain-ziggurrat.
Seven and seven libation-stands I set up,
And into their bowls I sprinkled sweet reed, cedar and myrtle.
The gods smelled the scent, the gods smelled the sweet scent,
and collected over the sacrifice like flies.

(After Gallery Kovacs 1989, 102)

was simply placed on the altar. Liquids on the other hand – water, beer, perhaps later wine – may have been offered in cups, but there is ample archaeological evidence in Early Dynastic altars of channels for liquid offerings (Figure 6:9), and the texts mention a ceremony known as 'beer-pouring', which reflects the same practice.[182] At the same time incense was usually burnt in special braziers, using valuable aromatics mostly imported from the forests of the Mediterranean littoral.[183]

The best evidence for the offering 'bowls' comes from ceremonial offerings made by or on behalf of the rulers (cf. chapters 2 and 14), but for the great majority of temples and occasions only the community could provide for these needs, and therefore a system of regular contributions to the temple was built up. A distinction needs to be drawn between contributions to the temple from the secular community, which are often described in English as 'offerings', and the actual food placed before the gods, the Biblical 'showbread'. These were very much traditional activities, which operated smoothly without the need for formal administration and so did not generate much written documentation for our benefit. The most comprehensive evidence comes from a Nippur archive concerned with the offerings accounts of Ninurta's temple called the Ešumeša.[184] The commodities brought in are not very varied: bread (**ninda**), 'lardy cake' (**ninda-ià**), emmer-flour (**eša**), beer (**kaš**), fish cakes (**utu₂**) and wine (**geštin**). These are known as **sá-dug₄**/*sattukkum* which means 'regular deliveries' (and has no particularly religious connotation until later). A similar, slightly more varied range of foods was recorded for the temple of Ningal at Ur, and in the Ur III period offerings lists include a wider variety, including all sorts of fruit, fresh and dried.[185] While the chief recipient in each temple was of course the head of the divine household, whether god or goddess, the other members were not neglected: family and servants, and even what we would consider furniture and fittings, not only cultic symbols and statues of rulers, but drain pipes and locks all received their share (Text 6:6).[186]

The questions which arise are where did this all come from, and where did it end up? We are entirely in the dark about the organization which brought these regular deliveries in, day by day. Lists tend merely to state the amounts received without mentioning their source, with the exception of the few which record royal largess in establishing permanent deliveries, presumably out of the royal estates. One can only presume, in a general sense, that, in addition to produce from the temple's own farms or commercial activities, its 'constituency' was somehow organized to supply the necessary contributions. In a village or small city temple, this will presumably have meant those households for which it was their religious focus; in a major shrine like the Nanna Temple at Ur, at the capital of the Ur III state, the offerings will have come from the entire domain, and one of the signs of

Figure 6:9 The Sin Temple at Khafajah, Level VI (ED II). View of north end of the sanctuary: altar-block, with pottery vessels each side to receive libated liquids. (Delougaz and Lloyd 1942, 41, Figure 37. Photo: courtesy the Oriental Institute of the University of Chicago)

Text 6:6 Gudea, Statue G: regular deliveries prescribed for Bau
When he had built the E-Ninnu, the house he loves, for Ningirsu his king, and had built
the E-tarsirsir, the house she loves, for Bau, his queen, as Bau's 'dowry' for the new house
Gudea, the ensi of Lagaš, the builder of the house, added:

2 fattened oxen
2 ... sheep
10 fattened sheep
2 lambs
7 ... of dates
7 bowls of ghee
7 palm-hearts
7 strings(?) of figs
7 fruit cakes
14 date spathes
14 cucumbers
1 **a.še** bird
7 dowry-birds
10 geese
7 **igi**-birds
60 little birds, on 15 skewers(?)
60 ... fish, on 30 skewers(?)
40 loads of ... vegetables
7 loads of ...
1 load of **manu**-wood (for fuel?)

the declining fortunes of that state under its last ruler, Ibbi-Sin, is the progressive reduction
of the list of provincial centres sending in offerings. Although such contributions are a
form of political statement, and may in practice constitute a form of taxation, in theory
they are more of an annual membership subscription: already back in Pre-Sargonic times
the independent rulers of Sumer sent contributions to the Ekur, Enlil's Temple at Nippur,
and under the Ur III kings the provision of offerings for the Ekur became a massive
operation, to the extent that Šulgi established Puzriš-Dagan a few miles to the east of
Nippur as a giant clearing house for all the animals passing through. The responsibility
for providing animals was divided between the provinces in proportion to their wealth,
with Lagaš shouldering two months, and others only one or a half. It is important to note
that the peripheral areas of the state did not contribute, only those which really belonged
to 'The Land'.[187] This role of offerings to a central shrine as a statement of membership
of a common organization is inherited by the Assyrian state where provinces under direct
Assyrian administration were expected to send in regular offerings (*ginā'e*).[188]

Festivals

There were of course special days in the calendar, when more offerings were made. One of these was the delivery of first-fruits – which may have been within the framework of regular offerings, but attracted special attention, with a procession by boat which involved a 'first-fruits symbol' (Figure 6:10).[189] The commonest of these were connected with certain days of the month, especially the 7th, 15th, and the 'crescent moon' or 'beginning of the month', as we learn from the temple accounts.[190] In addition, each temple and god will

Figure 6:10 Isin–Larsa period pot from South Mesopotamia, incised decoration of two-prowed boat with divine symbols. (AO 4800. See M.-C. de Graeve, *The Ships of the Ancient Near East*, 1981, Plate II.6. Photo: Musée du Louvre/AO)

have had their own particularly solemn festivals of special significance. In Isin–Larsa times a number of 'royal hymns' were composed, which make it clear that one such festival was the 'sacred marriage' in which the high-priest of Inanna – usually the king himself – enacted the part of Dumuzi by sleeping with the high-priestess (see chapter 14). It seems likely that this represents an ancient custom, and that similar rituals may have been enacted in other cities, but again our sources are very scrappy on this point, since the scribes who compiled the administrative documents on which we mainly depend were only interested in the figures. Similarly, we learn very little about the social side of such festivals, some of which must obviously have involved gatherings of people from far and wide, feasts, processions, music, dance and markets (Figure 6:11). Sometimes the god and his congregation left the temple and went out into the countryside, no doubt to participate in some agricultural rites; later on this kind of festival, called an *akītum*, became associated particularly with

Figure 6:11 Drummers at a religious ceremony in Lagaš. Fragment of carved stone bowl, *c.* 2100 BC. (L. Heuzey, *Les Origines orientales de l'art*, 1915 Planche 11)

the New Year ceremonies at Babylon, but in the third millennium it could happen at different times of year in different places.[191]

Even more exciting must have been the occasions when the gods left their home town to visit their friends and relatives. Cylinder seals of the Early Dynastic period show gods – and sometimes visibly divine statues – being poled along the river in a high-prowed boat (Figure 6:10), and the myths which tell of gods and goddesses visiting each other clearly reflect actual ceremonies in which the divine image was physically transported up or downstream. This is already mentioned in the Pre-Sargonic Lagaš texts, with visits not only between neighbouring Girsu and Lagaš but as far afield as Uruk. From the dry Ur III documents, we find that most gods of the south visited Nippur, and Eridu, Enki's city, was also a frequent destination. Sometimes the visit seems to be for festivals which were a regular part of the annual calendar, but there were also special occasions, such as the consecration of a temple at Girsu.[192] These divine exchanges expressed a sense of sharing a common religion and culture, and must have deep roots in the political pattern of South Mesopotamia in earlier times. They are rarely mentioned after the Ur III collapse, but this does not necessarily mean the practice was abandoned, and we do know that the gods continued to leave their temples to go on local journeys when required by their constituents to settle legal disputes (see chapter 15).[193]

Staff and servants

To return to the offerings, we have now to enquire what happened to them after they had been received within the temple. As suggested by the apocryphal but revealing story of 'Bel and the Dragon', in which Daniel demonstrates to Cyrus how the offerings on the altar vanish overnight (to the benefit of the temple personnel and their families), the gods did not consume everything placed before them, and, even if they had, they would not have exhausted all the incoming commodities, since these were scaled more to the number of the staff to be supported than to the appetite of the individual god. The archive from the Ešumeša Temple (see above) for the first time gives a clear idea of the redistribution of the commodities within the institution. The same products listed on arrival are mostly distributed to the staff of the temple – to the priests and priestesses, but also to the scribes and other administrative personnel and to the craftsmen, water carriers and doorkeepers. It is unlikely that the majority ever served as 'offerings' in the sense of being physically placed before gods in the sanctuary. Similar arrangements undoubtedly existed elsewhere. At Ur, as at Nippur, people connected with the temple are recorded as having a right to receive bread 'returned from the sanctuary',[194] and a long administrative document from Larsa is concerned with specifying where the temple income on the occasion of a particular festival should go, not only the food and drink, but textiles, wool and silver items.[195]

In origin it is evident that the prime recipients of these allocations were the regular staff of the temple, of which the Nippur list gives a good resumé. In the course of time, however, as in the temples of contemporary Egypt, many of these posts became sinecures, the tenure of which could be passed on, whether by inheritance, sale or even rental. Borrowing a term from medieval Europe, Assyriologists refer to such offices with their perquisites as 'prebends'. The practice was already in operation in Ur III times, but it became highly elaborate during the Old Babylonian centuries (Text 6:7). The individual allocation was

Text 6:7 Purchase of prebend of temple-sweeper in the Sin Temple at Ur
Apil-Ašnan son of Lu-dingira has bought from Qišti-Ea son of Lipit-Ea and his mother Alittum the prebend of courtyard-sweeper of the Temple of Sin, for 12 days per annum, in the Great Court, service rota of the month of Abum (V), first period. He has paid 2 shekels of silver as its entire price.

He has sworn by the name of Rim-Sin the king that he bears responsibility for claims that arise, and will not make claims in future.

Before Ah-kalla, cultic official; Lu-Nanna, priest; Apilša, courtyard-sweeper; Lu-Amar-Suenaka, courtyard sweeper; Uselli son of Ku-Ningal; Sig-ersetim son of Silli-Emah; Ellu-mušu, courtyard-sweeper.

23rd day, Month of Šabatum (XI), year Rim-Sin (II), King of Ur, founded the . . .

(After Charpin 1986a, 190)

known as the 'lot' (*isqum*), and although, as we saw in chapter 5, at Nippur there was a convention that the temple offices were the prerogative of the eldest son when the paternal estate was divided, this was not always the case, and in the course of time the prebend was subdivided until individuals might hold an office for no more than one day in the year. The nominal character of their tenure is emphasized by the fact that each individual might hold more than one office at a time.[196]

The right to a share of the redistributed offerings was not the only perquisite that went with particular offices. In the third millennium especially, the temples owned land, sometimes very extensive estates, and the cultivation was organized along three main lines. Some was under direct cultivation by the temple itself, presumably using its own workforce or members of society working under some communal obligation. Another major part of the land was assigned to the office-holders of the temple for their sustenance, and can be called 'prebend fields'. This system is well attested for the Ur III and Pre-Sargonic periods at Lagaš, but it is already present in even earlier texts; as one might expect, the area assigned varied in proportion to the importance of the holder. Finally, there was the surplus land which the temple rented out (see chapter 9).

The evidence from Nippur and Ur now enables us to have a much clearer idea of the composition of a temple's personnel, previously obscured behind the bewildering variety of technical terms. The list of recipients in the Ešumeša Temple can be seen as including three groups, cultic, administrative and domestic, including craftsmen (Text 6:8); a similar, shorter, list exists for the Nanna temple at Ur.[197] As far as the cultic procedures in the temple were concerned, certain persons were needed to attend directly to the gods' needs: to place the offerings before them, to keep them properly clothed and housed, and to carry out spoken or enacted rituals. But the majority of the temple staff had routine chores to perform: to sweep the courtyard, to guard the doors, and to see to the administration of the staff and property of the temple (Text 6:8). Both cultic offices (what we would call broadly 'priests') and domestic jobs (like 'doorkeeper') could be treated as prebends, but it is evident that some of the posts must have been firm appointments or it is difficult to see how the institution could have functioned. One criterion we can use here is indeed concerned with the prebends: very broadly, prebendary offices which could be passed from one hand to another every few days should be viewed in a different light from those where the identity and experience of the individual was critical. At Ur the commonest cultic title was **gudu₄**/*pašīšum*, usually attached to a specific divinity, which can be translated as 'priest of god X'; although there is little doubt that it entailed ritual functions, this post was generally divisible. The indivisible posts are primarily administrative and specialist.[198] It is easy to understand the reason for this, since a goldsmith or reed-worker cannot be replaced by just anyone, and the administration requires scribal expertise and a certain continuity. In this context it is reasonable that even the basic Sumerian and Akkadian word for the head of a temple, **sanga**/*šangûm*, is translated by some as 'temple-administrator', in preference to 'priest' with its cultic connotations.

One group of cultic staff had special skills: the diviner, the snake-charmer, the acrobat, the singer and the 'lamentation-priest'. Their presence in the Old Babylonian temples is foreshadowed in the Ur III period; Gelb (1976a) has discussed a text which lists these 'specialists' in the temples of the Lagaš area: there was a total of 180 'musicians' and 62 'lamentation-priests', but within the musicians were included snake-charmers and bear-wards, all part of the ritual circus act.[199] Gelb is also able to use their classification in administrative lists going back to the Pre-Sargonic period to show that the **gala**/*kalûm*, conventionally translated as 'lamentation-priest', 'had certain feminine characteristics'; there is no evidence that any of them were eunuchs, but he concludes that they showed homosexual or transvestite characteristics. It is hardly coincidental that Ur-Nanše the singer, the sex of whose statue from Mari has been much debated, is shown beardless, and

Text 6:8 Some of the staff of Ninurta's Temple at Nippur

The High-Priest	The house supervisor
The **lagar**	The accountant
The lamentation-priest	The treasurer
The purification-priest	The cupbearer
The high priestess	The overseer of the oil-pressers
The … priestess	The scribe
The *nadītum*	
The chief *qadištum*	
The diviner	
The snake-charmer	
The **bar-šu-gal**	
The **nu-èš**	

The miller
The door-ward
The fuller
The fuel-carrier
The water-carrier
The oil-presser
The cow herd
The (copper-)smith
The steward
The boatman
The boat-tower
The weaver
The courtyard-sweeper
The barber
The water-pourer
The mat-maker
The runner
The stone carver
The king's butler
The palace guard

(After Sigrist 1984, 160)

castration for cultic purposes was practised in western Europe hardly more than a century ago. That becoming a **gala** was a significant step is reflected in the fact that it was attended by special ceremonies, as we learn from texts recording offerings of sheep made, usually in the ninth or tenth month, 'on the day when he entered into the **gala**-ship'.[200] We can only guess at the physical characteristics that may have marked the **gala** out, but in early times at least it is probable that the truly cultic staff of the temple were distinguished not merely by their dress, but also by some physical attributes. On the Warka Vase, and on some Early Dynastic relief carvings, the person presenting an offering, or making a libation to the god, is nude (Figure 6:12). This practice is not depicted in the Akkadian period or later, but it may survive in the practice of shaving the priest's head. The barber (šu.i/ gallābum) is one of the members of the temple staff, and Gudea is shown bald-headed, when he is not wearing the ruler's turban. Undoubtedly the priests also practised ceremonial washing, and the descriptions of the preliminaries to the sacred marriage, which include elaborate bathing, are perhaps illustrated by iconographic scenes showing the king on his way to the bath with a towel over one shoulder.[201]

Figure 6:12 Door plaque from Ur. The lower register shows the priest, followed by people bringing offerings making a libation outside the temple, whose door is flanked with typical 'ring posts'. The upper register ('later') no doubt shows the same people inside the sanctuary before the enthroned deity. (U. 6831 = BM 118561. See Woolley 1955, 45. Photo: courtesy Trustees of the British Museum)

Cloisters

One of the questions we cannot begin to answer about the temple is how many of its staff were 'living in'. The Ur III and Early Dynastic sources make it clear that some temples had large bodies of regular employees, effectively slaves. In the Old Babylonian period this no longer seems to be the case, and indeed it is possible that it was only so earlier because of palace intervention on the temple scene (see p. 300). In any case, large numbers of employees will hardly have lived in the temple itself. It is a difficult point to resolve archaeologically, since it is often doubtful where the temple ends and secular housing begins (as with the 'North Palace' at Ešnunna, or the suspected temple at Abu Salabikh). Where we have a clearly demarcated enclosure, as at Khafajah or even Ur, there is not room for more than perhaps a priest and his household. At Khafajah one may be certain that someone, no doubt the head of the temple's hierarchy, lived within the oval, in House D; but there is no other evidence, written or excavated, which is so clear – with one exception, and that concerns the priestesses.

Next to the temple of the moon-god Nanna at Ur, Woolley excavated a well-preserved and monumental building which is our best example of an institution known as the **gipar** (Figure 6:13). Enclosed within the square of its four walls is the temple of Ningal, the wife of the moon-god Nanna, and a self-contained residence, with kitchens, bathrooms, store-

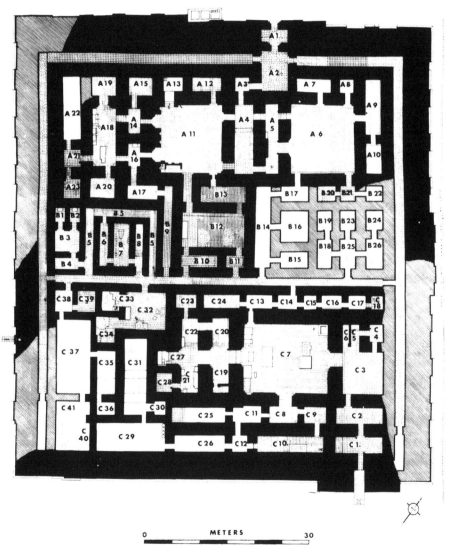

Figure 6:13 Plan of the **gipar**, residence of the high-priestess at Ur. (Woolley and Moorey 1982, 185)

rooms, ceremonial rooms and even a burial crypt. This was the home of the **en** priestess (in Akkadian: *entum*), who was dedicated to the service of Nanna and his consort Ningal. The earliest **en** known to us was a daughter of Sargon of Akkad called Enheduana. She is also the most famous, since she is one of the very few authors of a Mesopotamian literary work whose name is known, but she was followed by a long line of important ladies, most if not all of whom were close relatives of the current royal family. Thus among others we find the daughters of Naram-Sin of Akkad, Ur-Bau of Lagaš, Ur-Nammu, Šulgi (and probably of subsequent Ur III kings), Išme-Dagan of Isin, and Kudur-mabuk – the last being sister to Warad-Sin and Rim-Sin of Larsa. The memory lived on for well over a thousand years, when the last king of Babylon, Nabonidus, in a consciously traditional gesture made his daughter priestess of the moon-god at Ur.[202]

The records we have from the Nanna Temple are mainly lists of food offerings made during the century or two after the Ur III Dynasty. Most are destined for the goddess Ningal herself, but some go to three minor deities who evidently belonged in the temple, and some to deceased priestesses identified by name. These were not deified, but it is clear from Woolley's excavations that they stayed within the four walls of the cloister even after death, being buried (as was customary for members of a secular household) beneath the floors of the rooms, where libations were poured and offerings placed for them. And Enanedu, sister of Rim-Sin of Larsa and last of the sequence, describes very explicitly how in her time the 'place of the "day of fate" of the old *entum*-priestesses had no wall erected, ... no guard placed, was not kept clear; but I, in my great wisdom, sought out a place for future "days of fate", and established a wide enclosure beyond the resting-place of the old *entum* priestesses, erected a great wall on the deserted site, installed a strong guard, and cleared the ground'.

One of the functions of these princesses was to remain inside the temple as representatives of their male (and perhaps also female) relatives: '[Nanna and Ningal] ... placed in my pure mouth a prayer of life, and grasped my hand stretched out [to pray for] the prolongation of the life of Rim-Sin my twin[?] brother'.[203] The more exact role of the *entum* in the cult is never explicitly described, but what does seem clear is that, both here and in other **gipar**s, a bedroom was incorporated within the shrine, in which one must presume some kind of sacred marriage ritual was enacted (see above, p. 123; chapter 14). In this light we should interpret statements such as the description of one of the *entum*s as having 'loins suitable by their purity for the en-ship'.[204] While this is not the place to enter a discussion of these rites, the point needs to be made that gods were presumably as jealous of their spouses as their human counterparts, so that we need not be surprised that the *entum* was protected from the outside world in this way.

The Ur **gipar** was not unique, and similar establishments seem to have existed in other southern cities. Rather different was an institution best attested in the Old Babylonian period at Sippar, another kind of 'cloister', Akkadian *gagûm*. The Sippar cloister was attached to the main temple of the city, that of the sun-god Šamaš. Nothing is known of it archaeologically, although thousands of cuneiform tablets must have been excavated illicitly from its ruins at the end of the nineteenth century, from which it is clear that it was a large walled enclosure separate from though close to the main temple. It included houses and streets, and even a garden plot, and must have been much bigger than the Ur **gipar** since it served as the residence of not just a single *entum* but a whole community of priestesses.[205] As at Ur, some of these were also of high birth (especially pre-Hammurapi!), and sometimes came from the ruling houses of neighbouring states. The king of Mari, Zimri-Lim, dedicated his daughter in this temple, and when she writes home plaintively for gifts to maintain her in the state to which she is accustomed, she expresses the philosophy of her role by saying 'Am I not your symbol (*šurinnum*), a suppliant who gives you a favourable report in the Ebabbar?' – a sort of living worshipper statue (see below).[206]

A girl who became a *nadītum* was said to be a 'daughter-in-law of Šamaš', having entered the god's household, but it is not known whether she had any cultic role to play. The word *nadītum* means 'fallow', and must refer to the ladies' unmarried, or perhaps more exactly virginal, condition. Whether or not any form of religious marriage was consummated, at Sippar they did not engage in secular marriage. There were however other *nadītum* communities, of which those of Marduk at Babylon and Ninurta at Nippur are best known to us. At Nippur there is no evidence to show if they lived in a separate cloister, but they were celibate.[207] A *nadītum* of Marduk at Babylon could marry: this was probably not a consummated marriage, but it has important social implications, since it meant that she could enter a different (secular) patrilinear household, and pass any property on to her sons. For although cloistered, the *nadītum* was not a total recluse. Even at Sippar most of our documentary information comes from their business and family relationships. Instead of marrying into another patrilinear household, she was entitled to a dowry to set her up in her new home, and the Code of Hammurapi permits her a life interest in any property given to her by her father, or, if willed to her in writing, an absolute right to it. Much litigation surrounded the subsequent disposal of her wealth: brothers often sought to reclaim it for the patriarchal estate, but an older *nadītum* would sometimes adopt a more recent arrival as a daughter, and pass her property on to her.

The *nadītum* phenomenon is an enigma, which requires explanation in terms of the social and economic conditions of South Mesopotamia after the collapse of the Ur III Dynasty, when relevant sources are very scarce, since the great majority derive from Sippar after its incorporation in the kingdom of Babylon. While we may guess that the Sippar cloister was a transformation of something altogether smaller, and comparable to the **gipar** at Ur (which goes back at least to the Akkad Dynasty), women called **lukur**, the Sumerian equivalent of *nadītum*, were attached to the court of the Ur III kings as some kind of subsidiary spouse,[208] suggesting that changes have occurred and we should not expect to find cloisters of **lukur** in operation at that time. Some of the wealthy Sippar families had several generations of *nadītum* from among their ranks, and it has been suggested that one motivation was to prevent the dispersal of the patrimonial wealth to other patrilinear groups, by assigning dowry-portions which the brothers could expect to reclaim for the family on the death of the *nadītum*. On the other hand, there must also have been strong incentives in the realm of diplomacy, comparable to the political exploitation of the **en**-ship at Ur, since we see international connections with Mari in the case of Zimri-Lim's daughter, and at least one Sippar *nadītum* had a family link with the Old Babylonian city at Tell al-Rimah in the north.[209] Any satisfying explanation must also take into account the lesser ranks of priestess, some of them referred to in the Code of Hammurapi, with whom complex marital and property agreements were drawn up.[210]

The visitors

The temples were created by and served the local community, but we do not know as much as we would like of the use the ordinary person would have made of the temple in her or his secular capacity. Each temple was the place to meet one or more deities, and people went there to make requests. Most gods had a dual role, as the particular god of a place, whether large or small, and as the patron of a particular branch of life. Thus the city god of Ur was Nanna/Sin, who was the moon-god, and with his crescent horns had a special association with cows. Indeed we know that some cows were kept within the precincts of the Ekisnugal (and quite likely ended up as sacrificial animals).[211] The sun-god, Utu/Šamaš, was the patron deity of the southern city of Larsa and of Sippar in the north, both ancient centres: as the sun, he was also the god of justice. The ordinary citizen could not expect that his personal concerns would engage the sympathies of a major deity without some intercession. The commonest scene on cylinder seals of the Ur III Dynasty and later shows the owner being introduced by his personal god into the presence of one of the great gods, which may in real life represent a visit to the principal sanctuary. However, one could not be there all the time, and in Early Dynastic times in particular it was the custom to place a statue in the temple to substitute for the subject (Figure 6:14). They stand or sit, have hands clasped or hold a cup, but any doubts as to the significance of these statues are removed by the inscriptions which some of them carry (Text 6:9).[212]

> **Text 6:9** Inscription on a statue
>
> To Bau, gracious lady, daughter of An, queen of the holy city, her mistress, for the life of Nammahani, the **ensi** of Lagaš, Nin-kagina, the mother who bore him, has dedicated as an offering (this statue) of the protective goddess of Tarsirsir which she has introduced to the courtyard of Bau. May the statue, to which let my mistress turn her ear, speak my prayers.
>
> (After Sollberger and Kupper 1971, 120)

Sometimes the worshipper carries an animal (see Figure 8:4, p. 168), which is no doubt to be sacrificed to the god, since in divine as in secular households it would be normal to accompany a request with a gift. At the same time sheep were frequently sacrificed in the process of consulting the omens. The omen-reader (*bārûm*) was defined by his technical expertise, rather than by any specific cultic role, but he might be a regular member of the temple staff. A variety of kinds of omen were used. Some were derived from natural phenomena, including astronomical events, but the person with a specific enquiry needed to consult the omens at a time of his own choosing and about the matter concerning him. For this the inspection of the entrails, and especially the liver, of a sheep was the most used. Although much of Assurbanipal's library at Nineveh in the seventh century BC was composed of diviners' handbooks, the compilation of observations and interpretations was only beginning to be written down in the Old Babylonian period, and before that it

Figure 6:14 Worshipper statues from a cache buried in the ED II Abu Temple at Tell Asmar (Ešnunna), *c.* 2600 BC. (Delougaz and Lloyd 1942, 188, Figure 149. Photo: courtesy the Oriental Institute of the University of Chicago)

is likely to have been a completely oral 'science'. The earliest written documents recording omens are in fact crude clay models of particular livers with their characteristic marks, which had been preserved in the palace at Mari (Figure 6:15), and it is easy to imagine how general rules were gradually derived from these specific cases to give the diviner guidance in interpreting the signs as they refer to the king, the country or the individual making the enquiry (Text 6:10). Dubious as the procedure seems to us today, there is no doubt that it was treated with solemn respect. Temples could not be built unless the omens were favourable, and high-priests and priestesses had to be 'chosen' by the god. Major decisions in private life, such as whether or not to engage in a business venture or go on a journey, were settled in the same way, and armies were accompanied, sometimes even led, by a diviner, who submitted the plan of campaign to the scrutiny of the gods (cf. Text 13:7, p. 251). From Mari too comes our best evidence for other kinds of divine message, in the shape of dreams and trances. Dreams could come to lay persons, but the trances were normally experienced by recognized ecstatics attached to a temple. These are best

Figure 6:15 Two of the earliest known liver omen models, from Mari. Each reproduces the approximate shape of the liver with its characteristic feature, and explains the occasion on which it was observed. (Photo: Mission Archéologique de Mari. Courtesy J.-M. Durand)

Text 6:10 Excerpt from an Old Babylonian omen collection
If the diaphragm is mildewed: the man's estate will be squandered.

If, to the left of the centre of the diaphragm in the middle, flesh like juniper-berries is situated: one covered with warts will be born.

If to the left of the heart on the right of the diaphragm one side is as big as the other side: the enemy will be seen but there will be help from the god for the prince.

If the diaphragm is shifted towards the apex: the country will gather in stronghold.

If the diaphragm is shifted towards the Yoke: the prince will repopulate his abandoned country.

If the diaphragm is thick: the support of the god is firm.

If the diaphragm is wide: the prince will establish a noble reputation.

If the diaphragm is white: the client will encounter ruin.

(After Jeyes 1989, 163)

attested at Mari, but it is not clear whether that is because they are more of a 'western' phenomenon or simply through an accident of the sources.[213]

The temple's staff were undoubtedly remunerated in some way for their information service, if only by the sacrificial animal itself, but this was not by any means the only gift made to the temples. In Mesopotamia, as in most other cultures, free-will gifts were made to the gods either to secure their favour or as a thank-offering. These were known in Sumerian as **arua**, which probably refers to sprinkling water as a symbolic act of dedication. Unlike regular offerings, which were consumed after receipt, these were chattels which remained temple property. Inscribed statues and stone bowls often state that they were dedicated in this way to the god, but we know, particularly from Ur III sources, that a whole range of contributions came to the temples in this way.[214] Apart from cultic furnishings for the sanctuary, lists include animals, silver rings, boats, grindstones, even wool and bitumen. Most significant were the people: kings might dedicate prisoners of war to various temples, but quite humble individuals too presented people to the temple, mostly women and children.

The kings are only at one extreme of the traditional relationship between the temple and the community; the wealth of the temples undoubtedly derives, as in so many cultures, from the generosity of wealthy and less wealthy citizens. Apart from the implications for the giver's prestige within the community, the incentive to give will often have had a specific motivation. Modern scholars often refer to **arua** gifts as 'ex-votos', implying that they had been promised or vowed to the god once the giver's request had been granted. Mostly we cannot tell if this was the case, but we do have a clear example of thank-offerings with the merchants who sailed down the Gulf to trade in Bahrain. When their argosies came safely home, they paid a proportion of their cargo to the Temple of Nanna at Ur, which had provided capital, but also might give a specially crafted silver boat in gratitude for a safe return, and the scribes noting the receipts sometimes mention that it was 'from the prompting of his heart', in other words a 'free will' gift.[215]

The temple as wealthy neighbour

In all these ways the temple accumulated capital of its own, as well as in the management of its own rural estates and craft industries, but it should not be viewed as a purely capitalist institution. The temple remained the expression of communal identity, and its responsibility to the community is neatly expressed by the provision of the Code of Hammurapi that it should supply the ransom for a captured member of the village (Text 11:11). With its sacred inviolability and continuity it constituted the safest place for the storage of wealth, and it was able to serve the community as a bank: at Ur the Nanna Temple supplied at least some of the trading capital for the Tilmun traders in Ur III and Old Babylonian times, while at Assur it seems as though the merchants formally dedicated some of their profits to the temples in order to re-use them as a kind of inviolable capital.[216] The social conscience of the temples emerges most clearly in the case of a small temple dedicated to Sin on the Old Babylonian mound at Khafajah. Here, as in the Šamaš Temple at Sippar, some of the loans of barley to individuals are free of the usual one-third interest, implying a role as a charitable neighbour in times of famine. More poignant are a few sale documents in which the high-priest of the temple buys children, significantly for no specified price: this seems to be a case of the temple taking on extra mouths to feed when their families were unable to support them, and reflects a long-standing tradition whereby the temples gathered under their wing the rejects and misfits of society – orphans, illegitimate children, and perhaps the freaks hinted at above (pp. 126–7).[217]

Not all the temple's interventions in secular life were entirely altruistic, however. As we have seen, in the course of the Old Babylonian period the offices with their perquisites were gradually converted into commercial shares in the community's own subscriptions to its ideological centre. As a solemn place, the temples acted as the forum for various judicial proceedings, in particular the taking of solemn oaths (see chapter 15), and it is not unreasonable to guess that a fee may have been charged to the participants. Divine intervention in human affairs was also achieved by taking the god on to the streets: in the case of boundary disputes, or in the distribution of shares in a threshed and winnowed harvest, it was a common practice to bring the god, in the shape of his symbol, out of his temple to settle the matter 'on location'. This naturally required some inducement, and (again in later years, perhaps) a 'journey of the divine weapon' could be hired out from the temple, and the right to receive the fee could be bought and sold like any other temple prebend.[218]

Further reading

A comprehensive and richly illustrated survey of excavated Mesopotamian temples is given by Heinrich and Seidl 1982 (in German). Two fairly recent accounts of Early Dynastic temples in the written record, and of scholarly opinion about their role in society, are B. Foster, in *Journal of the Economic and Social History of the Orient* 24 (1981) 225–41 and K. Maekawa, *Mesopotamia* 8–9 (1973–4) 77–87. Chapter 4 of A.L. Oppenheim's *Ancient Mesopotamia* (Chicago 1964) gives a general survey of the practice of Mesopotamian religion. Charpin 1986a (in French) is of fundamental importance for various aspects of the Old Babylonian temple. For more detailed facets of temple life the notes to each section give the principal sources. For temple land, see now Diakonoff's new interpretation of *UET* 5 666 (e.g. *AfO* 35 (1988) 193–4). R. Zettler's *The Ur III Temple of Inanna at Nippur* (Berlin 1992) is an important contribution to the subject.

7

The palace

It is a common opinion among ancient Near Eastern historians that the Mesopotamian palace is a later development than the temple: that the construction of a separate seat of secular administration is the visible expression of the formation of a permanent secular authority separate from the temple. As we have already seen, in some Early Dynastic cities the government rested in the hands of the chief priests, who no doubt ruled from the temple precincts. If, with Jacobsen, we assume that before history the 'king' (Sumerian lugal or 'great man') was similar to a Roman dictator, chosen by a city in time of stress as a temporary leader, we should not be surprised if no secular palaces are known from those times. However, such a construct of the early formation of secular power subscribes trustingly to the idealized statements of later Mesopotamian sources, and even if valid for South Mesopotamia cannot be extended uncritically to the adjacent world. It is arguable that it was precisely the strength of the communal ethos of South Mesopotamian civilization that was responsible for the sophistication of its social forms. If so, the palace should perhaps be seen more as an intrusive element from less complex societies than as any sort of natural progression inherent in the traditional Mesopotamian scene.

The palace building

It is almost axiomatic that the separation of secular from religious authority would have required the construction of a ruler's palace independent of the temple. Since both the historical and the archaeological record from before the ED III period are very scrappy, it is not possible to verify this, but what indications we do have do not contradict it. Our earliest known Mesopotamian palaces are at Kish (Figure 7:1). Like their successors, both are significantly demarcated from the rest of the city by a solid defensive wall, but their location within the city is also suggestive. Palace A lies near the temple buildings, but the 'Plano-Convex Building', which was probably much larger, is about 2 km away (Figure 7:2). Reasons for this are not far to seek: a Mesopotamian temple, almost by definition, is established at the core of the settlement it serves and its emplacement is immutable and sacrosanct. In contrast, new rulers like to build themselves new premises, and in an ancient city the space needed by a large secular institution would only be available at the expense of existing buildings, so that a site away from the centre was often chosen. This can be illustrated very clearly in two later cases, at Ešnunna and Uruk: at Ešnunna the Akkadian, Ur III and Old Babylonian palaces are in the new, southern sector of the city, away from the old housing quarter and traditional temples on the north-western mound (Figure 4:3).

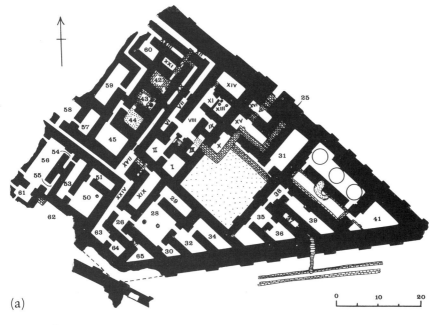

(a)

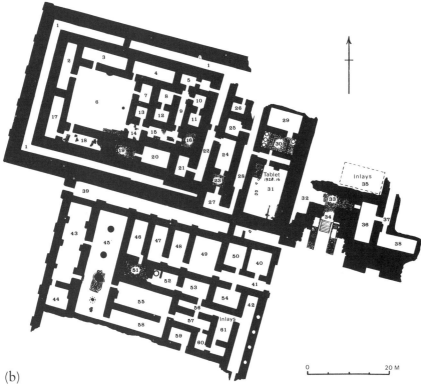

(b)

Figure 7:1 The two Early Dynastic palaces at Kish. (a) The 'Plano-Convex Building': heavy enclosure wall and narrow internal passages. (b) Palace A: monumental entrance, encircling passage round one unit and columned and decorated reception rooms. (Moorey 1978, 34 and 57)

Figure 7:2 The site of Kish (A = Palace A, P = Plano-Convex Building). Note scale. (Moorey 1978, 14)

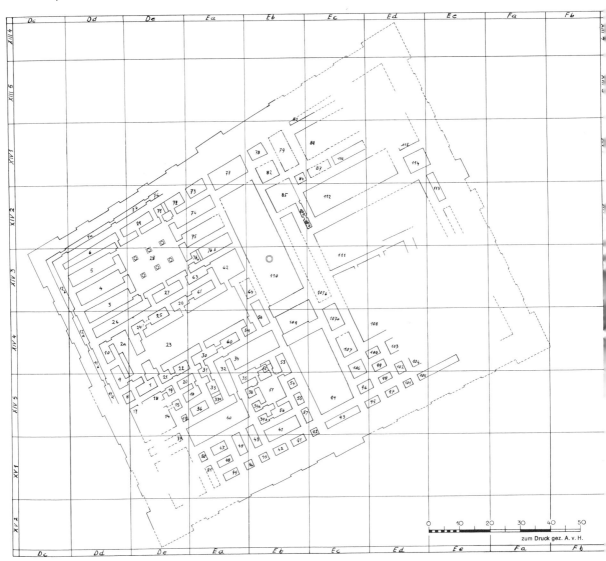

Figure 7:3 The palace of Sin-kašid of Uruk, *c.* 1900 BC. (Lenzen 1966, Tafel 35. Courtesy Professor Dr R.-M. Boehmer)

At Uruk, where traditionally religious and secular power seem to have been united, and the vast 'Stampflehmgebäude' within the Eanna temple precinct was probably in effect the 'palace' of the Early Dynastic dynasty (Eichmann 1989, 60–2), the Old Babylonian ruler Sin-kašid built his palace well away from Eanna, on the western side of the city.

These examples are perhaps especially suggestive by comparison with cities further north and west. For, even if it is difficult to assert with confidence that the palace was a newcomer to the southern cities, as one moves up river towards the hills the central role of the temple seems to diminish, and archaeological evidence suggests that a system of patrimonial princedoms is more the norm, in which the temples are little more than shrines attached to the seat of government at the centre of the town. Thus at Mari the Ur III palace, which survived in use until Hammurapi, stands on the emplacement of an Early Dynastic building with recognizable similarities to the Kish Palace A, but the military frieze of the same date comes in fact from a neighbouring temple. Further afield, at Ebla, the massive Early Bronze Age palace lies beneath the central acropolis of the city; and in the Kaneš correspondence it is clear that the Anatolian princes lived on the acropolis of their small towns, in buildings referred to as *ēkallum* ('palace') by the Assyrian merchants. It may not be coincidental that Palace A at Kish, with its columns, has a distinctly north-western look to it, suggesting that at least some architectural influence was moving west–east at the end of the Early Dynastic period. But in our state of ignorance it would be foolhardy to rule out the possibility that similar secular monumental buildings existed already in the Uruk period as well.

The need for caution is underlined by archaeologists' failure to locate most of the principal palaces of southern Mesopotamia at times when we know they existed. One reason may be that they were more transitory than the temples and hence form less conspicuous features within the ancient mounds. The city of Akkad has yet to be discovered, and we have no major Ur III palace.[219] At Babylon, Hammurapi's palace lies under the water-table, Išme-Dagan's at Isin and Rim-Sin's at Larsa have not been located – at least not by archaeologists as opposed to robbers. Even at Ešnunna the later Old Babylonian palace was eroded to its foundations, and in fact the only good representative in the south is Sin-kašid's new building at Uruk, where also virtually only the baked-brick foundations survive (Figure 7:3). Fortunately in plan it is very similar to the 'house of Zimri-Lim' at Mari, and this inevitably must serve as our prime example, since here we have not only a well-preserved architectural monument, which excited the admiration of its contemporaries (Text 7:1), but also a huge volume of cuneiform archives which illustrate the life of the palace in a wealth of fascinating detail.

Text 7:1 Letter to the King of Mari from the King of Aleppo
Say to Zimrilim, Hammurapi your brother says: The ruler of Ugarit has sent me a message saying 'Introduce me to see the house of Zimrilim'. Hence I am now sending you his servant.

(After Dossin in C. Schaeffer, *Ugaritica* 1, 1939, 15–16)

Although we see the Mari palace in its final state (Figure 7:4), as it was sacked by Hammurapi's army in the eighteenth century BC, much of the building had probably been erected in the Ur III period, some two hundred years before (on the site of an Early Dynastic palace with similarities to the Kish Palace A). In Sumerian the palace is called the 'big house' (é-gal); this was borrowed into Akkadian as *ēkallum* and becomes the word for palace throughout the ancient Near East. Like a house, it served a variety of functions: as a residence – for the king, his family, their personal servants (but probably not the officials); as a place of storage for the household's immediate needs and for the royal treasure; as a workshop for domestic activities as well as weaving and perhaps other crafts; as a forum for state ceremonial; and as a centre of government and administration. As an

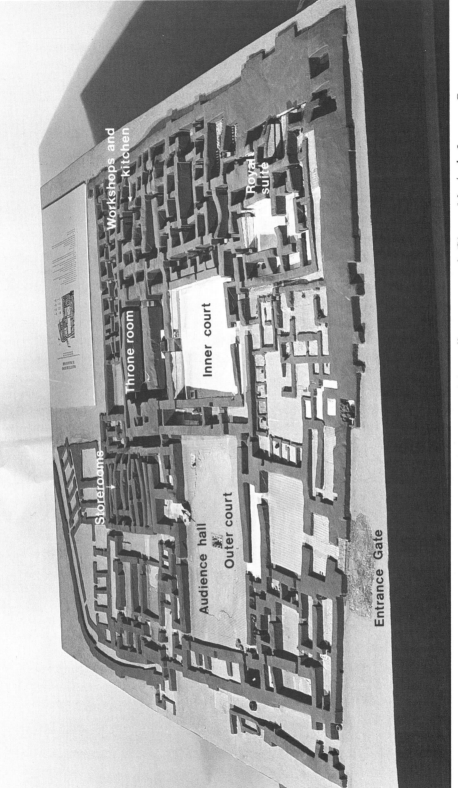

Storerooms

Throne room

Workshops and
kitchen

Inner court

Royal
suite

Audience hall
Outer court

Entrance Gate

Figure 7:4 The Palace of Zimri-Lim at Mari. Maquette in the Louvre of the walls as excavated. (Photo: Musée du Louvre. Courtesy J.-Cl. Margueron)

organization expands, so its various functions become increasingly specialized and sep-arated; and just as the growing specialization of a city can be observed in the differentiation of its archaeological remains, so with a palace as it grows the separate functions can be more easily recognized. All these functions are identifiable in the Mari palace, so that no apology is needed for recurring time and again to this example.

Throne room and audience hall

To this day the Near Eastern household has a room set aside to receive those from outside the family, usually larger and better furnished than any other room in the house, and often physically separate. The 'guest room' (*mudhīf*) of a traditional Iraqi house is not an optional extra, it is the essential forum where one household and its members are accessible to the rest of the world. On a small scale it is an 'audience chamber', partly symbolic but also practical: in accordance with his greater social responsibilities, both to the village itself and to outsiders, a headman will boast an extra large *mudhīf*, reflecting the fact that even for the sedentary population of South Iraq the tribal past with the sheikh's tent is not far away. By contrast, while Early Dynastic houses have a reception room, it is an integral component of the courtyard unit, and the audience chamber of the palaces is usually an enhanced version of this. In some cases, such as in the outer courtyard at Mari or at Ešnunna, a separate ceremonial unit can be made out. This may well be an echo of a different way of life, but it also begins to overlap with the question of deification of the ruler, to which we shall return later (chapter 14).

Naturally such a room, as a state's 'shop-window', was the place of greatest ostentation. Already in Early Dynastic times palaces were decorated with propaganda scenes, as the stone and shell mosaic friezes of Kish and Ebla make clear. Later, at Mari, the principal audience chamber on the outer court had been painted with ritual scenes, probably of Ur III date or shortly after. These were on the inner walls, above head height, while lower

---

Text 7:2 Zimri-Lim to a senior palace administrator

Say to Mukannišum, your lord says: I have heard your tablet which you sent to me. About the first-quality Yamhadian tapestry on the subject of which I wrote to you before, you wrote: 'I have sent(?) that tapestry ... to Babylon ...' ... that tapestry ... another tapestry ... [damaged passage] ... and that tapestry is (still) left in your hands. Now send that tapestry to me quickly.

And about the ibex-horns and the birch-wood on the subject of which you wrote to me, I will request them from Bunu-Ištar and send them to you.

(Rouault 1977, No. 12)

---

down the walls would have been hung with textiles, woven or knotted rugs (see Text 7:2). This is a reasonable deduction from later parallels, from the absence of painted decoration lower down the walls, and in particular from the main painted scene of the inner courtyard, which actually has a border reproducing the bunched tassels of a woven rug, showing that it was a replacement (either temporary or permanent) for a textile (Figure 7:5). We may reasonably infer that in many of the palace apartments of which the walls are now plain

Figure 7:5 The 'Investiture Scene', a wall-painting fallen into the main inner courtyard of the Mari palace. At the centre the king, with rounded hat of Amorite style, is entrusted with his office by the goddess. The significance of some of the other detail is not known. Note the border of tassels above and below showing that the painting is in imitation of textiles. (Photo: Mission Archéologique de Mari. Courtesy J.-Cl. Margueron)

plaster, there were figured tapestries proclaiming the luxurious standards of the state and at one and the same time conveying an iconographic message. In the ceremonial rooms the scenes are concerned with the religious legitimation of the ruler, and with his military prowess and, just like the sculptured slabs of the Neo-Assyrian palaces a thousand years later, they were at least partly addressed to the visitor, for it would have been here that the ruler received his subjects and guests.

Court ceremony

An audience with the ruler was an important event. We can only imagine the hurdles the average citizen would have to overcome before he was finally ushered into the throne room by the king's vizier (**sukkal**; Text 7:3). Ease of access was no doubt in proportion to the importance of the visitor, and, inversely, to the size of the king's realm. Both subjects and strangers would expect to bring an audience-gift, as visitors universally do in oriental

Text 7:3 Enmerkar and the Lord of Aratta: Enmerkar's emissary arrives back in Uruk with
the message from Aratta

The Lord of Aratta having put words in his mouth as if they were his own, the envoy
'turned his thigh' like a cow. Like a sand-fly he went in the cool of the dawn. He stepped
into the brickwork of Kulaba [the centre of Uruk] with a joyful foot. Into the Great Court,
the throne-room court, the envoy hastened. To his king, the Lord of Kulaba, he repeated
(the message) as it were his own, he roared it out like a bull.

(After Cohen 1973, 126–7)

contexts today – a tradition which extended even to the underworld, for some grave-goods
were meant for the new arrival to present to the different persons of importance encountered
there. Naturally most people came with a request of one kind or another, and even where
it concerned a legal decision it would not have been regarded improper for a gift to be
made merely for the favour of the king's attention (see Text 7:4). When rulers or their

Text 7:4 From the 'Poor Man of Nippur'

[This comic story begins with an impoverished citizen of Nippur who gets his own back
on the establishment in the person of the mayor ...] Gimil-Ninurta took counsel with his
miserable heart: 'I shall take off my cloak, for which I have no change, and I shall buy a
sheep in the square of my city, Nippur.' He took off his cloak, for which he had no change,
and in the square of his city, Nippur, he bought a 3-year old goat! He took counsel with
his miserable heart: 'If I were to slaughter the goat in my yard, there would be no feast,
for where is the beer? And my friends will hear of it and be offended, my family and
kinsmen will be angry with me. I will go to the mayor's house and bring him the goat ...'
[He goes to the mayor's house and] when Gimil-Ninurta came into the presence of the
mayor, he grasped the goat's neck in his left hand, and with his right hand he saluted
the mayor: 'May Enlil and the city of Nippur bless the mayor, may Adad and Nusku make
him prosper greatly.' The mayor said to the citizen of Nippur: 'What injustice have you
suffered, that you are bringing me a present?'

(After Gurney 1956, 150–3, lines 11–21, 34–40)

representatives came from another state, they too brought presents, often items of great
rarity or consummate craftsmanship. As within society in general, such gifts were understood to be on a reciprocal basis, and the etiquette of gift exchange was an important
constituent in various stages of diplomatic negotiation. 'There was no such thing as a free
gift', and both parties were acutely conscious of the implicit messages of the procedure
itself and of the quality and quantity of the items sent (see Text 7:5).[220]

The making of gifts is only one part of the reciprocal relationship between a host and
a guest: the host has the obligations of hospitality, and any visitors from outside the state
would certainly be fed and housed at royal expense, even if they were not accommodated
within the palace itself. The king's table was equally a part of the the paraphernalia of
royalty (Figure 7:6). The Mari archives include thousands of ephemeral texts giving us a
daily record of the royal menu from behind the scenes, as officials listed the issues of flour,
bread, beer and wine, fruit and vegetables, fish and meat. In the domestic quarter of the

Text 7:5 Letter from the King of Qatna to Išme-Dagan, the son of Samsi-Addu
Say to Išme-Dagan, Išhi-Addu your brother says: This should really not be said, but I will
say it and appease my heart. You are a Great King: you requested from me 2 horses, and
I sent them to you, and you sent me 20 minas ($\simeq$ 10 kg) of tin. You sent this little lot of
tin since you did not want a proper agreement with me. If you hadn't sent anything at
all, for the sake of my father's god would my heart have been sore? With us here in Qatna,
the value of horses of that kind would be 600 (shekels) of silver – and you have sent (a
mere) 20 minas of tin! What would anyone who heard this have to say? Would he not
slander us? This house is your house. In your house what is lacking? Does not one brother
give another brother his desire? If you had not sent the tin, my heart would not have been
the least sore. Are you not a Great King? Why have you done this? This house is your
house.

(Dossin 1952, No. 20)

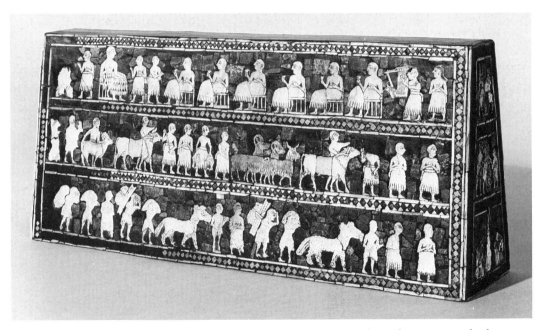

Figure 7:6 The 'Royal Standard of Ur', peace side. Provisions making their way to the banquet,
shown with its musical accompaniment in the upper register. The function of this object is not
known. For the other face see Figure 13:1. (BM 121201 from royal tomb PG 779 at Ur. Photo:
courtesy Trustees of the British Museum)

palace were the storerooms and ovens, while kitchen equipment, such as the pottery
moulds (Figure 7:7), bears witness to elaborate culinary standards. Some of the royal
correspondence is concerned with the provision of suitable storage for ice, floated downstream from the mountains for the delectation of the royal palate.[221] Recently some

Figure 7:7 Collection of moulds from the palace kitchen at Mari, *c.* 1750 BC. (Photo: Mission Archéologique de Mari. Courtesy J.-Cl. Margueron)

contemporary recipes for complex dishes have been recovered, confirming that gastronomy was recognized as a civilized skill.[222] Apart from the daily menus of the king and his family, there were special events such as religious festivals, including the ancestral offerings, and banquets for foreign envoys. The commissariat no doubt also supplied members of the administration and fed the messengers and visiting dignitaries. One of the commoner types of Ur III document is lists of rations given to messengers, monotonously recording bread, beer and onions – and occasionally other items like oil, fish or spices (see Text 7:6).[223] Occasionally we find mentions of more distinguished guests, such as the Hurrian ruler of Nineveh and his entourage of over 100 followers.[224]

The royal family

The palace was the principal residence of the ruler, and of his family, and in a real sense the king's family are one of his principal resources (cf. Figure 6:6). Sons, nephews and cousins can be trusted with loyalty to the dynasty (if not to the king's person), and the nepotism we shall return to below is as much a matter of policy as of charity. Similarly the tradition of appointing a daughter of the king as priestess of Nanna at Ur, reaching back at least as far as Sargon and his daughter Enheduana, must have had important

Text 7:6 Samsi-Addu to his son at Mari

Say to Yasmah-Addu, Samsi-Addu your father says: the second day after this tablet of mine (is sent) the Tilmun envoys will leave from Šubat-Enlil. [There follow details of the company.]

30 sheep, 30 litres of best oil, 60 litres of sesame oil should be decanted into skins; 3 litres of juniper and box(?) seed for the 10 Tilmunite men and their servants; 1 water-skin and 2 sandals each for the 5 slaves . . .; 1 water-skin and 2 sandals each for the 7 craftsmen; 1 water-skin and 2 sandals each for the 20 men who are going with them from Šubat-Enlil; [2] water-skins and [. . . each] for the 10 pack-asses: Total 52 water-skins, 64 sandals, 1 big leather sack, (and) 10 leather straps of 9 metres should be prepared, according to this tablet. . .

Pay them whatever provisions they ask of you.

(Dossin 1950a, No. 17)

symbolic value in political terms.[225] Such appointments are often mentioned in the year formulae, and, as we have seen, the daughter of Zimri-Lim of Mari was dedicated as a *nadītum* in the Šamaš temple at Sippar. Another event which may find a mention in the year formulae, underlining its state importance, is the betrothal or marriage of a daughter to a foreign ruler. This is of course the replication at a higher level of the sort of alliance between families common in both sedentary and nomadic communities. Early in its history the Ur III dynasty sealed an alliance with Mari when Ur-Nammu took a bride from there, called significantly Taram-Uram 'She loves Ur';[226] later in the dynasty similar alliances were concluded with eastern states, and are mentioned not only in the official context of the year formula but also in mundane administrative notes to do with expenditure on the journeys and celebrations involved.[227] We do not often hear of the reciprocal event, the taking of a foreign wife by the Mesopotamian ruler, although this no doubt also happened. In much the same way, later and further to the west, Zimri-Lim's close relations with the house of Aleppo were sealed by his marriage to the king's daughter, while his rival Samsi-Addu secured the daughter of the king of Qatna, not coincidentally Aleppo's chief rival in the west, for his son Išme-Dagan (Text 7:7).

These scattered references to interdynastic marriage are also important for the light they shed on the queens. We rarely learn the identity of a king's mother. This is a shame, because it would help us to a better understanding of foreign diplomacy and of the principles of succession. If the mother of a new king had entered the royal household as the result of a diplomatic marriage (whether as first wife or not), she would naturally be a foreigner and this could radically affect the attitudes of the king and hence foreign policy. As for succession, it seems that the throne was not automatically passed from father to son. In two well-known cases (and others) brother succeeded to brother – Rim-Sin to Warad-Sin and Šu-Sin to Amar-Suen. There was no shortage of choice: later Ur III documents give us the names of over fifty princes and princesses ('sons' or 'daughters of the king') fathered by Šulgi, Amar-Suen, Šu-Sin or Ibbi-Sin.[228] We also have the names of

Text 7:7 Letter from Samsi-Addu to Yasmah-Addu at Mari about paying the bride-price
        for the King of Qatna's daughter

Say to Yasmah-Addu, Samsi-Addu your father says: 4 talents of silver will be given for the
bride-price of the daughter of Išhi-Addu. Laum will make out a tablet for 1 talent of silver,
and I shall give 3 talents. Išhi-Addu knows the conventions: for the 4 talents of silver for
his daughter's dowry he will give a present worth 10 or 5 talents of silver. From that
present what will I get? Isn't it you who will get it? I shall give 3 talents 52 minas and 10
shekels of silver. Now I am sending Baqqanum to you. Entrust 52 minas 10 shekels of
silver into the hands of Baqqanum, and appoint security guards for that silver and let him
bring it to me. And the remainder of that silver, $7\frac{5}{6}$ minas of silver – the balance to make
1 talent – make it into a chain and a silver ring over there, and the person who goes to
Qatna will take it with him.

(After Dossin 1950a, No. 46)

some of their wives or concubines, but their relative status remains obscure, and we simply
do not know whether the sons of concubines had any prospect of being preferred to those
of the 'official' wife.

Like an ordinary household head it is possible that some of the king's concubines were
mere slave-girls, but some seem to have been of intermediate status and are known as
lukur, the Sumerian term in some way equivalent to the Akkadian *nadītum*, some even as
lukur kaskala ('*nadītum* of the road'), which must presumably be interpreted in the light
of later parallels showing that the king was accustomed to take at least part of his harem
on campaign with him.[229] While the women were certainly segregated from the toing and
froing of the main business of the palace, the Mari texts make it clear that they could be
far from inactive or cut off from their menfolk, and, rather unexpectedly, that many of
them were taken on without change by a usurping dynasty.[230] In the late second millennium
the palaces of the ancient Near East were characterized by a highly developed harem
system, with the combination of concubines and eunuchs familiar from more recent Near
Eastern regimes. Strict regulations are recorded for the conduct of the palace staff in respect
of the harem and its occupants.[231] Whether the same ethos is applicable to any of the
earlier palace regimes remains uncertain. Eunuchs probably existed, but we have no clear
association between them and the domestic administration of a palace, and it is hard to
be sure whether these women were segregated within the palaces to the extent that one
would associate with the term a 'harem'.

Royal responsibilities

In the Old Babylonian period, if not earlier, the great majority of palace activities seem to
have related more to the king's position as a rich and powerful member of the community
administering his own estates, than to affairs of state as we would perceive them.[232]
Whether within the four walls of the palace or outside, there were craft industries,
agricultural estates and commercial ventures to be administered. The bulk of the documentation that has come down to us results from such activities, and will contribute to

several of the following chapters. Some of the kings at least were extremely energetic in overseeing both these internal palace activities and the conduct of public affairs. Šulgi was presumably the driving force in the obsessive centralized management of the Ur III state, while many letters from Hammurapi himself have survived, revealing his attention to small details of government administration, a practice which survived into the later years of the dynasty when the kings were personally concerned in the organization of the shearing of the palace flocks.[233] On occasion the king would leave his palace and visit parts of his kingdom. Sometimes, of course, this took place as part of a military enterprise, but in the interests of national fusion rulers have always felt the need to show themselves in the corners of their kingdoms. We have stewards' accounts from a visit of the king of Akkad to the south (Text 7:8), and letters to Zimri-Lim when he was away from Mari both from

Text 7:8 Šar-kali-šarri in the south

(x) **gur** of barley; 0.0.2 ghee; 0.0.1 honey; 0.1.3 dates; 2 pots of milk; 0.0.3 malt-gruel; 0.0.5 beans; 0.0.5 peas; 0.0.2 gazelle-dung legumes; 0.0.4 sesame; 0.0.2 less 3 **sila** big nuts; 5 **sila** small nuts; . . . .; [x] strings of dried apples; [x] strings of dried figs; [x] minas cedar (-resin?); [x] minas cypress(-resin?); [x] minas myrtle; . . . when Šar-kali-šarri went to Sumer.

(After Steinkeller 1991, No. 27)

officials looking after the palace in his absence, and from his womenfolk. Indeed, he even undertook a journey of several months outside his own frontiers, through his father-in-law's kingdom at Aleppo as far as the Mediterranean at Ugarit.[234]

Most of this sort of work could however be delegated, whereas the king also had formal roles in the spheres of religion, justice and war, which he needed to fulfil in person. The public inscriptions of the kings make these responsibilities very clear, and they are all closely bound up in the ideology of political power which we shall be discussing in chapter 14. However, if we ignore the theoretical side for the time being, what were the practical implications of these roles? As the ultimate judicial authority within his realm, the king had to consider appeals made to him: in practice we find that he would tend to refer such appeals back to the existing authorities, and even where judges were royal appointments they were given posts within the existing judicial framework and assigned to a particular city. The same considerations affect the role of the king in religious affairs: Sargon, Šulgi or Hammurapi could not participate in person at every local ritual which had previously required the presence of the ruler, but it was evidently important to subscribe to traditional legitimation procedures, and this concern undoubtedly underlines the frequency of 'Royal Hymns' in the Isin–Larsa period with their close connections to the king's role in specific temple rituals. In Ur III times the kings made full use of their relatives to help spread the burden of cultic duties: a son might for instance be chosen as the high-priest of An at Uruk. However, where it came to the essence of their position as ruler, they usually did make the effort at the beginning of their reigns to attend ceremonies at Ur, Nippur and Uruk which involved three symbolic acts in the installation of a new ruler which survive to traditional monarchies today: 'coronation', 'enthronement' and taking a mace or 'sceptre'.[235]

Governors and generals

As soon as a polity was enlarged beyond the boundaries of one city-state, 'branch offices' were needed. Each previous independent state constituted a convenient province, which could be accurately delimited territorially, on the basis of the previous boundaries of the separate city-states (see Text 7:9). State capital became provincial capital, and the obvious

> **Text 7:9** From an Ur III record of provincial boundaries
> From the Numušda Tower to the Numušda Shrine, from the Numušda Shrine to the Hill Tower, from the Hill Tower to the Ser-ussa Canal, from the Ser-ussa Canal to Ibilum Village, from Ibilum Village to the Abgal Canal, cross the Abgal Canal and then go 560 ...s – it is the ... of the boundary: (this is the) North side.
>   From the ... of the boundary to Me-Belum-ili: (this is the) East side.
>   From Me-Belum-ili along the bank of the Abgal Canal as far as the mouth of the Ilum-bani Canal, cross the Abgal Canal, (then) from the mouth of the Ida-umma Canal to the Imnia Canal: (this is the) South side.
>   From the Imnia Canal to Nagarbi, from Nagarbi to Marsh-town, from Marsh-town to the Hill, along the Hill back to the Numušda Tower: (this is its) West side. Ur-Nammu the King has decreed the boundary of Meslamtaea (the god) of Abiak.
>
> (After Kraus 1955, 49)

solution was to adopt both the physical and the administrative establishments of the former regime. Thus under the dynasties of Akkad and Ur III the title of the earlier **ensi** was inherited by the new governor. This not only had the advantage of flattering local susceptibilities by seeming to preserve the traditional system in each city, but enabled the new regime to adopt wholesale a functioning administrative set-up. Of course the local continuity did not usually extend to the highest echelons of the new provincial governorate. While on occasion the existing **ensi** may have been confirmed in office, more normally he was nominated by the king, frequently from outside. Under the Ur III kings some governors are known to have been transferred from one province to another, in one case from Assur to Susa.[236] After his defeat of Lugal-zagesi Sargon records that he appointed **ensis** from among 'the sons of Akkad', and indeed at least three known governors do bear an Akkadian name.[237] These were royal princes, and under the Ur III kings too we have instances of high posts in the civilian and military administration entrusted to members of the royal family, the most notable being perhaps Babati, the uncle of Šu-Sin, who held a pluralist portfolio of a variety of high military and civilian posts (Text 7:10).

> **Text 7:10** Seal legend of Babati, Šu-Sin's uncle
> Šu-Sin, mighty man, King of Ur, king of the four rims (of the world), presented (this seal) to Babati, archivist, royal accountant, military governor of Maškan-šarrum, civilian governor of Awal, ... [lacuna] ... of the gods Belat-Suhnir and Belat-Teraban, the brother of Abi-simti, his (Šu-Sin's) beloved mother.
>
> (After Whiting 1976, 178–9)

Babati's titles 'civilian governor' and 'military governor' need some clarification. The adoption of an earlier administrative organization may have been convenient but was not in itself a complete solution. It is now clear that the Ur III state had two administrative hierarchies. The traditional civilian governorates, from which the great bulk of our documentary archives derive and which were no doubt largely staffed by the local elite, ran parallel with a military hierarchy also based on the provincial centres (although we have no idea whether to expect two separate palaces). Much less is known about the military administration because of the lack of documentary evidence, but its senior members do seem to have been drawn from circles close to the ruling dynasty, for obvious reasons of ensuring loyalty. It was presumably responsible for the recruitment and maintenance of a military force within the province, but also for the execution of the peace-time tasks of communal labour to which the Mesopotamian armies were often assigned. This duality in the Ur III government must surely have led to internal differences, and may help to explain how the Isin–Larsa period states could inherit so much from Ur III in the administrative and cultural spheres despite the dynasty's political and military dissolution.[238]

In the wake of that dissolution the old system of provincial governorates inevitably disappears in a welter of petty kingships, but as larger states coalesce the same policies are adopted. In the Mari region and the north the kingdoms are administered in districts (ḫalṣum), such as Terqa or Sagaratum, each with their governor. We have an extensive correspondence between Zimri-Lim and some of his governors, just as we have between Hammurapi and two of his top officials in the newly annexed kingdom of Larsa. An alternative was to retain some limited form of sovereignty under a trusted nominee. This was Samsi-Addu's choice when his kingdom expanded and he delegated the throne of Mari to his younger son, that of Ekallatum to his elder son. A letter from Mari gives us Zimri-Lim's view of the dilemma, or at least choice, confronting a king who had gained control of another territory – to preserve it as a client kingdom with one's own appointee, or to assume the throne oneself (see chapter 14, p. 273).

Whichever choice was made, the transfer of the administration will normally have been accompanied by the physical take-over of the palace. Hammurapi would certainly have taken over the palace of the kings of Ešnunna – just as they, in a reversal of the process, had converted the provincial residence of the Ur III governor into their own royal establishment. The Amorite dynasty of Yahdun-Lim occupied the palace of the Akkadian šakkanakkus who preceded them at Mari, and Samsi-Addu and his family used the same building during their interregnum. With the building, a regime often inherited an accompanying staff of domestic servants, craftsmen and officials. At Mari both the archaeological and the documentary evidence attest to an army of cooks, butlers, domestic servants and craftsmen of all kinds, and the third-millennium archives from the south often record the palace's involvement in the collection, production and distribution of goods, which will concern us further in chapter 10. It is not difficult to imagine the organization of the menial work, but when we come to consider the nature and activities of the administration itself we are much worse off, though only temporarily. The sheer volume of undigested documents from early Mesopotamian waste-paper baskets has prevented scholars from making full use of them, although some worthy attempts have been made. Archives still have to be reassembled and the bureaucratic procedures reconstructed, which is not always easy, as the system takes itself for granted. Hence, although it is clear that the concepts of authority and responsibility were strictly formalized. both the terminology and the hierarchy of civilian administration remain to be worked out.[239]

The bureaucratic cadre

Rather than rehearse a list of untranslatable officials, we shall conclude this chapter with some general comments on the palace staff, both at the capital and in the provinces. Some officials undoubtedly concerned themselves with the protocol and etiquette of the court. Like the military elite, many of these will have belonged to the ranks of the ruler's or governor's own relatives and followers, and have merged imperceptibly into a body of courtiers with less definite functions. On the other side there was a bureaucratic cadre, which may have been drawn more from the traditional city elite. When we look at the thousands of documents recovered from the Mari palace, many of them highly ephemeral and dating to the last years before its destruction, we get the impression that the palace must have sheltered a considerable bureaucracy. Yet even here it is difficult to quantify it.

The functions of the palace scribes were both to record the business transactions of the palace and government, and to serve as the means of transmission of information, whether within the palace administration or between it and the rest of the world. It remains very uncertain whether scribes were just secretaries, taking dictation and reading out incoming mail to the executive officials, or whether they combined their literate skills with an independent administrative function. *Some* mere secretaries were needed at Mari, since some high officials were indeed illiterate. However, in this respect it is not safe to treat Mari as typical, although it is virtually the only early second-millennium palace whose archives we possess. Here, as in other northern states, where writing and literacy were probably much less generally diffused within society, it seems more likely that scribal expertise was concentrated in and fostered by the palace for its own ends. In the Ur III period the title of scribe (**dub-sar**) is used almost as though it were a class, not a function. Given the emphasis placed on the written documentation of almost every aspect of life within the state's control, it would not be surprising if many officials were literate. Later, in the Old Babylonian kingdoms of the south, one may guess that a scribal class supplied the middle ranks of the administration, whatever the regime in power, although as we shall see the palace tried to pare down its intervention in society, operating more and more as a private business.[240]

Further reading

As with the temples, E. Heinrich, *Die Paläste im alten Mesopotamien* (de Gruyter 1984) is an invaluable source for the archaeological record. See also J.-C. Margueron, *Recherches sur les palais mésopotamiens de l'Age de Bronze* (Geuthner 1984). The exchange of gifts between states is discussed by Zaccagnini 1983a (for the later second millennium see his article in the same volume as Larsen 1987). Of the several contributions on royal women see e.g. Michalowski 1982 and Steinkeller 1981a. Steinkeller 1987b is by far the most useful general account of Ur III government. There is no survey of Ur III bureaucratic procedures, but the two principal studies, each based on a collection of texts, are Jones and Snyder 1961 and J.-P. Grégoire, *Archives administratives sumériennes* (Paris 1970). See also the surveys of T.B. Jones in *Jacobsen Festschrift* 41–61 and R.K. Englund, *Organisation und Verwaltung der Ur III-Fischerei* (Berlin 1990), pp. 13–90.

Part III

The economic order

8

Crops and livestock

The Near East has the seminal role in the history of agriculture, witnessing the first domesticated plants and animals, associated with a sedentary village lifestyle which persists to this day. Although lacking metal and forming pottery by hand, the early farming cultures of northern Iraq and the mountain fringes were not technologically backward, as the quality of their fine painted ceramics, their stone vessels, their flint implements and not least their architecture bears witness. Archaeological research in the last forty years has understandably concentrated on seeking out the earliest phases of these cultures and teasing out the origins of the new strategies for subsistence. Hence much work remains to be done on the nature of the large and probably prosperous later farming communities of Halaf and Ubaid times, when the South Mesopotamian plain was settled – should we say colonized? – and the critical steps toward urban life were taken. Consequently we can say little about possible changes in the agricultural regime in the period between incipient agriculture (say 8000 BC) and the Uruk period some four millennia later.[241] In early historical Mesopotamia we are looking at agriculture in another social context, one in which the rural world constantly interacted with the urban, and agricultural strategies were often directed by the urban sector towards its own economic requirements at the expense of the traditional subsistence pattern. We tend to think of the exploitation of animals and plants as being an old-fashioned, unchanging way of life, but in the absence of machines and artificial substances the tractive power of the larger animals (oxen and equids) and the by-products of all of them were important to the technology of the urban sector of the early states, and the exploitation processes are accordingly geared to urban needs.

*The hallmark of third-millennium agriculture is the maximization of production. Similar trends can be observed in all societies where an essentially peasant economy is being transformed by the creation and the resulting demands of cities and associated elites, accompanied both by population growth, with the consequent need for increased resources, and by political conditions tending to the exploitation of the rural sector. There are two broad strategies for this, **intensification** and **expansion**: the first seeks to get more out of the existing agronomic regime, as for instance by energetic application of fertilizer or more intensive use of the ground by planting more frequently or by mixed crops; the second expands the area of land under agriculture, and will usually involve considerable input of new labour, either by a modification of the existing social structure, or by the introduction of new labour sources. The newly won land will often by its nature require different techniques or strategies. The extraordinary wealth of documentation at our disposal for the third millennium BC is a direct consequence of urban policies of maximization, and* *enables us to see many detailed ways in which this second, managerial, agricultural revolution worked itself out, with consequences which transformed Old World farming in ways we are only beginning to suspect.*

The basic regime

The marshes of South Iraq teem with life, and textual and archaeological evidence shows that the fish, wild fowl and turtles were enthusiastically exploited by the ancient inhabitants long after agriculture had been established in the area (Text 8:1).[242] To this day, too, a

> ***Text 8:1*** Account of Ur III delicacies
> 145 **rigi** birds; 29 **u-az** birds; 16 **u** birds; 126 water-fowl; 18 'dowry-birds'; 176 ducks; 60 ducklings; 12 swallows; 11,441 **um** birds; 705 **gamgam** birds; 30 **ubi** birds; 86 **dadar** birds; 20 herons; 466 **esig** birds; ... [12 other types of bird] ...; 18,413 little birds; 2617 cured birds; 180 crows; 391 duck eggs; 152,298 little bird eggs; 2186 turtles; 2714 turtle eggs; 300 tortoises.
>
> Total 197,873 – completed account, aggregated deliveries, received by Nin-unumun-ki-ag.
>
> From the 5th month of Šulgi 30 to the 2nd month of Šulgi 33 – making 35 months.
>
> (After Owen 1981, 30–1)

variety of plants are collected, such as liquorice, the root of the rush and sedge tubers.[243] There is no compulsion, therefore, to turn to cereal cultivation, and it is a reasonable assumption that the earliest South Mesopotamian farmers had brought their skills with them from an environment less hostile to agriculture. That was well before 4000 BC, and by Early Dynastic times the farming practices developed thousands of years earlier in North Mesopotamia had long been adapted to the special conditions of the southern plain. Most of the agricultural landscape consisted of irrigated fields devoted to cereal crops, planted in the autumn and harvested the following April–May, but smaller areas were given over to legumes, including lentils, and flax, which could be grown either for its linen fibres or for its oil-bearing seeds. Vegetables requiring more frequent attention were grown in separate plots, often under the canopy provided by plantations of date palms, interplanted with lower fruit trees such as apple and pomegranate. Lexical texts give us every reason to suppose that a wide spectrum of herbs and spices was cultivated as well.

Animal husbandry was also inherited from the neolithic. Each species was kept for distinct reasons, among which value as a food source was by no means always paramount. Numerically and economically sheep were the most important, and were usually herded together with goats, as today. Their value lay primarily in their milk products and their wool, much less as a source of meat. Similarly cattle were kept mainly for ploughing and pigs as a source of fat. Given the restrictive factors of land ownership and water supply affecting cereal cultivation, animal husbandry often represented the farmer's best opportunity to build up capital, and the size of individual herds may well have varied widely between members of the same community.

This lightning survey is largely reconstruction, based on current practices and hints in the written sources: archaeological evidence at present is minimal since it has not been collected from historical sites. The improved methodology of animal bone and plant remains analysis has scarcely been applied to urban contexts in the Near East, but in future there is a real prospect of matching the patterns of plant and animal exploitation attested in the texts with the excavated remains, and several examples in this chapter will demonstrate that philologists have no grounds for complacency over their ability to reconstruct the agricultural regime on their own. For the present, though, we can describe the life of the countryside only through the eyes of the city-dweller, since this is how the information we possess has reached us. Our written sources derive from a non-rural context, and thus they can reflect agricultural conditions only as and when they affect or are affected by the urban population.

Sheep and shepherds

One reason why the sheep is so prevalent in the Near East is that it is well adapted to complement agriculture: flocks can graze on the fringes of the cultivation where surplus water has encouraged plant growth, and on the half of a village's fields left fallow during alternate years; and, in a practice still common today and well attested in the Old Babylonian period, flocks may even be allowed on to growing crops, with the farmer's permission (Text 8:2). This does not drastically reduce the yield, and has the advantage

> **Text 8:2** The Code of Hammurapi, §57
> If a shepherd has not made an agreement with the owner of a field to let the sheep graze on the crop, but has let the sheep graze on the field, the owner of that field shall harvest his field, and in addition the shepherd, who had let the sheep graze on the field without the owner's consent, shall pay the owner of the field 20 **gur** of barley per each **bur** of field.

of providing automatic manuring and encouraging extra growth by 'tillering'. Probably the great majority of small farmers had a flock of sheep usually mixed with some goats, which would have been led out to graze daily within the village's lands and brought home every evening, as long as the fallow fields and young shoots were sufficient to sustain them. In the summer months, though, it seems likely that larger flocks at least would have had to roam considerable distances to find grazing, taking the shepherds far from home.[244] If they were not tended by a member of the family, they would have been entrusted to a professional shepherd. Sheep were also owned by urban families as a form of capital investment: from Old Babylonian times we possess a good number of contracts between owner and shepherd which illustrate both the composition of the flocks and the conditions of employment (Text 8:3). Flocks vary from just 4 to over 200 animals; ewes are in the majority, but enough males were kept to suggest mixed-purpose herding, with a primary interest in the wool but some animals kept for slaughter. Some owners had no goats, but

Text 8:3 Contract with a shepherd

92 ewes; 20 wethers; 22 young sheep; 24 lambs; 33 nanny-goats; 4 billy-goats; 27 kids:

Total 158 sheep, 64 goats, which Sin-šamuh has entrusted to Dada the shepherd. He takes liability for them, and will replace any lost animal. If Nidnatum his shepherd-boy makes off, he shall be responsible for the loss. Dada will pay (the boy) 5 **gur** [1500 l] of grain. (3 witnesses. 18th day of 4th month, Samsu-iluna Year 1).

(After Finkelstein 1968b)

in other cases they come to more than 25 per cent of the total. The terms of the contract reflect the inescapable fact that the shepherd is beyond the control of the owner: the accounts were drawn up at the spring shearing when the wool was weighed and the main lambing season was over, and a new agreement was made for the coming year. This used an annual productivity ratio in respect of birth of new animals set against expected deaths. The shepherd normally kept all the milk products, and a fixed amount of wool per adult animal plus any animals in excess of the agreed ratio, while tradition also allowed him a food ration and a clothing allowance, as well as the pay of a subordinate.[245]

If the conditions seem unduly favourable to the shepherd, it is also a safe investment for the owner of the animals. Disasters, which could always occur, would usually weigh on the shepherd, not the owner, but some of the contracts include a provision which agrees with the Code of Hammurapi by distinguishing clearly between losses caused by a lion or by disease, which cannot be held against the shepherd, and those which can be attributed to negligence. The shepherd's wandering lifestyle made it difficult to be sure of such facts. Proof that the animal had not simply been sold can be supplied by production of the allegedly dead animal's tendons, or perhaps intestines; in nineteenth-century Iraq the ears served that function.[246] In the Code this is to be backed up by subjecting the shepherd to an oath in the temple, a practice already attested at Lagaš in Ur III times and doubtless going back much earlier.[247]

These Ur III shepherds were tending state or temple flocks, and of course large institutions faced the same contractual problems as individual owners. Similar procedures were used by the state offices at Larsa under Rim-Sin: since the numbers were larger, the contract is

Text 8:4 The rubric of an annual account from Larsa

Calculation (of) sheep and wool:

Capital and birth in Year Rim-Sin 21.
Entry to the shearing in Year Rim-Sin 22, with 80 female and male lambs born out of 100
    sheep, and 15 carcases deducted out of 100 sheep, and 2 minas wool the allocation
    per 1 sheep.
Receipts, issues, losses and deficits.
Completed account for 1 year.

Samum, Warad-murrim, Silli-Šamaš, herding contractors.

(After Kraus 1966, No. 5)

made with a 'herding-contractor', the *nāqidum*, who in turn employs shepherds, but the division of profit and responsibility is very similar. Annual account tablets tell us the exact figures: the shepherds were allowed a 15 per cent natural loss on the adult ewes, to be offset against an expected 80 per cent birth rate (Text 8:4). As with the private flocks, the numbers of males and females were roughly equal. The males (mostly castrated) will have been kept for slaughter, and the accountants list withdrawals of animals 'for an offering to Adad', 'to the king', 'for the omen-priest when Gimillum was ill', and similar purposes. It was however in the wool that the palace was primarily interested. Two minas, or about 1 kg, of wool was expected from each animal.[248] Texts from Ur mention amounts of wool which make it clear that the state flocks must have been numbered in thousands during the Ur III period, and this is confirmed by the Drehem archive (see Text 8:5). As early as

Text 8:5 Puzriš-Dagan animal account over 60 months

28,601 oxen
404 deer
236 wild sheep
29 ...
38 horses
360 onagers
727 onager-donkey hybrids
2204 donkeys
347,394 sheep (and goats)
3880 gazelles
457 bears
1 ...

384,344 opening balance

[After listing record of expenditure, the list concludes:]
Completed account of Naša, from the 12th month of Šulgi Year 44 to the 10th month of Šulgi Year 48, making 60 months including 2 intercalary months.

(After Calvot 1969, 101–3)

ED IIIa a (presumed) temple at Abu Salabikh recorded nearly 14,000 sheep and goats on a single administrative document; and at the end of the 1st Dynasty of Babylon the king himself is sufficiently concerned with the palace's wool production that he personally supervises the arrangements for the annual shearing.[249]

In secular society there is no doubt that in quantitative terms sheep were only secondarily a supply of meat, although it played an important social role as a component in offerings, and as a traditional large gift – for agricultural rent to a landlord, for omen taking, as an audience gift, and for weddings. This aspect was also institutionalized in the Early Dynastic period in the hands of a specialist profession of 'animal fattener'.[250] The regime of these earliest 'battery farms' emerges clearly from Ur III texts recording issues of barley, rations of 1 **sila** (c. 1 litre) rising to $1\frac{1}{2}$ and for the last few days 2 **sila**, as the sheep, as expected mostly males, reach the final stage of readiness for their ultimate destiny.[251]

Figure 8:1 Door plaque from near gateway to Temple Oval at Khafajah, late Early Dynastic (*c.* 2500 BC). The processions of sheep and goats belong in a tradition of temple iconography reaching back to the Uruk period. (Frankfort 1939, Plate III A. Photo: courtesy the Oriental Institute of the University of Chicago)

The self-conscious modification of a traditional agricultural regime under the control of the urban administration is also attested in deliberate efforts to improve the genetic stock by cross-breeding. The texts mention different kinds of sheep, especially the fat-tailed breed still popular in the Near East, and a variety of breeds or species feature in the

Text 8:6 Animals offered to the gods: an Ur III text
1 calf, offspring of a wild bull, unweaned – Enlil;
4 oxen, grain-fed, head ox (?)
6 oxen, grain-fed, 1 cow, offspring of a wild bull, unweaned
1 calf, offspring of a wild bull
4 sheep 20 goats
1 fleeced sheep, grain-fed
2 sheep, offspring of a mountain sheep, grain-fed, good, second-rate
2 adult goats, offspring of a mountain-goat, grain-fed, good, second-rate
1 nanny-goat, offspring of a mountain-goat, grain-fed, good, second-rate – Ninlil;
1 ox, grain-fed, head ox(?) – Nanna, in the Ninlil Temple.
Festival of harnessing the oxen.
Supervisor: Enlil-zi-šagal.
21st day of the month.
Issued by Šu-Mama.
(Date: 21.ii.Amar-Suen Year 7)
[Note on edge:] 14 oxen 10 sheep.

(After Jones and Snyder 1961, No. 64; cf. Steinkeller 1989b)

iconography (Figure 8:1). Once again it is the Ur III texts which in their passion for accuracy betray the details: animals in lists are recorded with different parents, showing that breeding experiments were underway in crossing domestic sheep, goats and cows with their wild counterparts (Text 8:6). These must have been imported from the mountains to north and east as the designation 'mountain sheep' emphasizes, an operation more readily organized collectively than by the initiative of single villages. The practice is potentially of importance in the genetic history of modern breeds, but collection of animal bones on sites of this date has been so rare that we cannot expect any trace of such experiments from the archaeological evidence without further work.[252]

Cattle

In many respects cattle resemble sheep and were treated similarly. They yielded leather and milk products, and the milking scene from the façade of the temple at Ubaid is the earliest certain attestation of this practice in the world (Figure 8:2). Cows were valuable and were not often sacrificed, except in state ceremonies, and they played no part in the taking of omens by extispicy (inspection of the entrails). Their primary importance was as a source of traction: the evidence of the texts is clear that they were used to plough the land before sowing and again in the seeding process. The plough was already in use in the Uruk period, as the existence of the cuneiform sign proves, and it has been suggested that

Figure 8:2 Mosaic stone frieze from the façade of the ED III shrine at Tell Ubaid near Ur. The scenes remain the earliest evidence for dairy farming, but the calves emerging from the reed-built shrine are another iconographic motif reaching back to the Uruk. (Photo: courtesy Trustees of the British Museum)

much earlier the osteological evidence from the middle Ubaid levels at Ras al Amiya is consonant with the use of oxen as plough animals.[253]

This role meant that every farming household wanted cattle, and they were often kept at home for when they were needed. In a simple agrarian economy there was no particular point in keeping large herds of cattle, since feeding them would be difficult and their by-products are not so easily processed domestically as wool. Lists of household property often include a flock of sheep, but rarely more than a few cows (Text 5:5). They were very much part of the family and in Old Babylonian households, and doubtless earlier too, were given names just like any other member of the family, often composed with the name of the moon-god, Sin.[254] Letters sometimes enquire about the health of the cows along with the rest of the household. Another reason for keeping them at home is their diet. Cattle need much more to eat than sheep or goats. Unlike them, they cannot survive by grazing across the Mesopotamian landscape, and of course they could not graze while at work. Hence their diet consisted of, or was supplemented with, barley, and reeds were also collected on a large scale to feed them.[255] As we shall see, Ur III administrators included the oxen's barley ration with the seed corn in calculating cultivation costs.

To what extent large institutions kept herds of cattle and why remains uncertain. There is little evidence for temple herds, although the iconography of the Uruk period suggests they existed. There is no doubt that many head of cattle passed through the accounts of the Ur III state at Drehem (Text 8:5), but it is possible that many of these derive from the provinces under military governorship on the north-eastern flank, where stock-breeding was especially prevalent.[256] Official accounts from Ur (from either a palace or a temple) suggest that dairy productivity was poor and, although recorded, was not of paramount concern. At Larsa the state cattle were administered by the same office as the sheep (see above), and accurate records of their milk and cheese output kept.[257] If these public herds exceeded what was needed by their ploughmen and for transport, it will have been with a view to leather production, which was an important industry, but we have no way of judging this. Nor at present can we determine the economic rationale behind a special situation in the late Old Babylonian period, when the state specialized in sesame and calf production, for conversion to commercial profit (see below, chapter 10).

The water buffalo (*Bubalus bubalis*) is at home today in most of the Near East, where there is plentiful water to suit its lifestyle, but was newly introduced in the early Islamic period. However, under the Akkad Dynasty a few seals like Figure 8:3 have representations of the water buffalo, carved with such skill that no doubt can persist as to the identification. A good case can be made for identifying the beasts in the texts as well (Text 4:4 above), and it is reasonable to assume that these animals were brought in from parts east, where they were at home, during this time of thriving contact between Mesopotamia and the Indus civilization. Unlike sesame, though, the introduction does not seem to have been a success, as the animal never again features in the texts or art.[258]

Figure 8:3 Impression from the seal of a scribe of Šar-kali-šarri, whose name is given the divine determinative. Late Akkad Dynasty (*c.* 2250 BC). The water buffalo and the *lahmum* figures have their feet on a landscape of a river flowing between mountains. (Musée du Louvre. Photo courtesy D. Collon)

Other draught animals

An embarrassing mistake made by Sir Leonard Woolley was only corrected thirty years later by the zoo-archaeologist Charles Reed peering through the glass in the British Museum: a sledge from the Early Dynastic tomb of Queen Pu-abi had been hauled by draught animals confidently identified by Woolley's workmen as donkeys. In fact, the jaw still displayed under one of the animals' copper collar was patently that of *Bos*, and her sledge must have been ox-drawn.[259] Woolley's assumption was the more understandable because the electrum rein-guide from the yokeshaft of this vehicle was cast in the shape of a charming equid, and similar equids are shown towing battle-chariots on the contemporary 'Standard of Ur' (Figure 13:1, p. 246). I use the term 'equid' deliberately, because the precise identification of these animals has provoked much discussion. For many years, during which philologists were blithely writing about 'donkeys' in early Sumer, received opinion among zoologists held that the donkey (*Equus asinus*) was introduced into Western Asia from North Africa later than the third millennium, and hence that the equids shown in Sumerian representations must be onagers (*E. hemionus* ssp.). This was despite reports that wild onagers are untameable, and another difficulty was that the cuneiform texts of the third millennium seem to mention several equid species.

A good solution to these problems has been achieved in recent years by a shift in zoological opinion, which now admits the possibility of donkeys indigenous to Western Asia, and by careful analysis of the textual references. It now seems clear that the Early Dynastic Sumerians both used domestic asses and succeeded in crossing them with wild onagers (called 'donkey of the steppe'), giving a domesticable (if sterile) offspring, a beast which combined the docility of the donkey with the strength and speed of the onager. The reason why this practice did not survive into the second millennium BC is clear: in the Ur III texts we begin to find references to small numbers of a new kind of 'donkey' – the horse, which was probably imported from the north or east. It offered all the same advantages in equal or greater measure, and the deliberate hybridization with onagers must have died out, to be survived only by the crossing of horse and donkey to get mules.[260]

Although the onager hybrid, and later the horse, could be used for agricultural purposes, their function par excellence was in the military field (Figure 13:1). Riding does not seem to have come in until the second millennium, and then it was not common; but the battle-carts of the Early Dynastic kings were towed by two or four onager hybrids. Horse-drawn chariots are a feature of the new order in the later second millennium, and do not seem to have played an important role before then, although horses were clearly highly valued, as they formed suitable ceremonial gifts for monarchs (Text 7:5, p. 146), and were used to tow chariots in temple ceremonies. Donkeys, on the other hand, were the traditional beast of burden. They hauled ploughs and carts, and donkey caravans carried the sacks of grain to Aratta over the mountain ranges, and over the Taurus to Kaneš with the tin and textiles of the Assur merchants (see chapter 11). Some of the nomadic tribes seem to have made asses their speciality (Text 4:8, p. 84), perhaps in particular the 'black asses', which were preferred by the Assur merchants.[261]

The pig

Like the goat, only more so, the domestic pig is studiously ignored by the scribes. Although archaeological evidence proves that it was a common sight on the streets of Mesopotamian cities in the third millennium, and cannot have been subject to the same strict prohibitions which exclude it from the modern Near East, it is never represented in official art (although rather fetching figurines are not uncommon, and pig-shaped pots are known)[262] and it features very rarely in the texts except as a source of fat or grease. Why the fat was thus prized remains uncertain: in Early Dynastic times it may have been a principal component of the diet, but it seems likely that if so it was displaced during the Akkadian period by sesame oil. Nevertheless, it remained a useful commodity (Text 10:2, p. 193), and the fat (admittedly from wild pigs) is still in use by the Neo-Assyrian army a thousand years later. Perhaps its hide was used, and its bristles, but we never hear of this, or of any other by-products. Although it may not have been esteemed, there is no reason to suppose that pig's flesh was taboo, as it became later: consumption of goats' meat is not mentioned either, and in at least one Early Dynastic grave at Abu Salabikh joints of pork were placed with other meat and grave goods.[263] Later hemerologies include prohibitions on eating pork, implying that it was indeed eaten in earlier times, and there can be little doubt that there were more pigs around than the written sources would lead us to expect.

Plant cultivation

The paramount place of cereal cultivation in Mesopotamian agriculture is implicitly recognized in the Sumerian composition called 'The Farmer's Instructions', which encapsulated the received wisdom of Ur III agriculture in the form of a farmer's instructions to his son – a remote forerunner of Hesiod's *Works and Days* and Vergil's *Georgica*, practical advice interspersed with reminders to carry out the proper rituals.[264] The year begins in late summer, when the field which has lain fallow the previous year needs to be prepared by breaking up the soil and irrigating it to soften the ground. There follows the sowing, first barley, then the smaller areas of emmer and wheat, and nowhere does Mesopotamian efficiency show through more transparently than here. The farmer required a seeder-plough (and the 'Farmer's Instructions' give details of how it should be maintained in good order: Text 8:7); cattle (or, in the third millennium at least, also donkeys) to haul

Text 8:7 From the 'Farmer's Instructions'
Your implements should be ready,
The parts of the yoke should be fastened,
Your new whip should hang ready from a nail;
Reattach the handle of your old whip,
It should be repaired by artisans.
The adze, the drill, and the saw, your tools, should be in good order.
Let braided thongs, straps, leather wrappings, and whips be firmly attached.
Let your sowing basket be gauged, its sides made strong.
All necessary things should be at hand. Carefully inspect your work.

(Civil n.d., lines 14–22)

the plough; seed corn; and barley for the animals to eat during the work. The seed was not broadcast, but dropped, seed by seed, in regularly distanced shallow furrows through the funnel fitted at the back of the plough (Figure 8:4). Already by the Early Dynastic texts from Lagaš – and very likely hundreds of years before that – farmers calculated with confidence the amount of seed corn needed for a given area: the distance between seeds was known, the number of furrows in a field could be varied by increasing or reducing the space between them, and on this basis the distance to be travelled by the oxen, the time taken and the seed corn and animal fodder needed could be estimated. On Ur III estates the norm was 10 furrows per nindan, giving a distance between rows of 60 cm, but this might be varied to 8 per nindan (= 75 cm between rows), the rate recommended by the 'Farmer's Instructions' and adopted as the norm in later centuries, or increased to 12 or more. The motive for these variations is hard for us to reconstruct, and involves complex interdependent considerations relating to availability of water, human and animal labour, grain for seed and fodder, and time.[265] It is clear that the prime consideration was to achieve the best 'yield rate' in relation to the seed corn expended, not the maximum per surface area of field.[266] The width between furrows promotes this in various ways: having the plants in parallel tidy rows, not haphazardly as with broadcast seed, facilitates the task of distributing irrigation water uniformly to the crop, makes weeding easier, and

Figure 8:4 Impression of cylinder seal excavated at Tell es-Suleimeh, north-east of the Jebel Hamrin on the left bank of the River Diyala, ED III (*c.* 2400 BC). Lower register: offering scene. Upper register: ploughing scene, in which the person behind the plough is filling the seed-funnel. (IM 83755, Al-Gailani Werr 1983, 49. Photo: courtesy Iraq Museum, Baghdad)

Figure 8:5 Field in Eastern Anatolia sown by seeder-plough in the 1960s. Note the straight rows, wide gaps between them, and the thick growth of each plant ('tillering'). (After J.G. Ross *et al.*, *Wheat Production in Eastern Anatolia. Investigations at Atatürk University, Erzurum, Turkey,* 1967, Figure 9)

gives each plant the best chance to bear. It is significant that a similarly wide stance is found today in regions using a traditional seeder-plough, as attested in eastern Turkey, for instance (Figure 8:5).

Harvest

Between seed-time and harvest the principal activities on the farm were weeding[267] and irrigating, on which see below. Harvest in South Iraq falls today in late April and May, with barley ripening earlier than wheat, and a slight difference between one end of the plain and the other. In any one area though, most fields ripen together, and it is the busiest time of the farmer's year. Manpower is always at its shortest. The large institutions will have mobilized all the population over whom they had rights to come and harvest temple and palace fields, leaving any private land to be reaped whenever and by whomever was available. One symptom of this shortage is the practice of making a loan conditional on the debtor's helping to harvest the creditor's fields, obviously at the expense of his own (Text 8:8; see p. 185). Once the crop was cut and stacked, it had to be threshed and

> **Text 8:8** Corn loan with harvester clause
> Sin-idinnam and Taribat-Sin, the sons of Aham-nirši, have received from Taribum, son of Ibnatum, 240 litres of grain (measured by) the *sūtum* of Šamaš, for harvesting. At the time of harvest he(!) will serve as harvesters like those to right and to left. If he does not serve, (he will be penalized) according to the ordinance of the king.
> (Two witnesses; 13th day 12th month Year 5 of Ammi-ditana)
>
> (After Lautner 1936, 152–3)

winnowed, and it was at this stage, when the heaps of grain lay in the open on the threshing-floors, and before transport to storage, that accounts had to be settled, old debts paid off and new ones incurred. In a rural community debts are mostly incurred in the lean months immediately before the harvest, and are to be repaid once harvest is in. Principally, though, it was the moment for settling accounts between landowner and tenant (see p. 185). As with animal husbandry, society also has conventions governing conditions of cultivation, some of which were inspired by a concern for social justice, and recognized 'acts of god': the Code of Hammurapi waives a debtor's rent in cases of crop failure, and prescribes the division of liability when a flood or rainstorm destroys the crop. Similar provisions were not new, and escape clauses of this kind are already envisaged in Ur III leases from Nippur.[268]

With ordinary loan repayments there was interest to calculate. Since the price of grain will have risen as supplies became scarcer, and fallen again with the harvest complete, some element of interest was eminently reasonable in commercial terms, estimated in silver – but for the poorer households, every litre of grain borrowed before the harvest reduced the following year's income by more than a litre. Rates of interest varied widely, and in fact in the Old Babylonian period two different kinds of loans existed, the *hubullûm*, or interest-bearing loan, and the *hubuttatum* or interest-free loan; another loan was called a 'favour' (*tadmiqtum*), and, although all these were regularly recorded on contracts, it is very likely that there was a strong social context governing the use of each type and determining between whom the contracts might be made.[269] One interesting archive was excavated in a small temple in the ancient city at Khafajah: here it is clear that the temple owned supplies of grain in different spots in the hinterland which it was ready to lend out to private clientele on favourable terms (cf. chapter 6).[270] In general, though, it is clear how 'economic coercion' operated even where no formal social dependence was recognized: in a downward spiral the mere fact of being in debt reduces the chances of paying it off, both by impairing the family's own cultivation by diverting its labour to the creditor's field at the optimum time for reaping, and by deducting interest in addition to capital from the family's grain supply for the following year.[271]

Other crops

Although many species of plant listed in lexical and medical texts were known to the Mesopotamians, any real knowledge of the food crops is limited to those for which legal contracts were drawn up, either between two individuals or between an individual and an institution, and those listed in administrative documents by the bureaucrats of temple or palace. It is difficult to know if the great range of plants recorded in the Ur III texts reflects a real expansion in the crops grown, by comparison with earlier (and indeed later) times, or whether – as seems more likely – the difference is merely in the recording. The most important crops apart from cereals were pulses, principally lentils and some species of pea or bean, various kinds of onions and garlic, flax, and sesame. All these might be cultivated in fields and the details recorded especially by Ur III scribes tell us something about the amounts sown and harvested, and when and where. The pulses and *Linum* (probably for flax more than linseed) were winter crops like the cereals. Onions were planted after the cereals, perhaps in December or January as today, and harvested before them, thus providing a useful interim activity.[272]

A great many other vegetables, fruits and spices were also grown, few of which can be confidently identified: again, more assiduous collection of archaeological evidence will help us in future. The Sumerian kitchen garden certainly had cucumbers, root vegetables and lettuces, and their orchards included pomegranates, apples, figs and vines. Sometimes these different crops could share the same ground. Modern Iraqi date groves are often interplanted with lower fruit trees – citrus, pomegranate and apple – and below this double canopy a third level of vegetables. This practice goes back into the Early Dynastic period, and in Ur III times figs, apples and pomegranates are mentioned mixed with dates, as well as a mixed date palm and tamarisk plantation, which can also be paralleled in modern south Iraq.[273] In the third millennium, stands of timber were also an important feature of the landscape. The principal indigenous trees are tamarisk, which can grow to a height of several metres, poplar and willow, all attested in charcoal remnants from Sumerian sites, and methodically exploited. More unexpectedly, we find from the texts that pine was extensively grown, perhaps especially for boat-making (Text 11:9, p. 218). In the absence of any archaeological evidence for this, the identification of the tree *ašuhum* as pine (*Pinus halepensis*) may be thought uncertain, but everything seems to point that way.[274]

As with the identification of some of the animals, this is only one of many 'best guesses' with which we have to live. All the various lines of approach need to be co-ordinated: botanical, agricultural, geographical and historical considerations all need to be taken into account and matched with the written sources. Etymology can help, but is also deceptive: no one doubts that *kisibaru* is the same word as modern Arabic *kuzbara* ('coriander'), or *kamiššaru* as *kummithra* ('pear'), but there are plenty of instances of words being transferred from one Linnaean species to another with no regard for the sensibilities of the lexicographer. The kind of problem we face may best be illustrated by the case of sesame. This is partly because of an academic debate which was started in the 1960s by the founding father of Near Eastern archaeobotany, Hans Helbaek. Although sesame, a word we have borrowed ultimately from Classical Greek, is agreed to be etymologically related to the Akkadian word *šamaššammū*, and this word had hence been not unreasonably translated 'sesame' by Assyriologists, Helbaek pointed out that no sesame seeds had yet been recovered from archaeological contexts until long after the Akkadian language had died out, and so he proposed that this plant, which we know from the texts to have been a major source of culinary oil, was in fact linseed – flax seeds being well attested in the Mesopotamian region for thousands of years before. The reactions of cuneiform philologists to this proposal ranged from rejection to conviction, but in fact it can now be confidently forgotten, since the Sumerian documents show that, like sesame today, **še.giš.ià** was planted in early summer and harvested in the autumn, whereas flax (**gu**) is found being grown as expected in the winter months. Hence some other explanation of its archaeological absence is needed: one part of the reason may have to do with the nature of sesame seeds and their treatment, which may reduce their chances of survival in archaeological contexts, but another factor is undoubtedly that *šamaššammū*, or rather its Sumerian equivalent **še.giš.ià**, is not mentioned in texts before the Akkadian period. This strongly suggests that the plant was newly introduced at about this time, probably from the Indus, where it is attested archaeologically, in the course of the lively trade between the two areas which may also have brought the water buffalo to Mesopotamia (see p. 164). Once adopted by the Mesopotamians, it remained popular, and in his description of Babylonia Herodotus wonders at the sesame plants and says that he 'will not say how high the tree-sized plants grow, being well aware that those who have not been to Babylonia would not believe me'. The principal use of the plant was to produce a fine oil, and this rapidly became a staple of their diet to the extent that in the Late Old Babylonian period commercialized production of sesame was one of the economic mainstays of the palace administration.[275]

One reason why sesame was so successful may have been its growing season: it was planted in the second month of the year (i.e. April/May) and harvested some three months later, so that as today it grows right through the heat of the summer, a feature shared by millet, which was probably also grown already.[276] In this way it made maximum use of labour resources during what was otherwise an off-season for work in the fields. Whether it was equally efficient in terms of land use is uncertain, because as far as I know there is no way of telling whether sesame was grown in fields given to cereals in other years, being planted immediately after the harvest. What is known is that a regular biennial fallow system was in operation in the third millennium.[277] This is the normal practice in the area today, and is essential to enable the land to recover nutrients by growing weed crops and from animal dung (see p. 159), and to avoid the saline effects of constant irrigation and evaporation. The texts have little if anything to say about manuring or other forms of fertilization. This is probably only because it was no concern of the official scribes, whereas the rotation of crops, under which a year of legumes restores nitrogen to the land and enriches it for another year of cereals, is not attested and seems unlikely to have been practised (being indeed not used in the area even today).[278]

Further reading

The *Bulletin on Sumerian Agriculture* 1–3 deals successively with cereals, legumes, oil-seeds and other vegetable crops, and fruit trees. Forthcoming volumes will cover trees and timber, and sheep and goats. For the agricultural cycle B. Landsberger's article on the seasons in *Journal of Near Eastern Studies* 8 (1949) remains the starting point (in German); see now LaPlaca and Powell 1990 for the Pre-Sargonic period. The date palm is covered by Landsberger 1967b. For equids (horses, donkeys, mules and onagers) see the contributions of Zarins and Postgate to H.-P. Uerpmann and R.H. Meadow (eds), *Equids in the Ancient World* (Beihefte zum Tübinger Atlas des Vorderen Orients, A.19/1, 1986).

9

Water and land

There is no denying that several of the world's pristine civilizations developed in environments similar to Mesopotamia where the production of food surpluses, and hence the emergence of a wealthy, stratified society, was dependent on irrigated agriculture. From his viewpoint in China, this led C. Wittfogel to attribute the increased complexity of such societies to the managerial imperatives imposed by the need to organize a large-scale irrigation system. This is a seductive hypothesis, and we shall see that in Mesopotamia large institutions could profit from the regime of the rivers; but it is no longer fashionable to see the need to administer irrigation as the chief formative influence – the 'prime mover' – converting a society of villages to one of cities, and indeed closer inspection of the third-millennium evidence does suggest that the irrigation system was in the hands of the traditional local authorities, not the creation of a newer political order.

The dependence of the water supply on the changing river regime, at one level, and on human organization at another, creates over the long term an impermanence in land conditions. Nevertheless, it does not reduce the importance of land as the primary 'means of production', merely increases its impact on the processes of social change. Athough much valuable detail has been recovered from the texts about the forms of land tenure and procedures through which changes in the system were made, these are no more than the framework within which major changes in property rights were at work, and basic questions remain to be solved before we can understand what was really going on.

The southern plain: using the rivers

The two rivers of Mesopotamia, Tigris and Euphrates, bear today the names they had as far back as we can read the texts, and doubtless long before. Within the Holocene their presence has dominated the land. As we can tell from texts, from archaeology and from geology, they have changed their courses, they have branched and rejoined, and they have no doubt also changed their rates and volumes of flow (which we cannot document directly), because of climatic changes and the rise and fall of the sea level in the Gulf (see chapter 1). Nevertheless, their presence has been constant and, whatever the uncertainties, it is impossible that the climate or the river regime have changed so much in the interval that the situation in the fourth to second millennia BC was significantly different. The rivers give drinking water for people and animals, irrigate the vegetation, and create a cool green world infinitely enticing by comparison with the bare lands away from the river; but they also impose their own terms. As we have already seen in chapter 1, agriculture (and hence settled life) is impossible without enough water for irrigation, and those who choose to live in the alluvial plains have to adapt to the regime of Tigris and Euphrates.

The obvious place to live in southern Iraq is close to a river. In primeval days sedentary life must have been confined to a meandering strip of cultivation bordering the main river courses, villagers only venturing east or west when rains or floods had covered the plains with fresh pasturage. It often comes as a surprise to visitors to find that in the south the land between the rivers ('Mesopotamia' in its strict sense) is desert or semi-desert wherever their waters do not reach. With population growth, expansion up and down stream will have become increasingly difficult, as distances became greater and neighbours' interests clashed. The obvious strategy is to move the area of exploitation sideways, and this can be done in two ways: by leading smaller water courses off each bank of the river at successive points, or by taking new channels off one bank well upstream to run roughly parallel and create a whole new strip. The early stages of this process are lost in prehistory, and because of alluviation it is unlikely that we shall ever recover enough of the Ubaid settlement patterns to illustrate the development of the Mesopotamian irrigation system. Site survey has suggested that adaptations of the natural system into localized branching networks were the norm well into the Early Dynastic. Only in the middle of the third millennium were 'the multiple, small shifting canals' (of late Uruk, Jemdet Nasr and Early Dynastic I times) 'consolidated into a much reduced number of larger and more permanent courses' (Adams and Nissen 1972, 38).

In the central plain virtually all such intervention seems to have concentrated on the Euphrates, and most of the early settlement to have depended on Euphrates water. There are various reasons for this. First, it is a slower stream, carrying less water and therefore easier to control. Then it is higher than the Tigris at the point where the two rivers enter the flood plain, hence offering a steeper gradient to those wishing to use its water. From earliest times the river tended to split into two or more branches shortly after entering the flood plain: recent research has identified the levées of two early branches close to ancient Sippar, and from historical references and the location of contemporary sites these can be reconstructed further downstream in the central area.[279] Finally, soil scientists have established that the silts brought down by the Euphrates are richer in chemical nutrients than the Tigris silts, and under controlled modern conditions have given 20 per cent better results to the farmer.[280]

How then does the farmer go about exploiting the rivers? Although the land looks quite flat, this is deceptive. As it sheds its load of silt a river will create a raised strip of land within which it flows, known to geographers as a levée. This is relatively steep closest to the river, flattening out with distance, but is scarcely perceptible at the best of times, and it is only by meticulous survey that it can be detected. If, as sometimes happens, the river abandons one of its channels altogether, the levée remains, and the old Euphrates' courses near Sippar have been mapped in this way.[281] These levées are important to the farmer. They are conveniently close to the river itself, and the marginally greater slope improves the drainage of the land, avoiding the saline consequences of standing water. The soil is also better because the levées are composed of the coarsest fraction of the river's silt load, which it drops first as it floods, which is more permeable (and contains more nutrients)

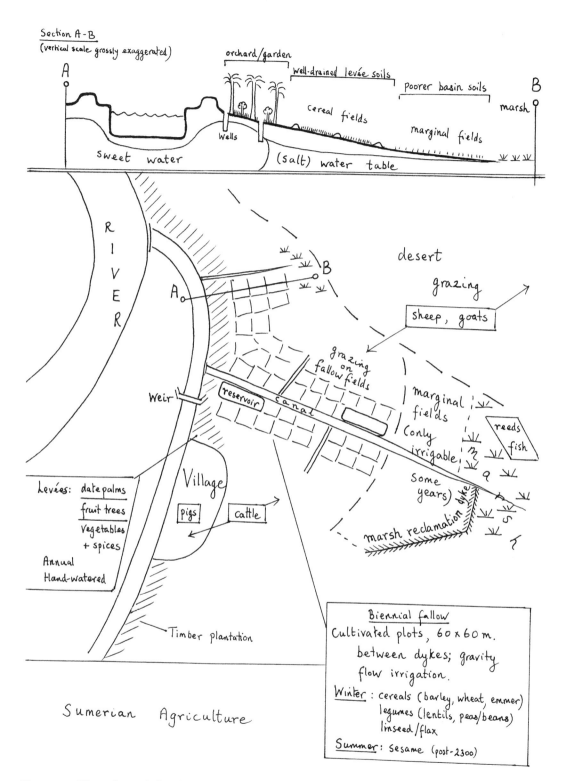

Section A-B
(vertical scale grossly exaggerated)

A

orchard/garden

Well-drained levée soils

Poorer basin soils

B

marsh

cereal fields

Wells

sweet water

(salt) water table

marginal fields

RIVER

B

A

desert

grazing

sheep, goats

grazing
on
fallow fields

Weir

reservoir   canal

marginal
fields

(only
irrigable

some
years)

reeds

fish

marsh reclamation dyke

Levées: date palms

fruit trees

Vegetables
+ spices

Village

pigs   Cattle

Annual
Hand-watered

Timber plantation

Sumerian   Agriculture

Biennial fallow
Cultivated plots, 60 x 60 m.
between dykes; gravity
flow irrigation.
Winter: cereals (barley, wheat, emmer)
legumes (lentils, peas/beans)
linseed/flax
Summer: sesame (post-2300)

Figure 9:1 Hypothetical sketch of an agricultural cell in South Mesopotamia.

than the finer silt which is carried further out into the basin. Finally, beneath and spreading out each side of the river bed there is a pocket of its own fresh water within the surrounding water-table which can be reached by wells sunk through the levée (see Figure 9:1).

The South Mesopotamian farmers were well aware of the varying quality of their soils and of the micro-relief of their land, and took them into account to make most efficient use of their resources (Text 9:1). Although the fall in the ground is imperceptible to the

---

Text 9:1 Summary of a land survey from the reign of Šulgi

Total: 94.1.2 $\frac{1}{2}$ **iku** – good
Total: 9.2.1   **iku** – middling
Total: 0.0.3 $\frac{1}{2}$ **iku** – middling, grass
Total: 28.0.0 $\frac{3}{4}$ **iku** – middling, empty
Total: 46.1.1 $\frac{1}{2}$ **iku** – ploughed, grain did not grow
Total: 3.2.3 $\frac{1}{2}$ **iku** – bridge
Total: 2.1.1 $\frac{1}{4}$ **iku** – good, brought out of the water
Total: 114.1.2 $\frac{1}{2}$ **iku** – medium
Total: 4.0.4   **iku** – flooded
Total: 52.2.5 $\frac{1}{2}$ **iku** – poor
Total: 22.2.4   **iku** – canal
Total: 0.0.3 $\frac{3}{4}$ **iku** – wells
Total: 2.0.3   **iku** – village
Total: 0.2.4   **iku** – orchard
Total: 4.0.2   **iku** – (ancient) mound
Total: 4.1.4 $\frac{1}{2}$ **iku** – dyke

Land surveyed in Girsu: Lu-Nin-ilduma and Ur-Lama surveyed. Under the supervision of Inim-Šara, the land-registrar.

(After Pettinato 1977, 73–4)

---

eye, water, once let onto the fields, will show the slope of the land and also reveal any minor unevennesses, enabling the cultivator to plan his water management. Date palms flourish best with their roots in water, and vegetables are less tolerant of drying conditions than cereal crops. It is thus natural that along the levées one finds a concentration of orchards and kitchen gardens, which would have constant access to water from the water course or wells, while the less demanding cereal crops are elbowed out further down the levées. The prime objective of the irrigation system was therefore to secure a dependable supply of water to the cereal fields, but this involved the solution of a number of associated problems for the irrigator which were of equal importance. Four principal concerns can be identified:

1 *supply* – to get the water to his land;
2 *storage* – to hold it there for as long as he wants it;
3 *drainage* – to dispose of the water when he no longer requires it; and
4 *protection* – to keep unwanted water away.

It is clear, then, that the problem is as much one of control as it is of acquisition of water supplies, and in fact the administrative concerns of the institutions seem to have been quite as much with storage and control as with supply. Let us consider these concerns in order.

Supply

Water for gardens or small areas can be taken by hand from wells or streams, and there is textual evidence for this practice in the third millennium,[282] but for cereal crops the most effective system is 'gravity flow irrigation'. Whether the predominant pattern of channels bringing water to the fields is formed of successively smaller branching canals, or aligned along major channels parallel to the main river courses, two controls are essential, 'outlets' and 'regulators'. Outlets, or sluices, need be no more than a hole opened in the side of a canal bank to divert water into a distributary channel, and provided they are watched need pose no major problems. Regulators are needed to arrest the entire main stream so as to raise the water to the necessary level. In the last century and probably in ancient times temporary barrages created from reeds were used for this purpose, but an efficient regime requires a permanent installation and there is both textual and archaeological evidence for solid structures of baked brick and bitumen (Figure 9:2; Text 9:2).

Figure 9:2 View and plan of baked-brick canal regulator excavated at Girsu. For interpretation on plan, see Pemberton *et al.* 1988, 221. (Parrot 1948, 213, Planche XXIVb)

Text 9:2 From brick inscription of Enmetena of Lagaš
When Ningirsu ordered his regular offerings in the temple Girnun and determined Enmetena's destiny in the temple Eninnu, and Nanše looked at him approvingly from Sirara, for Ningirsu Enmetena built the regulator of the Lummagim-du Canal, from 648,000 baked bricks and 1840 standard **gur** [≃ 2650 hl] of bitumen.

[Baked brick and bitumen are waterproof materials suitable for use in hydraulic projects]

(After Cooper 1986, 66–7 q.v.)

The Mesopotamian farmer has a problem not shared with his counterpart on the Nile. The amount of water available is more critical in the autumn, when the fields need to be flooded to prepare the ground for ploughing and sowing, and for the periodic irrigations over the winter, than in spring, when the cereal crops are fast ripening. Unfortunately, the two rivers are at their lowest in the autumn, and begin to reach their peak at just the stage when the crops no longer need to be watered. Hence all efforts must be made to use the water in the river and its distributary canals efficiently. Access to the canal was of course essential for each cultivator, and inheritance texts show how carefully water rights needed to be defined when a paternal estate was being divided between brothers.[283] Conditions today suggest that there will have been periods when no water was available to the individual farmer but, unlike vegetables, cereal crops do not require daily watering, and the rotation of water supply to all those who need it gives four to six irrigations as the crops are growing, which is ample. It is obvious that some social organization was needed to co-ordinate this rota, and it may have been the task of the *gugallum*, usually translated 'canal inspector' or the like. He was probably responsible also for the maintenance of the canals, a job which is carried out in the summer after the harvest: reeds can clog the stream

Figure 9:3 Disused canal in southern Iraq to show height of banks of spoil each side.

in slower-flowing sections and must be removed, and the silts must be thrown out from the bed of the canal, creating steep banks each side (Figure 9:3). The importance of this work is reflected in the mathematical problems calculating the amount of barley rations required for the clearance of a stretch of canal of a given length to a specified depth.[284]

It is important to consider the scale of organization required for different kinds of irrigation project. Although the institutional administrative documents mention canals being cleaned, or as topographical features, there is hardly any mention of digging such canals afresh. The creation of a new canal, of the order of 2 to 3 m in width, with its associated regulator, would have been a major investment of effort, and must always have been a collaborative venture, undertaken jointly by one or usually more villages. Larger projects, such as the construction of a massive regulator, were of sufficient importance to be celebrated in the formal inscriptions of the Pre-Sargonic **ensis** of Lagaš (Text 9:2).[285] Really major schemes, involving the redirection of the Euphrates or Tigris, are mentioned in royal inscriptions and date formulae only after the Pre-Sargonic period, and presuppose political control of a large area (Text 9:3). Projects spanning more than one of the original

Text 9:3 Royal canal digging: inscription of Rim-Sin I of Larsa

The eternal water, heritage of the Land, the water which the Tigris and Euphrates had brought from of old, the spring flood which will never fail, the Mami-šarrat canal, the canal of abundance of the Land, carried away half the waters of the Tigris and Euphrates and poured them into the sea.

The lord Nunamnir, whose word is important, turned towards the shepherd who pleases his heart: having called me joyfully, he decreed a good fate for me. Enlil, the Great Mountain, gave me the great mission of digging a canal to bring abundant waters to Sumer and Akkad, to make their extensive fields grow the dappled barley, to let the orchard wells increase the [...] of honey and wine, and to let their marshes joyfully provide fish.

... on the banks I carried out the rituals. The towns and villages, the numerous people whose shepherdship Enlil has given me, having assembled them from top to bottom (of the Land), I made them work by my great power. I fashioned the (canal's) two banks like awe-inspiring mountains. I established abundance at its mouth, and its tail I extended. I made the fresh grass thrive on its banks. I called the canal Tuqmat-Erra, and thus restored the eternal waters of the Tigris and Euphrates.

(Sollberger and Kupper 1971, 205–6)

city-states depended on the administrative unification of the plain, or on the collaborative subordination of local interests to the larger common benefit. It will be obvious, and is a point to which we shall recur, that this has serious implications for agriculture when the fragile political order is shattered.

What applies to construction also applies to maintenance of the system. Both rivers and ditches rapidly silt up, and therefore someone has to organize clearance, and has to control the number of field outlets so that the water level is maintained to the end of the system. This requires a co-ordinated approach between those taking water from each stream, and as we have mentioned was probably controlled by a village or district official called *gugallum*. Despite the evident importance of his role, this official is only rarely mentioned in administrative texts. Presumably this is because the state, as opposed to the village administration, did not need to interfere with locally based organization of this kind. It is hardly necessary to underline the relevance of this conclusion to theories about the interaction of hydraulic control and the political order.[286]

Storage

When the water is available it can be allowed to flood the field completely at the beginning of the season, and each plot is surrounded by a low field bank to allow the level to rise, and to hold the water in the furrows later in the season when the crops are already growing. One element of the irrigation system is called a **nag-ku(d)** in the third millennium, and seems to have consisted of narrow basins constructed alongside the canals, some being 90 m or more in length and over 2 m in depth. So far most scholars agree, but their purpose is more controversial. They are usually considered to be 'reservoirs', and this remains the most obvious interpretation, although there are various difficulties. The **nag-ku(d)**s recorded for Ur III Lagaš and Drehem are considerably smaller (e.g. 15 to 255 cu. m) than those at contemporary Umma (e.g. 2700 cu. m), suggesting a different purpose.[287] In either case, simple calculations make it clear that the capacity of reservoirs of this size would not have been sufficient to make a substantial contribution to the general cereal regime, and the rate of evaporation in southern Iraq means that they would not have served to retain quantities of water for other purposes over the summer months, for use when the river levels had dropped in the autumn. Perhaps, then, the water was intended for garden crops, especially vegetables, which could not tolerate the ten-day to two-week intervals between canal irrigations imposed by the need for a communal schedule for distribution. At other points we know that gardeners were regularly involved in drawing water from wells and perhaps from the canals or river by hand, and this task was a long and tedious one, as evidenced by the fact that in Pre-Sargonic Lagaš it was entrusted to the blind.[288] Whether or not this is the correct explanation of the **nag-ku(d)**, it remains the case that the third- and second-millennium farmers invested much labour in the creation and maintenance of these constructions, and we must presume that they contributed significantly to the maximal exploitation of the available resources, despite the fact that nothing comparable exists today or is apparently attested for South Iraq in Islamic times.

Drainage

Anyone who has been in South Iraq in the winter will be aware that, however difficult it is to get water *to* the land, it is just as difficult to get it *off* the land. The surface of the plain 400 km from the head of the Gulf is less than 20 m above sea level, and the complex history of each area means that it is not a single regular slope, but divided into a patchwork of old and new canal banks and basins. If surplus irrigation water is not drained from the land, the water table will rise, bringing with it salts which are pulled to the surface by capillary action and gradually render the soil useless to the farmer. As water dries from the land the salts left on the surface gleam like snow, and even today they may be collected and marketed for culinary use by rural families as an extra source of income. The Babylonians were well aware of the significance of such extreme salinity, since one of the poetical images for describing a famine is the whiteness of the fields, and already in Early Dynastic times land surveys refer to areas of salt (Figure 9:4). Since the 1950s an influential theory promoted by Jacobsen and Adams suggested that increasing salinity in the south was responsible for an apparent shift away from wheats in favour of barley over the second part of the third millennium, and later, in the eighteenth to seventeenth centuries BC for an almost complete abandonment of the major urban centres in the south. While this cannot easily be disproved, a closer examination of the evidence fails to substantiate their case in detail, and it is doubtful whether there was such a general rise in the levels of

Figure 9:4 Saline soil in southern Iraq today.

salinity; but this does not diminish the certainty that saline fields were a problem at a local level, of which the farmers must have been well conscious and against which they must surely have developed a strategy. Part of this strategy is the fallow system, but unfortunately there is nothing in our sources to tell us if the farmers were also aware of the paramount importance of field drainage, and if so, how they attempted to achieve it.[289]

Protection

The constant reference in law codes and legal documents to crop loss through flooding shows that this was a significant risk to the farmer. High water comes in April in the Tigris, and about a month later in the Euphrates, which has further to come from the melting snows. The water level of the rivers on their levées may be well above the surrounding plain, and, once it escapes, the flatness of the terrain means that huge expanses can be drowned. The natural regime of rivers in the alluvium would yield a meandering course, and aerial survey has revealed ancient meanders on the modern land surface which probably belong to a fourth-millennium branch of the Euphrates.[290] However, the natural shifting of the rivers is not convenient to the farmer, and more recent water-courses are confined by man's attentions to much straighter lines, although even so land sale documents have to allow for the possibility that the river will eat away or add to the plots being sold.[291] When the flood waters come, they could only be helped on their way by ensuring that all regulators were fully opened – as described in the story of the great flood (Text 9:4) – and keeping a close watch on the sluices and other potential points of weakness.

Text 9:4 The Epic of Gilgamesh: the gods bring the Flood
Just as dawn began to glow there arose from the horizon a black cloud. Adad the Storm-God rumbled within it, before him went Šullat and Haniš, heralds advancing over mountain and plain. Erragal pulled up the poles, and as he goes, Ninurta lets the (water) flow through the regulators.

(Tablet XI, after Gallery Kovacs 1989, 100)

There was of course a lesser, but less seasonal, danger. The carelessness of a single farmer in controlling the flow of water from the canal could easily have a disastrous effect on neighbouring fields, washing away the elaborate furrow system and quite likely uprooting young crops (Text 9:5). All these problems could be contained by earthen dykes, and the administrative documents offer such plentiful documentation of communal labour on the construction and maintenance of these earthworks that it is clear that they were

Text 9:5 The Code of Hammurapi, §§55–6
If a man has opened his channel for irrigation, and has been negligent and allowed the water to wash away a neighbour's field, he shall pay grain equivalent to (the crops of) his neighbours.

If a man has released the water and allowed the water to wash away the works [i.e. furrows and soil preparation] on a neighbour's field, he shall pay 10 **gur** of grain per **bur**.

one of the most important components of the system. They were found both along the banks of the canals, the natural consequence of excavating and re-excavating the channels, and out on the fields where they were needed to contain the flood water on plots to be soaked and to keep it from where it was not wanted. The basic unit of surface area, called in Akkadian an *ikum* and measuring about 60 × 60 m, is related to the Sumerian word for a dyke, suggesting that this was the normal size for a dyke-enclosed plot. Such banks need not have been massive, but the data of the agricultural labour texts reveal that there were also much bigger banks, which presumably enclosed larger-scale water management units and demarcated them from their neighbours. The ultimate dykes were between state and state, and it was along a border-dyke, which had an important practical as well as symbolic function in separating Umma's land and water from those of Lagaš, that Me-salim fixed their boundary and erected his stelae. Another major project is mentioned by Ur-Nammu, who heaped up a dyke about 45 km long to hold off the marsh waters and reclaim the land for agriculture.[292]

Agriculture and society

The possession of cultivable land is fundamental to the structure of Mesopotamian society, and we are fortunate to have a great deal of documentary information on the subject. However, although much detail is clear, it is not at all easy to reconstruct a general picture. For one thing, the sources themselves derive directly from the administration of land, and hence reflect some parts of the system better than others: they inform us of matters which concern the large institutions or the law, but not of private, unwritten practices and transactions. Then there is the conflict between the ideal and the actual: laws are hard to change, and society frequently finds ways of adjusting practice to its needs without abandoning legal forms appropriate to earlier regimes. Land tenure in ancient lands is usually a palimpsest: old systems do not die, they fade away, submerged by reform and environmental change, as the relative proportions of different sorts of holding shift. Hence fundamental changes in the structure of society may only become apparent if we have quantitative, rather than qualitative, data from which to work. The sources may hold clues, but research has not yet progressed this far.

Private land

These problems are naturally at their most acute when dealing with land owned by individuals or families. Although it is no longer thought that there was no private land in the Pre-Sargonic state of Lagaš, the complete absence of field sale documents from the Ur III period has led some scholars to deny the existence of private field ownership at that time too. Since private land is clearly present before this, that would imply that the Ur III state 'nationalized' the entire country, which is improbable, and others have more plausibly interpreted this absence rather as an embargo on land sale, and have observed that in the south of the country, in the archives from Ur and Larsa, land sales are extremely rare in the Isin–Larsa period as well.[293] In interpreting the negative evidence of the sources there are two problems: the biases in their recovery and their silence on the general issues at stake. Thus in Ur III times the only substantial group of private documents is from Nippur, while from the Old Babylonian period we hardly have any public documentation relating to land outside Hammurapi's correspondence with his officials at Larsa, which makes it very difficult to compare the two systems. Even if we accept that virtually no land sales took place in the Ur III and Isin–Larsa period, that would not have to imply that the state had arrogated all land to itself, or even that land sale was forbidden, since there could be social rather than legal reasons. Even in the later Old Babylonian period, house and garden sales are more frequent than field sales; perhaps this is because selling one's cereal fields was only a last resort, but there may well have been traditional restraints on field sale which derive more from family structure than from government decree. And even if there was a legal or administrative embargo, what was the situation in practice? Land sale was technically forbidden at Nuzi in the later second millennium, but in fact it was regularly accomplished through a legal fiction by which the purchaser was adopted by the original owner.

We have already seen in chapter 5 that the nominal ownership of land could be vested in kin groups rather than individuals, and inheritance documents from the Old Babylonian period do not always include land holdings among the divided property, suggesting they were treated separately. At Nippur in the Old Babylonian period we have no documents that definitely record the sale of land outside the patrilinear descent group.[294] Kinship groups at Ur jointly rent fields and date groves at Ur.[295] In the Old Babylonian period at Dilbat and at Sippar there is considerable evidence for a family or a *nadītum* building up large holdings of agricultural land which can only have represented a business venture, but in general we do not know enough about society, especially in the third millennium, or about the background to individual transactions to be sure of the significance of land sales.[296] It seems a reasonable assumption that a family only parted with all its land under duress, though one can imagine situations in which a household found itself with more land than it could manage. The massive land sales recorded on the Obelisk of Maništušu and at Girsu in the Old Akkadian period seem likely to reflect political duress, but historians tend to assume that economic duress is usually responsible.[297] We have already seen the downward spiral of debt for the rural poor (p. 170), and the debts of one year can lead to pledge of the family's fields in another, followed by compulsion to sell their land, and ending with them as share-croppers on their own former property. This is a situation which can be documented in Nuzi and Assyria slightly later in the second millennium, but it is not clear if it applies so generally to early Mesopotamia, partly because the incidence of pledge seems to be less.[298]

If sales were normally forced on the owner by his poverty, it may partly explain why 'the price of land was extremely low at all times', but other reasons are also needed. Diakonoff's explanation is that it was not worth a purchaser's paying more than three times the value of a piece of land's annual crop, because he could get as much by loaning the amount of the payment at $33\frac{1}{3}$ per cent interest; but we cannot be sure if this rational explanation ignores factors less obvious to us.[299] Sometimes perhaps the bare formalities recorded in the sale documents do not give us the whole of the economic nature of the transaction (e.g. informal payments not included in the purchase price as such, community or state obligations tied to the land, or technical aspects such as access to irrigation). Also, during the Old Babylonian period at least, such sales resulting from indebtedness might be annulled by the promulgation of an *andurārum* edict (see below, chapter 10).[300]

Lease of land

The infrequency of land sale naturally meant that any imbalance between manpower and fields to be cultivated had to be corrected by temporary arrangements. The initiative for such a contract might come from the land-owner, such as the wealthy *nadītum* who wished to capitalize on her estates, or from the small farmer who – whether landless because newly arrived on the scene or recently obliged to sell his own fields – needed a minimum subsistence plot.[301] In a society sufficiently concerned for natural justice to accept the government's annulment of crippling indebtedness, it is not surprising to find that rental conditions were quite standardized in Old Babylonian times, and that at least an attempt was made by Hammurapi to regulate the demands of landlords.[302]

Land was often rented for two to three years at a time, and the rental payments can be prescribed in a variety of ways: the tenant might pay either a share of the crop or an amount agreed in advance (an absolute figure or so much per hectare); some contracts simply specify that the payment will be 'like neighbouring fields'.[303] A payment was probably also needed towards the communal expenses of maintaining the irrigation system, perhaps in the earliest times a kid, but later in silver.[304] Special arrangements were accepted where a tenant took on previously uncultivated land, a three-year contract being normal, with more favourable terms than usual to compensate the tenant for the additional labour. Similar guidelines are included in the Code of Hammurapi (and before him, of Lipit-Ištar) concerning the lease of land for new date plantations, in cases where the tenant has failed to carry out the work as anticipated (Text 9:6).[305]

Text 9:6 The Code of Hammurapi, §§60–1
If a man has given a field to a gardener to plant an orchard, and the gardener planted the orchard, he shall grow the orchard for four years, and in the fifth year the owner of the orchard and the gardener shall divide equally, the owner of the orchard choosing his share.

If the gardener did not complete planting the field but left bare ground, they shall put the bare ground into his share.

For tenant and landlord alike the grain harvest in April–May is the critical event of the agricultural year. There is a chronic shortage of manpower, and this is another way in which the downward spiral of the indebted farmer can be accelerated: one of the conditions of loan texts in the Old Babylonian period (and we cannot know how much further back in time the practice goes) is that the borrower commits himself to work for a specified number of days on the creditor's fields. In this way the wealthy can ensure that their crops are harvested at the optimum time, increasing their economic advantage over the less successful sector of the rural community. The final scene of the drama is played out on the threshing floors, where the year's harvest is standing ready for transport to store. This is the moment for the division of the crop in the agreed proportions, usually one-third to the landlord and two-thirds to the tenant, although rates of one quarter and a half are also attested.[306]

Where the agreement had specified a share of the crop, there was a natural obligation on the tenant not to reduce the landlord's income by indolence or incompetence, and, as with the relationship between shepherd and owner, society had established certain conventions governing this. The allocation of losses sustained by storm or flood, enshrined in §§45–6 of the Code of Hammurapi, was already an eventuality dealt with by contracts in the Ur III Dynasty.[307] In this case too the law would estimate the theoretical yield by comparison with the neighbouring fields. Clearly there remained a danger of collusion between neighbours, especially in the case of large estates with multiple small tenants, and the temptation to dissemble the true level of the harvest must have been hard to resist and impossible to control. Against this background we can understand the practice attested in northern Babylonia of using an oath by a peripatetic divine symbol to guarantee the tenants' claim of honesty.[308]

Institutional estates

This practice was also adopted by the officials of the Šamaš Temple at Sippar when dealing with their tenants, which brings us to consider the temple and palace estates. The classic description of a Sumerian city-state goes back to Father Anton Deimel, who observed that the lands of the Bau Temple at Girsu were divided into three categories depending on who actually undertook their cultivation. There was the 'property of the **en**', cultivated directly by staff of the temple for the benefit of the temple, 'subsistence fields' allocated to members of the temple staff for them to cultivate for their own benefit, as part of their remuneration, and finally land excess to the temple's requirements, which was rented out to private individuals in return for a share of the crop or fixed annual payment. At Girsu at the end of the Pre-Sargonic period the proportions of land devoted to these three categories cannot be reliably estimated, but large areas are involved (according to Deimel's original calculations, 200–300 sq. km), and although we no longer think that the temples of Lagaš controlled the entire territory, they did undoubtedly constitute a major component of the economy and society.[309]

How valid this picture would be for other cities and other periods is difficult to say, but we do at least know that the three-way division of the land between the temple, its staff and tenants persisted for about three centuries into the Ur III period at Girsu. Here a new

	Farmed directly by the temple	Prebend lands	Rented lands
Early Dynastic Bau Temple	**níg-en-na** 'property of the en'	**GÁN šukura** 'ration field'	**GÁN apin-lá** 'tenant field'
Ur III Namhani Temple*	**GÁN gud** 'ox fields'	**GÁN šukura** 'ration field'	**GÁN níg-gál-la** or **apin-lá** 'tenant field'
Percentages in Amar-Suen 2	67%	25%	8%
Area in bùr	291.6	104.25	32.6
Area in hectares	1889.57	675.54	211.25

*see Maekawa 1986, 100

Figure 9:5 Terminology of temple lands held under the three main types of tenure in the ED III and Ur III periods. (Source for Ur III: Maekawa 1986)

text gives us figures for each category from one temple (Figure 9:5): the prebend land and rented land have not changed their names, only the temple's own land is now called 'ox-fields'. The prebend system was obviously very important in securing the distribution of the temple's wealth back into society. It was already developed in the Early Dynastic III period at Abu Salabikh, where holdings are assigned to the gods, the **ensi** and officials, including a number of scribes, and the same term, no doubt implying the same basic system, has been identified in the archaic texts from Ur, of Early Dynastic I date, alongside fields 'of the en'.[310] In the Old Babylonian period prebend land is held not only from temples but also from the palaces, which evidently found themselves in the same position as the temples earlier, of having more land than they could cultivate directly with their labour resources.[311]

Tenure and lease of prebend land

Since prebend land was officially assigned as the remuneration for performing an office, whether in the temple or the palace, it naturally could not be sold and was not inherited, at least automatically, within the family. However, the holder of a prebend may not always have had the labour within his family to cultivate his entire holding, and at least as early as the Ur III period we find that prebend land could be leased out to a third party. This practice, which obviously could have been going strong for centuries, is well attested also in the Old Babylonian period, and on terms indistinguishable from those for the letting of private property (see above, pp. 184ff).[312]

Although in principle prebend land would revert to the institution on the death of the holder, no doubt in course of time some such holdings tended to be passed down from father to son, since, as we have seen, some of the priestly offices themselves could be inherited. Another exception is provided by land held from the state in return for military service, known in Akkadian as *ilkum* (see chapter 13). Since the purpose of the arrangement was to ensure the army a supply of recruits, the obligation could satisfactorily be transferred to the sons of the original holder, who inherited the rights to the land at the same time. As with other prebend land, *ilkum* fields could be rented out.[313] The state was not so keen on the inevitable attempts to dodge the system, and we are particularly well informed about the position in the reign of Hammurapi because we have many letters between him and his governors in the newly conquered state of Larsa, where a programme of land assignment was being actively undertaken (Text 9:7). The king deals in person with frequent problems and disagreements, and no doubt some of the experience so gained is reflected in clauses in the law code (see chapter 15).

Text 9:7 Letter to Hammurapi's governor at Larsa
Say to Šamaš-hazir, Enlil-kurgalani says: May Adad keep you alive! About the field of Ahum-waqar: As you know, he has been enjoying the use of the field for 40 years, and now he is going on one campaign in the king's corps, but Sin-imguranni has now taken the field away from him and given it to a servant of his. Look into the matter and don't allow him to suffer an injustice.

(After Kraus 1968, No. 73)

Institutional advantages

We saw above various ways in which the Mesopotamian environment could be exploited to maximum effect (pp. 174ff). It is now clear to see that the combination of the agricultural regime with the social structure gave significant advantages to the larger enterprise at the expense of the small farmer. There are various factors involved. On the purely technical side both irrigation and cultivation are more efficient on a large scale. The construction and maintenance of canals and other water controls are better arranged in bigger units, and the technology of ploughing with teams of oxen favours long furrows, which minimize the number of turns required. This favours a field layout of long narrow strips, which also ensures as many farmers as possible have direct access to the canal banks (Figure 9:6). Ur III texts show that this was indeed the shape of their fields, and the same can be observed both ethnographically today and textually in Neo-Babylonian times.[314] Such a layout can be achieved by communal consent, but it is much easier to create and administer as part of a single enterprise.

There are also advantages of scale to be reaped from sharing equipment and labour, which can be deployed with more efficiency the larger the estate and the greater its variety of land and crop. Just as government-backed collectives in Iraq can bring in a

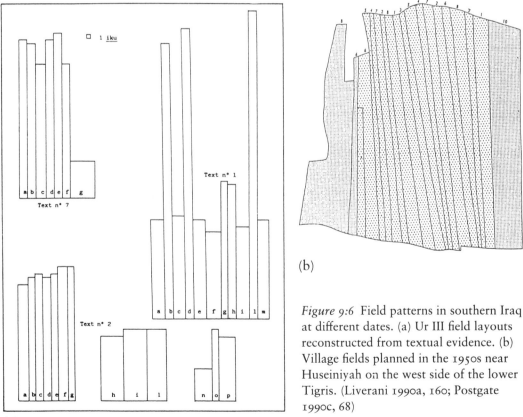

(a)

(b)

Figure 9:6 Field patterns in southern Iraq at different dates. (a) Ur III field layouts reconstructed from textual evidence. (b) Village fields planned in the 1950s near Huseiniyah on the west side of the lower Tigris. (Liverani 1990a, 160; Postgate 1990c, 68)

combine-harvester beyond the means of any individual farmer, so the early institutions were able to invest some of their capital in improved equipment. The shift in the course of the third millennium from sickles made of clay (in the Uruk period) and flint (in the Early Dynastic) and other stone and wooden implements to copper tools must have been an initiative of the temples, improving their own efficiency and enhancing their advantage over private enterprises (see chapter 12). Moreover, the larger the scale of an agricultural operation, the greater its resilience in the face of unfavourable conditions: an individual farmer, tied to a specific plot which he and he alone owns, cannot move away to a new plot if a water shortage or rising salinity threaten his crop; nor can he decide to diversify to cash crops and abandon his subsistence wheat or barley. A larger organization can do both: it can, and did, classify its land carefully by the quality of its soil, and its scale allows it to plan for diversity in crops. It can spread the risk by cultivating land in different ecological areas. And worse than this, when salinization does become a serious problem, to get enough to feed his family the farmer's only options are to try and squeeze more out of the same area by planting more thickly, or to violate the fallow regime, which simply accelerates the deterioration of the land. In recent times in South Iraq the same factors have been observed to make the ownership of private plots a less favourable option than being a tenant on a large estate.[315]

The capital wealth of the institutions also gave them a freedom to exploit marginal areas which would require too much risk for the individual, and to invest some of their surplus in reclaiming or creating new irrigated plots. In the south, such areas of marginal viability form the fringes of each irrigated cell; a similar situation can be observed with the rainfall regime in the north, where there is a wide belt of land which can be ploughed and sown by large land-owners for whom the risk of losing a complete year's harvest is more than compensated for by the good years, whereas the single farmer does not have the economic resilience to survive a bad year. In the administration of land and water, just as in the details of animal husbandry and agriculture, the benefits of a centralized authority must have been evident and the results are apparent today. The institutions had economic room to manoeuvre which enabled them to experiment – whether with new breeds of animal, species of plant, or technical equipment like sickles or ploughs. They were able to intensify production by efficient administration and the economies of scale, as reflected in specialized sheep-fattening establishments or the mathematical precision of variable sowing rates; and they could also expand the sustaining area by large-scale civil engineering projects of land reclamation and canal construction.

Of course, virtually all these advantages of the institution over the individual can be transferred to or replicated within the private sector if there is sufficiently close collaboration. We have to presume that at all times the villages were capable of concerted action at least to the extent of controlling water use and maintaining their local irrigation system. There was probably also agreement about the location of the fields to be left fallow each year, since there are practical advantages in keeping them together. Beyond this, the flexibility given to large family holdings by farming the land jointly, rather than defining the precise limits of each brother's or cousin's plot, will have conferred some of the same advantages of scale; but no village or extended family could compete with the massive irrigation schemes of the Ur III kings. Nor was the private sector in a position to cope with major shifts in the environment, such as the drying up of the eastern Euphrates channel.[316]

Further reading

For the best general overview of the South Mesopotamian environment from the archaeologist's standpoint see Adams 1981, especially chapter 1. Detailed description of modern agricultural conditions is given in Buringh 1960, on soils, and Poyck 1962, on agrarian matters. Vols 4 and 5 of the *Bulletin on Sumerian Agriculture* offer a recent collection of articles on irrigation and cultivation. For land tenure the volume edited by Brentjes (1987) gives a very useful survey of different periods (in German); there are many other useful articles, including Steinkeller 1981b and Leemans 1975. Ellis 1976 covers the Old Babylonian period but by no means exhausts the subject. R.C. Hunt, 'The role of bureaucracy in the provisioning of cities', in Gibson and Biggs 1987, 161–92 gives a valuable theoretical account of the relations between city and countryside.

10
The domestic economy

Many of the cuneiform tablets from Mesopotamia are concerned with the movement of commodities of various kinds, and it is self-evident that in a society with clearly defined urban and rural sectors some mechanisms are needed to achieve the distribution of food, raw materials and finished products to their consumers. The exchange of commodities in early societies has often been classified by economic historians and anthropologists under three broad headings or 'modes' of exchange: reciprocal, redistributive and commercial.[317] At its simplest, the reciprocal mode sees goods exchanged between two parties who are alike consumer and producer, on a basis of reciprocal obligation which is deeply embedded in society. A transfer in one direction is not usually reciprocated on the spot, but creates an acknowledged social relationship which will eventually lead to a transfer in the opposite direction. In time, such a relationship may be institutionalized, and form a dependable part of the two economic systems. The redistributive mode is associated in the ancient Near East with the temples and palaces, which are seen as gathering to themselves large reserves and distributing these to their dependants: the scale of such operations enables part of a population to be employed on maximizing food production, and another part to specialize in crafts or administration. They are therefore important in the process of state formation, but it would be dangerous to assume that this is the only route to civilization. The commercial mode is the nearest to most modern societies, with the paramount influence of supply and demand creating a market (whether physically present in a 'market square' or not) where goods can be exchanged between strangers in accordance with a freely varying price structure. Its role in the ancient Near East remains a source of controversy, and its undeniable existence among the merchants of Babylonia and Assur does not mean that the same forces applied throughout contemporary society. While one mode may seem more 'primitive' and another more 'developed', they are not mutually exclusive, and one of the complexities of early Mesopotamian society is precisely the co-existence of these three modes and their variations.

Prosperity and poverty

While temples accumulated treasures of gold, silver and lapis lazuli, the average Old Babylonian citizen's chests were filled with humbler possessions. Inheritance texts list textiles, furniture, animals and a few slaves (Text 5:5, p. 97); the Babylonian bride's trousseau included some more tempting items (Text 10:1), but on the whole we do not get the impression that families built up huge vaults full of possessions.[318] Some part of the

Text 10:1 From an Old Babylonian marriage contract
1 slave-woman called . . .; 1 slave-woman called Šarrat-Sippar-. . .

6 shekels gold as ear-rings; 1 shekel gold as her throat ornament; 2 armlets, silver, weight 4 shekels; 4 bracelets, silver, weight 4 shekels.

10 dresses; 20 head-dresses; 1 blanket; 2 coats; 1 leather sack.

1 ox; 2 three-year-old cows; 30 sheep; 20 minas of wool.

1 copper cauldron of 30 litres; 1 grind-stone for legumes; 1 grind-stone for grain.

1 bed for sleeping; 5 chairs; 1 barber's box; 1 *nushum* box; 1 . . . box; 1 box with a . . .; 1 round box.

60 litres sesame oil; 10 litre jar of first-quality cosmetic oil.

1 wooden tray; 1 wooden . . .; 2 wool combs; 3 head combs; 3 wooden spoons; 2 loom-woods; 1 full container of spindles; 1 small pot-stand.

1 woman called . . .-belessa; 1 man called Qišti-Ilabrat.

All this is the dowry of Liwwir-Esagil, *nadītum* of Marduk and *kulmašītum* priestess, daughter of Awil-Sin, which Awil-Sin her father, son of Imgur-Sin, gave her and which they brought into the house of Utul-Ištar, the Priest of Ištar, son of Ku-Inanna, for Warad-Šamaš, his son. After $\frac{1}{2}$ mina of silver, her 'bride-price', had been tied into her hem, it was returned to Utul-Ištar, her father-in-law. In future her sons are her heirs, they swore by the life of Šamaš, Marduk, and Ammi-ditana the king.

(After Dalley 1980, 60–1)

accumulated possessions was of course convertible into the household's daily meals and other consumables. The list of contents of the Babylonian larder is simple, and the staples are summarized for us by royal statements about the cost of living which list their prices (Text 10:2). In addition to this there were of course fresh fruit and vegetables, the occasional meat, and a long list of the spices, many of them grown locally, for which the Near East has always been renowned. In much the same category come a miscellaneous group of expensive imported aromatics, mostly resinous, which were certainly used in the temple rituals but perhaps also had a place in palace and everyday life.[319]

At the level of the household we know very little about how these products were bought and sold. There are enough hints, in the shape of references to small shops, to a 'street of purchases', to a travelling salesman, and to a 'gate of exchange', to allow us to be sure that in later Old Babylonian times at least a small-scale private sector existed serving the daily needs of the ordinary citizen, but we get no concept of its scale, or its relative

Text 10:2 Opening section of the Ešnunna 'Law code'

1 **gur** [300 l] barley	for 1 shekel (8 g) silver
3 litres best oil	for 1 shekel silver
1.2 litres vegetable oil	for 1 shekel silver
1.5 litres pig's fat	for 1 shekel silver
40 litres bitumen	for 1 shekel silver
6 minas (3 kg) wool	for 1 shekel silver
2 **gur** salt	for 1 shekel silver
1 **gur** potash	for 1 shekel silver
3 minas copper	for 1 shekel silver
2 minas worked copper	for 1 shekel silver

| 1 litre vegetable oil, on withdrawal(?), its barley 30 litres |
| 1 litre pig's fat, | on withdrawal, its barley 25 litres |
| 1 litre bitumen, | on withdrawal, its barley 8 litres |

[The meaning of ša nishatim, given here as 'on withdrawal', remains unknown.]

(After Yaron 1969, 20–3)

importance within the economy as a whole.[320] Put another way, we do not know if the surplus produce of private citizens, whether farmers themselves or urban landlords, was largely reserved for reciprocal exchange purposes within the immediate circle of the family, village or ward, or regularly disposed of to commercial agents. The concept of a middleman was certainly current, as we shall see, and we may be sure that the commercial mode was more prevalent in the city than in the countryside.

There were of course families or years with no surplus, and as the economic horizon of a community expands, and the commercial ethic grows in strength, so the wealth differential within the community will widen. Whether urban or rural, a family confronted by a poor

Text 10:3 An Old Babylonian letter

Say to Mattaki, Illuratum says: may Šamaš and Marduk give you life. About the bronze hatchet and the bronze ingot which were left with you as a pledge, I had forgotten about them until the boy who brought the corn mentioned them. I did not have any corn available and did not send any, but at the sheep-shearing I will send you 2 shekels' worth of wool. Don't give the bronze hatchet or the bronze ingot to anyone – they are entrusted to you. On the day I send the wool, send me the bronze hatchet and the bronze ingot.

(After Frankena 1966, No. 93)

year will have to borrow. We have already seen that a temple might act as creditor, but the great majority of recorded loans are between private citizens. In Old Babylonian times the general practice was to charge an annual interest of one-fifth (i.e. 20 per cent) on silver and one-third (33 per cent) on barley loans, and this was probably enshrined as fair practice in the Code of Hammurapi.[321] Earlier there are fewer documents: private loans were not recorded in writing before the Akkad Dynasty, and are rare in Ur III (though perhaps only because of the bias of the sources).[322] Yet loans took place, as we can tell from the arrangements made to protect the creditor against the borrower's failure to pay: no doubt from earliest times the institution of pledge was practised. Just as envisaged by Deuteronomy, this could involve individual objects like garments or animals (Text 10:3);[323] but the items which tend to be recorded in our Old Babylonian documents are those for which a purchase document would have been drawn up in the case of sale – persons and real estate (Text 10:4).[324]

> **Text 10:4** Silver loan secured by pledge of the debtor's son
> Bakšišum has received [x] shekels of silver from Mannum-ki-iliya. He has placed his son as pledge. If Bakšišum (wishes to redeem[?]) his son, he shall pay the silver together with its interest. If (the son) dies or escapes, he will take his silver from Bakšišum. (7 witnesses, including a smith.)
>
> (After Harris 1955, 61, No. 5)

It is evident that the loss of disposition of either a member of the family or a piece of land was not the best situation in which to ameliorate the finances of a distressed family, especially when we remember that loans were often made on condition of the supply of harvest labour (see above, chapter 9). In South Mesopotamia, famine conditions were usually occasioned not by the climate but by political disruption of the delicate agronomic regime. Cities besieged behind their walls might starve, and the Flood story mentions saline fields as a cause of famine.[325] The severe inflation in the city of Ur at the end of Ibbi-Sin's reign, when grain urgently had to be shipped downstream from Isin, may surely be put down to political causes, but we cannot be sure that this was not part of a general failure of the southern cities to match their cereal production to their population. We have already seen how the large institutions or land-owners are better placed to withstand deteriorating conditions, and in these circumstances inevitably the poor grew poorer and the rich richer. In the end, the household head is left with no legal solution but to sell his land, if permitted, to his creditor – who could no doubt pay the lowest price – and finally to sell himself and his family into servitude, remaining in many cases as the dependent tenant on lands which had once been his own.[326]

It is certain that Mesopotamian society viewed economic exploitation askance. Hammurapi's boast that his Code was enacted so that 'the strong should not wrong the weak', goes back through the Ur III code to the Reform texts of UruKAgina, who is the first king known to us to declare the duty of the Near Eastern ruler to protect the orphan and widow. The king's responsibility for the welfare of the population was not confined to impartial administration of justice but extended to attempts to correct the economic inequalities that had arisen in society. One symptom of this is the prominence given to prices in official inscriptions. The list of commodity prices at the start of the Ešnunna code is not the only example. Hammurapi apparently does not attempt to fix prices in this way, but he does follow earlier rulers in prescribing legal levels for the hire of specialists like a surgeon or builder, of equipment like carts (see Figure 10:1) and boats, and of animals (Text 10:5). Earlier kings also proclaim the success of their reign by quoting prices: Sin-iqišam of Uruk, Sin-idinnam of Larsa, and others.[327] Although we may permit ourselves

Figure 10:1 Old Babylonian terracotta model of a cart from Tulul el-Khattab near Baghdad. Four terracotta wheels will have been fixed each side of the two axles, and the holes in the side-beams no doubt took perishable uprights forming the sides of the vehicle. (IM 87213. Courtesy Iraq Museum, Baghdad)

some scepticism as to the efficacy of such proclamations, since prices attested in contemporary documents are normally distinctly higher, they are a clear sign that the kings were expected to alleviate economic hardship.

In part the king's responsibility for prosperity reflects his role in those annual religious ceremonies usually designated 'fertility rites', and royal inscriptions often celebrate the prosperity attending a reign (see chapter 14). However ineffectual their efforts at price control, there is certain proof that another class of royal enactment did have its effect. This was the periodical annulment of debts, a practice which was passed on to the Levantine world, is attested in the Bible, and can hardly have failed to influence early Classical Greece with the famous 'seisachtheia' of Solon.[328] Known in Akkadian as *andurārum*, probably meaning 'freedom of movement', its Sumerian equivalent was **amar-gi**, which meant 'return to mother', and referred to the liberation of members of a family enslaved for debt. The earliest reference to this practice goes back to Enmetena, well before the Akkad Dynasty, at a time when private credit transactions seem not to have been committed to writing (see Text 10:6). Perhaps the most striking feature of this edict is that the persons freed and sent home by the ruler of Lagaš come from neighbouring city-states. This suggests that debt relations could be incurred across frontiers, and indeed this is implied by a passage in the Stele of the Vultures which talks of an enormous grain debt owed to Lagaš by its rival city of Umma. That indebtedness of this kind outreached political frontiers is almost certainly the explanation of an enigmatic passage in which King

Text 10:5 Code of Hammurapi, §§234, 239, 242–3, 257–8

If a boatman has caulked a boat of 1 **gur** [300 l] for a man, he shall give him 2 shekels of silver for his 'gift'.

If a man has hired a boatman, he shall pay him 6 **gur** of grain a year.

If a man has hired (an ox) for 1 year, he shall give its owner 4 **gur** of grain as the hire of a rear ox, and 3 **gur** as the hire of a front ox.

If a man has hired a farmer, he shall give him 8 **gur** of grain a year. If a man has hired an ox-herd, he shall give him 6 **gur** of grain a year.

Text 10:6 From a building inscription of Enmetena of Lagaš

Enmetena annulled debts for Lagaš, restoring mother to child and restoring child to mother. He annulled grain loan debts.

He annulled debts for the sons of Uruk, of Larsa, and Bad-tibira, restoring them to the hands of Inanna at Uruk, to the hands of Utu at Larsa, and to the hands of Lugal-Emuš at the Emuš.

Enmetena, who is commissioned by Inanna – his personal god is Šul-utul.

(After Cooper 1986, 58–9)

Ilušuma of Assur claims to have established the freedom (*andurārum*) of the 'Akkadians and their children' from Ur, Nippur, Awal and Kismar, Der as far as the City (of Assur).[329]

  We cannot be sure that these earlier measures did more than revoke personal enslavement for debt. Later, in the Old Babylonian period, the debts cancelled may include straight-forward loans or real estate sold under economic duress. Kings often mention their promulgation of acts of judicial reform which included the annulment of debts. This applied to contracts between citizens within the private sector, and we can be sure that they could indeed be annulled, since the possibility is specifically envisaged in some documents, and we have plaintive correspondence about it from some of the unlucky creditors (Text 10:7).[330] Charity begins at home, and the palace's own debtors, whether farmers or shepherds, have their debts remitted. Far the most explicit document we have relating to these edicts is that published by Ammi-ṣaduqa. From this we learn that there are certain types of debt which the edict specifically excludes, those which are not so much debts as business investments, whether capital transferred from one party to another, or equal partnerships. These are the everyday relationships of a sophisticated commercial community, and it would clearly have been outside the spirit of the edict to dissolve such liens, which could be either between one merchant and another, or be-tween the palace and a merchant. A closer examination of one of the relevant clauses will give us an insight into one of the principal economic mechanisms of early Mesopotamia (Text 10:8).

Text 10:7 A plea for the king to correct a miscarriage of justice
When my lord raised the golden torch for Sippar, and instituted the 'Rectification' for Šamaš who loves him, Taribatum the Controller of the soldiers made the Judges of Babylon and the Judges of Sippar sit in Sippar, and they examined the cases of the people of Sippar. They heard [i.e. read] the purchase-tablets of fields, houses and orchards, and those that were annulled by the 'Rectification' they broke. ... [A damaged passage gives details of the plaintiff's property deals] ... and I took my tablets to the Assembly. Riš-Šamaš, a resident of Sippar, Kudiya the stool-bearer, and Sin-nadin-šumi the survey-scribe examined my tablets, sealed them, and had them transferred to Šalim-tehhušu, to his house, for him to examine. Šalim-tehhušu, the Overseer of the Barbers, without even hearing my statement, broke my tablets in his warehouse in Sippar. They told me, and I bowed my face [i.e. was distressed] and took the fragments of my tablets from his house and showed them to Riš-Šamaš, Kudiya and Sin-nadin-šumi. They said: 'What can we say to the Overseer of the Barbers?' So now I have come to you, (as to) a god: may my lord judge for me the case of tablets which are broken without the knowledge of the Judges or the principal party, and so all Sippar will see that before my lord the weak is not given over to the strong, and the strong [are not allowed] to oppress the weak.

(After Finkelstein 1965, 233–6)

Merchants as agents of the palace

Text 10:8 From the Edict of Ammi-ṣaduqa
If a merchant, who retails goods of the palace, has left a sealed (receipt) with the palace in exchange for goods from the arrears of a tenant, which he received from/in the palace, and has taken a sealed (receipt) of the tenant, but the goods referred to in his sealed receipt were neither given to him at the palace, nor received by him from the tenant, because the king has remitted the arrears of the tenants, that merchant shall declare on oath before the god 'I did not receive anything referred to in this sealed receipt from the tenant', and after he has made this declaration he shall bring the tenant's sealed receipt, they shall meet together, and make their mutual deductions, and from the goods referred to in the sealed receipt, which the merchant left with the palace, they shall remit the amount referred to in the sealed receipt which the tenant left with the merchant.

(After Kraus 1958, 32–5)

At first sight the provisions of Text 10:8 may seem complex and incomprehensible, but in fact we have enough examples of the kinds of receipt mentioned to make perfect sense of what is going on, and Ammi-ṣaduqa's enactment serves as confirmation that we have understood not only the detailed individual transactions, but also the general set-up. The complexity of the enactment reflects complexity in the real world, and the best introduction to the Old Babylonian commercial scene will be to elucidate the situation envisaged by the edict. Step by step, the situation can be described as follows:

1 The tenant owes an annual rental for his land to the palace, probably in barley.

2 He fails to pay this rental on time.

3 The palace 'sells' to the merchant the barley owed by the tenant, and includes this amount with other such debts in a document which the merchant seals, to acknowledge his obligation to make payment at a future date.

4 Because the tenant still owes the amount in question, the palace cannot give the barley itself to the merchant, only the right to that barley. The merchant also gets a document, sealed by the tenant, acknowledging both the debt and that it is to be paid to the merchant. Under normal conditions, this is then a matter between the two parties, and the palace plays no further role in the affair.

5 However, Ammi-ṣaduqa then promulgates his edict. This has the charitable effect of cancelling the tenant's debt to the palace, now due to be paid to the merchant, but it does not remit sums owed by merchants for merchandise (and rights to merchandise) which they had received from the palace for retail as part of their regular business activities. Hence the merchant finds himself owing the palace a payment for a good which he can no longer extract from the tenant, and the edict regulates the situation entirely justly by remitting his debt too.

To understand the motivation of the different parties to these transactions, it will help to consider it from their different angles. For the palace the advantages are clear. First, by selling the goods to the merchants it is able to free itself of the task of disposing of surplus goods by entrusting them to an agent in return for a payment in silver. Second, by making the sale a 'paper transaction' it transfers the difficulties of debt collection to the same agent, and, third, it is freed from the need to transport and store the barley (or other goods).

The merchants will also have profited, but their role is best illustrated by moving back in time about a century, and downstream to Larsa, shortly after its incorporation into the kingdom of Hammurapi. Texts, presumably from the palace archives, which must have been illicitly excavated at the site itself, continue to surface in museums, giving us increasingly fine detail of the organization, but already the broad outlines are clear. In Text 10:9, Ili-iqišam has a concession from the palace for a certain quantity of merchandise, and this has passed, in some way not made explicit, to four persons who now sell it to

Text 10:9 Sale of a concession to palace goods
Mari-ersetim, Sin-kašid, Beli-ašared and the sons of Baba have sold sale-goods (worth) $2\frac{1}{2}$ minas silver – sea-fish, dates, garlic and wool – the concession of Ili-iqišam – to Ibni-Amurru for $\frac{5}{6}$ mina of silver. He will receive the wool from him at the plucking.

On 30th day of the 5th month he will pay $\frac{5}{6}$ mina of silver to the palace.

Before Sin-idinnam, the priest of Šamaš; before Awil-Šamaš; before Taribum; before Awil-Aya. He impressed his seal.

30th day of the 6th month, Samsu-iluna Year 5.

(After Jean 1931, No. 106)

Ibni-Amurru. He pays them one-third of the face value of the goods, and receives the goods: that is to say, he physically receives the fish, dates and garlic, but the wool will not become available to him until the shearing, which takes place around the Babylonian New Year, in seven months' time. In return, he is to pay the sum owed to the palace at the end of the fifth month, i.e. in eleven months' time.[331]

Two features of this transaction favourable to the merchant are immediately apparent: he pays only two-thirds of the nominal value of the goods, and for one of those thirds there is a long delayed repayment date. As for the repayment date, this is only one possible arrangement; sometimes the contract specifies 'at the payment of the "allocation"' (*ina šaqāl sūtim*), in other cases it may simply say 'when the palace requests it', or 'when the messenger (*našpar*) comes from the palace'. Amounts sometimes remained unpaid for more than one year: one contract from Samsu-iluna Year 3 Month VI, deals with amounts of dates from the first and second years of his reign.[332]

As for the difference between the sum actually paid by the merchant and the face value of the goods, in the Larsa texts the separate payments are regularly exactly one-third, and the transactions are sometimes quite explicitly described as 'at a third'. The later Sippar texts do not give the same detail, but no doubt a similar arrangement was in force. Quite *how* advantageous this apparent 50 per cent profit was for the merchants is another question, which cannot be answered at present: for one thing they had the expenses of transport, storage and distribution to meet, and in the later texts at least it is clear that these were considerable, since the merchants were expected to come from Sippar to Babylon to take delivery of the merchandise (Text 10:10).[333] Then of course we are not told the exact significance of the starting price, which I have called the 'nominal value', and which may have been known as the 'palace price' (*kār ēkallim*).[334] Our texts do not usually specify the amounts of each commodity, merely the silver value, no doubt because they were tied to a known equivalent. Precisely for this reason, they seem unlikely to be prices current in the market situation where the merchants would be making their sales or loans, but were rather formal values assigned by decree, and '(black) market' forces may well have been operative. Hence there is a possibility that the starting price for the calculations was unrealistically high, and the 50 per cent profit illusory.

Text 10:10 The palace gathering its due from the merchants
Say to Sin-idinnam, Hammurapi says: with reference to what I wrote to you about sending to Babylon Šep-Sin, the Overseer of the Merchants with 1800 **gur** of grain instead of sesame and his arrears of 19 minas of silver, and Sin-muštal, the Overseer of the Merchants, with 1800 **gur** of grain instead of sesame and his arrears of 7 minas of silver, and about receiving wool, and sending Overseers of Five with them, on which you said that the Overseers of the Merchants said 'At present it is harvest-time. Let us go after the harvest' – well the harvest has now arrived! The moment you see this tablet of mine, send to Babylon Šep-Sin, the Overseer of the Merchants with his 1800 **gur** of grain and his arrears of 19 minas of silver, and Sin-muštal, the Overseer of the Merchants, with his 1800 **gur** of grain and his arrears of 7 minas of silver, and together with them a reliable servant of yours ...

(After Frankena 1966, No. 33)

Regardless of the vexed question, to which we shall return in chapter 11, of whether the merchants were employees of the palace or merely agents, the general purpose of these transactions is clear. The palace had quantities of staples in excess of its needs, and wished to dispose of them without the expenses of storage, distribution and petty administration. It therefore made the goods over to the merchant community in exchange for silver, and since the concessions were made in advance of the delivery of the goods, the merchants were effectively acting as debt-collectors for the palace. For the merchants, it gave relatively secure access to known quantities of staple goods, on easy repayment terms.

The term 'staples' requires some qualification. At Larsa the merchants are receiving fish, dates, garlic (and occasionally other alliaceous plants), and wool. Since the fish is dried, and the other products also keep well, all these products can in effect be stored as capital. The fish and the dates are especially characteristic products of the 'Lower Province'. In the northern region, round Babylon, a century or so later, there were just three types of merchandise regularly made available by the palace: wool, sesame and cattle. Since these are sold off by the palace, they are undoubtedly in one sense a 'surplus'; but the effort put into the production of wool suggests that the palace was deliberately generating this surplus for commercial motives, and the same could be equally true for the other products.

One category of staple agricultural product is conspicuous by its absence, the cereals. The palace must certainly have received large and sometimes excessive quantities of grain (principally barley) from its tenants and its directly cultivated lands, but neither at Larsa nor later do cereals feature regularly among the merchant transactions. The reasons for this are not yet clear. One reason could be that the palace might have maintained huge stocks of grain against a poor year and famine conditions – but this cannot be documented, and indeed we hear surprisingly little about storage in early Mesopotamia in general. Another reason may have been that grain was more readily convertible, sometimes functioning as a currency like silver. This would of course make it a less marketable commodity than those retailed by the merchants: wool and the textiles made from it were certainly trade items, and perhaps dates, fish and onions were traditional specialities of the south which could find a fresh market in the north – while in the north we may be witnessing a deliberate market-oriented initiative, with the cattle intended particularly for the leather industry (as well as plough animals), and sesame grown for export as a fine-quality oil. In any case, one has the impression that the whole operation was carefully controlled by the palace, and indeed by the king in person: the wool-shearing correspondence includes letters from the kings themselves[335] and in the Hammurapi–Samsu-iluna period the amounts to be remitted by the merchants were prescribed in 'the royal tablet' (*kanīk šarrim*) and could be very considerable (Text 10:10).

The Ur III system

A series of elaborate periodic statements of income and expenditure by merchants at Umma gives us a detailed insight into merchant activity in the Ur III period, although as so often the superb detail is offset by the difficulty of reconstructing the wider context from the telegraphic data we are given (Text 10:11). Each account tablet sets out the

Text 10:11 Excerpts from an Ur III merchant's balance-sheet

1 mina 9$\frac{1}{2}$ shekels 7 grains silver, remnant from Year 6 of Amar-Suen;

10 talents 30 minas wool, its silver(-value) 1 mina 3 shekels;

9 talents 40 minas wool, its silver(-value) $\frac{5}{6}$ mina 8 shekels, a second(?) amount;

5 talents wool (for?) gold, its silver(-value) $\frac{1}{2}$ mina, loss on it: 10 shekels;

under the supervision of Lu-Enlila.

30 **gur** [9000 l] dates, its silver(-value) $\frac{1}{3}$ mina 5 shekels.

Total 4$\frac{1}{3}$ mina 5$\frac{1}{2}$ shekels minus 2 grains of silver – the opening balance.

Out of this:

1 talent 9 minas – cedar, its silver 6$\frac{5}{6}$ shekel 10 grains

29$\frac{1}{3}$ minas – juniper, its silver 2$\frac{1}{3}$ shekel 20 grains

9$\frac{1}{3}$ minas – cypress, its silver $\frac{2}{3}$ shekel 20 grains

3$\frac{1}{3}$ minas – myrtle (**gír!**), its silver $\frac{1}{3}$ shekel 15 grains

1 **ban** [10 l] juniper twigs – its silver $\frac{1}{6}$ (shekel)

4 **sila** [4 l] best sweet oil – its silver 4 shekels

0.1.4 5 **sila** [105 l] dry bitumen – its silver 1 shekel 9 grains

5 wild-goat horns – their silver $\frac{1}{3}$ shekel 15 grains

2.3.0 [780 l] sprouting malt – its silver $\frac{1}{2}$ shekel

8 talents [240 kg] gypsum – its silver $\frac{1}{4}$ (shekel) 5 grains

Total 2 minas 10$\frac{1}{6}$ shekels 13$\frac{1}{2}$ grains of silver, expenditure; remainder 2 minas 15$\frac{1}{4}$ shekels minus $\frac{1}{2}$ grain silver.

Completed account of Ur-Dumuzida, merchant, for Amar-Suen Year 7.

(After Snell 1982, 18–22)

merchant's total receipts and expenses since the last statement. The income side of the account includes the credit balance (if there is one) from the previous statement, and the final summary gives the balance to be carried forward to the next. The period of accounting does not seem to have been fixed, but it may have been roughly annually or every six months.[336]

The merchandise listed on the 'income' side of the statement shows clearly that the merchants are engaged as later in retailing surpluses on behalf of an institution. The principal commodities are: wool, fish, oil, wheat, figs, dates, barley and silver. The presence of silver (and perhaps also barley) in this list shows that a different motivation was also at work, especially in some cases where the entire capital was of silver. Since, as we shall see, silver functioned as a currency, the palace did not need merchants to dispose of a surplus of it: in this case the issue to the merchant is to enable the acquisition of the items on the 'expenditure' side of the statement, which are much more varied, and appear to represent the commodities which the palace could not produce itself from its own estates, hence usually imported from outside South Mesopotamia. As well as bitumen and gypsum, feathers and fruit, a major component of these purchases is a range of resins and aromatics, frequently listed in a fixed order, and obviously imported since they mostly derive from western trees like cypress or cedar. In this way the Ur III accounts encapsulate in themselves the function of the merchant as a cog in the economic machinery, converting the palace's surpluses of basic commodities into luxuries. A similar process is attested by Lagaš texts recording farm animals acquired for the palace from outside sources.[337]

In some cases it is clear that in Ur III times the merchants were operating on behalf of the palace, although the 'take-over' of the temples by the state in the Ur III period sometimes makes it difficult to be sure for which institution they are formally employed. Earlier, before the Akkad Dynasty, the same uncertainty surrounds the activities of merchants from the Bau Temple at Lagaš, which does seem in effect to have been adopted by the palace for its own purposes. Administrative texts from there show that merchants were employed in the same way and for the same purposes: in one case large quantities of fish brought in to the temple by a fisherman are partly deposited in the storeroom, but partly issued 'as purchase-goods' to a merchant, but in another a merchant taking delivery of copper, tin and dried fish 'as purchase-goods' is given it 'from the palace', and copper imports from Tilmun are also paid into the palace.[338]

Currency

The phrase 'as purchase-goods' is difficult to translate, since the multiple functions of the merchant make it possible to understand it either as 'things with which to purchase (other things)' or as 'things to be retailed'. In some cases, however, the inclusion of copper or silver among the commodities issued makes it clear that the transaction is aimed more at the purchase of commodities than at their re-sale. This brings us to consider the question of currency.

Silver

One of the most striking features of the Ur III balance-sheets is their use of silver as a unit of accounting. All the incoming goods are assigned a value in silver, by weight, which is totalled to give the capital sum at the merchant's disposal, the sum for which he has to account. Similarly, the items bought in are priced in silver, thus enabling the total value of the merchant's expenditure to be deducted in a single sum from his capital, and the remaining balance, negative or positive, to be expressed in silver, which is then ready to be carried forward to the next accounting period. In the same way in the Larsa texts the value of goods received by the merchant is usually stated as a single amount of silver, and the actual quantities of the different commodities involved are often not actually specified.

This procedure is readily understood, but what concerns us here is to ask whether it implies a general use of silver as a currency, or whether it is an accounting practice restricted to the merchant class. The function of currency has been much discussed by historians and anthropologists. Three different functions are sometimes distinguished:

1 standard of accounting;
2 medium of exchange;
3 means of payment.

Polanyi was right to insist that these three roles should be kept distinct: the existence of currency in one of them does not necessarily imply its existence in another, nor does use of an item in one role mean that it served for the others.[339] In the context of the Ur III merchants' accounts we have seen that silver was the standard of accounting, and although we can hardly suppose that each of the individual receipts was physically converted to silver, and each purchase made in return for silver, the mere fact that silver could be included in its own right as part of the capital shows that it could also serve as a medium of exchange. That at this time it also served as a means of payment – a quantity of silver being handed over as simple payment for a good received or service performed – is demonstrated by sale documents and loans, where prices are usually specified in silver, and by administrative texts recording payments to labourers in silver.[340]

This all fits in well with the picture of silver usage in the Old Babylonian period and for the peripheral city of Mari, and we shall see in the next chapter that this use of silver could be considered international. While we are a long way from coinage, invented in Lydia in the first millennium BC, in societies which use a metal as currency it is common for it to be presented in a conventional form, whether or not it is authenticated by means of a stamped design. In Mesopotamian texts, silver is usually just weighed, but in some Ur III texts it is clear that 'rings' of silver with a uniform weight were in use by the administration (Text 10:12). Rings are mentioned in similar texts with weights ranging from just 1 shekel (= 8 g) to 10 shekels, although the great majority are of 5 shekels. A text from Ur lists the manufacture of 240 silver 'rings' of 5 shekels, being made from 20 minas. There is indeed some archaeological evidence for the form of such rings: they come from contexts as early as the Dynasty of Akkad, weighing in one case 1 mina (= 60 shekels), in another $\frac{1}{2}$ mina (Figure 10:2). Their distinctive feature is that they are coiled into a spiral, which would not have been worn as an ornament but would be easily broken up to give the precise weights required by the variety of everyday transactions. No doubt larger amounts came in solider form, such as small ingots, but few such have survived. The records of commercial transactions do not usually specify the form in which silver was handled and the spiral ring may have been more widespread than it seems at first sight.[341]

Text 10:12 From the Ur III public accounts
2 rings of silver at 8 shekels each, when the king drank beer for the (inauguration[?] of) the brewing-house of the divine Šulgi. Uta-mišaram the official. Disbursed by Puzur-Erra in Al-šarraki. 11th month, Amar-Suen Year 1.

(Michalowski 1978, 55)

Figure 10:2 Silver rings, from Tell Taya, time of Akkad Dynasty. (Courtesy Dr J.E. Reade)

Other currencies

In the early second millennium, silver was the preferred currency of the merchant classes and perhaps of the administration, but even in Old Babylonian times it was not the only one. Alongside it the administration and the private sector regularly used barley to fulfil much the same function, and other commodities are also attested, while other metals such as copper and tin are found in use as means of payment, usually with an accepted ratio between them.[342] Copper is used like this already in the Fara period, and in Anatolia by the Assyrian merchants, who also used tin in the same way. Only silver is attested as a standard of accounting (although gold served this purpose later, in the Amarna age, probably as a result of influence from Egypt), and archaeological evidence for pre-formed standardised units of metal is confined to the existence of the ingots in which the metal was conveyed from the smelting site.[343]

Determining the precise function of metal pieces is always delicate since they had a practical value as the raw material of finished artefacts as well as any value assigned to them by society as currency. We should not assume that metals were the only possible currency, however. Other early civilizations retained symbolic items to serve as currency for centuries before they were displaced by precious metal or coinage. In many parts of the world shells have served as currency, and this includes Old Kingdom Egypt and pre-Han Dynasty China.[344] Nor was there usually a single kind of currency, and just as knives also served in this way in early China, so it is no particular surprise to find that in the north of Mesopotamia the palace used 'axes' of precious metal, while in Old Assyrian texts cups (*kāsum*) feature in much the same role.[345] These finished items were weighed, but in some cases the craftsmanship which went into them cannot have been disregarded, and they therefore shade off into elite exchange goods, more at home in a reciprocal than a commercial mode of exchange. It is noticeable that they feature in the texts more and more as one moves away from the commercial world of South Mesopotamia, but silver and gold do seem to retain their validity as currency in their own right, as we shall now see.

Further reading

No general work covers this topic as a whole, with the exception of the very general but valuable observations of Diakonoff 1982. Particularly useful are Renger 1984, and, on the merchants' role, Charpin 1982b (French) and Snell 1982. For the economic measures of the kings, Kraus 1984 (German) is indispensable. See also Yoffee 1977, Veenhof 1988, and Powell 1990.

11

Foreign trade

The exchange of goods is at first sight one of the easier facets of society for the archaeologist to detect. Metals and stones have perforce to be imported into South Mesopotamia, and survive relatively well in archaeological contexts. It is in theory possible to trace such raw materials to their geological origins, although there remain formidable practical difficulties. More productive of recent years has been the archaeological recovery of industrial activities in places far from Sumer but evidently engaged in the same trading network: in Oman for copper, south-west Iran for carved stone bowls, eastern Iran for lapis lazuli, the Indus for carnelian. To judge from these examples, long-distance trade was mostly in the processed raw materials rather than in finished products. Occasionally, though, a find stands out as the work of a foreign workshop, such as the Indus-style seals which have been found on Mesopotamian sites. Finally one must not ignore the physical evidence for the transactions of trade: documents, seals (and more especially sealings) and weights all derive from the procedures of commercial exchange and are sometimes our only evidence when the nature of the commodities exchanged has wiped them from the archaeological record. The multifarious ways in which the lively foreign trade of South Mesopotamia can be detected have meant that the subject has attracted a good deal of attention in recent years, but the archaeologist also needs to understand the complementary evidence of the documentary sources, both because they create our expectations, and because they reveal salutary object lessons about the validity of some archaeological assumptions.

It is of course misleading to write about trade as though it were a single homogeneous system. Quite apart from the specialization of different routes mentioned below (p. 219), we need to distinguish the differing roles of trade in different social contexts. If we group items traded broadly into essentials, staples and luxuries, it is easy to see that each group has different correlates in society: the market for high luxuries must be an elite one, and a small one, while the staples trade plays to a certain sector of society which was involved in metal tool production or in the creation of textiles for export, and need not have seriously affected the lives of a majority of the population. On the other hand, everyone in society was concerned in one way or another with the supply of things like salt or grindstones, and we should not underestimate the value of long-standing exchange arangements for essentials in paving the way for more ambitious ventures. While the textual material tends to direct our attention to the more conspicuous items of consumption, archaeology is less socially discriminating and can help to restore the balance.

The evidence for early trade

From well back in neolithic times obsidian, the rich man's flint, was widely distributed throughout the Near East. The volcanic glass is almost indestructible and in the Near East only a few sources are known, to which pieces can be assigned by scientific analysis. The sources from which neolithic Mesopotamia imported include the Van region and central Turkey.[346] This is not surprising since the diffusion of pottery styles suggests a similar range of cultural contact, and one can only speculate at present about the social nature of the obsidian trade and about the possible exchange of other commodities of the time which have not survived in the archaeological record. Later, evidence for specialized trading ventures in the Ubaid period comes from Yarim Tepe in North Iraq, where a Soviet team recovered several hundred grindstones in a single room (Figure 11:1). The obvious assumption that this reflects a specialized trading venture is supported by later historical sources which show that grindstones were indeed manufactured from the volcanic lava in this general locality.[347] Evidently Yarim Tepe was a stage on the overland route east to supply the region of later Assyria; an Old Babylonian letter from Mari mentions a boatload of grindstones on their way to the cities of the south, doubtless having taken a western route down the Habur from the same sources.[348]

One of the most striking features of the Uruk culture, and one that has become fully

Figure 11:1 Grindstones and grinders from the Ubaid settlement at Yarim Tepe, North Iraq (*c*. 4500 BC), excavated by the Soviet expedition in 1977–78. These are a representative selection of more than 300 from a single room. (Photo: courtesy Professor R. Munchaev)

apparent only in recent years, is the range and uniformity of its distribution. Both red burnished and other technically superb fine wares turn up on sites as far apart as Godin Tepe on the Iranian plateau and Habuba Kabira at the Euphrates bend in Syria, in each case associated with some of the 'hardware' of trading procedures, rudimentary inscribed 'numeral tablets' and clay sealings. While the Uruk presence in Iran appears to be grafted on to the existing society, at Habuba Kabira we seem to be witnessing an entire fresh colony, a walled city complete with temples whose plan, construction techniques and decoration are lifted intact from South Mesopotamia.[349] The political dimension to this surprising discovery remains beyond our reach at present, but the obvious assumption that it was a trading colony is supported by the clay sealings found in and around the houses, both here and in the sister settlement of Jebel Aruda upstream.[350] It is obvious that like Emar in the second millennium BC the city owed its importance to its position on the Euphrates, at the head of the long boat journey through Mari (founded about this time) to South Mesopotamia. We can only guess at the nature of the goods traded; later parallels may suggest that textiles came upstream in exchange for timber and aromatics from the mountains of Syria and Turkey, but they also warn us not to place too much faith in what may appear to be 'reasonable' reconstructions from purely archaeological evidence.

Lapis lazuli found at Jebel Aruda is tangible proof that there was an eastward branch of the Uruk trading system, since the prized blue stone came from the Afghanistan mountains. Two remarkable sites excavated in the 1970s attest to the international importance of the lapis lazuli trade (Figure 11:2). At Shortughai in the Oxus valley on the Afghan–Soviet frontier a French team recovered evidence of the exploitation of the lapis sources by people with links to the Indus culture of Harappa and Mohenjo Daro; while the westward branch is represented by the Italian excavations at Shahr-i Sokhta, now stranded in the desert of south-east Iran but a pivotal caravan city on the route through Elam to Sumer and Akkad in the third millennium BC. Careful and imaginative exploitation of the archaeological evidence by the excavators has revealed an interesting specialization of the industry in semi-precious stones. The stone-workers of Shahr-i Sokhta imported the raw materials and prepared them for export by shaping and trimming, the exact processes varying from stone to stone (Figure 11:3). Turquoise was known and used at the site but was not an article of their trade, which concentrated on the lapis lazuli and carnelian.[351]

The precise course of the route westward is not known, and indeed the political geography of the Iranian plateau was probably very complicated and shifting. The capital of Elam, Anšan (Tall-i Malyan), no doubt controlled much of the trade much of the time, and Shahr-i Sokhta was not the only centre. A northern route is represented by the site of Tepe Hissar, while another industrial venture has been revealed south of Elam at the site of Tepe Yahya, where carved chlorite bowls were produced for the export market in the early third millennium. These bowls have also been found, and were probably actually manufactured, on both shores of the Gulf, and the presence of Mesopotamian pottery in this region testifies that sea-borne trade was already practised from the Ubaid period on.[352]

Most of these trade links were too early to surface in Mesopotamian documentary sources, but some left their mark on the collective memory of Sumer and Akkad. A story about Enmerkar, the ruler of Uruk, tells how he engaged in negotiations with the ruler of

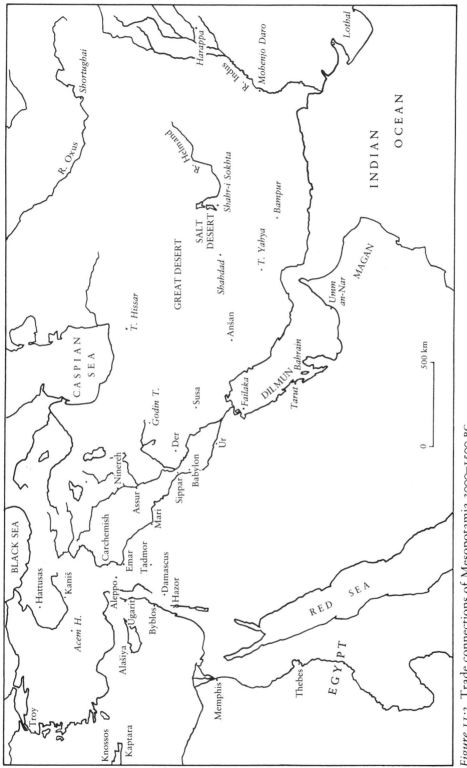

Figure 11:2 Trade connections of Mesopotamia 3000–1500 BC

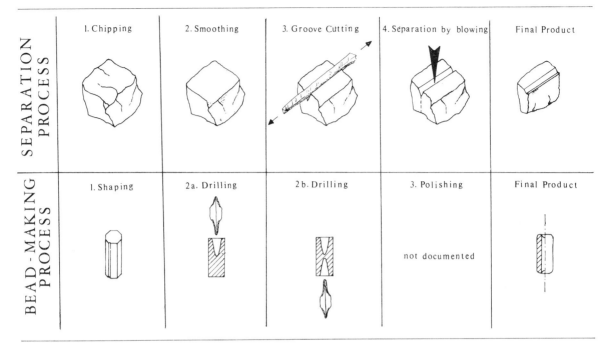

Figure 11:3 Shahr-i Sokhta: stages of preparation of lapis lazuli as reconstructed from archaeological evidence by the excavators. (Drawing by I. Reindell, reproduced courtesy M. Tosi from *Studi di Palentologia, Paleoantropologia, Paleontologia e Geologia del Quaternario* 2, 1974, 158)

a land behind seven ranges of mountains to secure the lapis lazuli, carnelian and other precious materials for the embellishment of the temple of Inanna. Messengers go back and forth, and in time a consignment of precious goods is exchanged for a donkey caravan of grain, suggesting that we are witnessing something more substantial than the exchange of diplomatic compliments between one ruler and his peer (Text 11:1). Indeed, a literary text

Text 11:1 Enmerkar sends supplies to Aratta

The lord then opened his main storehouse, ... the barley for the granary he measured out in full, adding (even) for the locust-tooth. After having loaded the pack donkeys – the reserve donkeys, having placed them at their sides – the king, the lord of broad wisdom, the Lord of Uruk, the Lord of Kulaba, dispatched them directly to Aratta. The people, like ants out of the crevices, in their entirety were moving on to Aratta ... After the emissary reached Aratta, the people of Aratta stepped up to wonder at the pack donkeys. In the courtyard of Aratta the emissary measured out in full the barley for the granary, adding (even) for the locust-tooth. As if from the rains of heaven and shining sun Aratta was filled with abundance. As when the gods reclined together on their couches, Aratta sated its hunger.

(Cohen 1973, 128–9, lines 323, 329–36, 352–60)

Figure 11:4 Jewellery and other luxury imported goods from an ED III grave at Abu Salabikh: lapis lazuli, carnelian, copper; at base, conch shells from the Indian Ocean. (Grave 168: see Postgate in J. Curtis (ed.), *Fifty Years of Mesopotamian Discovery*, 1982, Plate 3b)

from well before the end of the Early Dynastic period reports that 'the foreign trader brought lapis lazuli and silver from the mountains',[353] suggesting that even these luxury items were regularly traded (cf. Figure 11:4). As it happens, the everyday documents of the early third millennium are only rarely concerned with foreign trade, but they do make quite frequent mention of traders. In contrast to the ubiquitous 'merchant' (*tamkārum*) of the second millennium, who operated on both the external and internal circuits, these early texts make a clear distinction between the ordinary merchant and the foreign trader, known in Sumerian as **gaeš** or **garaš**. Unlike the merchant (**damgar**) he is not attested in the documents from Fara, although he features in the lexical list of professions and is regularly present in the Pre-Sargonic Lagaš documents.[354]

Assur trade with Kaneš

Although international trade had clearly been flourishing for over a millennium, it is in the resurgent cities of Babylonia and at Assur, after their emergence from the restraints of the Ur III empire, that we have the most complete image of a foreign trade network of a complexity and sophistication that foreshadows similar phases of mercantile prosperity in other places and at other times, and merits detailed description.

In the late nineteenth century, scholars were perplexed by an unfamiliar kind of cuneiform tablet apparently reaching the antiquities market from Kayseri in central Turkey.

When it was eventually identified as being in an early dialect of Akkadian akin to later Assyrian, this puzzlement increased, but any doubts were settled in the 1920s by the Czech orientalist Bedrich Hrozny – renowned as the decipherer of Hittite – who began excavations at the Bronze Age mound of Kültepe in the Kayseri plain (Figure 11:5), and discovered in situ more of these cuneiform tablets in the Old Assyrian dialect, establishing beyond doubt that they derive from the archives of a community of merchants from the city of Assur some 1600 km away to the south-east. Now, seventy years later (and even though thousands more tablets from recent excavations remain to be published), it is possible to describe the nature of the trading venture fairly succinctly. It was organized by merchant houses at the city of Assur, who exported tin and textiles by donkey caravan, across the plains of North Mesopotamia, and over the Taurus onto the Anatolian plateau. There they reached their own trading colonies, usually installed in local housing below the citadel of the main cities, and sold the goods they had brought in exchange for gold and silver, with which they then travelled back to Assur.[355]

What were the economic realities of this trade for the merchants who organized it? Presumably the demand for tin in Anatolia was mainly for alloying with copper to make bronze. Recent research has revealed ancient tin sources in the Cilician Taurus, more or less on the direct route of the Assur caravans, but even if they were yielding at this time, we must presume that the Assyrians had access to cheaper and/or more reliable supplies.[356] Quite where, remains unsolved: from the east, at any rate, whether from the Iranian plateau across the Zagros or from Susa and Elam to the south-east; the Kültepe documents say nothing about this, but there is perhaps a hint of it in the presence of Assur merchants

Figure 11:5 Kültepe: view of excavations on the city mound.

at Nuzi across the Tigris. Large quantities of tin are also mentioned in texts found at Shemshara, high in Iraqi Kurdistan on the Lesser Zab.[357]

At Sippar too, at the northern end of the Babylonian plain, there was a colony of merchants from Assur: their principal interest was almost certainly in the 'Akkadian textiles' for which Babylonia was renowned, and which formed the second main commodity of their trade with Anatolia.[358] It is true that Assur produced its own textiles, some of the merchant houses employing a team of weavers, but the references in the letters to the need to procure Akkadian textiles makes it clear that the local product was only second-best (Text 11:2). Obviously both at Assur and in Anatolia sheep were kept and their wool used, but the quality and quantity of the South Mesopotamian textiles was unmatched. There was sound sense in the combination of tin and textiles, because the animals could bear only so much weight, and the regular packages of tin, divided equally with 65 minas ($\simeq 32.5$ kg) on each side, left plenty of space for the large volume taken up by four to six textiles.[359]

Text 11:2 Assur merchant explains lack of textiles to his Kaneš partners
As to the purchase of Akkadian textiles, about which you wrote to me, since you left the Akkadians have not entered the City (of Assur). Their country is in revolt. If they arrive before winter, and there is the possibility of a purchase which allows you profit, we will buy for you and pay the silver from our own resources. You should take care to send the silver.

(After Veenhof 1972, 98)

The documents found come in the great majority from the houses of the merchant colony at Kaneš. What they tell us about directly are principally the matters which needed settling between the merchants at Kaneš and their counterparts back home at Assur (Text 11:3). These may concern the formation of partnerships to put up a large capital sum (*naruqqum*) in gold, the adjustment of business debts at both ends, family affairs like inheritance arrangements, and requests for help in private or business matters. Incidentally we hear about events en route, and about the further distribution of the goods within

Text 11:3 An Assur merchant to his agents at Kaneš
Say to Assur-na'da and Assur-taklaku, Ili-alum says: 16 cloths (*kutānum*), 18 black textiles, 2 fine textiles, 1 garment, 1 Šilipkian textile, 2 head-scarves, $32\frac{1}{2}$ minas of tin under my seal, 10 minas for current expenditure, 2 black donkeys: of these goods one-third is an interest-free loan of our father, the remainder is my loan. You have paid in person my consignment-tax to the *kārum* – don't deposit any (other) consignment-tax!

2 fine textiles, 1 Šilipkian textile, 2 head-scarves, 1 mina 4 shekels of tin, as a share of my ex voto for Assur; 1 cloth as my ex voto for Ištar; 1 cloth as my ex voto for Ilabrat; 1 cloth as my ex voto for Šamaš; 1 cloth for Ili-na'da; 1 cloth for . . .; 1 cloth, 1 mina [of tin(?)] for the slave-woman; . . . of the garment for the little girl: all this Assur-taklaku is bringing you. Sell it at the best price and send me the silver.

(After Garelli 1966, 112–13)

Anatolia, either to native courts or to other *kārum* or minor trading depots called *wabartum*. It is clear that the Kaneš *kārum* was the nerve centre of the Assyrian trade, at least during the four generations or more of the earlier phase represented by Level II of the excavations. It was of course an important native capital city, but the choice of Kaneš, rather than for instance Burušhattum, residence of a Great King, or other cities like Ankuwa (= Ališar) or Hattusas (= Boğazköy), both of which have yielded a few tablets from their own *kārums*, has probably most to do with the geography of the access routes across the Taurus range.

While we are certainly right to consider the Kaneš trade as being in the hands of private firms, they were not by any means free from outside controls. On the one hand conditions were imposed by the native Anatolian rulers, and on the other equally strict controls were exercised by the Assyrians themselves. At Assur itself taxes were levied on each consignment as it left the city, and further taxes were exacted on arrival in Kaneš by the merchant body itself through the institution of the the *kārum*. These funds were applied to the maintenance of the *kārum* there, which had a formal constitution of rotating officials, was able to pass legal judgments on the Assyrians, and kept a firm eye on them to ensure that they did not infringe local regulations and endanger relations with the Anatolians.[360] There were taxes to pay on the imported goods, and the *kārum* did its best to ensure that if smuggling did take place it was undetected: there was apparently a narrow defile which was habitually used for this purpose. One particular temptation concerned the items traded: within Anatolia the Assyrians were not allowed to do trade in local Anatolian textiles – presumably to avoid competition with local traders – and there were certain luxury items which individuals were not permitted to carry, being apparently reserved as a monopoly of the 'City House' (*bīt ālim*) at Assur (Text 11:4).[361]

The classic age of the Assyrian colonies lasted for about four to five generations, before the throne of Assur itself was usurped by the Amorite outsider, Samsi-Addu. After a disruption, of uncertain nature and duration, in the course of which the colony was destroyed, trade resumed again but on a somewhat different footing.[362] The rigid control

Text 11:4 Warning not to smuggle …

Imdi-ilum, Ennam-belum and Assur-sululi (at Assur) to Puzur-Assur (in Kaneš): [The first part of the letter is about textile consignments and payment of dues] … The son of Irra sent his contraband to Pušu-ken, but his contraband was caught, whereupon the palace seized Pušu-ken and put him in jail. The guards are strong. The queen has sent messages to Luhusaddia, Hurrama, Šalahšuwa and to her own country concerning the smuggling, and look-outs have been appointed. Please do not smuggle anything. If you pass through Timilkia leave your iron which you are bringing through in a friendly house in Timilkia, and leave one of your lads whom you trust, and come through yourself and we can discuss it here.

['Iron' (*asium*) was a very valuable commodity at this date, presumed to derive from pure meteoric sources.]

(After Kienast 1960, No. 62; cf. Veenhof 1972, 307–8)

of the Assur *kārum* seems to have lapsed: there is evidence from Acem Höyük, a major capital south of the salt lake in the central plain, plausibly identified as Burušhattum, that links were maintained with the Samsi-Addu Dynasty, but correspondence shows that the rival Zimri-Lim Dynasty at Mari also had interests in Anatolia (Text 11:5). The archives from Alişar and Boğazköy date from this time, known archaeologically as

Text 11:5 Trade with Anatolia in the Mari letters

(a) . . . I am able to requite the favour of my lord. Any luxury goods which they bring from Kaniš, from Harsamna, or from Hattuša, of foreign craftsmanship, I can send.

(After Dossin 1939, 70–2; cf. CAD, vol N/ii, 328)

(b) . . . Askur-Addu [known to be King of Karana, at or near Tell al-Rimah] has allowed (a caravan) into his land; from it 50 donkeys and their personnel have passed on to Kaniš, but the remainder have been retained at his court. . . .

(After Dossin 1939, 73)

'Kaneš kārum Ib', and there are other differences reflecting the wider scope of the Meso-potamian links, such as the introduction of the post of 'overseer of the merchants', which is otherwise known to us only from Babylonia, and may imply tighter control by the ruling house at the expense of the merchant body. In any case, the trade with Assur itself does not seem to have survived much longer, although we are unable to say whether this is the consequence more of upheavals within Anatolia (such as the embryonic phases of the Hittite kingdom), or of events in Mesopotamia and Syria.[363]

One of the startling aspects of the Assyrian colonies is that, were it not for the cuneiform tablets which turn up in such large numbers, archaeologists could not have guessed that they were excavating the houses of a sizeable foreign community. The Assur merchants seem to have imported just their commercial wares and values, not their architecture or pottery or any other hardware which would survive in the ground, so that their houses and contents have no distinctive features. Yet in social terms the colony seems to have remained insulated from the locals: although Assyrians might take native wives, their commercial contacts with the Anatolians were strictly confined to the eastern goods they imported. There seems to have been a ban on trade in Anatolian textiles, we come across no joint ventures with the locals, and, although there is the occasional local serving a spell of debt-slavery, they did not act as domestic servants to the merchants.[364] The limits of Assyrian influence are perhaps exemplified by the fact that, once the colony disappeared, their writing tradition, which had been used in some cases by the locals, disappeared with them, and the Hittite Old Kingdom adopted Babylonian script and dialect, presumably from Syria. This is a disconcerting object lesson for the archaeologist: since Assur itself acted only as a middleman in the tin trade, and textiles do not survive, there is no conceivable way in which we could have hypothesized the Kültepe trade from the economic and social constants of the two geographical areas, and it acts as a reminder that the archaeological record is only a very imperfect reflection of the variety and unpredictability of human initiative.

In this case, it immediately induces speculation about the antecedents of the Assur venture. Virtually nothing is known about Assur and the rest of North Mesopotamia in the Ur III period, beyond the names of a few local rulers. Written sources for Syria and Anatolia are also lacking, but there is no doubt that sites like Kültepe, Acem Höyük, and Kara Tepe near Konya were already important cities in the third millennium, with the wealth and incentive to participate in international trade. Hence scholars are now inclined to view with less scepticism a story about Sargon of Akkad, in which he surmounts formidable obstacles to rescue a colony of Akkadian merchants from oppression at the city of Burušhanda (= Burušhattum). The principal text of the legend comes in fact from the fourteenth-century archives of the Pharaoh at El-Amarna, but recent discoveries have emphasized that such texts were translated into Hurrian and Hittite, being especially popular in the west, where the cities they mention, like Burušhanda or Uršu, were familiar places, not the shadowy memories they must have become in Mesopotamia. It is reasonable, therefore, to guess that trade links between the Anatolian plateau and Syria and Mesopotamia were well established at least as early as the Akkad Dynasty, and not as government ventures but by independent trading families.

The south

Moving now to Ur at the other end of the Mesopotamian network, the situation at Assur is turned on its head: there we had none of the documentation from Assur, while here we have the home-based archive but not the other end of the venture. The documents were excavated by Woolley in the merchants' housing quarter at the south-east side of the city at Ur. As first described by Oppenheim and Leemans, merchant families undertook sea-borne trade down the Gulf to Bahrain (at that time known as Tilmun), where excavations have proved the existence of a contemporary sea-port with connections further south and east.[365] Imports coming up from the Gulf were various luxury items, and at least one very important staple, copper, which came in considerable quantities (Text 11:6), although this was not the only source, as Text 11:7 illustrates. Thanks to extensive survey and excavation

> **Text 11:6** Memorandum on copper imported by Ur merchants from Tilmun
> 13,100 [+ x minas of copper (weighed by) the Tilmun] stone, which . . . received in Tilmun.
>
> Out of this: 5,502 [+ x + 2]$\frac{2}{3}$ minas of copper (weighed by) the Tilmun stone they gave to us, its weight by the Ur stone being in total 611 talents 6$\frac{2}{3}$ minas of copper.
>
> Out of this: 245 talents 54$\frac{1}{3}$ minas of copper, which Ala... has given us; 4,271$\frac{1}{2}$ minas of copper, the debt of Ea-nasir; 325 minas of copper, the subsequent debt of Nawirum-ili which was taken:
>
> In total 450 talents [13,500 kg] of copper by the Ur stone, which he has given; remainder 161 talents 4 [$\frac{1}{3}$ minas of copper].
>
> (After Leemans 1960, 38–9)

Text 11:7 A list of metal items including Cypriot and Tilmun copper

1 gold sun-disc of 10 shekels
1 gold sun-disc of 3 shekels
4 gold sun-discs of 1 shekel each
1 gold emblem of 1 shekel
2 gold emblems of $\frac{1}{3}$ shekel
1 gold sun-disc of $\frac{1}{3}$ shekel
3 gold sun-discs of $\frac{1}{6}$ shekel each
4 gold emblems of 15 grains each
Total: ... shekels of gold.

[3 broken entries]

2 bronze rings
2 bronze vessels
12 minas of refined copper of Alašiya and of Tilmun.
10th month, Samsu-iluna Year 5.

(After Millard 1973)

in recent years we are now tolerably certain that the copper came from the mineral-rich mountains of Oman, and there seems no reason now to doubt that this is the land meant by 'Magan'.[366] Similarly, the identification of Meluhha as the lands of the Indus civilization is no longer controversial, and some at least of the luxuries came from there. A particular type of decorated carnelian bead originating from the Indus is in fact best attested from Mesopotamian sites; and doubts as to connections should be entirely dispelled by the Indus-style seals and Indus weights discovered in Bahrain and in Mesopotamia itself (Figure 11:6).[367]

Figure 11:6 Impression of cylinder seal from Tell es-Suleimeh, early second millennium BC (cf. Figure 8:4). Although the cylinder seal is a typically Mesopotamian product, the animals and their style of cutting are characteristic of the Indus culture. (IM 87798, al-Gailani Werr 1983, 49. Courtesy Iraq Museum, Baghdad)

In the opposite direction, the majority of Mesopotamian exports were manufactured goods and perishable commodities which have not survived archaeologically. In the Ur III period, exports to Magan included textiles and wool, leather, sesame oil and barley, and the Old Babylonian list is similar though less complete. The earlier Larsa texts, mostly dating to Sumu-ilum, are records of gifts or tithes to the city's main temple from the luxury goods brought back by traders who had gone to Tilmun 'on their own' (Text 11:8); these therefore do not tell us about the items exported, but list items such as copper, ivory, exotic woods, carnelian and other stones, pearls, sea-shells and manufactured items.[368] Texts from the long reign of Rim-Sin mention silver, textiles and sesame oil as exported to Tilmun. It is noteworthy that, whereas the rulers of Pre-Sargonic Lagaš and of Akkad talk of direct trade with Meluhha, Magan and Tilmun, in Ur III times the Mesopotamian ships reach only to Magan, and in Old Babylonian times no further than Tilmun. This may reflect conditions in the Gulf, where it is obviously possible that the inhabitants of Tilmun were taking a more active role themselves and preventing access to Magan or making it unnecessary, but it may also have to do with a shift within Mesopotamia from publicly supported ventures to private enterprise, which would probably imply less capital investment. Old Babylonian boats seem to have a capacity of up to 40 **gur** (i.e. *c.* 12,000 litres), while the Ur III temple accounts mention ships of 300 **gur** ($\simeq$ 90,000 litres), and we know that their construction was a concern of the **ensi** (Text 11:9).[369]

While the sea-trade is the most spectacular, it is only one element in the pattern. Boats or rafts plied the Tigris and Euphrates, contributing to the wealth of Assur and Mari respectively, and overland trade was by no means exclusive to the Assur merchants. Some of the desert tribes engaged in commerce, including trade in slaves (Text 11:10).[370] Different cities no doubt had different specialities: shortly after the Ur III Dynasty a correspondent is asked to buy carnelian at Akšak, near the Tigris–Diyala confluence, where it is apparently available.[371] As at Assur, foreign trade in Babylonia, as well as internal redistribution, was

Text 11:8 Record of tithe to Ningal Temple at Ur
[1] copper ingot of 4 talents; 4 copper ingots of 3 talents; 11 shekels of oblong pieces of bronze; 3 carnelian kidney-shaped stones; 3 'fish-eyes' [pearls?]; 8 . . .s; 9 **sila** [9 l] of shells; 3 agates(?); 5½ minas of ivory sticks; 30 tortoise fingers; 1 copper . . . stick; 1 ivory comb; 1 mina copper in place of the ivory levy; 3 minas of *elligu* stone; 2 grains of antimony; 3 shekels of of *arasum*, 2(?) shekels of *hulumum* . . . from an expedition to Tilmun, tithe for the goddess Ningal, from those who went there on their own.

(After Leemans 1960, 25–6)

Text 11:9 Ur III memorandum on materials for ship-building
178 big date-palms; 1400 big pines; 36 big tamarisks; 32 big *še-hi* trees; 10 tamarisks of 3 cubits each; 276 talents palm-fibre ropes; 34 talents palm-leaf ropes; 418 talents of rushes; 207 talents [1695 l] of fish-oil; 300 . . . .; 4260 bundles of . . .-reeds; 12,384 bundles of dried reeds; 3170 **gur** [951,000 l] of purified bitumen.

For caulking Magan boats. Under the **ensi** of Girsu.

(CT 7 31a, after Lambert 1968, 9; cf. Landsberger 1967b, 7)

Text 11:10 Royal command of Samsu-iluna of Babylon
Say to Ibbi-Šahan, Samsu-iluna says: Nobody shall buy a man or a woman who is a citizen of Idamaras or of Arrapha from the hands of the Sutians. (Anyone) who buys a citizen of Idamaras or of Arrapha from the hands of the Sutians shall forfeit his silver.

(After Frankena 1968, No. 1)

in the hands of the merchant guilds. There were *kārums* run by the merchants of Sippar at Mari and elsewhere,[372] and the Code of Hammurapi shows that merchants were expected to travel abroad (Text 11:11). It is clear that concentration on specific routes and commodities was not unique to the Kaneš trade. The Gulf trade too was probably underpinned by the need for metal (copper rather than tin), and only secondarily involves the other products. As in Ur III times there is a lively trade in aromatics, which had the advantage of high value for little weight, and we find individual merchants trading them from Larsa in the south to the cities of Zabban and Arrapha on the northern overland route which extends over the Jebel Hamrin as far as the mountain fringes at Šimurrum (Text 11:12).[373]

Text 11:11 Code of Hammurapi, §32
If a merchant has ransomed a soldier or a fisherman who was taken captive on a campaign of the king, and enabled him to regain his village, if there is enough to ransom him in his household, he shall pay his own ransom; if there is not enough in his household to ransom him, he shall be ransomed from the (resources of) the village temple; and if there is not enough in his village temple to ransom him, the palace shall ransom him. His field, orchard or house shall not be sold for his ransom money.

Text 11:12 Legal dispute about a lost donkey
Tablet about 1 pack-ass which Ilšu-abušu hired from Warad-Enlil and Silli-Ištar his brother in the town of Šimurrum, and lost:

On the subject of the pack-ass Ilšu-abušu, Warad-Enlil and Silli-Ištar went to law, and the judges dispensed justice to them in the Gate of Šamaš inside the city of Sippar. On behalf of Ilšu-abušu the judges committed Warad-Sin and Silli-Ištar to (swear by) the emblem of Šamaš. Without an oath-taking Ilušu-abušu the son of Sin-nasir, Warad-Enlil and Silli-Ištar reached agreement at the emblem of Šamaš in the Gate of Šamaš. Because he did take their donkey, Ilušu-abušu shall not make any claim against Warad-Enlil and Silli-Ištar for the 6 shekels of silver (paid) at Zaban [near the Diyala] or the 10 shekels of silver (paid in) Greater Sippar.

(Concluding formulae; witnesses; 5th day, 6th month, Year Apil-Sin 5)

(After Schorr 1913, No. 305; cf. Leemans 1960, 90)

The merchant's place in society

While we have been able at different periods to identify the functions of the merchant in the movement of commodities, we have not seriously addressed the question of his general role in society, and how much it changed over the thousand years or more. Discussions have tended to revolve round whether he was an independent operator, merely an agent of the temple or palace, or a combination of these extremes. Unfortunately, a decision is often difficult, because the majority of the texts we possess are from the institutions themselves, and reflect only those activities of the merchant which concern them. Nevertheless, there are indications of private enterprise, like the merchants who went to Tilmun 'on their own' (see p. 218), or were in a position to make considerable ex voto offerings to a temple, and it should be possible to offer some kind of answer.

The function of a merchant, like that of a shepherd, takes him away from the town and the direct supervision of its administrators. This is most obviously true for foreign trade, but even within the country we have seen that the raison d'être of the merchant was the *distribution* of commodities, getting them to the places where people would buy them. This could not be done by officials from within the four walls of the palace or temple, and therefore, however close the link between merchant and institution, he must have been entrusted with the goods and have accepted (full) responsibility for them. How we describe his relationship with the institution is mostly a problem imposed by our modern terminology: that he has a recurrent engagement, does not necessarily mean that he is a full-time 'employee'; similarly, if in the employ of the palace he conducts his own business at the same time, he does not thereby cease to be a 'palace employee'.

There are good reasons why foreign trade should not be under the direct control of the state. At one time some Assyriologists believed in the existence of an 'Old Assyrian Empire' stretching as far as central Anatolia. Nothing could be less true: trading ventures which pass through foreign lands need as much neutrality as they can muster, and, like Jews and Armenians in medieval Europe and the Near East, the merchants of Assur were probably successful before Samsi-Addu largely because they did not represent a participant in the contemporary power struggle. 'Trade before the flag' is a universal human experience, and there is always a tendency to underrate the range and frequency of long-distance contacts. The legend of Semitic merchants at Burušhanda, well beyond the confines of Akkadian territorial domination, is entirely plausible from this point of view.

Within The Land too there are advantages in an independent merchant body, and the favourable terms on which the palace dealt with them is sufficient evidence that they had some degree of independence. We should not, however, underestimate the importance of the palace connection for the merchant community. Their status seems to have given them entitlement to purchase the individual concessions to palace staples, but in the Ur III period and probably earlier it is clear that when they receive silver and copper they are being paid to undertake a commission, not being issued with a commodity for disposal on the open market, so that the initiative comes from the institution.

It seems, therefore, that down to and including the Ur III Dynasty the merchant class was indeed partly in the direct employ of the institutions. Some scholars have suggested that the Ur III state had a total monopoly on external trade, but our sources are still too one-sided to allow us to deny that the merchant class could have been engaged in independent trading of its own.[374] The political changes following the fall of Ur and the establishment of local dynasties must have had their effect on the economic scene, and as we have already seen at Ur the initiative for the Gulf trade seems to have shifted from the palace itself to the merchants. This is easy to understand: the bureaucratic pyramid of the Ur III system could not have survived the collapse of the state, and the local kings would have had neither the capital nor the administrative staff to re-establish a comparable level of inter-state commerce. Yet the demand for both foreign trade and internal redistribution did not disappear overnight, and the merchants are likely to have stepped in to perpetuate the system on their own initiative. When the veil first lifts, in the Larsa period from the time of Hammurapi, we find that role of organizer has indeed been assumed by the association of merchants called the *kārum*.

In origin this word means the 'quay' or 'wharf' where canal traffic was unloaded and business transacted, but it came to refer to the association of merchants, and was used even in the heart of Anatolia where no river or harbour was present. The *kārum*'s role in the Old Assyrian state has already been described, and in Babylonia there are clear similarities. At Larsa under the 1st Dynasty of Babylon the head of the *kārum* (the *wakil tamkārī*) acted as a regulator of the relations between the palace and the individual merchants, or, rather, between associations of five merchants each with their representative (*wakil hamuštim*). It seems likely that the bilateral agreements between the merchants and the palace were concluded on an equal basis between the chief merchant on the one hand and an important palace official on the other, and it does appear as though the chief merchant assigned concessions without charge to his members, in his officially recognized capacity.[375]

There is therefore good reason to think that the *kārum*, although independent, was officially recognized by the palace. Indeed in various cities, including Sippar, we find that the *kārum* was exploited by the local governments to fulfil some of the functions which had previously lain within their own direct control. The *kārum* could act as a legal authority, even outside the commercial world of its members, and as an arm of local government in purely administrative matters (Text 11:13). This devolution of power is understandable: as long as each temple or palace controlled its own restricted area there need be no call for an organization independent of them, but during the Ur III period the local palaces were shorn of much of their power, so that when the system collapsed there were no arrangements in place for the local rulers to inherit, and the initiative was very likely to pass to the merchant community, who needed only to continue their earlier activities under a different guise. The incoming Amorite rulers, some perhaps fresh from the desert, must have depended on the expertise of the merchants. [376]

Text 11:13 Order of Samsu-iluna to the authorities at Sippar
Say to Sin-idinnam, the Sippar *kārum*, and the Judges of Sippar, Samsu-iluna says: I have been told that the boats of the fishermen are going down to the Big Meadow and the Meadow of Šamkanum and catching fish. I am sending you one messenger, and as soon as he reaches you (give instructions that) the boats of the fishermen which are (catching fish) in the Big Meadow and the Meadow of Šamkanum shall not go down there again.

(After Frankena 1966, No. 62)

Further reading

On the early systems see for instance Algaze 1989 (Uruk period), and Kohl 1978 (third millennium). For the Old Assyrian system, in addition to the works cited in note 325 see Larsen 1987, with bibliography. For the Old Babylonian trade Oppenheim 1954 and Leemans 1960 remain indispensable. Ratnagar 1981 gives a valuable survey of the evidence for Indus connections. *Iraq* 39 (1977) has a collection of articles on 'Trade in the Ancient Near East'.

Part IV

The social order

12
Craft and labour

Central to all accounts of urbanization or state formation is the concept of specialization: the distribution of essential functions among the population so that some concentrate on one task, some on another, whether it be administrative or productive. This diversification of function can be horizontal – corresponding to specialist craft or agricultural activities – or vertical – leading to a hierarchical bureaucracy. The earliest texts from Uruk IV include lexical lists which mention a range of crafts and professions which shows how far specialization of both kinds had progressed. In historic times they are closely though not indissolubly associated with temple and palace. The institution both profits from control of specialized activity, and makes its own contribution by providing the conditions under which technical expertise can flourish. Although the Near East lacks the marvellous visual record of Egyptian wall-paintings and models, it seems usually to have been ahead of Egypt in the development of technology. Each innovation cannot be traced to its source, but Mesopotamia undoubtedly played an important role in providing a social context which favoured the exploitation of new potential. As with agriculture, this involved the control of some sectors of the population by others. Rather than focus attention on the definition of social classes as such, we shall concentrate more on the types of work attested in our sources, falling broadly into specialized crafts on one side and and mass labour schemes, which merge with the organization of military service, on the other.

Materials and manufacture

While technology may have higher-profile applications, notably transport and war, for most of time its solidest impact on society has been in the realm of agriculture. In Mesopotamia, as essential a tool as the sickle can illustrate this close relationship. Even in the Natufian, 8000 BC or earlier, flint blades were set into bone handles to create a sophisticated one-handed implement for cutting stems. In South Mesopotamia in the Ubaid period we see the introduction of an apparently implausible substitute, the clay sickle, which nevertheless survives into the Uruk period, and certainly had the advantage of easiness and cheapness of manufacture with an inexhaustible supply of the raw material. In the Early Dynastic, however, it was replaced by a revival of the composite flint sickle, flint blades, now serrated, set into a wooden handle with bitumen. These were displaced in turn by copper sickles, introduced in Early Dynastic times and the norm by the Ur III period (Text 12:1; Figure 12:1).[377] There is little doubt that copper sickles were more satisfactory, and no doubt that the institutions also played an important role in the

Figure 12:1 Tell Sifr, copper sickles and a spade, corroded together. (Moorey 1971, Plate XX.b)

Text 12:1 Memorandum from the administration at Ur
1083 old copper sickles
60 copper hoes
For refurbishment, the smiths have received from the store-room.

1st day, 12th month, Ibbi-Sin Year 9.

(Legrain 1937, No. 383)

substitution of metal tools for the traditional wooden hoe (**giš-al**),[378] and in the introduction and refinement of the plough and its seeder funnel. So here again we see the institution's advantage in farming matters, since the temple or palace must have always had better access to the better tools (Text 12:2). It is obvious that they were better placed to invest labour and capital in the development of a metal industry, and to initiate and organize the search for and importation of metal supplies, whether from Oman, Cyprus or Anatolia (see chapter 11).

Metal-working

A discovery made in the earliest days of Mesopotamian archaeology illustrates the range of metal equipment in use by an institution in the early second millennium BC. In 1854 at the site of Tell Sifr, ancient Kutalla near Larsa, W. K. Loftus's workmen came on a large stack of copper vessels and tools, many of them packed tightly together in rush or palm-leaf matting (Figure 12:2). They are almost all agricultural tools, including fourteen spade

Text 12:2 Annual balance-sheet of a farm near Ur III Nippur

[The tablet begins with an unfinished list of days worked by the farm employees]

5.3.0 [1680 litres] grain; 1 shekel silver; 5 bundles of garlic, their silver value $\frac{1}{2}$ shekel; 50 [litres] leeks, their silver value $\frac{1}{6}$ shekel $7\frac{1}{2}$ grains – from Ur-Šulpae.

5 shekels silver 1.3.2 [500 litres] grain – under the supervision of Sidu.

$2\frac{1}{3}$ shekel silver, individual wages; 5 copper hoes; 3 copper adzes; 3 copper sickles; 1 copper wire(?) – from Adda-kalla.

0.1.1 $7\frac{2}{3}$ **sila** [$77\frac{2}{3}$ litres] grain, the overseer of the hired brewers.

Totals: 9 shekels $7\frac{1}{2}$ grains silver
       7.2.3 $7\frac{2}{3}$ **sila** [$2257\frac{2}{3}$ litres] grain
       [blank] workmen
       3 copper hoes; 3 copper adzes; copper sickles; 1 copper wire(?)

Out of this:

177 workmen('s daily) wages for hoeing and weeding; $1\frac{2}{3}$ shekel 20 grains silver rental of a harrow; $2\frac{5}{6}$ shekels silver wages for ploughing the field; 0.4.4 $3\frac{1}{3}$ **sila** [$283\frac{1}{3}$ litres] seed corn – field called ...

$14\frac{1}{2}$ workmen for 1 day (daily) wages for hoeing and weeding; $\frac{1}{3}$ shekel rent of a harrow; $1\frac{1}{3}$ shekel ox for sowing; 0.2.1 3 **sila** [133 litres] seed corn – field called Uš-gidda ....

(After Biggs 1975)

blades, twenty-nine sickles and a variety of other implements including rings which probably belonged to a plough. Implements of this kind are all too rarely found on excavations, and Loftus' discovery helps to explain why. In among the complete tools were scrappy pieces and 'an ingot of copper and a great weight of dross from the same smelted metal'.[379] Moorey concludes that this collection had come back into the temple at the end of the season to be checked and reworked where necessary. This is surely correct: the records of the institutional metal-workshops automatically record the weight of metal items, and it is clear that artefacts were regularly recalled to be melted down and re-formed.[380] Metal was never wasted, and on urban sites one relatively often finds collections of miscellaneous items – weapons, tools and scrap – which were obviously assembled for their metal content.

We are in the Bronze Age, when the metal-worker was the craftsman par excellence: a specialist, whose expertise could not be reproduced in every household, but whose products were transforming the nature of society through their effect on agriculture, warfare and transport. While copper was already known way back in the neolithic, it seems first to have been exploited in quantity during the fourth millennium BC, throughout the Near East. The cuneiform sign for a 'smith', which is also significantly used for the verb 'to pour' (implying the practice of casting in moulds), is found already in the Uruk IV tablets. Evidence for this technology comes from the contemporary artefacts. Much work has been done, though much remains to be done, in the detailed study of metal-work and in scientific

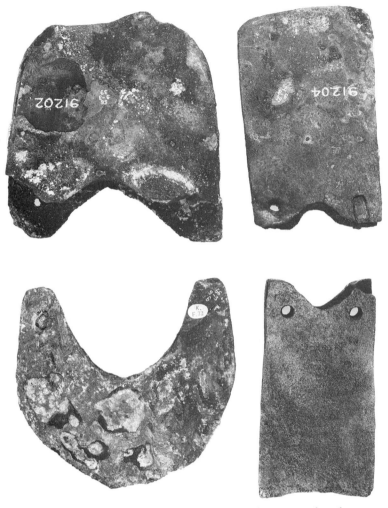

Figure 12:2 Tell Sifr, different kinds of copper digging-tools. The crescent-shaped blade, bottom left, preserves herringbone traces of the palm-mat wrapping. (Moorey, 1971, Plate XXI.a)

analyses of its materials. Tin bronze was already in use by the middle of the third millennium, but not universally, and recent work has revealed extensive use of arsenical copper, as well as showing that pure copper could be used for elaborate cast artefacts for which bronze had been thought essential.[381] Very few major pieces of this kind have survived the recycling processes just described, but the quality of some of the metal-work from the Akkad Dynasty is superb, and implies mastery of large-scale and sophisticated techniques.[382] From the documents it is certain that the institutions maintained considerable metal-working establishments, although none have yet been identified by excavation.[383] In fact archaeological evidence for metal workshops is rather scarce in general. Two early second-millennium workshops are known, one in the *kārum* at Kaneš,[384] and another in the small town of Tell adh-Dhibai, now inside modern Baghdad but then in the kingdom of Ešnunna. There the excavators found the equipment of the copper-smith, complete with clay moulds, crucibles, tuyeres and bellows.[385] We have no way of knowing whether this was a private enterprise or attached to an institution, but there is no reason to think that simple metal-working was beyond the capacity of the private sector, and many important crafts were well within the reach of individual homesteads.

Crafts in the private sector

Naturally the relative importance of the private and institutional sectors was not constant. In Early Dynastic times we are probably right to assume that the temples were the principal patrons of the crafts, whereas under the Ur III kings or at Mari the palace may have been more important. In Old Babylonian times the Ninurta Temple at Nippur still had craftsmen among its regular employees (smiths, textile workers, stone-workers),[386] but temples might also employ independent workers ad hoc, for a particular piece of work, and when gold work was needed in the temple at Ur it proved necessary to import the craftsmen from Larsa.[387] The example of metal-working shows that one simple way of classifying craft activity is to look at the origin of the raw materials involved. There is at least a presumption that where these can be extracted from the immediate environment, it would favour the survival of a craft as a home-based/domestic activity, while imported materials would have been more readily accessible to larger organizations, both because of the capital outlay required for their acquisition and because of the greater ease with which they could make contact with foreign sources. Thus the manufacture of reed-mats, or furniture made from palm-ribs, could remain within the capacity of single households, even though the Ur III state characteristically intervened in it,[388] whereas the working of metals or semi-precious stones is likely to have been initiated, at least, by the institutions. The craftsman buried with his stone-working tools in an Early Dynastic grave at Ur may therefore have been a temple or palace employee, but there is no way to be sure.[389]

Unfortunately the activities of the private sector are veiled from us in almost all respects by the silence of the sources, implying surely not that they were absent but that they functioned without written documentation. Hence we do not know whether crafts were organized as guilds, in the sense of more or less exclusive associations of workers engaged in the same craft outside the employ of the institutions. Some crafts boasted a patron deity, such as the brick-god Kulla,[390] and it is possible to speculate that those engaged in them were kept together by common worship of the god; however, it is by no means certain that such gods had temples of their own, and that their existence was more than a theoretical construct. There is a natural expectation that trades were passed on from father to son, but, except for merchants, examples of this seem to be very hard to find.[391] A family connection would tend to concentrate members of the same craft in one part of a city. As we have seen in chapter 4, there is some archaeological evidence for craft quarters and some priests, scribes and merchants lived in their own vicinities at Ur and Nippur, but city quarters named after trades are not well attested, the only probable evidence for this being the name of a gate at Assur. Finally, in contrast to the Neo-Babylonian period when contracts of employment were regularly drawn up, the only apprenticeship agreements we know of are apparently those for a singer and a cook recorded in a scribal form-book from Old Babylonian Isin (Text 12:3).[392]

> **Text 12:3** Formula for an apprentice's contract: a scribal exercise from
>   Old Babylonian Isin
> Lu-Inana, son of Nur-Kubi, has been given by Nur-Kubi his father to Wusum-beli for two years, to teach him the profession of cook as(?) an apprenticeship. When Wusum-beli from his ... [remainder lost].
>
> (After Wilcke 1987, 106, col. ii')

The institutional mode

The shipping industry can serve as an example of the effect of the institutions on traditional crafts. Boat-building certainly goes back to the Ubaid period in Mesopotamia, and simple reed boats are still in use today, while with only the addition of bitumen from up the Euphrates at Hit, the 'guffah' or basket was no doubt within the means of the ordinary household. But large ships – and, as we saw above, in the Ur III period their capacity reached 300 **gur** – were probably dependent on public institutions to commission them and to supply the timber (often pine from plantations in the south) with which to build them (Text 11:9 above).[393] In Old Babylonian times the boats mentioned in the texts are smaller (see chapter 11), and this undoubtedly reflects the reduced state involvement in the Gulf trade.

The advantage of institutions was not just in matters of capital investment; as with agriculture, the scale of their organization will have afforded the individual craftsman the 'leisure', the freedom from economic pressure, to experiment and to introduce new methods. Specialization creates the expert, and enables the formulation of a body of expertise which could be standardized to a form in which it could be transmitted within the institution and disseminated outside it, to the private sector. The 'Farmer's Instructions' is one example of the codification of a set of guidelines; no comparable manuals survive from early Mesopotamia in craft areas, although glass-making and horse-training manuals make their appearance, along with the skills themselves, in the later second millennium.[394] Clearly craft expertise was transmitted orally, and indeed old traditions record the existence of specialist jargons, familiar hallmark to this day of a brotherhood, which have not left any documentary traces of their own.[395]

The nearest we come to craft manuals in early Mesopotamia is the body of practical examples used in school exercises. As in Egypt, the bases of Mesopotamian mathematics were field mensuration and volume calculation. The value of field survey techniques for an efficient administration of farming enterprises is obvious, and it became a necessity when accurate land sale documents were needed (Figure 12:3).[396] The surveyor's skill could also be brought into play to assist irrigation officials in estimating volumes of work to be achieved and the quantities of rations required; or army commanders to calculate the time needed to construct a siege-ramp of a given height (Text 12:4). Architects too used

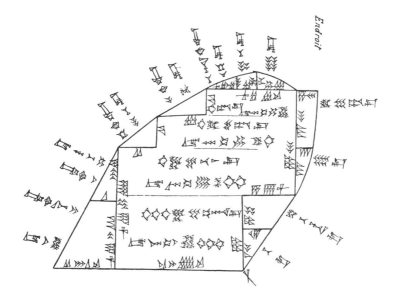

Figure 12:3 Scribe's plan of a field, cuneiform text with Thureau-Dangin's reconstruction to scale (Ur III period). (Liverani 1990a, 149)

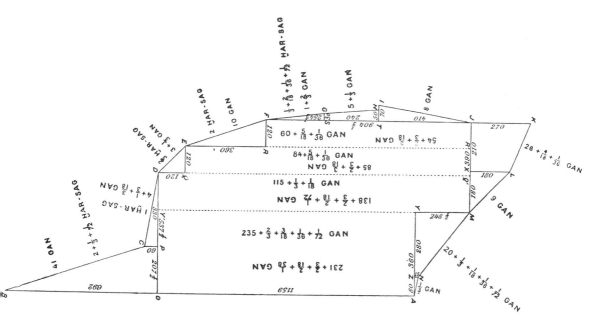

Text 12:4 A mathematical exercise
With (a volume of) earth of 1.30 [i.e. 90] I shall capture the city hostile to Marduk:

From the foot of the earth(-ramp) I went forwards 32, length. The height of the earth(-ramp) is 36: what is the length I have to advance in order to capture the city, and what will be the dimension in front of the ...?

You take the reciprocal of 32, you find 1.52.30. Multiply 1.52.30 by 36, the height, and you find 1.7.30. Take the reciprocal of 6, the base of the earth(-ramp), you find 10, multiply 1.30 (the volume of) the earth by 10 and you find 15. Double 15, you find 30. Multiply 30 by 1.7.30 and you find 33.45. Of what is 33.45 the square? It is 45 squared.

45 is the height of the wall. By how much does 45, the height of the wall, exceed 36, the height of the earth? It exceeds it by 9. Take the reciprocal of 1.7.30, and you find 53.20. Multiply 53.20 by 9, and you find 8. 8 is the length that you advance forwards.

(After Thureau-Dangin 1932)

mathematics: the expertise shown by the builders of temples, as reflected on the ground, was achieved by careful planning (cf. Figures 5:3 and 6:8 above). Brick sizes were known, lines were kept straight, right-angles accurate;[397] and Gudea, **ensi** of Lagaš, is sufficiently proud of his own architectural expertise to have himself shown with a plan of the temple on his knee next to a measuring rod (Figure 12:4).

The institutional sector

From an Ur III archive found in a secondary context at the southern end of the temple area at Ur we learn that a number of crafts were grouped under a single administrative umbrella – mostly, but not exclusively, producing luxury goods.[398] The separate departments were: workers in wood and ivory, gold and silversmiths, fine stone-workers, carpenters, (copper)smiths, leather-workers, rope-makers and workers in reed. All these are grouped together under one term, 'craftsmen' (**giš-kin-ti**), and come under one administrative officer. The government office in question is not named – it may simply have been the temple workshops under royal supervision – but its functions are clear: the labour has to be recruited and controlled, the raw materials of manufacture have to be supplied, and the finished products have to be distributed to their destinations. These archives suggest that the materials like gold, silver and lapis lazuli were kept in the 'chief store-house' (**ganun-mah**), and at Lagaš in the Pre-Sargonic period there was a 'craft storehouse'.[399] This need not have been exclusively for precious items, and in the Ur III period texts from Tello give an idea of some of the more mundane items which government scribes might have to list in their stock-taking (Text 12:5), while some from Umma give detailed catalogues of reed-workers' output.[400]

The detailed documentation of state manufacturing activities was not an innovation of the Ur III kings, but under them it reached an extreme. Their minute control of production

Text 12.5 Excerpt from an inventory of government supplies

Total: 0.4.1 **gur** 2 **sila** cumin

Total: 2.2.4 **kumul** spice (?)

Total: 5760 **sag-kur** fish

Total: 15.5.0 **gur** smoked fish

Total: 39.3.0 **gur** onion plants

Total: 4.5.0 **gur** onion seed

Total: 16.2.0 **gur** 7 **sila** 10 **gin gaz**-onions

Total: 4.2.0 **gur zahadin**-onions

Total: 1680 bundles of . . . -plants

Total: 84 talents of mixed vegetables

Total: 1.0.2 **gur** of flax seed

Total: 1826 talents of **abal** bitumen

Total: 3 talents of 'white' bitumen

Total: 4 talents of . . .-bitumen

Total: 2.3.0 **gur** of dried bitumen

Total: 144 'weaver's textiles

Total: 156 poor quality textiles

[broken section]

Total: 1 talent of palm-fibre

Total: 5547 palm-leaves

Total: 154 palm-ribs

Total: 185.0.4 **gur** 8 **sila** salt

Total: 72 **gur** soapwort

Total: 15 talents of gypsum

Total: 7.0.3 **gur** of pomegranate-rind

Total: 3600 palm-fronds

Total: 900 **gur** straw(?)

etc.

(Reisner, TUT 121, after Pettinato *et al.* 1985)

and labour is exemplified by their four different qualities of sesame oil or by the scribal account of the vessels a pottery workshop produced in a day, with the exact time allocated to each type of pot.[401] As in other areas of society, the Ur III state made constant efforts to standardize and rationalize. The resulting practices were introduced throughout the different cities of Sumer and Akkad and hence survived beyond the life of the political system which engendered them. The unified office of craft administration attested at Ur seems to have been adopted with little change by Išbi-Erra, the first king of the Isin Dynasty, who considered himself as inheritor of the Ur III mantle. The leather industry at Isin in the early years of the dynasty (even before the final demise of Ibbi-Sin) is attested from a bureaucratic archive, and recent studies have shown that it worked in close harness with other crafts, just as at Ur.[402]

Figure 12:4 Gudea, Statue B. The long inscription relates his construction of the Temple of Ningirsu, and on the **ensi**'s lap is a plan of the temple, with the graduated architect's ruler resting on it. (AO 2. Photo: Musée du Louvre/AO)

State employment schemes

In the Ur craft archive the lists of raw materials and finished items are balanced by records of the labour which produced them. Daily rosters show that the same craftsmen turned up regularly for work day by day, and they are occasionally registered as 'sick' or just absent. This does not of itself tell us whether they were slaves, semi-free or fully enfranchised citizens, yet the social status of these government employees is a point of obvious significance. To pursue this question further it is time to consider conditions in the textile industry, which was quantitatively at least the most important at all times, depending on the huge flocks of sheep for wool, more than on flax for linen. Both fibres were within the productive potential of individual households, and indeed the 'wool ration' issued to third millennium employees of the temples implies that they were expected to manufacture their own threads and weave their own garments. Such domestic activities cannot be illustrated from the textual sources, but we can see at Assur how home-based production could be enhanced to meet a commercial demand.[403] Predictably, though, most of our evidence relates to institutionalized textile production. The 600 tonnes of wool recorded in a text from the capital city in the Ur III period is entirely consistent with the contemporary Lagaš archives where a factory of over 6000 workers, the great majority women and children, is located in Guabba alone. The records of these state establishments, which have been studied in rare and exemplary detail, demonstrate the level of self-conscious organization and specialization fostered by the Ur III system. Types and grades of cloth are specified with great precision, and the quantities produced are recorded along with the work-days required.[404]

Once again, these Ur III workshops are without doubt the most organized, but they are not without parallels. The massive textile enterprise in the province of Lagaš is fore-shadowed by the Pre-Sargonic archives from the same city, where institutional textile production was divided into a 'wool place' (ki siki) and a 'flax place' (ki gu), reflecting the different processes needed.[405] A combination of textual and archaeological data suggests that the 'North Palace' at Ešnunna was in part devoted to textile production, perhaps as an enterprise of the neighbouring Abu Temple. There is less evidence for large-scale centrally controlled production after the Ur III period, but we know, if only from Assyrian letters, that 'Akkadian' textiles were a major item of commerce, and the work was not entirely on a domestic scale, as an archive from a small Old Babylonian temple at Ishchali and a single surviving record from a state workshop at Larsa demonstrate (Text 12:6).[406]

Conditions of service

The production of textiles is exceptional in that it required a large trained workforce on a permanent basis. Other undertakings were either the relatively small highly skilled craft workshops, or mass labour schemes usually of a temporary or at most seasonal nature. Any society in South Mesopotamia requires a concentration of effort on certain tasks at certain times: at harvest, at sheep-shearing, on irrigation works, on public works such as monumental or defensive constructions, and occasionally for war. Although in the nature of our sources we hear more about these events when they are administered by an institution, there can be no doubt that some such organization was required, far back in prehistory, for the communally administered projects, and it would be rash to assume that collective labour was exclusively institutional, with no responsibilities in the hands of local communities.

Our written sources also bear witness to collective labour for the institutions on tasks which would be carried out on a small scale in the private sector. Examples of this are the pounding and grinding of grain, a daily task for any independent household, or the making

Text 12:6 From the labour accounts of a textile workshop at Larsa
1 robe, fine, *laharītum*, 6 minas (3 kg):

    4 months – plaiting
    2 days – cleaning
    2 days – trimming
    1 month – sewing up
    2 days – beating
    2 months – teasing
    4 days – stripping and … ing
    1 month – sewing, teasing and finishing
    4 days – stretching and pressing
    1 month – hair taking
    2 months – releasing
    1 month 10 days – blowing

384 textile-workers (days), quota for 1 fine *laharītum* robe of 6 minas.

[There follow similar entries, then a sub-total:]

134 textile-workers (days), quota for 1 2nd-quality robe of 6 minas; 536 textile-workers (days), quota for 4 2nd-quality robes of 6 minas each; 3390 (daily) quotas (and) 150 holidays = 3546 textile-workers (days), quota and holidays, deducted giving a remainder of 1134 textile-workers (days) from Ipqu-Adad.
    [After Lackenbacher 1982, ii.12–26 and iv.20–31; the translation of the technical terms is quite speculative]

of bricks, a simple job which any family could do.[407] The work itself will not have differed much from age to age, and was always a necessary component of society. What did change was the form of social coercion or contract under which the labourers were obliged to perform. One Old Babylonian archive consists of inscribed clay bullae recording bricks received from and barley paid out to brick-yard workers, and similar bullae are known for hired workers in various other trades such as harvesters, shepherds, builders and reed-mat workers.[408] Quite what these bullae were attached to is not clear, but they seem to be characteristic of the relationship between the casual employee and the (probably) public institution, and suggest the existence of a free market in labour in the Old Babylonian period. 'Work contracts', which specify work to be carried out in return for a stated payment, do not seem to be frequent in early Mesopotamia, and, like the crafts, this relationship was therefore probably largely conducted without documentary contracts.[409]

Inevitably, then, most of our information about conditions of employment comes from the state and temple sector, where records were kept by the office controlling the work. Sometimes we have attendance lists, but the commonest form of record is the list of wages. These tedious documents are far from fully exploited as yet, although great strides have been made in recent years, but once they are much will become clearer. There are three classes of information they can give us about the remuneration of workers: the nature and amount of the payments, the frequency of the payments, and the terminology used to describe both the workers and the payments. With this information, it should in due course become possible to make informed statements about the nature of state employment, and to assess the legal and social standing of the employees and the nature of their lien to the employers.

Wages and rations

The rations issued to state employees in the Ur III period have been studied several times in recent years.[410] They are mostly grain, wool or cloth, and oil, but other commodities are sometimes mentioned. The texts distinguish clearly between the age and sex of the workers, and it is also clear that the nature of the responsibility could also define the level of remuneration, with heads of teams, or workers on better-quality cloth, getting more.[411] How significant these calculations are for the standard of nutrition and economic condition of these employees depends of course on whether they had other sources of income, and traditional views on this are subject to some revision. Gelb initially set up a clear dichotomy in the terminology between 'rations' (še-ba, etc.) issued to slave or dependent workers, and 'wages' (á) paid to free persons working for hire. This distinction has not entirely stood the test of time, and it is not justifiable to assume from the receipt of 'rations' that the person is in fact in a servile status. The difference in the terminology of remuneration seems to revolve rather round the regularity: those terms composed with the verb **ba** ('to apportion') 'usually seem to indicate a long-term work relationship between the employer and the employee with payments on a monthly basis' (Waetzoldt 1987, 119).

The same conclusion results from the observation that some of the ration-receivers also worked for the state at other times of year in a different capacity. In Lagaš both the 'workers' (erín) of Ur III times and the 'royal subjects(?)' (šub-lugal) of the Pre-Sargonic Dynasty did their state service in turns, a month at a time. When they were officially called up they are described as 'serving (their) turn' (erín bala guba) and received rations; they were also employed outside their formal term, when they were said to be 'sitting out (their) turn' (bala tuša). When they were officially off duty they were acting as free agents, being paid 'wages' (á), and in the Ur III period at least often borrowing barley from their state paymasters in advance of pay-day.[412] These workers were not the principal agricultural employees of the state, who were full-time farmers (engar),[413] and were employed during the winter months on tasks such as dike-repairing and canal-clearing. There are indeed indications that many of them in the Ur III period were city residents, because the texts note their absence from work with the comment 'not having left the city'.[414]

A different type of state service is represented by the personnel lists of a grain-milling establishment at Sagdana near Girsu which employed male (guruš) and female (gemé) workers (cf. Figure 12:5). Although the scribes do not record rations paid out, the workers are classified according to the level of ration they receive, so that they would conventionally

Figure 12:5 The grinding room in the early second-millennium palace at Ebla. (Photo: courtesy P. Matthiae)

have been considered as 'semi-free'. However, a recent study has shown that they were drawn from a variety of social backgrounds, including prisoners-of-war, members of miscellaneous professions, as well as the principal group known as 'tenants' (or perhaps better 'squatters'). The significant points which emerge are that some of them are there for only a few months at a time, and that some of them have families, so that here again it is clear that less of the Ur III labour force was necessarily of servile status than has sometimes been thought.[415] Some of the **guruš** class, who were obliged to work for the state, were only so obliged for part of each year, and presumably more or less free to do their own work at other times. This puts a very different complexion on the nature of the Ur III state, which has sometimes been viewed as maintained by 'the mass of serfs (**guruš**)...., who represented the main productive labor employed in agriculture and processing of agricultural goods in large public households'. It is now conceivable that these state employees also fell within Gelb's category of 'free peasants and craftsmen working outside of the public households', who need not therefore have 'constituted a negligible force in the productive effort of ancient Mesopotamia' (Gelb 1979, 92).

As to be expected, something of the same arrangements was inherited by the Old Babylonian kingdoms. One king of Isin prides himself on having reduced service for the *muškēnum* class to four days a month (Text 12:7). This is the equivalent of the old **guruš**

Text 12:7 From an inscription of a king of Isin, probably Enlil-bani
In Nippur I established justice, and promoted righteousness. I sought out nourishment for them like sheep, and fed them with fresh grass. I removed the heavy yoke from their necks and settled them down in a firm place. Having established justice in Nippur and made their hearts content, I established justice and righteousness in Isin and made the heart of the Land content. I reduced the barley tax, which had been at one-fifth, to one-tenth. The *muškēnum* served (only) four days in the month. The livestock of the palace had grazed on the fields of ... , who had cried out with the appeal 'Oh, Šamaš' – I turned the palace livestock out of their ploughed fields and banished those people's cries of 'Oh, Šamaš'.

(After Kraus 1984, 29–30)

class of the Ur III Dynasty under another name. The *muškēnum* features as one of the three classes of society (between free men and slaves) in the law codes, but scholars have always had difficulty locating them in society outside the framework of the codes.[416] The best guess at present sees them as semi-free, tied to their land by obligations of service to the palaces, but this need not have ruled out access to private sources of income, and in the Old Babylonian period one has the impression that the social order was not as rigidly stratified as the codes would suggest: certainly some free members of the state also had obligations towards the state, as the same codes record. This class of obligation was known as *ilkum*, which may be understood as 'temporary service', since it could include civilian as well as the military duties which are met in the next chapter. Best known from the Code of Hammurapi and from his correspondence with the administrators of the south after his conquest of Larsa, it was closely related to the tenure of land, and was probably in origin a secular version of the prebend system (see above, chapter 9); there are traces of the same system in Ur III texts.[417] The evidence of the Code and contemporary documents and letters makes it clear that some classes of holder were exempted from military service, but even those who were conscripted were no doubt often employed in civil engineering schemes rather than strictly military tasks, and it remains uncertain whether *ilkum* obligations were the same as those under which the *muškēnum* were called up.

Further reading

Powell (ed.) 1987 is the most important collection of papers on labour in the ancient Near East. Almost the only studies of a craft in action are from the Ur III period: Limet 1960 (French) on metals, Waetzoldt 1972 (German) on textiles, and Neumann 1987 (German) on the craft establishments at Ur (previously treated in Loding 1974). Of works on the craft archive at Isin, van de Mieroop 1987 is at present the most convenient.

13
War and peace

So far our description of Mesopotamian society has treated it almost as though a closed and stable system, but the political history sketched in chapter 2 is enough to show that this is far from reality. It may not be too bold to say that, in the view of Sumer and Akkad, the forces of disorder pressed on their borders, so that order at home could be achieved only by a readiness to fight abroad. To judge from the year-names of the 3rd Dynasty of Ur, the state was engaged annually in some military action, as under the Assyrian or Roman empires, but we are not entitled to assume the same for other regimes without good reason. Unfortunately, though, we have little to go on: with war, perhaps more than any other subject, we are the prisoners of what the Mesopotamian rulers wanted us to know: both their royal inscriptions and the public art are essentially propaganda, and we must be more cautious than ever about reading between the lines. There is the danger of allowing a single triumphant event to colour our perception of an entire disastrous, or essentially peaceful, reign. The situation is made worse because there is little in the way of compensating documentation of an archival kind: the obsessive bureaucracy of the Mesopotamian palaces did not up sticks and tag along on campaign; and we don't have the archives of any military quarter-master. Hence we are unable to gauge the extent of the communal investment in offensive and defensive military measures, or the impact of organized campaigns or civil disorder on the lives of the bulk of the population.

Military service and conscription

The cylinder seals of the Uruk period include scenes of battle and bound prisoners (cf. Figure 2:3, p. 25), and the monuments of Early Dynastic times leave us in no doubt that battles were fought and armies conscripted. Some of the attendants buried with the kings of Ur were surely military guards in life as well, and the textual sources paint a similar picture: all the traditions about the century or two before Sargon hint at frequent armed confrontations, both within The Land and against external invaders, and the early records from Šuruppak list military contingents and chariots, while others from Zabala near Umma list issues of various weapons.[418] However, there is little at this early date to tell us who the soldiers were, what their place was in society. In such conditions it would be naive to suppose that cities did not maintain some kind of full-time professional army, but it is difficult to prove, because in times of emergency any able-bodied member of a state would have been conscripted to fight. Disappearances from periodical listings of civilian employees in the records of the Bau Temple under UruKAgina probably reflect the death or incapacitation of those men in the fighting against Umma, and show that the non-professional soldier would indeed be called on in times of need.[419] Similarly, titles, such as **nu-banda**, which later became a military rank, are still part of the civilian hierarchy in the Bau Temple, and as in later times the word for 'troops' is used indifferently for men engaged on any tasks under state control, whether military or civil, just as they themselves would have been redeployed indifferently as occasion demanded from the agriculture and communal labour essential to a southern city-state into a military role.

Our earliest clear reference to a permanent military force belongs to the Akkad Dynasty. Sargon talks about 5400 soldiers eating bread before him, not all of whom are likely to have been mere courtiers.[420] The first mention of the formation of a specific military contingent comes from Šulgi, who says he formed a unit of spearmen from the citizens of Ur.[421] It is at first sight surprising that at all periods documents deriving from the administration of the army are few and far between. The explanation must be sought in the separation of military from civilian government, which we have seen most explicitly in the Ur III period (see chapter 7), but which for practical reasons was probably normal. Where such texts do exist, they belong to the intersection of military with civilian administration, and hence tend to be concerned with the conscription of soldiers into the armed forces, and, predictably enough, with their efforts to avoid it. The responsibility for locating and producing the necessary conscripts is likely to have been deputed to the community and its civilian officials, and the scant textual sources we have point in that direction.

The best-known mechanism for conscription is the institution of *ilkum*. This is the subject of several clauses in the Code of Hammurapi, and of much correspondence between him and his senior officials in the newly annexed province of Larsa. The basis of *ilkum* was the obligation to serve in the royal army in return for the right to hold land. Despite some scepticism on the point, it is certain that *ilkum* could when required entail participation in a military campaign, but in times of peace it often involved state service on less warlike activities (Text 13.1). Hammurapi legislates in his code that soldiers who

Text 13:1 Excerpt from a letter to an official of Hammurapi at Larsa
Say to Šamaš-hazir, Lu-Ninurta says: Pirhum has informed me as follows: 'In my family we perform one campaign as couriers and one campaign as cowherds, but (the service due on) my family land is used up on (supplying) the cowherds.' Investigate whether in fact (their service) is used up under one heading, and if they have two campaigns in their family divide it in half between them so that he does not pester the palace.

(After Kraus 1968, No. 64)

failed to turn up when commanded to join a royal campaign would be executed. Although there are scattered earlier references to a similar system, both in Ur III and Isin–Larsa times, its origins are by no means certain. In my view, not everyone in Old Babylonian times was liable to *ilkum*, as it was an obligation linked to the usufruct of state land allotted with the specific intention of establishing a duty to serve the king, a specialized form of 'palace prebend'; it would not have applied automatically to families with their own property held under traditional land tenure systems.[422] Under the 3rd Dynasty of Ur a comparable, but probably separate, system was established in the eastern territories beyond the frontiers of Sumer and Akkad, where soldiers were allocated plots by the military administration for which they were expected to reimburse the state by paying the 'rental of the territory' (**gun mada**).[423]

The distribution of state land to soldiers in return for an obligation to military service is a practice recurring in many different forms in different times and places. In Mesopotamia as elsewhere land held in this way was usually heritable, and the duty to serve was imposed on sons and brothers alike. The precise details elude us, and the potential for the system to be undermined with the passing of generations is obvious. The Code of Hammurapi permits certain classes of society, like priestesses and merchants, to sell their *ilkum* plots (presumably held by the family before them), but this was expressly forbidden to others, suggesting that it had in fact been occurring (Text 13:2).[424] Another dodge was to get

Text 13:2 Code of Hammurapi, §§36–7
The field, orchard, or house of a soldier, a fisherman, or a (palace) tenant shall not be sold.

If a man buys the field, orchard or house of a soldier, fisherman, or (palace) tenant, his tablet shall be broken and he shall forfeit his silver. The field, orchard or house shall return to its owner.

someone else to serve in your place. From Hammurapi's own reign we have at least one legal contract in which a man hires a substitute 'for the royal campaign for his month'.[425] This might predate the Code itself, which expressly forbids the hiring of substitutes to perform military duties. Even so, it was no doubt only a matter of time before the regulation's effect was eroded, because a similar contract is preserved from the very first year of the following reign, and a later archive from a small village near Kish shows that the conscript might trade days and months of *ilkum* service like commercial debts and credits, both with someone explicitly designated as his 'substitute', and with others.[426]

A set of census tablets probably written at Khafajah on the Diyala in the time of Samsu-iluna confirms that the substitute system was formally acknowledged. One document records the 'houses' where the men were to be found in different towns of the Diyala region, in some cases noting that they have 'decamped to Ešnunna' – no doubt to avoid being drafted (Text 13:3). They also specify the category of their service obligation,

Text 13:3 Excerpt from census of troops in Neribtum (= Ishchali)
1 man Ahu-šina, young, who is living in the house of Ipqatum, the man of Sippar;
1 man Warad-Kubi, son of Inbuša, who is living in the house of Etel-piša, the divination
      priest;
1 man Belšunu son of Utul-Ištar, who is living in the house of Belanum son of Wardum;
1 man Lipit-Tišpak, son of Mar-iltum
      Kurhitti-muštešer, his brother
      Kubburum, pupil at the school, his brother
      who are stationed with Nabi-Sin,
      who is living in the . . . ;

1 merchant Ubarum, young Pirhum, his brother, who is pasturing Damqi-ilišu's goats;
1 merchant Awiliya son of Belšunu, overseer of the merchants, who is living in the house of Hudu-libbi ....
1 gardener Etirum, son of Išme-karab, man of Dur-Rimuš, who is to be found in the house of Ibni-Amurrum, in the country, but has decamped to Ešnunna;
1 gardener Warad-Ištar, son of Inbuša, man of Dur-Rimuš, who is to be found in the house of Ibni-Amurrum, in the country, but has decamped to Ešnunna ...

(After Greengus 1979, No. 305)

distinguishing the 'soldier proper' (**sag aga.ús**/*qaqqad rēdîm*) from the 'substitute' (literally 'additional', **dah**/*tahhum*; cf. Text 4:5 above) and the 'extra' (**diri**). Shorter lists show that there were, as we should expect, about the same number of 'soldiers proper' and of 'substitutes', and that the 'extras' (perhaps we would say 'reserves') were less numerous.[427] A similar document from somewhere else listing the potential soldiers in the same three categories, shows that they were usually sons and brothers, and belonged together in units commanded (or at least brought together) by one of the 'soldiers proper' among them.[428]

The royal corps

In Old Babylonian times some, if not all, of those actually called up under the *ilkum* system entered the 'royal corps' (*kiṣir šarrim*; Text 9:7) and served on a 'royal campaign' (*harrān šarrim*; Text 13:4).[429] The emphasis on the king is presumably because this system

> **Text 13:4** Hammurapi to Sin-idinnam at Larsa
> Say to Sin-idinnam, Hammurapi says: 240 soldiers of the royal corps, who are under Nanna-mansum, of the district under your command, who have set out from Assur and Šitullum ... [broken passage] ... let them make a march and stay with the troops of Ibni-Amurrum, their group. That contingent must not delay: send them quickly to me so that they may make their march.
>
> (After Frankena 1966, No. 23)

transcended any traditional conscription organized on the basis of community membership. A local official, also working in the Diyala region and reporting to his superior on the progress of the local harvest, has under him different groups, including 'crews of the royal corps', 'Amorite crews' (lit. 'sons of Amurru') and 'crews of the city-ward'.[430] This is a rare hint of the separate existence of a community-based service obligation, but it is also of interest in the separate status it gives to the Amorites. This undoubtedly has historical roots, reflecting a separate tradition of military service based on membership of the Amorite tribes which established their dynasties immediately after the Ur III collapse. Even in later centuries, the highest military title in the South Mesopotamian states is the 'chief Amorite' and there were separate 'Amorite captains'.[431] No doubt the census list of Amorite families from Ešnunna (Text 4:5, p. 82) had a military incentive, and the retention of this ancestral duty may help to account for the differentiation between Amorites and Akkadians which survives even as late as the Edict of Ammi-ṣaduqa. The same differentiation is known from the Mari texts, and it is probable that there were also parallel systems of conscription for nomad and sedentary. The royal correspondence of both Samsi-Addu and Zimri-Lim is full of the problems of recruiting from the tribes, but here too there was also the 'royal corps', and in a letter to Yasmah-Addu from one of his officials we see that 'reserves' from the sedentary villages (here called 'back-up men' LÚ.EGIR) were designated for the royal corps, and not to be called up for any other purpose (Text 13:5).

Text 13:5 Letter to Yasmah-Addu from one of his officials
Say to Yasmah-Addu, my lord, Bunu-Ištar your servant says: my lord wrote about the pack-asses, saying: 'Have 100 pack-asses brought from Našilanum to Karana.' This is what my lord wrote, but those people are reserves for the king's corps, and among troops on an … campaign, which of them leaves his donkey behind? In accordance with my lord's message, I did send into the country, but they did not find a single donkey, they had all gone with the troops, there was not a single pack-ass. Also, the troops who live in the country are reserves for the king's corps, and the king [i.e. Samsi-Addu] has issued strict instructions not to touch them.

(Dossin 1952, No. 70)

Types of soldier and their weapons

Like most armies, then, Mesopotamian ones were not homogeneous bodies of men, but included different contingents corresponding to a variety of social groups, and these differed also in their expertise and equipment. While the ordinary soldier was known as a *rēdûm* in Old Babylonian times, Hammurapi also mentions another class of soldier doing *ilkum* duty in the same breath, the 'hunters', who must originally have followed a non-agricultural lifestyle and no doubt had their own equipment peculiar to it (Text 13:2). In Akkadian, as in modern Arabic parlance, 'to hunt' and 'to fish' are the same word; in the south of Mesopotamia they were no doubt fishermen, but we also find them accompanying the armies in the Mari letters, in the districts of Šubat-Enlil or Tuttul in the Habur and Balih regions where hunters seem more likely. Whether they came from nomadic tribal contexts or, perhaps more likely, were a sector within the more sedentary population, they were assigned fields and probably belonged to the royal corps.[432]

No doubt the hunters used the slings and nets in which their peace-time work had made them expert (like the Roman retiarii). It is evident that the weapons used by the different groups must have depended largely on their home environment. Those who live in the desert and move their homes are not likely to develop an armoury requiring industrial expertise and large supplies of metal. Thus it is no surprise that the sedentary farming communities of the south are the ones with elaborate military equipment, such as the chariots – or rather, carts – and heavy protective armour of the Stele of the Vultures and the Standard of Ur (Figures 13:1; 13:3). Pragmatic considerations aside, military units universally express their corporate identity in their style of dress, and the contingents from different social backgrounds undoubtedly wore different clothing and used different weapons. A light Amorite dress is clearly identifiable in the Mari wall-paintings, on royal

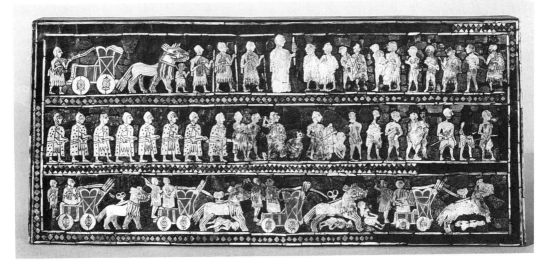

Figure 13:1 The 'Royal Standard of Ur', military side. The battle scenes in the lower registers lead to the presentation of captives to the ruler, who is shown slightly larger than the others, top centre. The best preserved example of such scenes in inlay technique, which have also been found in public buildings at Kish, Mari and Ebla in the Early Dynastic period. For the other side, see Figure 7:6. (Photo: courtesy Trustees of the British Museum)

stelae (Figure 13:3), and on contemporary cylinder seals; and it is perhaps no coincidence that several centuries earlier the stelae of the Akkad Dynasty, with their north-western connections, show the kings and their troops in a similar light battle dress, very different from the traditional Sumerian infantryman.

Here again, the written sources are surprisingly silent about the types of weapon and protective clothing with which the state's craftsmen must have been busily engaged at times. In the south in the third millennium, to judge from the few available representations of battle, the chariots were the elite arm. The four-wheeled carts of the Standard of Ur were apparently towed by four animals and carried two fighters, who attacked with copper-tipped javelins kept in a quiver at the front of the cab. The ruler rides in one, and they are shown trampling down the prostrate enemy on cylinder seals. Chariots were a conspicuous component of the burial goods of kings and other wealthy citizens, and enough pride was taken in the equids trained to tow them that a poet could not incongruously liken Šulgi himself to one. Nevertheless, the vehicles must have been unwieldy, with their solid wooden wheels and primitive construction, and difficult to maintain. One must suspect that their value was largely symbolic, and that it was partly indeed their cost, and the mystique involved in the very expertise they demanded, that gave them a social role like that of the medieval charger or the late second-millennium chariotry of the Near East, both intimately bound in with a noble class. They lost this paramount role under the Akkad Dynasty (whose armies perhaps lacked the urban background, and certainly campaigned over long distances, in terrains very different from the flat plains of Sumer

(a)   (b)

Figure 13:2 Stele of the Vultures (so named from another fragment showing them preying on the dead; see also Figure 13:5), from Girsu, *c.* 2450 BC. Troops of Lagaš arrayed against the enemy from Umma. With a long inscription of Eanatum. (de Sarzec 1884–1912, Planche 3 bis and 4 ter)

Figure 13:3 Stele of Daduša, King of Ešnunna at the time of Hammurapi. The inscription relates his military exploits, while the relief scenes in four registers show him facing a goddess who stands over the walls of a fortified city, smiting an enemy, and having captives led before him. The lowest register has the severed heads of his opponents (cf. Figure 13:5). (Photo: courtesy Iraq Museum, Baghdad)

and Akkad). By the Old Babylonian period, although heavy wagons are an important resource, chariots seem virtually to be confined to ceremonial occasions or ritual use in the service of the gods (now with the recently introduced horse to tow them), and cavalry, in the sense of bodies of troops riding on horseback, does not appear till late in the second millennium.[433]

In any case, the humble infantryman was doubtless the backbone of the armies at all times, even if he gets less coverage in the iconography and texts. The foot-soldiers of Early Dynastic Sumer used a variety of weapons, to judge from the monuments. The Stele of the Vultures, erected by Eanatum of Lagaš to commemorate his victory over his neighbour at Umma, illustrates three classes heavily armed (Figure 13:2): one contingent of the Lagaš troops shoulders axes, another carries solid adzes (with the blade transverse to the handle), which could well double up as an agricultural tool. These are well attested archaeologically, and the head of a typical adze could weigh more than 1.25 kg of solid copper.[434] The remainder form a phalanx with large shields (probably leather with metal studs) and spears. Of the three, it is probably the spears that proved the most effective arm, since contingents of spearmen persist in Ur III times and are singled out for mention by Šulgi.[435] On his 'Victory Stele' Naram-Sin holds one of the very few military bows, although like slings they were certainly age-old, and already in the Uruk period we see the ruler engaged in shooting arrows at lions. The best illustration of a bow in use in war comes from Mari in the Early Dynastic period, along with a large and no doubt very welcome shield (Figure 13:4).[436]

All these are *piercing* implements. Another class of weapon conspicuous by its absence is the slicing blade. To those brought up on tales of single combat from medieval and ancient Europe, the classic hand-to-hand weapon is probably the sword, with its capacity to cut by slashing as well as thrusting, but this is an invention of the later second millennium BC, and, despite the bronze swords in use in the Aegean and the Levant, in Mesopotamia it remained a rarity until the Iron Age. The reasons for the late arrival of the sword are partly technical: copper or bronze does not take a sharpened edge as well as iron, and a strong blade in solid metal is an expensive item. The sword's antecedents are represented on one side by the dagger, on the other by the rather home-made looking blades which were wrapped round the end of a wooden shaft and can be seen held by a warrior from

Figure 13:4 Incised shell plaque from Mari, Early Dynastic III. Archer with spearman holding protective wicker shield. (Mission Archéologique de Mari. Courtesy J.-Cl. Margueron)

Kish (Figure 2:5, p. 29), or indeed tucked into Naram-Sin's belt on his great stele. Intermediate stages between these two are best attested in the Levant, in the early second millennium, but the transitional 'sickle-sword' is a familiar divine weapon on Babylonian cylinder seals too.[437]

Much remains to be discovered about the detail of developments in military equipment. Partly this is because not enough effort has been made to match the textual data to the archaeological evidence, but it is also partly because archaeological evidence itself is scarce: the business end of virtually all these weapons will have been copper, or where possible bronze, but, except as grave goods, few such weapons survive, since damaged or broken blades were regularly salvaged for their metal. For these reasons it is difficult to assert the absence of certain items with confidence, but it does seem likely that the heavy armour of overlapping metal plates, known from the later part of the second millennium, was not in use, only leather or perhaps sometimes heavy felt being used as protective clothing over the body and head. The metal armour may indeed partly have been a response to the increased power of the newly introduced solid sword blades, as well as to the penetration of arrows from improved composite bows.

Nature and causes of conflict

Armies fought for many reasons and in different conditions. The historical record includes the meeting of armies in a pitched battle, beduin razzias, the invasion of barbarian hordes, long-distance campaigns to foreign countries, and siege and sally round fortified cities. The character of a successful force is defined by the task confronting it. The dependence of the city on its agricultural base makes the defence of territory of prime importance, and makes it vulnerable to defeat by siege or by the destruction of its food reserves. On one occasion in the squabbling of Amorite princes round Mari we hear that a land's harvest was burned.[438] This may have been an exception, a 'foul' according the rules of the time, but it underlines the seasonal imperative, that a sedentary community cannot draw on its full human resources without damaging its subsistence base, for fields have to be irrigated and harvested, so that certain times of year are better for fighting. Nomadic groups are not bound by these constraints, having no sedentary homes or fields to defend, and this is one reason why they were particular thorns in the villagers' sides.

The mobile past which may lie behind the lightness of the equipment of Amorite (and perhaps also the Akkadian) armies must also have affected their geographical horizons. Sargon and Naram-Sin's legendary marches into the west are less surprising when we learn that the king of Aleppo was prepared to send troops to the far side of Babylonia to help his fellow Amorites against the threat from Elam (Text 13:6). The political and military scene in the second millennium spanned over 1000 km from the Mediterranean to the Gulf. Messengers from Tilmun passed through Mari, and Samsi-Addu's correspondence with his sons shows that routes were carefully planned, with knowledge of local geography and, of course, of logistical requirements (Text 13:7). From Babylonia itself detailed day-by-day itineraries have survived for the route from Babylonia up the Tigris to Assur and west across the North Mesopotamian plains to Emar on the Euphrates.[439] Information

Text 13:6 Letter from the King of Aleppo to the King of Der
Say to Yašub-Yahad, Yarim-Lim your brother says: May Šamaš (the god of justice) investigate my conduct and yours, and render judgement! I behave to you like a father and brother and you behave to me like an ill-wisher and enemy. What requital is this for the fact that the weapons of Adad and Yarim-Lim rescued the city of Babylon, and gave life to your land and yourself? Had it not been for Adad and Yarim-Lim the city of Der would have been blown away like chaff 15 years ago, so that one would be unable to find it and you would not be able to act like this. Indeed, Sin-gamil, the King of Diniktum, like you is rewarding me with hostility and obstructions. I have moored 500 boats in the quay of Diniktum, and for 12 years I have supported his land and himself. Now you are rewarding me with hostility and obstructions like him. I swear to you, by Addu, the god of my city, and Sin my personal god, I shall not rest until I have destroyed your land and yourself! Now I shall come at the beginning of spring, and I shall advance to the doors of your city gate, and shall acquaint you with the bitterness of the weapons of Adad and Yarim-Lim.

[Der is east of the Tigris on the route to Susa, and Diniktum a port on the Tigris]

(After Dossin 1956)

Text 13:7 Routes for a force of 20,000 men across the desert to Qatna
[Samsi-Addu to Yasmah-Addu:] ... You wrote to me about your route with the army. Marching with the army is not [...], and you are still young and have not gained experience of [...]. Let La'um and Mutu-Bisir read (the earlier[?]) tablets, consult with them, and take your decision in the light of theirs. Mutu-Bisir has experienced [those routes] ... [After a passage concerned with gathering intelligence on the water supplies] Send me a report on the whole matter: Which route is best for the army's march? Is the upper route best? Is the central route best? Is the lower route best? Is it best for the army to go from where you are? Or should the army set out on the march from Abattum, or from Halabit, or from where you are? Send around to have them establish properly for you the situation with regard to the water supplies available on those routes, and send the information to me .... and the divination experts who are going with you, Zimri-Dagan, Naram-Sin, ..., and Apil-ilišu son of Ibal-pi-El, should take their decisions and [read the omens] before you in Qatna.
[Note that Mutu-bisir's name actually means 'Man of (Jebel) Bishri']

(After Durand 1987a, 163–5)

was collected by spies or informers, and in the amazing political kaleidoscope of Hammurapi's era it was obviously important that it should be transmitted at speed, and, as well as couriers, the Mari texts reveal the use of beacons in cases of dire need.[440]

Siege warfare is a major feature of the military scene. The earliest city walls are those of Habuba Kabira, the Uruk period trading settlement on the Euphrates in Syria, although, as one might have predicted, walls of that time are now also attested in the south.[441] In the story of Gilgamesh and Akka, the Uruk population look out at the Kish encampments from the walls, and it is Gilgamesh's appearance on the battlements that seems to clinch the result (cf. Figure 13:3). Once a city was captured, further resistance was often pre-empted by the razing of its walls; and the rebuilding of the walls was a symbol of revolt. As with body armour, so with architecture, offensive innovation balances the measures of the defender. As early as the Ebla texts, we have mention of battering rams, and the Mari correspondence is full of references to siege towers, some of which would be pre-assembled and floated downstream (Text 13:8).[442] Failing a wooden scaffold to

Text 13:8 An early Old Babylonian letter from Ešnunna

Say to my lord: The troops are well. The city is safe. The garrison of my lord is strong. Even if the Amorites should make war for ten years and bring ten battering rams, ten siege towers, (and) twenty ladders(?), I will remain strong in my city. My lord should not worry.

(After Whiting 1987, 46)

surmount the battlements, the next best solution was to build a ramp. This too is described in the Mari letters, and the three-dimensional geometry of constructing siege ramps was one of the exercises of the Babylonian mathematical curriculum (cf. Text 12:4 above).

For the siege of Nurrugum (an unidentified but evidently important city in northern Mesopotamia) Samsi-Addu reckoned to gather an army of 60,000. This may excite some scepticism, but in fact the Mari texts, which are not propaganda documents, not infrequently talk of bodies of 1000 to 10,000 men (Texts 13:7, 13:9). Hammurapi also deals with comparable numbers, but further research is needed before Ur III and earlier texts can yield similar information, despite the '5,400 men' Sargon is reputed to have maintained at Akkad, and the large bodies of men at Šuruppak, of whom a group of more than 600 are explicitly described as 'going to battle'.[443] In any case, the significance of such numbers is hard to assess until we have a better idea of the size of the entire sedentary and nomadic populations of the time.

Text 13:9 Samsi-Addu reports on international troop movements

Say to Yasmah-Addu, Samsi-Addu, your father says: About the troops which are waiting with you. I did write to you about sending them to me. Send those troops to me quickly, and you wait in Mammagira with the rest of those troops which you are retaining with you. It is not a good idea for you to wait in Šapanašim or Talhaya: Mammagira is a good place for you to wait.

Another matter. I wrote to have my troops which are waiting in Babylon moved on, and they have brought those troops on here. With those troops, 3000 Ešnunna troops with their Ištar-standards, these two (bodies of) troops have arrived. Those troops have joined up with the troops who were here – these two forces have gathered together. The matter of the Turukkeans will be dealt with quickly. When the matter of the Turukkeans has been dealt with, I shall take the head of the army and go up to the land of Zalmaqum. So now the matter of the Turukkeans will be dealt with, and the matter of the campaign to the Upper Land will be dealt with. This is for your information.

I sent you this tablet on the 3rd day of Kinunum.

(After Charpin and Durand 1985, 316–17)

The aftermath

Whatever the motive of warfare, the participants reaped benefit or loss. The spoils of war were various. After a battle, cities, houses and individuals were plundered, and conventions as to the distribution of the plunder were acknowledged, as some fascinating Mari letters reveal.[444] Some portion was reserved for the king, and, earlier, the kings of Akkad presented at least a token of their booty to the shrines: stone bowls plundered by Rimuš from Iran and inscribed 'booty of Elam' have been found at Nippur, Ur, Sippar and even further afield, and at least one bowl of Naram-Sin from the 'booty of Magan' at Ur.[445] The Sumerian myth of Ninurta recounts how on his return from a victorious campaign against the forces of disorder, he and his troops marched towards the Ekur, Enlil's shrine, and after some negotiations were able to present their spoils (Text 13:10). Not to make a dedication to the appropriate temple would doubtless have constituted hubris, and this is a tradition which survives into Assyrian times, not to mention the classical world. We may perhaps see such gifts as the counterpart of the ex votos presented to the temples by grateful merchants on their return from a journey. Whether the temples themselves suffered despoilment often depended on who the enemies were: the Ur laments describe the desecration of the innermost sanctuaries at Ur, and the casting down of the decorations

Text 13:10 Ninurta's battle spoils on his approach to Nippur

The warrior Ninurta, in his valorous strength, completed (his triumph):

On his shining chariot, which inspires terrible awe,
He hung his captured wild bulls on the axle,
Hung his captured cows on the cross-piece of the yoke,
Hung the Six-headed Wild Ram on the dustguard,
Hung the Dragon, the warrior, on the seat,
Hung the **magilum** on the frame,
Hung the Bison on the beam,
Hung Kulianna on the footboard,
Hung the 'White Substance' on the front of the yoke,
Hung Strong Copper on the inside pole pin,
Hung the Anzu bird on the front guard,
and Hung the Seven-headed Serpent on the shining ...
Into his 'Chariot Fit for Battle'
Lord Ninurta set foot.
Udanne, the all-seeing god, and
Lugal-anbadra, the bearded lord, go before him, and
The awesome one of the mountains, Lugal-kurdub,
The ... of the Lord Ninurta, follows behind him. ...
The Anunna, the great gods, are unable to confront him,
As the sovereign swept on like the Deluge ....
When at Enlil's command he directed his way to Ekur.

(After Cooper 1978, 63–7)

of the temples, but this was on the part of the invading Elamites and their allies from the hills.[446] Similarly, the Hittites had no compunction in taking the statue of Marduk himself into exile when they put an end to an era by their capture of Babylon, but within the cut and thrust of local warfare in Sumer and Akkad one gains the impression that the temples of another city were respected – after all, they belonged to members of a single pantheon, gods acknowledged throughout the land. There were of course exceptions, and even today we seem to sense that the lament over the destruction of the temples of Lagaš by Lugal-zagesi is laden with genuine revulsion at the breaking of a convention usually honoured in its observance (cf. Text 6:4 above).

Human spoil

One of the most important spoils of battle were the people. In the Ur III period some texts record long lists of ex votos, known as **arua**, and some of these are women and children from the campaigns of the kings. The absence of males is significant. Gelb presumes they were often killed, or mutilated.[447] True, in the third millennium official propaganda commemorates the piling of enemy corpses into heaps and their burial under a tumulus of earth (Figure 13:5),[448] but we cannot be sure if they were killed in the heat of the battle

Figure 13:5 Stele of the Vultures: forming a burial mound of enemy corpses after the battle. (de Sarzec 1884–1912, Planche 3c)

or executed, and some prisoners were certainly taken as slaves. Actually on the march, we know that prisoners-of-war were held in neck-stocks (see Figure 13:6) or simply had their elbows tied behind their backs, but this was only a temporary measure, and there had to be a long-term way of constraining them and keeping them under control. Heavy chains were expensive, though not unknown. One solution was blinding: despite the humanitarian qualms of twentieth-century scholars, the large-scale blinding of prisoners-of-war is well attested at other times and places, and the existence of 'blind men' among the slaves of Lagaš in the Early Dynastic period does not need to be doubted.[449] They could serve perfectly adequately, like Samson on the grindstone, to move water from a well or canal to the fields or gardens, with just a bucket and rope. Slaves could of course be marked, and in Old Babylonian times we know that they were given a special hair-do (*apputtum*; Texts 5:13; 5:14), but this serves purely for identification, not for constraint.[450]

Figure 13:6 Fragments of an Akkadian victory stele: prisoners in a neck-stock and exotic booty (the vase, bottom left, is probably of Anatolian origin). (Reconstruction by J.F.X. McKeon, *Boston Museum Bulletin* 68 1970, 230. Drawing by Suzanne Chapman)

Whether imprisonment was used is a more difficult question. Maintaining numbers of foreigners in captivity is only sensible if there is an intention to repatriate them eventually, whether in return for ransom or in the context of political negotiations in which they take the role of hostages. Such a situation is probably reflected in the presence of Hurrian prisoners-of-war in the Nippur region during the Ur III period: they will have constituted a diplomatic bargaining counter.[451] It also must lie behind a group of texts concerned with prisoners (asīrum) during the Old Babylonian period. Some of them record the issue of government rations to these people, who include named individuals and numbers of women and children; others seem to be 'death certificates', formally witnessed by the responsible officials. The significant point is that the archives came from cities in the south like Uruk and Larsa, whereas the prisoners are often stated to come from a variety of towns and countries, including Isin, Ešnunna and Elam. It now seems clear that they were victims of the upheavals in the south of Mesopotamia after the death of Hammurapi, some at least of whom were awaiting financial or diplomatic manoeuvres to secure their release.[452]

Peace and alliance

Text 13:11 From an agreement between Šadlaš and Neribtum
Decree of Šadlaš and Neribtum

§1 Son of a freeman – $\frac{2}{3}$ mina silver
Slave of a freeman – 15 shekels silver
Slavewoman – 10 shekels silver
Old man and old woman – like a child(?) – tariff.

§2 Anyone of the land of Šadlaš and its pastures,
and of the land of Neribtum and its pastures,
who fled from the hostilities and has been cut off –
his master shall not seize him.

§7 A son of Šadlaš and its pastures,
a son of Neribtum and its pastures,
who went to make profit before the hostilities
and was taken prisoner, shall be released.

§9 If a theft of cattle or sheep took place, and
if it can be brought to and tried before judges,
if it is a citizen of Neribtum –
an oath of the citizen of Neribtum by Sin of Kamanum;
(if it is a citizen of Šadlaš) –
an oath of the citizen of Šadlaš by Sin of Ur-Iškura.

§11 Ammi-dušur shall not enlist a soldier of Sumu-numhim
Sumu-numhim shall not enlist a soldier of Ammi-dušur.

(After Greengus 1979 No. 326)

Text 13:12 Samsi-Addu delayed by treaty negotiations

Say to Yasmah-Addu, Samsi-Addu your father says: I have heard the tablet you sent me, in which you wrote 'Yarim-Lim is not present so I did not come to my lord. I am now staying at Qattunan until my lord reaches Šubat-Enlil. I shall await my lord at Qattunan'. This is what you wrote. The ruler of Ešnunna has written to me about making a treaty [lit.: touching his throat]. There are some words which I have removed from the tablet of the oath, and I have written to Ešnunna. The Ešnunna men are blocked(?) and until now no message has (reached here[?]). Since I am delayed in the City (Assur), don't wait for me at Qattunan, but go to Haššum of Membida: there is the centre of the land, and there all the Haneans gather. Get there, let the Haneans gather to you, set about making a census of the Haneans and do the census.

I sent you this tablet on the 12th day of Addar.

(After Dossin 1950a, No. 37)

The repatriation of citizens was certainly a concern of states at the time. One of our earliest treaties, between the rulers of Šadlaš and Neribtum, two small post-Ur III kingdoms in the Diyala region, is more of a memorandum of disengagement terms than a treaty proper. It is particularly concerned with the fate of citizens of the two states who find themselves the wrong side of the frontier at the end of the fighting, but also covers other claims consequent on the disorder (Text 13:11). Such written treaties from our period are very scarce, although diplomatic correspondence makes it clear that they did exist and were carefully drafted for each occasion (Text 13:12). On the other hand, much diplomacy was conducted on an oral plane, not least within the world of the Amorite tribes. The very words for concluding a treaty in the Mari age, 'to kill asses' (*hayārī qatālum*), reflect the traditional and ritual nature of the procedures, referring to mimetic actions as part of an oath-taking ceremony. Oaths and the vengeance expected on an oath-breaker were the only sanction to be expected between two sovereign polities and their representatives, whether these were the **ensis** of Umma and Lagaš, or two Amorite sheikhs. In Sumer too divine involvement was sought: to cement the acceptance of the frontier originally delineated by Me-salim, the great gods were summoned to witness, and the news of the oaths sworn by the two parties to the agreement was conveyed to their home shrines by doves.[453]

The same involvement of divine sanction can be seen with prospective agreements promoting future co-operation rather than settling past differences. Some kind of alliance probably lay behind the well-known letter to a god found at Mari, where the cause of the Samsi-Addu family against the dynasty of Zimri-Lim is traced back to the breaking of an agreement between Ila-kabkabu and Yaggit-Lim. The writer uses the strongest words of his opponents' action, emphasizing that the breaking of an oath was a religious sin which justified extreme action against the sinner (Text 13:13). Nevertheless, the sanction was not always entirely effective, and alliances could be extremely transitory in the shifting world of Near Eastern politics (Text 2:7, p. 46).

Text 13:13 Apology addressed to a god

[To the god ... who pro]tects the worshipper, the lofty one, my lord, [speak]! [The words of] Yasmah-Addu, your servant and worshipper: Since my birth there has been no one who has sinned against the god. Everyone has observed the god's ordinances. In the past, Ila-kabkabu and Yagid-Lim between then took a binding oath by god. Then Ila-kabkabu did no wrong to Yagid-Lim but Yagid-Lim did wrong to Ila-kabkabu. When you learned of this you attacked him (thus) going to the aid of Ila-kabkabu. Ila-kabkabu destroyed his wall (and) conquered [...] Yahdun-Lim [...] the wrong of Yagid-Lim [...] Ila-kabkabu and [...] Samsi-Addu [...] Yagid-Lim.

(Dossin 1950a, No. 3; see also Charpin and Durand 1985, 293–5; Sasson 1987)

International politics

The complexities of the political map are reflected in a lively diplomatic scene. Messengers travelled widely both within and beyond the frontiers, and there were recognized conventions for their treatment. Envoys from Tilmun at Mari received gifts, shoes, provisions (Text 7:6, p. 148). Some messages were of course oral, but, despite their extra-urban roots, even the Amorite kingdoms made extensive use of the written document to control their officials and communicate with their allies, and reports to Zimri-Lim from his representative at the court of Hammurapi show that the cuneiform tablet was an important factor in international politics, enabling ambassadors to conclude agreements which might otherwise have been possible only by the meeting of the two rulers involved. Not that such meetings were impossible. Not only did the king of Ugarit want to pay a visit to the palace at Mari, but it seems that Zimri-Lim himself made a journey to the Mediterranean which was a diplomatic, not a military, expedition.[454] The crossing of frontiers in this fashion must have required clear understanding of the protocol, and careful advance organization. Kings must have travelled with their entourage, some of whom will have been armed. On one occasion an important Hurrian ruler from North Mesopotamia travelled with a substantial escort to visit the Ur III king, and some of the VIP *asīrum* prisoners also have an entourage with them.[455] Relations between states required the exchange of more than words. Gifts were normal, and their language was very specific. Just as in the Amarna Age, there was no hesitation in requesting a gift, and sometimes in complaining about one received (cf. Text 7:5, p. 146). As we have seen in chapter 7, the ultimate exchange was of women, and this of course provided a much stronger bond, not least because the woman's children would tend to favour their mother's country. Such exchanges, and in particular the treaties, oral or written, constitute in themselves an acknowledgement that there is a legal entity on each side. This brings us to consider the theory as well as the practice of power.

Further reading

For the practice and equipment of war, see Yadin 1963; for wheeled vehicles M.A. Littauer and J.H. Crouwel, *Wheeled Vehicles and Ridden Animals in the Ancient Near East* (Leiden). On the treatment of defeated populations see Gelb 1973. For warfare and diplomacy in the Old Babylonian period, Sasson 1969 and Munn-Rankin 1956 remain useful general surveys despite much additional material recently published. For a sociologist's view of ancient Near Eastern warfare see M. Mann, *The Sources of Social Power, I: A history of power from the beginning to* AD *1760*, chs 5 and 8 (Cambridge University Press, 1986).

14

Religion and politics

International negotiations require that authority be vested in the person or group repre-senting each party. The practical nature of this authority and its theoretical basis varied widely with their social and ethnic origins. Whereas the tribal hierarchy of the Amorites conforms quite well to what we know of similar societies at other times and places, the urban culture of the old sedentary population had developed an explicit ideology to describe the relationships between ruler and ruled, and between politics and religion. Religion as such is not our subject, but in the spheres reflected in our documents Meso-potamian religion is politics. From the earliest times historical statements are couched in religious metaphors, and this alone is enough to show that their ideological statements were important on a purely secular level. While most such statements concern the king or kingship, this is by no means the only political concept in play: the system has to incorporate the ideas of territory, of popular will, of tribe and dynasty. Statements, whether in 'literary' or 'historical' texts, may reflect popular belief, scholastic speculation or blatant propaganda, and we do not really have the insight into the context of such texts which would enable us to discern their true nature. Nevertheless, even blatant propaganda tells us something: it shows the climate of opinion and how much attention the rulers paid to it, and it reveals the importance attached to tradition and precedent in the maintenance of the order on which their civilization depended. Thus their political philosophy needs to be understood for two reasons, rather like the system of writing: partly because it is the filter through which the record of historical events is transmitted to us, but partly also because it was itself one integral cog in the mechanism of society.

Installation of a ruler

That the subject of political power is a complex one is immediately apparent from the diversity of terms referring to rulers in the early third millennium. Perhaps the commonest is the Sumerian **ensi(ak)**, e.g. at Lagaš, but some cities had a ruler with a priestly office (**en** at Uruk, or **sanga** at central Sumerian cities like Umma and Isin), while some also held the title **lugal**, which, as we have seen, sometimes implied domination over other rulers. Reams have been written on the subtleties of the distinctions, but for our present purposes we can dodge the issue by using the neutral term 'ruler'.[456]

There is general agreement from a variety of different sources on the rituals accompany-ing the installation of a ruler, although they differ in detail. After the Flood, the Sumerian epic tells us that kingship was brought to earth, represented by three symbols: a hat, a stick and a stool (or, to give them the names they have acquired in this context in English, the 'crown', the 'sceptre' and the 'throne'), and these recur time and again in the hymns addressed to kings, along with other royal insignia (for instance, Text 14.1). In the iconography too we see the ruler identified by certain symbols: even in the Uruk period there is one figure who wears a flat cap and a 'net skirt', who wields authority. Later, in Neo-Sumerian art, the ruler alone is depicted with a close-fitting hat with a turned up band (see Figures 14:1; 14:2). When shown seated on a stool cushioned with a fleecy rug,

Text 14:1 From a hymn to Rim-Sin, King of Larsa

At Larsa ... where the **me**s of rulership have been cast, you have been chosen rightly for the shepherdship of Sumer and Akkad,

....

May An fix the holy crown on your head,
May he install you grandly on the throne of life,
May he fill your hands with the sceptre of justice,
May he bind to your body the mace which controls the people,
May he make you grasp the mace which multiplies the people,
May he open for you the shining udder of heaven, and rain down for you the rains of heaven.

(After Charpin 1986a, 275–6)

Figure 14:1 Impression of the cylinder seal of Šulgi-ili, a servant of the king's daughter. He is brought into her presence by his protective goddess on the left. Imitating the king in similar scenes, the princess sits on a dais to receive him, like a deity but on a fleece-covered stool rather than an altar. (A.255, L. Delaporte, *Musée du Louvre: Catalogue des cylindres orientaux, II. Acquisitions*, Paris, 1923, Planche 77:2)

Figure 14:2 Stele of Gudea of Lagaš: the **ensi**, bare-headed on the left and identified by his name carved on his robe, is led into the presence of Ningirsu, only fragments of whose throne survive, by his personal god and other figures distinguished as gods by their horned crowns. (Photo: Vorderasiatisches Museum, Berlin)

he is presumably on his 'throne', and sometimes holds a mace, just as the foremen of groups of workers or soldiers hold a stick. Official literature tells us that the rulers were solemnly invested with these symbols of their office in the temples (Text 14:2),[457] and that these events really took place is known from administrative documents recording sacrifices made on the occasion of the coronation of Ur III kings.[458]

Duties of the ruler

Offerings

Let us begin by looking at the ritual acts expected. The earliest texts we have naming rulers are the stone bowls in which offerings were made to temples, and these were acts with overtly political overtones, since the act of making this formal offering constituted a

Text 14:2 The inauguration of the king at Uruk
He entered into Eanna.
He drew near the resplendent throne dais.
He placed the bright scepter in his hand.

He drew near the throne dais of Nin-men-na ('Lady of the Crown')
He fastened the golden crown upon his head.

He drew near to the throne dais of Nin-PA ('Lady of the Scepter')
Nin-PA, fit for heaven and earth . . . .

After she had discarded his 'name (of) smallness,'
She did not call his **bur-gi** name
But called his 'name (of) rulership.'

(After Jacobsen, in Frankfort 1948, 245–6)

claim to hegemony, and the acquiescence of the temple personnel in accepting it must have been an acknowledgement of it. From En-mebaragesi in the Diyala region (Figure 2:6), through Me-salim at Adab and Lugal-zagesi at the Ekur itself in Nippur (Text 2:3) the length of the inscription grew, but the underlying idea was the same. The formal importance of the proceedings is underlined by the mention of the 'King of Kish' in the Keš Temple hymn, and probably also by the information that the ruler adopted a special name, known as his **bur-gi** ('bowl presentation'?) name, for the act (cf. Text 14:2).[459] While it is never spelled out for us, it is not unreasonable to assume that two ideological motives were here converging: the ruler as representative of the people will have been responsible for making offerings on their behalf to the god(s) of their city, without which the gods' favour could not be retained. On the other side, it is clear that the kings took the credit for the economic prosperity and social order which follow from successful harvests, and it was thus very much in their interests to secure the divine favour, from which prosperity would follow. This circular concept – prosperity is the result of and hence evidence of divine approval, and pleasing the gods is the means to secure prosperity – is the religious counterpart of the secular argument which runs, quite simply, success is self-justifying. Already in the ED II period some of the personal names bear witness to the association between the king and prosperity (e.g. **lugal hé-gál** 'the king [has created?] plenty').[460] This is exemplified by the end of Lugal-zagesi's inscription on his vases, with its emphasis on the prosperity of The Land under him, and is a recurrent theme in other Sumerian inscriptions (Text 2:3).

Care for the temple

The majority of the formal inscriptions of Mesopotamian rulers result from another, more substantial, activity on behalf of the gods, the building of temples. That it was an important part of the ruler's role cannot be doubted, if one looks at the images of Ur-Nanše carrying the basket of earth (Figure 6:6) or Ur-Nammu with the builder's tools over his shoulder, or reads of Gudea's commission from the gods to rebuild the Eninnu, and of his part in moulding the first brick. Gudea in particular explains at length that his reconstruction of the Eninnu, Ningirsu's principal shrine at Girsu, was undertaken to please or appease the god and so rescue Lagaš from the effects of a water shortage (Text 14:3). The building

> **Text 14:3** Material rewards for building Ningirsu's new temple
>
> When for me, able shepherd Gudea,
> You have started (work) on Eninnu, my royal abode,
> I will call up in heaven a humid wind,
> that shall bring you abundance from on high,
> so that in your time the people shall spread their hands on plenty.
> Prosperity shall accompany the laying of the foundations of my house.
> All the great fields will raise their hands for you,
> dikes and canals will crane their necks for you,
> and for you the water will rise
> to the high ground which the waters do not reach.
> Cream will be poured abundantly in Sumer in your time.
> Good weight of wool will be given in your time.
> (Gudea Cylinder A, col. xi, after Jacobsen, in Frankfort 1948, 257–8; Jacobsen 1987, 401–2)

was a communal activity: while the ruler might mould the first brick and carry the first basket, the rest of the population took part too, and Gudea brought contingents in from outside the city itself (cf. p. 83). To please the god and ensure his or her continued presence, or, in earthly terms, to satisfy local pride, the building had to be splendid. To span the roof, timbers would often be imported from abroad. The walls were decorated, and the tradition of communal investment in the temple, which must have its roots in prehistory, is still echoed in the legends of Early Dynastic times, telling how the lapis lazuli and other luxury items were explicitly imported from the east for the adornment of Inanna's temple, not for the ruler's private glorification (cf. p. 114).

The most important piece of furniture was of course the divine image. Perhaps because of their rarity, and certainly because of their very special nature, divine statues have not survived from our time and place, though they undoubtedly existed. Textual evidence is also frustratingly silent, until the end of the Ur III Dynasty when accounts from the goldsmith's workshop prove that the kings were engaged in restoring a divine image.[461] One of the commonest Ur III year formulae is concerned with the induction of a deity into the temple, which probably means installation of a new divine statue. In the Old Babylonian period it certainly does, since the materials of which the new image is made are described (cf. Text 6:2, p. 118). The deities needed continuing support, and rulers often made provision for them by decreeing regular offerings (see chapter 6).

The ritual duties

These acts need be seen as no more than the proper demeanour of a wealthy secular patron, not something necessarily linked to a religious role, but the rulers were also expected to participate in a variety of ritual activities. Some of course were already priests, and both coronation and the presentation of offering-bowls were ritual, though not necessarily recurrent, duties. Some are regular festivals, others may be ad hoc rituals, such as were needed to avoid evil presages. In later Mesopotamia we have long orders of service or programmes for rituals involving the king. In earlier times ritual instructions were not usually written down. The few that were and have reached us also involve the king, and that the later ceremonies in which he participated had deep roots is shown by the occasional early mention of his role in ceremonies like ablution or the purification of the army before battle.[462]

The stress which the official literature places on the ruler's responsibility for the prosperity of The Land is undoubtedly linked to the belief that it depended on the correct fulfilment of certain rituals. As we have noted already (p. 150), the king himself could obviously not take on the ritual duties of each earlier city ruler, so that the appointment of members of the royal family to the position of high-priest was a political compromise which asserted the regime's acceptance of the traditional order, while relieving the king of the impossibility of participating in person. In later times the king of Babylon was required to participate in an annual New Year ritual, which took place in a special building called the 'festival house' (*bīt akīti*). Previous *akītum* festivals are attested in various cities and at various times of year, but all seem to belong outside the city, thus to be agricultural festivals associated with fertility.[463]

The details of the ruler's role in the various local festivals are not known, but he was certainly involved in one, eloquent fertility ritual which has attracted much modern attention. During the Isin–Larsa period the kings participated in a ritual enactment of sexual intercourse designed to promote prosperity. The majority of our textual evidence takes the form of hymns to the ruler, the most explicit of which depicts the ruler as embodying the god Dumuzi (known as Ama-ušumgal-ana), the spouse of Inanna, the

Text 14:4 The king joins Inanna for the Sacred Marriage rite

In the palace, the house of counsel of the Land, the lock of all countries . . . for the 'Lady of the Palace' they have installed a dais, (and) the king that is the god dwells with her – so as to care for the life of all countries, to inspect the first right day, to perfect the **me** on the day of no moon, at the New Year, on the day of the ritual, they laid out the bed for my lady. They purified the bed-straw with cedar essence, and laid it down for her bed. Beside it they arranged her bedspread. When the bedspread had joyfully improved the bed, my lady bathed for the pure loins, she bathed for the loins of the king, she bathed for the loins of Iddin-Dagan. Holy Inanna rubbed herself with soap, she sprinkled oil and cedar essence on the ground. The king went to the pure loins with head high, with head high he went to the loins of Inanna. Amaušumgalana shares the bed with her, in her pure loins he is entertained.

(After Römer 1965, 133–4, lines 167–88; cf. Reisman 1973, 190–1)

goddess of love and war and patroness of the city of Uruk. The detailed description, of which the central episode is quoted in Text 14:4, leaves no doubt as to the nature of the ceremony. We read how the king arrives in Uruk,[464] how the ceremony is introduced by jugglers and musicians, offerings brought for the feast, and the bedchamber prepared. The king is dressed in special robe and headgear, and brought before the goddess by another god, Nin-šubur. At some point the king is endowed with the insignia of royalty,[465] and the political implications of the ritual are underlined when the goddess 'decrees the shepherdship of (all) countries as his destiny'.[466]

As Frankfort remarks, we are 'free to speculate' as to how Inanna herself was represented in this rite, although there is good reason to guess that a class of priestess known as **nu-gig** may have taken her place.[467] There are less clear indicators that similar rituals may have been enacted between the ruler and other deities following other local traditions, and many details remain unclear: whether it was normally a component of New Year ceremonies, whether it was re-enacted annually or only after the accession, whether any of the representations of sexual intercourse in contemporary iconography refer to this ritual, and whether the same proceedings took place in earlier years for which we lack explicit descriptions.[468] Some writers have taken the deification of the Ur III kings from Šulgi onwards as the logical consequence of their representation of the god described so unequivocally in the sacred marriage rite, but this is not self-evident, and it is necessary now to turn to consider this phenomenon in more detail.

Divine kings

A ruler's claim to divinity can be expressed in three ways: his name may be preceded by the cuneiform sign for god, in the same way as other deities' names are, his headdress may be represented with horns, the mark of a god in the iconography, and in a variety of ways evidence may be seen that he was worshipped by the population in a cult of his own. The most extreme version of this is undoubtedly the temple built to the divine Šu-Sin in the city of Ešnunna (Tell Asmar), excavated by the Chicago expedition to the Diyala region in the 1930s. The inscribed doorsocket of the temple tells us that it was to him that it was dedicated, and in its architectural features the building resembles the shrines of other gods.[469] Ur III cylinder seals offer a depiction of this scene, but they do retain a very marked distinction between the real god and the king: the king's seat is not the converted altar of the gods, but a stool over which a fleece has been spread, and he wears his royal hat, without any trace of horns (Figure 14:1). Evidence for the worship of the king also comes from administrative documents which record offerings made to the statue of the king: in many cases, the statue is of a deceased ruler, and it is difficult to be sure whether we are looking at the regular funerary rites accorded to ancestors, but where the king is still alive this explanation is clearly inadequate.[470] Moreover, in the case of Šulgi we have plenty of references to the priests who took care of his worship,[471] and the divine role is emphasized by month names, and a good number of personal names, composed with 'Šulgi', or the name of one of his successors, where a god's name would normally stand.[472]

The questions remain why certain rulers claimed divinity, and how this anomaly was understood. Modern scholars have suggested that participation in the sacred marriage was one route. This hardly accounts for the innovation, since it seems probable that the ritual itself is of considerable antiquity, and yet Naram-Sin is the first ruler to make this claim. Another, attractive, hypothesis is that any rulers who were the offspring of a sacred marriage could legitimately claim both divine and royal parentage.[473] Gudea, for instance, says that he had no mother and no father and was the son of the goddess of Lagaš, Gatumdug; however, elsewhere he also states that he is the son of Ninsun, of Bau and of Nanše, which makes it hard to be sure of the implications of such statements. He, however, did not lay claim to divinity, so that the Ur III practice cannot be solely explained in this way.[474] In the case of Šulgi we are fortunate to have a partial explanation: in one of his rare surviving historical inscriptions, written in both Akkadian and Sumerian, he refers to himself as 'god of his land'.[475] This plain phrase has to be interpreted in the general context of political theory, and must first be compared with the words of the original claimant of divinity, Naram-Sin. His claim is vividly expressed in the horns on his helmet in the magnificent victory stele carried off to Susa by a marauding Elamite a thousand years later and thence to the Louvre. In a recently discovered inscription from a massive copper symbol-base in northernmost Iraq he describes himself as the 'god of his city' (i.e. Akkad).[476] This inscription recounts his successive victories over rebellious cities in the south, and his role as 'god of his city' is placed in close parallelism with the role of the great gods of

Text 14:5 From an inscription of Naram-Sin

Inasmuch as he established the foundations of his city under duress, his city requested him as god of their city Akkade, from Ištar in Eanna, from Enlil in Nippur, from Dagan in Tuttul, from Ninhursag in Keš, from Enki in Eridu, from Sin in Ur, from Šamaš in Sippar (and) from Nergal in Kutha, and built his temple in Akkade.

(After Farber 1983, 68)

Mesopotamia in respect of their ancient shrines (Text 14:5). While the precise formulation is beyond our reach, what emerges clearly is that in both cases the ruler's claim to divinity is in very specific relationship to a political entity, an entity which, being newly created by historical circumstances, has no patron deity to fulfil that role.

The divine metaphor

To understand why this was felt necessary or found acceptable, we need to look more closely at the relationship between the Mesopotamian pantheon and the human political order. The circumstances which made one man ruler or gave one state hegemony over another can be described on two levels, the worldly and the heavenly, but there is a close link between them. We have already seen in chapter 6 that each city's identity was encapsulated in its patron deity, and, just as an individual's misfortune or fortune is ascribed to a personal god, so it is with a city, events on earth mirror those in heaven. Political success means divine favour, and Hammurapi's prologue to his code gives the classic formulation of the divine metaphor (Text 14:6): Babylon has gained control of the whole of Mesopotamia, and this means that Marduk, patron deity of Babylon, has been

Text 14:6 From the Prologue to the Code of Hammurapi
When exalted Anum, king of the Anunnaki (the major gods), and Enlil, lord of heaven and earth, who decrees the destinies of the Land, decreed for Marduk, first-born son of Enki, the role of Enlil to the entirety of people, making him the greatest of the Igigi-gods, called Babylon by its exalted name, made it pre-eminent in the world, and established in it a permanent kingship whose basis is founded like heaven and earth –

at that time Anum and Enlil called my name to improve the living conditions of the people, Hammurapi, attentive prince, revering the gods, to make justice appear in the land, to abolish the criminal and evil, to stop the strong from oppressing the weak, to rise like Šamaš (Sun-god, God of Justice) over mankind and to illuminate the land.

entrusted by Enlil, the patron deity of Nippur and the king of lands, with the 'Enlilship'. In turn, Marduk entrusts his flock to Hammurapi, the shepherd of his people: a metaphor which implies not two, but three parties, for a shepherd was usually employed to look after other people's sheep. For the modern western mind, the heavenly version is the later, an ex post facto rationalization of events on earth, but it is a powerful metaphor which persists well into the first millennium BC, and deserves to be examined in some detail.

Divine selection

Let us begin by considering the position of the individual man as ruler (or indeed the very occasional queen). Texts from the southern Mesopotamian cities make it clear that patrilineal descent from a previous ruler was not considered an exclusive or adequate qualification, although we know that both in north and south sons often did follow their fathers as ruler. Not unexpectedly, the protestations of some other form of selection are

Text 14:7 From the 'Reforms of UruKAgina'
… The oxen of the gods ploughed the garlic plot of the **ensi**, and the best fields of the gods became the garlic and cucumber plots of the **ensi**. Teams of asses and spirited oxen were yoked for the temple-administrators, but the grain of the temple-administrators was distributed by the personnel of the ruler … These were the practices of former times.
   When Ningirsu, warrior of Enlil, granted the Kingship of Lagaš to UruKAgina, taking him by the hand from among the 36,000 people, he replaced the customs of former times, carrying out the command that Ningirsu had given him: [there follows a list of reforms]
(After Cooper 1986, 71)

most frequent in the case of a break in the succession (Text 14:7). While we need not doubt the genuine reforming zeal of UruKAgina at Lagaš, we may also suspect that his emphasis on his virtue reflects the need to display his religious acceptability, and that his assertion that he has been divinely selected is the more strident because he did not come to power by inheritance. Similarly, Ur-Nammu, when setting up his dynasty at Ur, lays great stress on the omens which had confirmed divine approval of his selection by, or from among, the people.[477] The gods are described as choosing the king, 'taking his hand', and sometimes indeed are credited with some role in his creation, birth and upbringing. The extreme version of this comes from Eanatum in the Stele of the Vultures (see Text 14:8). With its specific and manifestly 'untrue' detail, we remain unable to read the meaning this text had for its contemporaries.

Text 14:8 The role of the gods in Eanatum's early life

... Ningirsu implanted the semen for Eanatum in the womb ... [his birth presumably related in a broken space] ... rejoiced over Eanatum. Inanna accompanied him, named him Eana-Inana-Ibgalakakatum [meaning: 'Worthy in the Eanna-Temple of Inanna'], and set him on the beneficial lap of Ninhursag. Ninhursag offered him her beneficial breast. Ningirsu rejoiced over Eanatum, semen implanted in the womb by Ningirsu. Ningirsu placed his span against him, for (a length of) 5 fore-arms [= cubits] he placed his fore-arm against him: (he measured) 5 cubits 1 span! With great joy Ningirsu gave him the Kingship of Lagaš.

(From the Stele of the Vultures, after Cooper 1986, 34)

The background to the metaphor of divine favour is obvious. In the absence of an unequivocal secular criterion for one man to be in authority over others, divine sanction was a clear necessity, and only by divine approval could the fortune of one person (or of one city) at the expense of others be explained. The selection for such high office is made by the city god, Ningirsu at Lagaš or Nanna at Ur, for instance. The individual human can hardly expect to come to the notice of the great god unaided, and it is clear that the personal god was envisaged as introducing the ruler to the city god (see Figure 14:2). When our texts refer to the personal god, they are describing something which, in our secular society, is usually referred to as 'luck', corresponding to the *daimon* of the Greeks, and the Gudea passage cited as Text 14:9 could be paraphrased as 'any king who has the good

Text 14:9 Request by Gudea to his successors as **ensi**

May any man whom Ningirsu has nominated to his personal god from among the people, as he nominated me to my personal god, not look unfavourably on the temple of my personal god. Let him mention its name – such a man will be my friend indeed, let him mention my name.

[Gudea, Statue I, col. iii.11–iv.7]

fortune to become **ensi**'. This, of course, explains how a ruler can at one and the same time be selected by popular vote or acclamation (as we shall shortly see) and by the decision of the gods. And it serves to underpin the simple philosophy that 'might is right', or that success is self-justifying.

Popular selection

In Jacobsen's seductive reconstruction of the earliest kingship, taken from the tale of Gilgamesh's resistance to the overlords from Kish, he is chosen by the assembled citizens as their leader. That a king could be chosen by the Assembly is confirmed by historical evidence from the later third millennium. The great revolt against Naram-Sin saw a citizen of Kish raised to kingship by vote of the city: his name is given as 'Kish assembled', and whether or not the event is historically accurate, it must reflect contemporary attitudes (Text 14:10). We have already seen that Ur-Nammu claims to have been selected from the people, and two of the Lagaš **ensis** tell us that they were 'taken by the hand' by Ningirsu from among the populace. Gudea also mentions his legitimation in the Assembly, under-

> **Text 14:10** Revolt against Naram-Sin in the region of Kish
>
> By the judgement of Ištar and Annunitum, he defeated them in battle ... and Kish assembled on the common boundary of TI–WI and Urumum in the (tract) Ugar-Suen on the common boundary to E-sabad, the temple of Gula, and raised Iphur-Kiši, the man of Kish, son of Summirat-Ištar, the lamentation priestess, to kingship.
>
> (After Jacobsen 1978–9, 6)

lining how important popular acceptance was, at least in theory. It is hardly surprising if the official inscriptions and administrative documents do not reflect dissenting views of the events of a succession, but the other side of the coin does show in the curses, which we meet as early as Eanatum, which envisage a ruler being unseated by a revolt of his own citizens.[478]

Ruling houses

As we have seen, Sumerian ideology did not admit a hereditary right of succession, although in practice sons often did succeed. This ideology did not necessarily apply in other cases. In the early years after the collapse of Ur III the political order was in disarray, and new rulers brought a different tradition with them, one which shows clearly in a Mari year-name 'The year in which Zimri-Lim acceded to the throne of his paternal estate', or accession years of the kings of Ešnunna described as 'The year PN entered his paternal estate'.[479] It is no coincidence that both these dynasties were Amorite. The social structure of nomadic tribal society in the Near East, as in other parts of the world, has always revolved round 'houses', representing a line of patrilinear descent but without the fixed territorial links of the sedentary dynasty.[480]

The ideology of the tribe could survive generations of sedentary rule. A tablet from the time of Ammi-ṣaduqa listing the recipients of *kispum* offerings gives us the king's ancestors for several generations before Hammurapi, even before the dynasty's installation at Babylon (Text 4:9, p. 85). The earlier names are those of some of the Amorite tribes, and from traditions incorporated into the Assyrian King List it emerges that Samsi-Addu's family traced their ancestry to the same origins, describing these forebears as '17 kings who lived in tents'.[481] We have already noted the dualism in the royal authority of Old Babylonian times as reflected in the retention of separate recruitment channels for Amorites and the older sedentary population. This dual role emerges very clearly even at Mari from Bahdi-Lim's advice to his ruler on his choice of four-legged transport (see Text 4:12). The Amorite dynasties inheriting the thrones of the traditional city-states thus had to reconcile the ideological metaphors formulated by centuries of written and religious tradition with the simpler, sheikhly, view of authority from their nomadic past. Hence, just as the list of

Hammurapi's ancestors acknowledges the role of previous dynasties (Amurru, Hana, Gutium) so we find that the new rulers at Mari continue to include the kings of Akkad in their own *kispum* ceremonies.[482]

The Old Babylonian myth of Amurru, from which we have already cited one famous passage (Text 4:7), is a vivid illustration of the efforts of the theologians to accommodate the new order. The success of the Amorites ('Amurrites' would strictly be better), with their distinctive origins and lifestyle, required to be worked into the traditional world order. As Kupper has shown, this led to the invention of an entirely new god, called simply Amurru. He was given an appropriate iconographic persona, being represented on cylinder seals in characteristic Amorite dress, with a curved shepherd's staff, and often attended by a gazelle. To fit him fully into the Mesopotamian scene, this poem was written to describe his arrival. It deals with his marriage to the daughter of Numušda, the patron deity of Kazallu, a city in the north-western corner of the plain. We do not know what the precise corresponding events were on the human level, but Ur III sources make it likely enough that this was one of the areas where Amorite pressure was at its most intense.[483]

As Kupper remarks, we are here confronted by an attempt to 'legitimize his presence in the Babylonian pantheon, by the device of his entering the family of a local deity' (1961, 75). We have no way of knowing whether this reflects popular belief or is just a construct of formal propaganda. At least on the official level, though, the attempt was successful, since Amurru still features among the major gods of the Assyro-Babylonian pantheon in the first millennium BC, but he was never completely at ease, because he did not have the same kind of geographical constituency as his colleagues. In place of the strong dynastic ethos of the mobile Amorites, the ideology of the settled lands was intimately bound up in the sense of place. We have already seen the close bond between the city and its patron deity, and the realities of agricultural life mean that each village must have known which lands it claimed, and to which city-state it belonged.[484] Hence we can expect that wherever cultivation extended the boundaries of the state were equally clearly defined, and the dispute between Umma and Lagaš is no doubt the consequence of their moving into previously unexploited lands where historical guidelines were absent. In the course of the bitter struggle between Lagaš and Umma over control of the 'desert edge' between them, one of the Lagaš rulers speaks of Lagaš territory as 'the field of Ningirsu', raising events to a heavenly plane and so legitimizing his claim.[485]

The traditional metaphor

This was fully in accord with contemporary theology. With foreign affairs, as with internal politics and the choice of a ruler, events on a human level were described in heavenly terms. This could apply to both peaceful and military relations. Armies were accompanied by divine standards;[486] when a truce was arranged between Lagaš and Umma, commemorated on the Stele of the Vultures, oaths were sworn, and in a symbolic rite doves had ointment smeared on their eyes and were sent to fly home to the shrines of the great gods of Sumer – Ninhursag at Keš, Enki at Eridu, Enlil at Nippur, the sun god at Larsa and the moon god at Ur.[487] Just as membership of a city community implies worship of the city god, and contributions to its temple, so there was a system of contributions to the Ekur, the central Mesopotamian shrine of Enlil. Attested already in the Early Dynastic period, it was institutionalized by the Ur III state with each province contributing in accordance with its wealth, both regular offerings and first-fruits.[488] Close political relations between two cities may well have lain behind the visits by gods up and down the river, and of marriages in heaven, although these are so far back in time that the historical events are beyond our reach.

As so often, ideas are given their clearest expression when a change in the status quo is to be described. A class of Mesopotamian myth is concerned with the selection of one young god to fight on behalf of the group against the forces of evil, and in the Epic of Creation, which became the national myth of Babylon, we read that Marduk fills this role. Other myths have Ninurta in this context, and a suggestive passage in the 'Angimdimma' myth shows him approaching the Enlil Temple in Nippur with the spoils of battle, a clear reflection of the booty from foreign lands presented to the Ekur by victorious kings as a sign of their prowess on behalf of The Land (see chapter 13). This could go back to an occasion when Lagaš led the defence of The Land, since Ninurta by this time incorporates much of the god of Lagaš, Ningirsu, and such cases of successful conflict between one of the Mesopotamian gods and the forces of disorder beyond the frontiers are easily assimilated into the theology. Disorder within The Land poses greater problems for the ideological metaphor. Among the booty carried back from battle in the Ninurta myth are a variety of curious beings (Text 13:10), and from Gudea's hymn on the building of his temple we learn that the symbols of these defeated beings were installed in the Ningirsu Temple itself. In even earlier texts from Girsu it emerges that some of them were worshipped in their own right, and it has plausibly been suggested that their appearance among the spoils of battle on the victor's chariot reflects the absorption of local cults into that of the city god.[489]

Similarly, political disasters have to be explained in divine terms, but the shared pantheon of the Mesopotamian world poses a dilemma for the religious exponent of history: how to represent the demise of one city in religious metaphor without submitting a member of the council of the gods to a similar demise. Thus the collapse of Akkad cannot mean that Ištar, the patron deity of the city, is at fault since she is one of the great gods, but for her city to suffer so much she must have deserted it, and this is how the events are pictured. In that case tradition was able to point a finger at the sin of Naram-Sin in ignoring the omens and acting without the clearance of the gods, but no such blame is levelled in the case of the Ur III collapse, which is represented simply as an unaccountable decision of Anu, king of the gods, and Enlil, king of the lands.[490]

Political tiers

It was Enlil, from his base at the ideological and geographical centre of The Land at Nippur, who dispensed kingship and it is evident that the concept of an 'Enlilship', implying the supremacy of one ruler and state over others, erects a two-tier system. Enlil's constituency encompasses the whole of Sumer, although it is not certain that originally the northern part of the plain was equally his, and this role goes back well into the Early Dynastic since it is already described by Eanatum on the Stele of the Vultures. While the whole of the southern plain can rarely have been united under one rule, in the way one might suppose the Sumerian King List implies, it certainly was seen as a cultural if not a political entity, known as 'The Land' (**kalam**) as distinct from '(all) countries' (**kur kur**), which included the outside world. A similar higher-tier cultural unit was recognized in the north-west, since Dagan was recognized by the Akkad kings and at the time of Yahdun-Lim as the patron god of the 'Euphrates banks', with his central shrine at Tuttul on the Balih.[491] As we have seen, the divine world needed to adjust itself to secular events, and the Ur III kingdom, a new phenomenon lacking a traditional patron, created its divine representative in the person of the king, a function which naturally lapsed with the demise of the dynasty. Thereafter, Hammurapi is indeed the first ruler who can make any plausible claim to rule the whole of The Land once more, and it is no coincidence that the 'Enlilship' surfaces with him once more. The prologue to his code of laws expresses with full clarity the official, traditional, version of events, presenting him as a true inheritor of the mantle of the traditional Mesopotamian ruler (Text 14:6).

As we have seen, this was only one side of the political coin, and a more pragmatic picture emerges from the diplomatic correspondence of the time. The kings and governors of the Amorite dynasties wrote simply and directly about the political conditions they were observing. We have read one description from Mari of the chessboard of major and minor kingdoms at the time of Zimri-Lim (see chapter 2; Text 2:6). When Hammurapi of Babylon defeated the major kingdom of Ešnunna, he received some gratuitous advice from Zimri-Lim: 'If the men of the ruler of Ešnunna consent to you, exercise the kingship of the land of Ešnunna yourself, but if they do not consent to you, appoint a noble who is living at your court to the kingship over them' (Dossin 1972). The presumption that Hammurapi will take account of the preferences of the defeated land is interesting, but possibly unjustified, since Zimri-Lim does not in fact put forward a third option, the one which Hammurapi in the event adopted, that of total annexation – abolition of the 'kingship of the land of Ešnunna' as a separate entity. Indeed, he was sufficiently unimpressed by Zimri-Lim's advice that shortly after he did the same to Mari. Neither city was ever important again. All the same, Zimri-Lim's letter focuses on the dilemma of many a conqueror, before and after Hammurapi: whether to annex territory and place it under direct administration, or to retain at least a semblance of local self-government.[492]

Hammurapi's choice was undoubtedly part of a deliberate policy of unification, expressed triumphantly in the prologue to the code. As ruler of a long list of once independent cities, he became the head of their judicial systems too. Royal inscriptions of all periods echo the clear statement of the code that the administration of the law was one of the principal duties of the Mesopotamian king, entrusted to him by the sun god, Šamaš, who was responsible for justice. Justice is inseparable from civil order and peace, and this aspect of the king's role is closely tied to the economic prosperity of his subjects. His legal reforms may work to banish 'Oh, Šamaš' – the cry of the wronged – from the land, but the king takes credit for years of plenty when the land lies at peace like cows in a meadow, well in body and soul, and hence he also undertakes economic reforms, in the shape of the cancellation of debts and attempts at price control.[493] We may have doubts as to their efficacy, but the propaganda at least makes it quite clear that the favour of the gods obliges the ruler to adopt the role of the shepherd, the benevolent guardian of his people. There are mutual obligations between ruler and ruled, and in the changeable world of Mesopotamian politics sheer despotism does not have a record of success. Although the political role of the city assemblies does not seem to have survived into the second millennium, through all the religious ideology of the royal inscriptions there runs the implicit awareness that the favour or disfavour of the gods was expressed through the actions of his subjects or enemies. As our next chapter will show, the king's role in the exercise of justice was only a gloss on a system which was already in place, and the religious metaphors which permeate the official propaganda of the Mesopotamian kings acknowledge that they owe their throne, and the people their prosperity, to the goodwill of the gods, who have to be wooed with loving care by the king as the representative of the people.

Further reading

The general view of Mesopotamian religion and politics conveyed here owes most to Thorkild Jacobsen – see his statements in Frankfort 1948 and, most recently, Jacobsen 1976 (especially chapter 3, 'Third Millennium metaphors. The gods as rulers: The cosmos as a polity'). On the titulary of rulers the standard work is Hallo 1957. For a recent account of *akītum* festivals and related matters see Black 1981. On the terminology of territorial concepts see Limet 1978 (French). Recent work on the divine ideology of politics includes Cooper 1983a (Introduction), Michalowski 1983, and Postgate forthcoming.

15
Laws and the law

Little has been written recently about the role of law in early societies from an anthropological standpoint, at least in a Mesopotamian context, and yet much remains to be said. Perhaps the Mesopotamian historians have thought too much about laws, at the expense of law. The Code of Hammurapi is justly famous, and has been joined by earlier, shorter, texts which also deserve to be considered as collections of laws. Not surprisingly, the nature of these collections, and the legal principles and practices they reveal, have been much studied. A great deal of this work is by legal historians, many of them of the German school, and trained in the traditions of Roman law; and the entirely proper concerns of that discipline have discouraged approaches from other angles. For the general historian, the laws are a poor mirror of the role of law in society: they are either traditional provisions, likely to be overtaken by social change, or attempts by the current authority to reform or update. Either way, they are likely to give a distorted picture of conditions, being either atypical or unreal. This chapter will therefore concentrate first on reconstructing how law operated within society, so as to have a context against which to assess the collections of laws to which the rulers have so insistently drawn our attention. Law need not be written down, and self-evidently could not have been in earlier times, so that it will not be possible to recover the full picture, but we are witnessing in Mesopotamia at this time the gradual assimilation of written practices by the legal system, and this is a process which deserves examination in its own right.[494]

The legal establishment

Mesopotamian judicial institutions had four major tasks: (1) to settle disputes between individuals or groups; (2) to enforce their decisions and inflict punishment on those who offended against society as a whole (i.e. in modern terms, criminals); (3) to administer certain enactments of the government; and (4) to act as a public agency in authenticating or officially recording certain acts as legally valid. These tasks were carried out by a pyramid of judicial authorities, on three levels: the local councils, the judges and courts, and the king. We do not have, and would hardly expect, any written formulation of the assignation of these functions. Neither the Code of Hammurapi (CH) nor any of its predecessors lays down the framework within which justice was to be administered. Thus they do not define the constitution of the courts or the functions of court officials. Except incidentally, the 'codes' do not identify the types of case within the competence of different courts or specify the kinds of evidence acceptable to them. Nor do they define what words or actions in everyday intercourse would be recognized by the courts as legally valid. Yet these are all things that must have *been* acknowledged, if not explicitly stated, within the existing legal system, and we shall see that they can in part be reconstructed from the surviving documentation of legal transactions of various kinds.

The local council

The court of first resort in early historical Mesopotamia was the local council. As we have seen, the towns and countryside were administered by the elders of a village (*ālum*) or town-quarter (*bābtum*), together with the 'mayor' (*rabiānum*), who was the link with central authority.[495] Their decisions and announcements were conveyed by the public herald, and these were not all in the realm of judicial administration. The council's public role is reflected in the Code of Hammurapi itself: in the case of an ox known to be dangerous, it is the 'ward' (*bābtum*) that conveys the formal warning to the owner (CH §251), and the code also tells us that the village was held responsible as a legal entity for actions within its surrounding territory: 'If a robber is not caught, ... the village and the mayor on whose land or within whose borders the robbery took place shall replace his losses to the man who was robbed' (CH §23). Here the village is not acting as a judicial authority but rather as a body collectively responsible for the guilty person(s); but that it was also directly involved in the administration of justice is clear from references in judicial records. The 'ward' is expected to establish the facts about the lifestyle of a woman seeking a divorce;[496] we read that one of the litigants in a land dispute 'assembled the members of the ward who knew them, and the members of the ward examined their statements',[497] or that 'the mace-symbol of Ninurta was present in the ward, and his witnesses were present'.[498] The members of the ward were not of course a permanent court and undoubtedly, like the mayor, had non-judicial functions, but the reasons for their involvement are obvious. They constitute at one and the same time a jury and a source of specialist local knowledge, which can uniquely contribute to the establishment of the facts of the case.

Judges and courts

All the same, although the local councils are found carrying out executive decisions, it is difficult to prove that the *ālum* or *bābtum* functioned as a legal court, because we have no documentation deriving directly from their activities. This is probably because even in Old Babylonian times – as obviously was the case in pre-literate times – no written documents were kept at this level, and matters decided at this level would not have been referred further up the system. Occasionally their role is revealed by correspondence which passed between the village and the higher authorities, such as a letter from Larsa which shows that the local council is entitled to pass judgement if it feels it can, but may pass the case up if it needs to. An official and the judges of Larsa write to 'the mayor and elders of Bulum: Watar-Šamaš has informed me that he bought an orchard 5 years ago and that the village is claiming it from him. Examine his case and pass judgement according to the edict. If it is too difficult(?) for you, send him and his adversaries to us'.[499] A case where the move to a higher court was induced by a litigant dissatisfied with the justice available at a local level is illustrated by another letter from the judges to the local council (Text 15:1).

Text 15:1 The city judges called into a village dispute
Say to the mayor of Laliya and the village elders, the judges say: Ili-idinnam has appealed to us. His deposition states: 'I gave 30 bushels of corn to my son to plant in a field, but they ate the corn and rented my field out to a tenant, and the tenant treated me contemptuously. I went before the mayor and village-elders and put the matter before them, and my son answered me before the mayor and village-elders. I said to him: 'I am going to put a stop to your wife and your mother-in-law, your witches'. He replied to me: 'I shall put a stop to your witch'. This was his deposition before us. Now that our tablet has reached you, send Ur-Šubula, his wife and his mother-in-law to us, so that we may pronounce justice on them according to the royal edict.

(After Walters 1970b, 29–31)

In this way a legal case might be taken to court: there is no Babylonian word for 'court', and the term is used here to imply that it was tried in the presence of a judge or judges. They sometimes sat in the temple, such as the Temple of Šamaš at Sippar, but the Code of Hammurapi tells us that the judges sat in the Assembly (Text 15:2; also Text 10:7); the two are not incompatible, as the Assembly may indeed have met in a temple courtyard.[500] By the early Old Babylonian period some men bore the professional title of 'judge'. In Hammurapi's reign and later, groups of judges were appointed by the king in the major

Text 15:2 Code of Hammurapi, §5
If a judge tried a case and made a decision and had a sealed document executed, but later changed his judgment, they shall convict that judge of changing his judgment: he shall pay twelve times the claim involved in that case, and they shall remove him in the Assembly from his judgment seat, and he shall not sit in judgment with the judges again.

cities; in Ur III times they mostly sat in groups of up to seven.[501] In most if not all cases such a court was at the capital of a city-state, which later became the capital of a province. As early as Old Akkadian times the courts kept records of their judgments, we have a good number of such records from Ur III Lagaš and Umma, and documents were also drawn up at the end of individual Old Babylonian cases, so that we know a good deal about the administration of lawsuits at this level.[502]

The ruler

As we have seen in chapter 14, in the ancient cities of Sumer the **ensi** was answerable to the gods for the maintenance of social justice, and was accordingly the head of the judicial system. Although there are certainly 'judges', they are his agents and there is no reason to doubt that the last word lay with him. With the Dynasty of Akkad the role of supreme judge was taken over by the kings. In Ur III Lagaš, for example, the **ensi**, now merely a provincial governor, continued to function as the chief judge of the province, but the king constituted a still higher authority. The four early codes (Ur III; Lipit-Ištar of Isin; Ešnunna; and Hammurapi[503]) are the most concrete reflection of this. Just as cases could be referred to the city courts from the local council, so they might be passed up to the ruler himself. In Old Babylonian times there are two ways in which cases might be referred to the king from the city courts: either by an appeal by one of the contestants in the dispute,[504] or because the matter was of such gravity that it automatically came before him. This latter is called 'a case of life' (*dīn napištim*), and there is a tradition mentioned in the Ešnunna code, and reflected in the famous Nippur homicide trial, that murder trials came before the king (Text 15:3). Here, in the event, the king at Isin referred the case back to the

Text 15:3 A murder trial at Nippur

Nanna-sig, Ku-Enlila the barber, and Enlil-ennam slave of Adda-kalla the gardener, killed Lu-Inana the priest. After Lu-Inana's death, they told Nin-dada, wife of Lu-Inana, that Lu-Inana her husband had been killed. Nin-dada, opened not her mouth, covered it up. Their case was taken to Isin before the king. King Ur- Ninurta ordered their case to be taken for trial in the Assembly of Nippur.

Ur-Gula, Dudu the bird-catcher, Ali-ellati the *muškēnum*, Puzu, Eluti, Ses-kalla the potter, Lugalkam the gardener, Lugal-azida, and Šeš-kalla, took the floor and stated: 'They are men who have killed a man; they are not live men. The three males and that woman should be killed before the chair of Lu-Inana son of Lugal-urudu the priest.'

Šuqallilum the . . ., soldier of Ninurta, and Ubar-Sin the gardener took the floor and stated: 'Did Nin-dada in fact kill her husband? What did the woman do that she should be put to death?'

The Assembly of Nippur took the floor and stated: 'A man's enemy may know that a woman does not value her husband and may kill her husband. She heard that her husband had been killed, so why did she keep silent about him? It is she who killed her husband, her guilt is greater than that of the men who killed him.'

In the Assembly of Nippur, after the resolution of the case, Nanna-sig, Ku-Enlila, Enlil-ennam and Nin-dada were given up to be killed. Verdict of the Assembly of Nippur.

(After Jacobsen 1959)

Assembly at Nippur for a verdict, reflecting the fact that he cannot attend to all such matters, and would normally delegate to his judges, who would pass their verdicts in accordance with the oral traditions in force, as well as any royal ordinances, taking due account of any local variations in accepted practice (such as different rules about inheritance). A different solution is attested at Babylon, where from early in the dynasty we hear of a 'royal judge'; later there were panels of judges appointed by Hammurapi and his successors at several of the main cities, such as Babylon, Sippar and Larsa. No doubt this was in part to impose some measure of central standardization.[505]

Judicial procedures

That justice in ancient Mesopotamia was administered in courts of law which we would recognize as such is perhaps most clearly demonstrated by their procedural guidelines. Even though they retain several features which we would consider archaic, there is a clear recognition that facts should be established before verdicts were passed, and that there was a fixed relationship between a crime or injury and the penalty to be exacted. The records of court proceedings make it clear that evidence was sought and carefully examined. It could be oral or written. Oral testimony was usually taken from the two contestants in a dispute, backed up by the oral statements of witnesses on either side. These statements may have been generally that they know something to be true (e.g. that A was a slave, or that Y was chaste), or more specifically that they saw something happen, whether this was a transaction between two individuals, or the perpetration of a crime. If the facts are unclear, the judges will take steps to seek clarification. They may write to the local authorities, to have witnesses sent, or they may request that the matter be further investigated locally. Text 15:4 shows the judges summoning before them the original witnesses to a house sale, as listed in the deed, and a long-running lawsuit at Nippur saw the

> **Text 15:4** Lawsuit over the payment of the purchase money for a house
> [The document begins with a complex past history of transactions between a priestess called Iluša-hegal and the current owner, a *nadītum* married to Addi-liblut. Iluša-hegal claims she has not received the full purchase price, but]:
>
> The judges requested from Iluša-hegal the witnesses that Belessunu the *nadītum* had not paid her the silver, or the debt-document which they had made out to her for the remainder of the silver, but they did not exist and she did not produce them; whereas Addi-liblut did produce the sealed deed for 1 **sar** of house, and the judges read it, and questioned the witnesses who were written in the deed and they gave evidence before the judges in front of Iluša-hegal that she had received 15 shekels of silver as the price of 1 **sar** of built house, and Iluša-hegal conceded it. The judges examined their case, and because Iluša-hegal had disowned her seal they imposed a penalty on her and made out this tablet renouncing her claim ....
>
> (After Schorr 1913, No. 280)

witnesses to one court case recalled to reaffirm the evidence they had given seventeen years earlier in a case of disputed paternity, and to bear witness to oral testimony given then by the grandmother, now deceased (Text 5:6, 98). Cases of this kind show that legally valid documents were acceptable evidence, even though courts preferred it to be backed up by oral testimony. In one case the judges accept a fifty-two-year old text even though it was in such bad condition that 'the envelope of the tablet was broken, so they extracted the tablet from inside to read it'.[506]

Oaths

When giving oral testimony before the court, witnesses were placed under oath as today, but this is so common that it is not normally mentioned. Oaths were also taken by parties to certain everyday legal transactions, usually simply a promise not to challenge the agreement. The courts did however have more solemn forms of appeal to divine sanction, brought in where a clash of evidence or an absence of evidence made it impossible to decide on a human level. This 'oath of purgation' is a feature common to most early legal systems, and involves the close interlocking of the human and divine sanction. In part, it is indeed the fear of perjury and the consequent divine vengeance that acts as a sanction, and this of course could operate quite independently of any judicial context; but in part the point is that the oath is taken, or not taken, under conditions specified by the court and as part of the court proceedings – so that whether or not someone was prepared to take the oath constituted evidence on a human level. As in Roman law, the oath 'generally appears to have related to matters within the sole or special knowledge of the party to whom it was offered'.[507]

Examples of this from the Old Babylonian period include cases relating to inheritance divisions, dissolution of business partnerships, or the rental of a date grove. In the Code of Hammurapi a shepherd who has lost sheep to the attack of a lion or an illness – something which would naturally take place away from other witnesses – 'may clear himself before the god, and the owner of the flock will accept the loss in the flock from him' (CH §266). This is a principle which goes back at least to the Ur III period, when shepherds at Girsu regularly took an oath in the temple of the god Nin-mar(ki) to absolve themselves for lost sheep.[508] The same practice was also followed where conflicting testimony was received from two parties to a dispute, without any other means for the court to decide the case. Then the court would ask defendants to clear themselves by sending them to the temple to swear a solemn oath, and cases are known where the truth was established by a refusal to incur divine wrath by taking an oath known to be false. When taking the oath it was usual to swear on the symbol of a god – like the dog of Gula, or the weapon of Marduk (Text 15:5a). Sometimes the divine symbol itself came to the dispute rather than vice versa: particularly where a dispute involved the entitlement to property, the judges might decide that divine sanction is needed on the spot, and the god's symbol was sent out for an oath to be taken by the parties to the dispute 'on location' (Text 15:5a, b). As we have seen in chapter 6, the renting out of the divine weapon was in fact a source of income for the priests, and in the later Old Babylonian period the symbol of Šamaš made a regular tour of the temple lands, submitting tenants to the dangers of perjury when they declared their yields to their temple landlords.[509]

While the solemnity of the oath was undoubtedly effective in many cases, the possibility of perjury was implicitly acknowledged by the existence of a still stronger sanction, the river ordeal, where verdict and sentence are merged economically into a single operation. In Hammurapi's time, following a tradition which goes back at least to the Ur III code, the river ordeal was reserved for cases where a grave accusation could not be tested any other way (sorcery, adultery and homicide). This use of ordeal to settle unprovable

Text 15:5 Swearing on divine symbols

(a) The divine hand of Dingir-mah, the divine Dog of Gula, the divine Spear-symbol of Ištar, these gods they placed inside the orchard, and Sabum swore to Matiya and Belu as follows: . . . .

(Faust 1941, No. 76, 1–10)

(b) Iddin-Enlil appealed to the judge of Larsa, and the mayor of the village of Kutalla and the village elders were present and (for) Iddin-Enlil the axe of Lugal-kidunna was taken up and it went round the orchard and he made a solemn declaration and took (the orchard).

(Tell Sifr 71, after Charpin 1980a, 188 and 254)

(c) (The elders) committed Apil-ilišu to the emblem of Šamaš, (to swear) by [or: in] the reed *kilkilu* in the gate(?) of Nungal inside the ring of flour, and he 'pulled out' the symbol of Šamaš . . . .

(CT 2 9; see van Lerberghe 1982, 255; for *kilkilu* see Reiter 1989)

accusations of a serious nature, and especially of witchcraft, is common to many societies, including Europe, all too recently. In Mesopotamia, its restriction to such cases seems to be a late development, since judicial decisions show that the river ordeal was used in the Akkad period to settle more trivial, civil affairs of disputed ownership or debt.[510] That an extreme sanction of this kind fell into disuse for such relatively minor matters is probably the result of the increasing advance of literacy within society: reliance on oral testimony as to a transaction would have led to more unresolvable disputes in the courts, whereas a written record would normally ensure that the dispute never reached the court, and would resolve the problem if it did.

Court officials and the execution of judgment

We have already noted in chapter 3 that some of the earliest sealed documents are the final records of court judgments, and most of our evidence for the conduct of trials comes from the documents drawn up at the close, which were called 'completed lawsuit' (**ditilla** or (*kanīk*) *dīnim gamrim*); in Old Babylonian times the 'tablet of solemn declaration' (*ṭuppi burtim*) is also important. These simply provided a record of the court's decision, and often specified actions to be taken to resolve the case, such as submission to the ordeal or another oath. Court officials were needed to supervise these final stages. In Ur III times the official of the courts, called a **maškim**, was a member of society drawn from the same background as the judges themselves.[511] They were presumably responsible for seeing punishment exacted, although the actual process of execution or judicial mutilation is not referred to by our sources. Outside the Old Babylonian courts the arm of the law was the policeman, simply called a 'soldier' (*rēdûm*), who might, for instance, be employed to carry a baby to court to have its birth registered, or to pay a visit to a house to recover property (see Texts 5:6 and 15:6).[512] Another frequently mentioned court official was the

Text 15:6 A letter from the Judges of Babylon

Say to Muhaddum, The Judges of Babylon say: May Šamaš and Marduk keep you in good health! Concerning the lawsuit of Ilšu-ibbišu, son of Warad-Sin, and Mattatum, we have examined their case and we have given them judgment in according with our lord's ordinances. We have instructed that they return to Mattatum all the dowry that Mattatum had given to her daughter and which she had brought into the house of Ilšu-ibbišu. We have despatched a soldier with her; let them give Mattatum anything intact that can now be found.

(After Stol 1981, No. 25)

'barber'; he may have been brought in originally to give slaves their distinctive hair-do, but later on he had responsibility for quite unconnected tasks such as destroying tablets invalidated by a royal edict (Text 10:7, p. 197).[513] The herald was also at the disposal of the court, although his role of conveying official information to the public had administrative as well as legal applications. On the loss of a seal it was the practice to publicize the loss and its date through the herald – so that documents sealed with it thereafter would be invalidated – and Hammurapi's Code mentions the herald's announcement of a runaway slave (cf. p. 107). He also made announcements about government call-up, and officiated at house sales (and no doubt other legal transactions) as early as the Pre-Sargonic period, impressing his seal (Figure 3:9, p. 61).[514]

Legally valid transactions

These earliest sealed documents are exceptional in explicitly recording the formal validation of the judicial establishment by the participation of the herald in the sale. Yet it is clear that later the courts accepted as evidence many types of written text not drawn up under their supervision or sealed and authenticated by them. The Code of Hammurapi itself requires that in some circumstances a written document must be made out, and in other cases it envisages that written evidence may exist and be admissible evidence.[515] The document in itself was not thereby constitutive, but remained evidentiary: that is to say, the law did not recognize the creation of the document as the essence of the transaction, but accepted it as proof that the transaction had taken place in a legally valid manner. Nowhere do we find any definition of what constitutes a legally valid transaction, but from practices observable on the documents themselves, and from incidental remarks in trial reports, certain criteria can be reconstructed. Whether the document is purely retrospective, in that it records a completed transaction such as a land or slave sale, or also prospective, in that it records an obligation incumbent on one party, it is evidence of a past event: evidence that certain words were spoken, certain actions taken, and that certain persons were present. These are the components of legal transactions which surely existed before anyone thought to write them down, and persist to this day in a tradition which derives distantly but not too indirectly from third-millennium Mesopotamia.[516] In a very speculative way, Figure 15:1 sets out some of the components of legal transactions as they may have changed through time. Only in very specific circumstances would the

Form of transaction	Constitutive practices for private transactions Authentication by		Sanctions
	presence of	seals of	
Pre-law, pre-literate (say, 5th millennium BC):			
spoken words	relatives	ceder of right	religious
symbolic acts	witnesses	witnesses	social
written words	officials	officials	official
Pre-literate (say, 4th millennium BC):			
spoken words	relatives	ceder of right	religious
symbolic acts	witnesses	witnesses	social
written words	officials	officials	official
Early literate society (2700–2100 BC):			
spoken words	relatives	ceder of right	religious
symbolic acts	witnesses	witnesses	social
written words	officials	officials	official
Later literate society (2100–1600 BC):			
spoken words	relatives	ceder of right	religious
symbolic acts	witnesses	witnesses	social
written words	officials	officials	official

═══	= always required		─── regular
───	= required in some cases		
- - -	= sometimes occur		- - - occasional

Figure 15:1 Chart to exemplify changing formalities for legal transactions.

writing of a document have been a required component of a legal action. We should view the role of the written text as secondary to a variety of spoken and enacted formulae, traces of which survive in our documents from preliterate times.

Spoken formulae

All legal systems have recognized forms of words. Lawyers like to call them 'solemnia verba', but it is the fact of making a certain oral statement before witnesses that the law recognizes. The best-known form of oral statement in our society is the marriage formula, in Islam perhaps the threefold repetition of the divorce formula. The same may well have been true in ancient Mesopotamia. The Code of Hammurapi says quite explicitly that 'If a man has taken a wife and not made a contract for her, that woman is not a wife' (CH §128), and this provision is already present in the Ur III code. Other 'contracts' referred to in the Code of Hammurapi are those between a shepherd and the owner of the sheep (CH §264) and between the owner of goods and a person to whom they are entrusted for safe-keeping (CH §§122–3). What the necessary components of such a contract were we do not learn. It has been shown convincingly that the contract (*riksatum*/**inim ka-kéš**) need not be a written document, as has often been assumed, but there must have been some ceremonies which surrounded the striking of an oral agreement to lend it legal validity.[517] In some cases in the Ur III **ditillas** it is clear that a betrothal involved swearing an oath by the life of the king.[518] For the actual marriage contract the approximate form of the words can be deduced from a later literary text and from the negative version quoted in the context of divorce ('You are not my wife'). The same could be applied to adoption, where merely saying 'You are not my father' (*ūl abī atta*) reverses the statements which would have been made at the time of adoption if the child was old enough, and leads to instant disinheritance.[519]

Enacted formulae

When referring to the formation of a marriage contract the Ešnunna code gives a little more detail than Hammurapi's, mentioning not only a verbal contract (*riksatum*) but also a formal meal offered to the bride's parents.[520] This serves to emphasize the fact that some formal gestures very often accompany legal transactions. We still shake hands to conclude a bargain, and place a ring on a finger in a wedding ceremony. Such acts are not legally constitutive, but when done in the presence of witnesses they may once have been. Of the variety of practices referred to by the texts perhaps the most explicit is the controversial 'crossing of the pestle'. In third-millennium texts this signified the transfer of ownership of a slave; probably because the slave was made to step over a pestle, as a symbol of servile labour.[521] Other symbolic acts mentioned in the legal documents include metaphorical mimesis like 'throwing a lump into a canal' (possibly to emphasize the solubility and hence impermanence of the land being bought), and gestures involving a part of the body, like striking the forehead as a sign of willingness to act as a guarantorṣ. In Ur III times the establishment of freedom from claims against the person seems to have been symbolized by the drawing aside of a cloth, while we have already noted acts involved in the wedding ceremony, along with the reversal of that bond by the cutting of a hem.[522]

All these acts are known to us from legal documents which refer to them. As time passes, they are mentioned less and less. This gradual phasing out of symbolic actions can be closely paralleled by a similar tendency in the development of other legal traditions. In Anglo-Saxon England the conveyance of land was solemnized in the eighth century by putting a turf on the altar, but this dies out, along with other symbolic acts, being less and less seen as constitutive. No doubt in illiterate times in Sumer and post-Roman Britain alike such symbolic ceremonies had a recognized and unmistakable significance which in some measure compensated for the absence of a written record; in both contexts there is a period of overlap during which the written record mentions that the act was carried out. While neither symbolic act nor written record were by themselves constitutive, it is easy to see that one would fade as the other gained in importance.[523]

Written evidence

There is plentiful evidence for the admissibility of written documents in court. They must have conformed to socially agreed norms, and as with spoken and enacted formalities there must be evidence that the document was created with the knowledge and consent of both parties. In pre-literate times almost the only evidence would be the testimony of eye witnesses; their presence is obviously essential and constitutive, and remained so later too. The documents themselves also required authentication. Usually, this was by the sealing of the tablet by the 'ceder of right' in the presence of witnesses. This we can deduce from the fact that in Old Babylonian times virtually every legal document was sealed (or otherwise acknowledged[524]) and witnessed, but it is not specified as a principle anywhere: we do not come across any law stating that, e.g., 'a man may use his brother's seal', or 'land sale documents should be sealed on the envelope . . .'. Nevertheless, the legal importance of the seal is clear from the herald's announcements in case of loss, and in one case a woman is penalized by the courts because she 'disowned her seal' (Text 15:4).

Sealing by the 'ceder of right' to prove his presence and consent is the norm in Old Babylonian times and persists into the first millennium BC – indeed we are doing the same thing each time we sign a cheque. The pattern did however take some time to establish. This can be shown from land sale texts, the first legal documents we can identify. The very earliest are written on stone (a practice which does indeed survive into the Akkad Dynasty – see Figure 5:5), and in some cases they have iconographic scenes carved on them, underlining their importance (Figure 3:14 above; 15:2).[525] A cylinder seal cannot be rolled on stone, but one can hardly doubt the legal validity of these documents, at least in an important evidentiary role. They are followed by the house and field sales from Šuruppak, of 2500 BC or so. These are all of very uniform appearance, written on well-made rounded tablets, with details of the property sold, of the payments made to the principal seller and baksheesh issued to relatives and neighbours, and of the witnesses. They are clay, but they are not sealed; at this stage, therefore, evidence of the consent of the seller can reside solely in the actions and spoken words of the transaction and the fact

Figure 15:2 Record of land sale in South Mesopotamia, *c.* 2700 BC Neither the text nor the iconography of this and similar stone documents is fully comprehensible (cf. Figure 3:14). (A. Parrot, AfO 12, (1937–9), 320, Figure 1; now in the Metropolitan Museum, New York, cf. V. E. Crawford, *Bulletin of the Metropolitan Museum of Art* 18, 1959–60, 245ff)

that witnesses and, sometimes at least, an official were present. The documents are perhaps strictly not even evidentiary, merely records of the persons who could be adduced as proof. Indeed, their consistent format, and the fact that so many were found in good condition, suggests that they derive from some central records office where they were stored together.[526]

The next step comes just at the end of the Early Dynastic period, in examples from Girsu. There are unsealed house sale documents, as earlier, but in a few cases the same text is written not on a tablet but on the clay which was used to seal a wooden peg (Figure 3:9, p. 61). The texts state that the herald has 'driven the peg into the wall and applied the oil to it'; another symbolic action, of course, but the point I want to stress here is that the city authorities are involved. Heralds also turn up among the witnesses of the earlier Šuruppak sales, and it is very likely, although not provable, that as in later Assur real estate sales had to be preceded by a public announcement to give a chance for any other claimants to object. The texts do not state whose seal was rolled on these clay sealings, but I have little doubt that it was that of the herald, hence an authentication of the transaction by the public authority.[527]

In the third millennium, therefore, sale documents were rarely sealed by the seller alone. It is in this light that we should view the curious '**burgul**' seals rolled on sale documents of the Old Babylonian period: these were made (perhaps of wood) ad hoc for the individual transaction, as we can tell because they have just the names of the witnesses present on that one occasion. The practice of witnesses sealing a tablet reflects the stress placed on the presence of witnesses in the third-millennium document, when the small payments made to them are laboriously recorded as an integral part of the transaction. This all emphasizes the concern of the community as a whole in the conveyance of real estate.[528]

The function of the seal impression as a sign of cession of a right, which converts a tablet into a bilateral legal instrument, rather than a record unilaterally authenticated by the law, was regularized during the Ur III period, where it was universally applied to administrative documents as well. Such texts, recording not a permanent change of ownership but an obligation to be fulfilled, are not known before the Akkad period at the earliest. There are written references to loans and indebtedness, but not a single legal contract; this can hardly be the chances of discovery. The making of a loan must in earlier times have been authenticated by witnesses and was no doubt accompanied by formal words or actions, but there is nothing in our texts that gives a hint as to the procedures, nor does the anthropological literature suggest obvious parallels. The implications of a legally admissible written contract for the extension of economic links between the urban and rural societies, beyond those enabled by existing social contacts, are important, even if difficult to quantify (cf. chapter 3).

Sanctions

Clearly it is no use having procedures recognized by society if the society is not in a position to apply sanctions to those who break or ignore them. In small communities the social sanction, by which I mean non-institutionalized communal attitudes or responses, often suffices, but the growth of the state inexorably sees the process vested in the hands of local or central administration, as the complexity of the society leads to mixing of groups between whom no social sanctions could apply. We have already seen the extensive use of oath-taking in the context of court administration, and the reinforcement of sale contracts with oaths promising not to challenge the transaction is mentioned as far back as the Akkad Dynasty. The oath is normally taken by the patron god or gods of the local city. Under Naram-Sin, the king himself is included in the oath, and an oath by the 'name of the king' is a regular component of a promissory contract in Ur III times, reflected by the inclusion of the king's name (though emphatically without divine status) in Old Babylonian texts.[529]

The oath must of course derive from times long before writing, and was no doubt accompanied at times with symbolic rituals. As in judicial and diplomatic contexts, an essential component, whether expressed or not, was the fear of the divine retribution that would fall on the oath-breaker. While in texts from South Mesopotamia the written formulae are laconic, some texts from 'peripheral' areas such as Susiana or the Middle Euphrates list frightful retributions that gods and man may inflict on the oath-breaker. This is probably a reflection of the relative strength of spoken and enacted symbolic practices and of the superficiality of the written word in these places. A similar trend may be observed in later Assyria, where far more picturesque threats await the breaker of a contract after the Aramaic incursions separating the Middle Assyrian from the Neo-Assyrian period.[530]

Royal reforms

Having outlined the operations of law in Mesopotamian society as a whole, we may now turn to look at the laws which have rightly attracted so much attention. The forty-two surviving columns of Hammurapi's stele called 'King of Justice' (see Figure 15:3) are the most informative single source for legal history before the classical world, but they raise enough questions to fill volumes, and there is indeed a considerable literature on the part

Figure 15:3 Stele of Hammurapi, excavated at Susa in 1900. The text is inscribed in the traditional vertical columns in the script of the Ur III Dynasty. Above, Šamaš, seated on his altar and with his solar rays springing from his shoulders, commissions Hammurapi to mete out justice to the people. (MDP I, Planche IX, opposite p. 142. Photo: Musée du Louvre/AO)

of legal historians, especially in German. One of the favourite topics is "What is the Code of Hammurapi?" – is it a code of laws, a literary composition of no practical application, or something in between? To answer that question, we have first to recognize that the Hammurapi text is only the most complete and longest of four such collections, of which the earliest belongs to the Ur III Dynasty, about three centuries before. They differ in details, but have to be treated as a single genre.[531]

They are not codes, if by that is meant that they deal comprehensively and methodically with all aspects of the law, but collections of individual provisions, some isolated and some grouped by their subject matter; but most of these provisions may be considered laws, in that they are fixing principles or practices to be applied in the administration of law, and we have seen that the legal mechanisms within which they would operate already existed. They are therefore modifications of an existing body of law – whether written or not – and are best considered as 'reforms'. Nevertheless, if we look in more detail at the contents, it is obvious that it is a mixed bag. Some of the laws are there because it is traditional to include them, and are repeated verbatim from one collection to the next. Others, such as those in the Code of Hammurapi regulating *ilkum* tenure or the property rights of priestesses, would seem to be a response to changes in contemporary society. These strongly suggest the hand of the royal reformer, and the king's role is also explicit in some provisions which are in the nature of executive orders, notably the hire-fixing clauses (see Text 10:5). The codes are quite distinct from the 'edicts' of economic reform, though: those are purely retrospective, cancelling debts up to the day of their promulgation. The 'codes' (to use the convenient if sometimes misleading term) are prospective, laying down rules for the future.

Whether or not the principles enunciated by the codes were originally extrapolated from actual cases, they are not collections of individual cases, 'case law' ('In the case of A vs B at Larsa on day x the king judged as follows'). As we have seen, records of cases were kept at least as early as the Akkad Dynasty, and the Nippur homicide trial was recopied as a school text, so that such a compilation would not have been impossible. The codes, however, are not descriptive, but prescriptive: they have derived general principles, and, if a particular judgment did lie behind any provision, it was stripped of any specific reference to the names, times or places involved. The process of extracting judicial guidelines from individual cases is indeed hinted at by the Ur III court records, which frequently explain the reason why the judges reached their verdict: 'because the witnesses contradicted his statement and demonstrated him to be a criminal'.[532] Occasionally later court records give reasons in this way, and even within the Code of Hammurapi a few provisions are given an explanation: 'because he denied his travelling agent' (CH §107), 'because he rejected his village and fled' (CH §136), 'because she took on a second child without the agreement of his father and mother' (CH §194), 'because he did not strengthen the house he built sufficiently so that it fell down' (CH §232). In some passages, such as the rules of compensation (see Text 15:7), we can see that the authors of the provisions have proceeded by analogy. Therefore it is clear from this level of abstraction that the intention is to lay down a set of laws universally applicable throughout the realm in future, much as one would assume from the terms in which Hammurapi himself describes his

Text 15:7 Code of Hammurapi, §§196–9
If a man has put out the eye of another man, they shall put out his eye.

If he breaks the bone of another man, they shall break his bone.

If he puts out the eye of a *muškēnum*, or breaks the bone of a *muškēnum*, he shall pay
1 mina of silver. If he puts out the eye of the slave of another man, or breaks the bone
of the slave of another man, he shall pay half his price.

stele's function (Text 15:8). In this context it is important to realize that the codes are promulgated by a king, in most if not all cases one who has recently annexed new territories over which the new laws are to be valid. Obviously a degree of standardization in legal practice within a single realm is only just – and the concern for justice is deep within the ideology of rule, as we have seen – but we must also remember that the claim to impose a single judicial code also conveyed a strongly political message, and the prologue of the Ur III code makes explicit reference to reforms of the metrology which had as much an administrative as a legal objective.

Text 15:8 From the Epilogue to the Code of Hammurapi
Let the wronged man who has a case go before my statue called 'King of Justice' and read
out my inscribed stele and hear my valuable words. Let my stele reveal to him the case,
so that he will discover his rights and appease his heart.

The famous clauses enunciating the Biblical principles of talion – an eye for an eye and a tooth for a tooth – direct our attention finally to some of the thinking behind the provisions. Compensation for accidental death and injury in the Ur III code is by monetary penalties; in the Code of Hammurapi it is by talion, scaled according to the social class of the victim. The appearance of these physical punishments only in the latest of the codes has provoked much discussion. In my opinion it represents the traditional law of the desert intruding on the older southern urban context in company with the Amorite dynasty to which Hammurapi was heir. The truth of this is unlikely to be known until and unless we find the practices of the kingdom of Babylon under its earlier Amorite kings, or of a comparable state in the northern sphere. It is equally clear, however, that Hammurapi's code incorporates and gives enhanced status to traditional devices for ensuring justice: if damage is caused to a farmer's crop by negligence, or if a tenant has deprived him of a fair return on his land by failing to cultivate it, the code provides that the culprit's liability should be assessed by comparison with the yields of his neighbours' fields (CH §§42, 55, 62). This is hardly an innovation, since already at Larsa under Rim-Sin legal documents provide that 'he shall pay like those to his left and right', a device so obvious that it doubtless reaches back into prehistory.[533] Similarly with the shepherd and his sheep: here the code distinguishes losses in the flock due to the shepherd's negligence, and those, like the attack of a lion or of a sudden illness, for which he could not be blamed. This same idea is already implicit in the oaths of purgation taken by shepherds in the Ur III period.

The code in practice

While the codes may thus have enshrined traditional practices, they presumably did so in order to formalize and standardize them. It is difficult to imagine that in such cases the provisions of the codes were simply ignored, and had no effect on existing legal practice. As we saw in chapter 8, the code holds the shepherd liable for deaths from foot-rot, and since exactly this is specified in herding contracts from after Hammurapi but not earlier, it could be that the standard form of contract was changed to conform with the code. It is hard to be certain, though, and indeed scholars have had the greatest difficulty in putting their finger with confidence on textual proof that any of the codes was actually applied in judicial practice. Partly this is undoubtedly because they were only a gloss on the large body of traditional (presumably unwritten) law, and can have dealt with only a fraction of the cases before the courts. Partly also there is a problem with the terminology, since some of the texts mentioning the 'royal ordinance' (ṣimdat šarrim) are certainly referring to economic edicts. The exact implication of the word translated as 'ordinance' has been the subject of lively discussion, but when the Judges of Babylon tell us that in a lawsuit between two contestants 'we have examined their case and meted out justice to them in accordance with the ordinance of our lord (the king)', or another judge is exhorted to 'give judgement in accordance with the ordinance which is before you', it is perverse to resist the conclusion that these ordinances were indeed royal laws committed to writing, and applied in practice to the exercise of justice.[534]

Further reading

There is no detailed survey of cuneiform laws or legal procedures in English. The principal English-language work in the field is Driver and Miles 1952, but by its nature it hardly serves as a general introduction. The French translation by A. Finet (1973) has much less comment but is of course more up to date. Fundamental works on court procedures are Falkenstein 1956 (Ur III), Walther 1917 (Old Babylonian), and Edzard 1976 – all in German. An important contribution is Malul 1988 on symbolic acts, which reached me after the completion of my text. For translations of the law codes consult Pritchard 1969.

16

Order and disorder

Mesopotamian history is longer than that of the western world and more homogeneous. While chapter 2 described the rise and fall of dynasties, I have treated the different components of the Mesopotamian social order as broadly constant, despite occasional instances of changes through time. This was a necessary over-simplification, and, to conclude, it is time to pull together some of the different threads, and see how political factors interacted with the social order, and the different sectors of society with one another, to create the changes we observe. Long-term trends within the fabric of society are often assumed by historians, but usually depend on intuitive judgements. Thus, reacting rightly against the Deimel 'temple–state' construct which was current until the 1950s, Diakonoff emphasized the role of the extended family and the local commune. Nissen goes further back in time, and even suggests that the undeniable importance of the temple in southern Mesopotamia does not date as far back as the Uruk period.[535] As far as the private sector is concerned, another frequently asserted trend is the development of private property at the expense of the state after the collapse of the Ur III Dynasty.[536] This again seems to draw its legitimacy from a silence which could be broken; it is extremely difficult to allow for the bias deriving from the absence of private documents in the Ur III period and the rarity of palace archives later. Similarly the relative importance of a semi-free class in the third millennium, by comparison with nominally free labour in the Old Babylonian period, may also be affected by the same biases, and seems less absolute than it did as more detail of the early labour relations is recovered.[537] Such issues depend so much on the quantitative role of different archives or types of text available to us that I prefer to shelve them, and leave time and future excavation to shed more light. Instead, we shall look at some of the processes which we can observe at work, not being too dogmatic about their relative importance but concentrating on the mechanisms by which changes took place.

Stability and disruption

The most obvious sources of social change are the periodic disruptions in the political order, the 'Dark Ages' or 'Zwischenzeiten' ('between-times'). These are invariably accompanied by the end of a dynasty and the dissolution of centralized political authority. The effects of this can be easily predicted and occasionally illustrated, more from archaeological than from written sources. The cultivation of most of Mesopotamia is a dangerously fragile system maintained by a combination of social and environmental factors. Changes are most easily observed in ecologically marginal areas. Thus, along the fringes of cultivation in North Mesopotamia a slight shift in the rainfall pattern could have a drastically visible effect on the limits of agricultural settlement; the same is true in the Hamrin basin, and archaeological surveys in both areas have shown very clearly periods of almost complete abandonment alternating with a thriving settlement.[538] There may indeed be climatic factors at work, but political ones are equally relevant. In a marginal environment a satisfactory agricultural regime can be sustained provided there is back-up from elsewhere. In the northern plains any large land-owner spreads his investment: a core of fields well within the dependable rainfall zone, round Nineveh or another major city, will provide the capital reserve to permit the chancier exploitation of marginal lands, and the same applies on a larger scale to a state. Moreover, the state has the political muscle to provide secure storage in the marginal areas, and to give military protection to crops, standing and harvested, which could well be vulnerable in times of disruption. At a private level, contractual or family relationships between the marginal farmer and his more secure landlord or cousin in the heartland will also permit the maintenance of agriculture out in this danger zone. Farmers on their own in these environments do not have a secure prospect: one or two years of poor rainfall, or the destruction of the local political set-up, will force them off the land, either back to a desert nomadism with their surviving sheep, or up to the mountains to seek a free niche there.[539]

In South Mesopotamia similar trends are at work, although the detailed mechanisms may differ. With the breakdown of government any agriculture dependent on the scale and resilience of a state-run enterprise would rapidly be abandoned – the exploitation of marginal land at the fringes of the irrigation system, specialized cultures such as timber which needed the demand created by general prosperity and a reliable employer to support the cultivators, and any field cultivation supplied by irrigation projects under central political control. Historians have in recent years tended to discount the paramount necessity of highly centralized organization to sustain the water regime, pointing to the rather localized scale of administration observed in southern Iraq this century, and we have already noted that in early Mesopotamia the canals may well have been maintained by the traditional local authorities, without central intervention.[540] Rural society may therefore have been able to fall back on a minimal, default level if central government disintegrated, but this does not mean that there were no changes in the landscape. Where an irrigation system had come under, or was created by, the direct control of the state, rather than the traditional local authorities, and especially where the scale of the works required a geographical control beyond the reach of local authorities, the agricultural regime must have rapidly deteriorated.

These cataclysmic trends have also to be set in context against the more subtle effects of agricultural deterioration and social change. The Arabic proverb 'one skein [of geese] has flown, one skein has raised its neck' (raff ṭār u raff šāl ar-rugba) refers to share-croppers fleeing the impossible demands of their landlords: just as there is a downward spiral for the average peasant, and the economic edicts suggest that this was normality, so the landlords themselves face a similar dilemma. Poor land or inadequate irrigation reduces both the tenant's and the landlord's share. When conditions get bad enough, unless political control is extremely tight, nothing can stop the farmers from leaving their homes and their debts. In pre-revolutionary Iraq, decamping tenants drifted to the town, but there is ample evidence in the ancient sources for fugitives either seeking a continuation of their way of life in a fresh context, or becoming outlaws, bands of whom worried the fringes of civilized society.[541] Then the landlord will be left with poor land and no one to farm it. Modern conditions suggest that in fact the lot of the tenant is, ironically, not as bad as that of the small independent farmer. The tenant of an institution or a large land-owner may be moved from field to field as his landlord dictates, but at least the spread of the landlord's holdings means that if a particular field or area becomes saline or loses its water allowance, there is somewhere else to go. The small farmer has no such option, and, if yields are diminishing on his land because of increasing salinity and poverty of the soil, the only way to wring more food from the ground is to sow more thickly or to violate the fallow regime and use some of the land two years in succession.[542] This of course merely compounds the problem, and the downward spiral to ruin is accelerated.

> **Text 16:1** From an inscription of Nur-Adad, nineteenth-century King of Larsa
> When he contented the heart of Ur, banished injustice and the cry 'O Šamaš', established the throne of Larsa and returned its scattered people to their place.
>
> (After Edzard 1957, 117)

Hence in the south too the standard response to political unrest can only be the widespread abandonment of villages and smaller rural settlements. This can be observed in the archaeological record as well; and the opposite side of the coin can be seen, which is the resettlement of the countryside in times of greater stability.[543] Signs of this are clear in the textual record too: kings refer to their resettlement projects (Text 16:1; also Text 16:10), and after the Mitannian interregnum at Assur, city families established rural outposts to the west of the city, named simply after their first settler or owner.[544] The same can be seen in the south in the early Old Babylonian period, with places called 'Town of PN' or 'Keep of PN'. Some of these are also in the control of and perhaps founded by urban landlords, but there are others whose origin is no doubt from newly settled nomadic groups, like the village called 'The tents'.[545] These are no doubt new foundations, with no continuity from the Ur III pattern of settlement other than that imposed by the irrigation regime. The disruption of land tenure need not have been equally severe in all provinces, and one might expect a gradual reassertion of traditional land rights by city-based families, balanced by the assimilation of the marginal zones by incoming Amorite families.

The passage of time during these events is minimal in archaeological terms: we are not yet able to distinguish late Akkad from early Ur III Dynasty, or late Ur III from early Isin–Larsa in the archaeological record, and to detect a disruption of this kind it is therefore essential for us to observe the continuity or discontinuity of the patterns of settlement. The political reach of early Isin–Larsa city-states did not rival that of Ur III, but the mechanisms of state involvement were established, and at a local level the two political orders must have had similar effects: hence the two rural settlement patterns can be expected to look fairly similar on the ground, and it is only the abandonment of one set of villages and establishment of a new set that could betray the period of disorder. It has been suggested that just such a superimposition of two similar patterns can be seen in the survey data for the south at the transition from the Uruk to the Early Dynastic, but only further refinement of ceramic sequences will give us the chronological control to integrate such evidence confidently with an historically documented process.[546]

The literature of early Mesopotamia reflects the population's keen awareness of the effects of a breakdown in social order (Text 16:2). Contemporary responses describe political calamities through the lamentations over Ur and other cities, and environmental disasters through the Flood story, which includes famine as well as flood, and seeks to give some explanation of the gods' destructive decisions. The consequences of natural or political disaster are death and starvation, leading to a diminution of the population. Hence divine determination to destroy mankind is blamed on the disturbance of the gods by the prosperous clamour of the cities, and the subsequent re-establishment of order is tempered by devices to keep the population under control in future: celibate priestesses, barren women, homosexuals.[547] We cannot judge whether the growth of population in fact posed a serious threat to stability, thus in a sense vindicating the aetiology of the poet, until we have much better control of quantitative components such as family structure or agricultural carrying capacity. Archaeologists have suggested that the growth of settlement in the fourth millennium BC exceeds what could have been achieved by the natural increase of a stable population, leading to theories of large-scale immigration, which cannot be discounted. On the other hand, the propensity of the rural population to adopt a more

Text 16:2 Section from the 'Lamentation over Sumer and Ur'
After An had frowned upon all the lands,
After Enlil had looked favorably on an enemy land,
After Nintu had scattered the creatures that she had created,
After Enki had altered (the course of) the Tigris and Euphrates,
After Utu had cast his curse on the roads and highways,
In order to forsake the divine decrees of Sumer, to change its (preordained) plans,
To alienate the (divine) decrees of the reign of kingship of Ur,
To defile the Princely Son in his (temple) Ekišnugal,
To break up the unity of the people of Nanna, numerous as ewes,
To change the food offerings of Ur, the shrine of magnificent food offerings,
That its people no longer dwell in their quarters, that they be given over (to live) in an
    inimical place,
That (the soldiers of) Šimaški and Elam, the enemy, dwell in their place,
That its shepherd be captured by the enemy, all alone,
That Ibbi-Sin be taken to the land of Elam in fetters, ...

That the hoe attack not the fertile fields, that seed not be planted in the ground,
That the sound of the song of the one tending the oxen not resound on the plain,
That butter and cheese not be made in the cattle pen, that dung not be laid on the
ground, . . .

(Michalowski 1989, lines 22–44)

mobile lifestyle and of the nomads to settle makes it extremely difficult to assess the real significance of apparent fluctuations.[548]

Polarization and diffraction

When order is restored, and the dust has settled, how much is new, and how much of the old order survives? This question can be addressed by both historian and archaeologist, and each can detect different aspects. The changes most accessible to the archaeologist are those of standardization and diversification: we know from royal inscriptions and economic documents that when The Land was reunited under a strong regime attempts were regularly made to standardize the instruments of government, law and trade. It is most conspicuous in the Akkadian metrological system and in Šulgi's reforms of the weights and measures (Text 16:3), the calendar, the transport system, scribal and accounting practices, etc., but

> **Text 16:3** From the Prologue to the Ur III code
> At that time by the strength of the moon-god Nanna, my king, I set free Akšak(?), Marad, ..., Kazallu and their settlements and farms, which had been subjected to the service of Anšan. I fashioned a copper bushel, and fixed it at 60 quarts, I fashioned a copper measuring-vat and fixed it at 10 quarts, I fashioned the regular vat of the king and fixed it at 5 quarts. I fixed the weight-stone of 1 shekel of silver at one-sixtieth of the mina; I fashioned a bronze (vessel) of 1 quart, and fixed it at 1 mina.
>
> (After Yıldız 1981, lines 125–47)

the same applies to other dynasties, such the 1st Dynasty of Babylon under Hammurapi, and to other areas of life. The kings are not reticent about their attempts to impose some degree of uniformity, and one of the benefits they bring to the people is 'unanimity'.[549] Such a concern is natural. Human nature requires that legal norms within a single realm should be consistent – even when, as probably reflected in the Code of Hammurapi, a harsher desert code of morality comes into conflict with the more commercial traditional urban approach. A new regime will wish to use a single set of bureaucratic and fiscal procedures throughout its territory, and it is natural that when the instruments of that control coincide with the normal instruments of daily life in the private sector, the state should seek to impose its own standards. Conversely, the local interests will wish on their part to adapt themselves to facilitate the exploitation of the new regime.

There are of course other less rigid forces of assimilation at work during periods of strong central control: within a single political frontier intercourse is easier, and still more eased by a common acceptance of a central norm. Individuals can move independently wherever the king's writ runs, and members of the administration and military will be appointed to different parts by the state itself, introducing not only common practices detectable in the cuneiform documentation, but also an artefactual repertoire and aesthetic preferences which could surface in the archaeological record. Hence we can observe a standardizing tendency in the script (compare the 'chancery' styles of the courts of Akkad, Ur III and Hammurapi), in language (and indeed, within a language, in grammar), but also in arts and technology.[550]

If stable government polarizes the culture in this way, the reverse process of diffraction associated with instability is just as significant. Geographical horizons contract and centralized direction evaporates. Standards of accuracy in metrological matters require not only common acceptance of, but also access to and enforcement of the norm, a luxury which a peasantry in turmoil will be unlikely to indulge in. The arm of the centralized bureaucracy will reach no further, and probably less far, than the political power of the moment, and indeed the individual administrative cells (provincial governorates), which were previously staffed by minions or adherents of the fallen regime, may have disintegrated altogether, leaving the field open to other institutional players. Moreover, not only the supply but also the demand for standardization disappears – all the currents which previously encouraged it flow in reverse: contact between cities is atrophied because of insecurity in the countryside; the commercial and administrative pressures for goods of dependable quality in uniform packing can no longer operate; and the strength of the judiciary and state to suppress dishonesty and cheating is much reduced. When all this is united with the disruption caused by economic uncertainties and population shifts, the disintegrating consequences are easy to imagine.

Archaeologists have been slow to consider these issues in the Mesopotamian context. It is obvious that the changes in pottery style and technology on which ceramic corpuses and hence ceramic chronologies are built up must have been radically affected by changes of this sort. The supreme example of centralized control is of course the Ur III Dynasty, and the homogeneity of the cylinder seals of the time is a clear instance of this. Again, the pottery is not sufficiently studied, but we can speculate as to what we might see. The effect of a new dynasty could be expected to be visible first as a major upheaval in local repertoires followed by a period during which a common standard is established throughout the realm, and the pace of change slackens, since bureaucracies like to keep to the status quo once they have established the form. Both fine luxury wares and standardized utilitarian containers would be expected to become more frequent. The advent of a period of disorder would reverse the process: the luxury wares would very likely cease to be made, local standards of size would begin to diverge, and much of the ceramic industry would revert to domestic needs and styles, with potting techniques gradually differentiated. A much more refined approach to these questions is needed before these trends can be observed and confirmed, but with its time depth and tight environmental parameters Mesopotamia between 2500 and 1500 BC offers a prime opportunity for such research. Again, the integration of such evidence with historically attested events would provide valuable criteria for interpreting earlier artefactual repertoires like that of the all-important Uruk period.

The cultural continuum

With so many disruptive influences at work, we may be surprised that Mesopotamian civilization retained any coherence over its three millennia or more. The forces of cultural conservatism resided in the cities, and are expressed in the antiquity and strength of the scribal tradition. In the seventh century BC, Assurbanipal of Assyria boasts of reading inscriptions 'from before the Flood', and Assyrian kings report on the exact number of years since a temple was previously restored, basing themselves in some cases on the foundation inscriptions of rulers a thousand years before. The Neo-Babylonian kings were also antiquarians, keeping antiquities in their palace, collecting ancient cuneiform tablets, and reporting on discoveries in the foundations of temples (Text 16:4).[551] The hallowed nature of the traditional temple certainly had much to do with the persistence of tradition. Already in the Early Dynastic period sites like Tell Ubaid and Tell Uqair, which had once been population centres in the Ubaid period, survived as holy places, capped by a temple and providing the focus for a cemetery. When major cities fell into disuse, their sites were still remembered. Eridu was probably abandoned as a viable town long before the temple, but its location was not forgotten. As far as we know the site of Akkad was remembered in later years, although it never features in everyday documents, and Larak, recorded by the Sumerian King List as one of the cities before the Flood, does not feature even in the earliest historical or economic contexts, yet in about 700 BC the Assyrian king Sennacherib mentions a settlement at the site.

Text 16:4 Nabonidus (555–539 BC) excavates Akkadian levels in the Šamaš Temple

Of that year, Ebabbara, the Temple of Šamaš in Sippar . . .
Whose . . . old foundation kings who preceded him
Had sought but not found . . .
Of his kingship, for a dwelling to gladden his heart . . .
The foundation of Naram-Sin, son of Sargon,
To him, his reverent slave, who seeks his shrines (for oracles),
He revealed it. In that year, in a propitious month, on a favourable day,
Not a finger-breadth bigger nor a finger-breadth smaller, on
The foundation of Naram-Sin, son of Sargon,
He laid the foundations of Ebabbara, the temple of Šamaš. He looked on
The inscription of Naram-Sin and restored it,
Not changing its position, and put it with his own inscription.
He looked on a statue of Sargon, father of Naram-Sin, within
That foundation: half
Of its head had broken off and had disintegrated so that he did not find
Its face. Because of his reverence for the gods and respect for
Kingship, he summoned the skilled craftsmen,
Renovated the head of the statue and restored
That face of it. He did not alter its location
But placed it in Ebabbara and established an offering for it.

(After W.G. Lambert 1968–9, 4–7)

Even some of the major cities of later Mesopotamia suffered apparent periods of desertion within their lifetimes. There is a consistent absence of archaeological remains at the southern cities after the reign of Samsu-iluna, even those which were active again in the Kassite era such as Isin, Ur and Uruk. This is matched by the disappearance of written documents. At Nippur, guardian during the Old Babylonian period of Sumerian cultural traditions, the scribal quarter seems to have been physically abandoned in the years – of unknown length – after Samsu-iluna until the firm establishment of Kassite power. A great body of unilingual Sumerian literature did not survive this break but most else did. The problem is, how? During all the 'dark ages' in Mesopotamia, we are confronted with an absence of written information, which is obviously symptomatic of conditions but also veils from us the nature of the events. The puzzle is how the cities transmitted their scribal culture to later generations when they were themselves moribund.

Part of the answer is that not all disruptions were the same or universal. We have no definite reason to suppose that Lagaš was directly affected by the intrusion of the Gutian destroyers of much of Sumer and Akkad. Later, the Ur III to Isin–Larsa 'Zwischenzeit' was accompanied by a take-over of palace organizations which need not have involved any physical displacement (e.g. at Isin itself, cf. p. 43) and would have positively sought a continuity of scribal expertise. Whatever the temporary consequences of a change of regime, the newcoming dynasty's interests were best served by continuity in the life of the city and countryside. The real hiatus is the consequence of total abandonment, and abandonment did not come as a result of instability alone; as we have seen, it might be as much the consequence of environmental factors. Eridu, today stranded deep in a sandy and rocky desert, is a case in point, the city of one of the principal gods, site of a shrine which has been traced right back into the early Ubaid period, to at least 4500 BC. Yet, as far as we know, no one lived there after the Early Dynastic period. The religious cults of Eridu and their maintenance could be seen as crucial to all Mesopotamians, since Enki/Ea had a central role in the pantheon, transcending his role as local god of that city. A recent study has shown in detail how the entire liturgy of Enki was transferred bodily to the nearest major city, Ur: his temple was not re-founded, but his priests moved, and the daily rituals were enacted in a shrine built for him within the complex of his host Nanna, the god of Ur.[552] This was not unique. Also at Ur we find that the cult of Ningublaga has been brought into the city from neighbouring Kiabrig, whose destruction is bewailed in the 'Lamentation over Sumer and Ur', while it appears that at Kish in the later Old Babylonian period there is evidence for cults originating at Uruk, presumably transferred to the security of northern Babylonia in the wake of the disruptions which supervened at the end of the reign of Samsu-iluna. In this context too we may see the existence of cults at Babylon which are extraneous: Ištar of Akkad has a temple there, but Eridu and Uruk cults are also perhaps reflected in the names of the city quarters.[553]

The role of the institutions

While the temples had a central role in the preservation of the culture's ideological identity, both they and the palaces gave society an economic buffer against the worst effects of disruption. Quite apart from their role as economic patrons and employers, whether in agriculture, industry or trade, the scale and diversity of their own resources gave them a resilience which imparted an element of stability to the society as a whole. For the society's long-term survival the institutions' role may well be crucial: where natural forces led to the drying of a major river course, the capital investment required to counteract this effect or relocate urban society to another stream would have been beyond individual villages. In the case of a complete relocation there would have followed a significant shift in the balance of economy to the favour of the institution. Fields along the old river-course would have been in the hands of the traditional private sector, whereas those newly brought into cultivation would become prebend land of the temple or palace, or at the least assigned where those in charge chose, giving the institutions influence over an important new slice of the economy.[554]

These general points apply equally to temple or palace, although it seems likely that in the early third millennium the temples would have been the principal actors, but later increasingly the palace. Indeed, while the balance of power between the institutions and the private sector is difficult to document, there do seem to be various indications during the period 2500–1500 BC of the formal transfer of power from the temples to the palace. This could be either by default, in that the palace regimes were better placed to recoup their position after a period of disturbance, or by deliberate reform by the secular ruler. Tension between temple and palace is first expressed in UruKAgina's reform texts, but the clearest example is perhaps Šulgi's 'nationalization' of the temples. Ur III scholars are now agreed that the major temples of Lagaš, and no doubt other cities, were placed under the supervision of secular officials (**šabra**) and used as an arm of the state economy. We even have one case where a secular institution was adapted to become a temple for the purposes of bureaucratic standardization.[555] A similar state usurpation of local institutions was undertaken by Hammurapi, no doubt in part in a concern for conformity. The temples had state accountants assigned to them, and the judicial functions which had often been exercised by the local temples were arrogated to the royal judges.[556]

Of course the administration of justice had been in the hands of the state already in the Ur III period, and it was only thereafter that the temples assumed – or, perhaps more likely, resumed – a judicial role. This is a reminder that administrative functions can be transferred in the opposite direction too. When state authority breaks down, social order can be maintained if some of its functions are assumed by some other agent. This is the context of the rise of the *kārum*. In the fragmented state of the country, the merchant community was still needed, and it seems likely that the *kārum* was formed by the urban elite in the absence of strong state direction into a chamber of commerce to regulate their affairs. Indeed in some cities it became a public organization and was invested with some of the former roles of the state, including political and legal decisions.[557]

The different sectors of society also borrowed procedural mechanisms from one another. One of the most persistent legacies of any social order will tend to be its habits, its manner of doing things, its bureaucratic idiosyncrasies. The practices of western European administration are still ingrained in many Third World countries which have long since eschewed the higher-profile ideological aspects of a foreign culture; in modern Mesopotamia, the Republic of Iraq, for years post-boxes were painted red and beer served in pints. More significantly, post-colonial African governments can be readily separated by their administrative style into the former French and British spheres of influence, regardless of the languages in use. In ancient Mesopotamia, the ways of doing things are also passed on to later generations long after the political order which instituted them has disappeared. In law, sealing tablets and writing dual texts is something which survives to the present day all over the world.

Palaces borrowed the terminology and probably the system of prebend land from the temples, and as time proceeded they increasingly adopted the commercial procedures and vocabulary of the private sector. More significantly still, the consensus administration of village and city communities constitutes a procedural pattern which was adopted both through time and space and across different sectors of society. Thus the amphictyony reconstructed for the early third millennium, if it is not a complete figment of modern scholars, would have as its subconscious, but perhaps also its conscious, pattern the communal organization of the individual city-states. Although political initiative was firmly in the hands of the secular regimes by the second millennium, and the role of the local assemblies surfaces in the documentation almost exclusively in legal contexts, we have seen that political ideology acknowledges the importance of popular consent, and I believe that this was not mere lip-service, but reflects the survival of a strong communal ideology, in both city and countryside.

The geographical context

When describing the collapse of civilization and the dissolution of social order, the Sumerian poet is in no doubt that it is the **mes** of Sumer that are dissolved (Text 16:2). As we have already seen (pp. 28ff), the limits of The Land are clearly perceived and broadly coincide with the southern alluvial plain. The cities of Sumer and Akkad shared a conceptual and material amalgam which can be observed in the written record and in the homogeneity of the artefactual remains. At times we may detect a divide between northern and southern regions, in language, social structure, or artistic style, but the similarities greatly outweigh the differences. The idea of a cultural unity which transcends any political entity is of course familiar from other seminal civilizations, such as Classical Greece and Renaissance Italy, and the phenomenon has been often observed, and recently dubbed 'peer polity interaction'.[558] The definition of a sphere of interaction places its neighbouring cultures outside it. The question is, how much of Mesopotamian civilization belongs further north, in the lands of later Assyria and northern Syria – lands which were reached via Mari and Assur, lively participants in the Mesopotamian scene, and whose relevance has been vividly underlined by the palace archives of Ebla?

We saw in chapter 14 that the ideological constructs reflected in royal inscriptions admit the existence of a separate, north-western interaction sphere. In the mid-third millennium Mari and Ebla may have been as close in their cultural and social character as Mari, Aleppo and Qatna in the time of Hammurapi. Northern Mesopotamia is even more obscure at this time, but all the evidence hints at a strong Hurrian presence, and the Hurrian incantations were part of the literary traditions of the early second millennium.[559] Southern statuary comes from Pre-Sargonic temples at Assur and at Tell Chuera, much further afield on the road to Harran. One of the most surprising aspects of the early second millennium is the emergence of closely similar dialects of Akkadian as the medium of communication of independent states throughout the Near East from Bahrain, to Shemshara in Iraqi Kurdistan and the cities of the Levant. This argues a receptive cultural context, and strengthens the sense that the north and west played a major part in the rise of civilization, the more so when one remembers that they too were heirs of the Uruk civilization.

Nevertheless, the links between north and south were of a different order from the internal coherence of Sumer and Akkad, as their own ideology makes plain. As far as our evidence takes us at present, it is in the south that the extremes of literacy, urbanization and bureaucracy were conceived and from there that they were diffused to the rest of the ancient Near East and beyond.

Further reading

Little has been written on long-term historical trends in Mesopotamia, but two stimulating contributions are those of Adams 1978 and N. Yoffee in N. Yoffee and G.L. Cowgill (eds), *The Collapse of Ancient States and Civilizations* (University of Arizona Press, *c.* 1988).

Epilogue

The bureaucrats and businessmen of early Mesopotamia have left us an unparalleled record of the society and economy of some of man's first cities and states. Thanks to them we can map out the road taken in the ancient Near East towards the organization of an urban society, but the map is still far from finished. Cuneiform specialists are too few and far between, so that those best qualified to synthesize the data we have are too busily engaged in the primary task of deciphering the tablets to give enough attention to reconstructing the general scene. I am acutely conscious that for virtually every chapter of this book there is enough unexploited material in the textual sources to turn it into a book on its own, and indeed while it was being written several substantial books or collections of articles were published which are of central importance to its themes. The rate of advance is not likely to slacken, so that it is a safe prediction that a revised edition will soon be needed.

It would be easy to single out specific issues where progress is likely to be made, whether through more detailed research or through new discoveries, but there are two general aspects in which a real advance would lift our understanding of early Mesopotamia to another level. The institutional records of the third millennium contain a multitude of precise quantitative detail about men and materials. As the reconstruction of the various activities is pursued, we can begin to make firm statements about the statistics of production and consumption, at least within quite narrow limits. Even now some disjointed information is available, but these isolated facts need to be worked into a framework with others until they are no longer isolated but achieve a significant role within a system. At that point, they will open a whole new window on the society, one through which we can assess the implications of quantitative data – discover what meant prosperity and poverty, or heavily and sparsely populated; how extreme the wealth differential; how precarious or productive the agricultural regime.

The other aspect is equally critical, and that is the degree of overlap between different sectors of society. These are issues we have alluded to but the time is not ripe to resolve them. Are the administrators of the temple also the secular elite of the city? How much of the city bureaucracy is indigenous, how much a civil service cadre deriving from the entourage of the ruling house? The solutions may sometimes be found in prosopography, but we would have to be very lucky to find archives relating to the same persons from different archives. At the highest level there are hints – like a high-ranking Ur III family at Nippur, or the overlapping of different archives from Šuruppak – but the further down the social ladder we go the less chance there is that the same people's activities are recorded in different contexts.   Nevertheless, the huge mass of Ur III documents or a single informative Old Babylonian letter could easily yield results of considerable interest at any time, and the quantity and variety of documents from within the palace at Mari may eventually give us an insight into the extent of its links with society outside its four walls. In the meantime, there is more than enough to keep historians busy with the integration of Mesopotamia's uniquely informative dual legacy of documents and archaeology.

Notes

1 Mesopotamia: the land and the life

1 The date of the domestication of the camel remains an open question, but there is no clear evidence that it had any significant effect until its appearance with Arab tribes in the desert and in the Zagros, in the early first millennium BC (cf. Luke 1965, 42–3, for the issue).
2 Luke 1965, 28ff with map, p. 317.
3 Salim 1962, 8–9.
4 Steinkeller 1982, esp. 242–3.
5 For Ebih, cf. Rowton 1982, 323.
6 Edmonds 1957, 53ff.
7 See Mason 1944, 372–3; Edmonds 1957, 147–9.
8 Thureau-Dangin 1912a, lines 15–16.
9 Wirth 1971, 92.
10 For accounts of the relevant isohyets, see D. Oates 1968, 3, citing Davies 1957; Wirth 1971, 88–93; Sanlaville 1985, 17–18; Weiss 1986, 76–80.
11 Layard 1854, I, 315.
12 Wright 1969, 9.
13 Note that the survey work of Adams in particular depends heavily on the ease of observation and access of the currently uncultivated sectors of the plain.
14 Some literature is cited by Brookes 1982, 199; cf. the chart Figure 14:14 in van Zeist and Bottema 1982, 321. It should be stressed again that the scarcity of observed data and the interdependence of a large number of variables make even the most plausible deductions about the ancient climate highly speculative
15 See van Zeist and Bottema 1982, 282ff.
16 Guest 1966, 89.
17 Guest 1966, 81–2.
18 Passage cited in Guest 1966, 88.
19 Nissen 1988, 55–6, after Nützel 1976.
20 Cf. Brookes 1982, 199.

2 Cities and dynasties

21 For the earliest levels at Tell Oueili and their relationship to the cultures using Samarran and later Ubaid pottery, see for instance the contributions by Calvet and J. Oates to Huot 1987, 129ff.
22 Nissen 1983, 60.
23 Evidence presented succinctly in Safar *et al.* 1981, Figure 72 on p. 148.

24 Speiser, in Jones 1969, 90.

25 Kramer, in Jones 1969, 117.

26 Often called the Lion Hunt stele; for a photograph, see for instance Frankfort 1954, Plate 9A or Strommenger and Hirmer 1964, Plate 18.

27 On the nature of the King List, see recently Michalowski 1983.

28 Translated by Cooper 1981; Jacobsen 1987, 345–55.

29 Cooper 1986, 19.

30 For the full text, see Cooper 1986, 54–7.

31 For Eanatum's claim, see Cooper 1986, 42; for the exchange of gifts between the wives of the rulers of Adab and Lagaš, see Sollberger 1957–8, 51 (and Lambert 1953, 58–9, for a, rather outdated, translation of the principal text (RTC 19)).

32 The best discussion remains at present Wright 1969, 31–2, but the whole phenomenon needs re-examination in the light of the new Jemdet Nasr evidence to be presented in Englund et al., forthcoming. The cities certainly involved are Uruk, Ur, Larsa, Adab and Keš. Wright has noted that the Ur sealings do not appear to include Lagaš, Kish or Umma, and this could well reflect the current pattern of political allegiances; but until we have identifications for the 'bird' and 'snake' cities it would be premature to base conclusions on this. The Jemdet Nasr sealings include Uruk, Ur, Larsa and Zabala in the south, and Urum, for which identity with Tell Uqair has been proposed; in any case, their provenance alone shows that at an earlier period the system embraced the northern half of the plain as well.

33 Collon 1987, 107, Nos 454–5.

34 Jacobsen 1970, 376, n35 (reprint of 1957 article).

35 Jacobsen 1970, 157–72 (first published 1943).

36 Martin 1988, 98.

37 Biggs and Postgate 1978, 109; Powell 1976, 104, n25.

38 Jacobsen 1970, 140.

39 Westenholz 1977, 21.

40 It is of course impossible to know when the last native speaker of Sumerian died; a discussion of the question is found in Cooper 1973; for an ancient satirical comment on the use of Sumerian at Nippur see the text edited in Reiner 1986.

41 For a description of the Akkadian language, see Reiner 1966; a recent introductory book is Caplice 1988.

42 Evidence for Semitic language in the Early Dynastic and the presence of scribes with Semitic names are discussed in Biggs 1967; see also Cooper 1973, 239–40. The scene was transformed by the discovery of the Ebla archives, some of the implications of which are considered in Gelb 1977, resumed and amplified in Gelb 1981, especially 52–7; and Biggs 1981, 122–4.

43 Discussed by Gelb 1981; note for instance shared month names: Gelb 1977, 12.

44 The precise linguistic affiliation of Eblaite has aroused much discussion. For a recent view stressing points of similarity with the Assyrian dialect of Akkadian see Parpola 1988.

45 See Wilcke 1973, 41–2.

46 For the possible connection with the place-name Warûm, see Kraus 1970, 37f; these issues are also discussed in Cooper 1973.

47 Because Sumerian calls itself **eme-gir** ('the gir language') and this could easily be composed with **ki** 'region' to give **ki-en-gir** (<**ki-eme-gir**); see Westenholz 1979, 118, an opinion which I share (though not universally accepted).

48 For an up-date on the issue of Sumerian vs. Akkadian, see Jacobsen 1978–9, 8–10. Note also

how the cities mentioned in the treaty rituals of the Stele of the Vultures, in the vase inscription of Lugal-zagesi (Text 2:3), and (as far as we can be sure) in the ED city sealings, are all south of Nippur and Adab, hence in **ki-en-gir**.

49 Following a practice regularized by the kings of Akkad and used until the end of the Old Babylonian period, years were identified by a salient event, often cultic (e.g. Texts 6:2a–d), but also military.

50 For metrology in general, see Powell 1989; for comment on the Akkadian system, see Powell 1984, 46.

51 On the Maništušu Obelisk (Figure 5:5; Text 5:4) see Gelb 1979; Foster 1982, 30–2; note 297 below.

52 For a recent succinct description of Ur III reforms, see Steinkeller 1987b, 20–1.

53 Tidnum is the name of one of the major Amorite groups, which features until the end of the Old Babylonian period, as for instance in the name Samsu-ditana.

54 See Wilcke 1969b.

55 Jacobsen 1953, 38 and n17; the evidence for prices has recently been reviewed by Gomi 1984.

56 For the Adab Old Babylonian texts, see Zhi 1989; for Al-Hiba (= Lagaš) see Biggs 1976, Nos 36–41. It is true that the apparent desertion may seem to be somewhat contradicted by the Edict of Ammi-ṣaduqa, which still lists the 'quays' (*kārum*) or chambers of commerce at sites like Larsa, but we are entitled at present to consider these as archaisms retained for traditional motives.

57 A long-term increase in the salinity of the whole of the southern plain, as proposed by Jacobsen and others, has been questioned recently (Powell 1985; see note 289 below).

58 For the role of Elam, see for instance Steinkeller 1982 (Ur III links with the east); 1988a, 52–3 (Puzur-Inšušinak); van Dijk 1978; and increasing evidence from Mari for Elamite participation in Mesopotamia in the age of Hammurapi (e.g. Charpin 1986b; Durand 1986).

59 Yamutbal was discussed by Stol 1976, 63ff; the recent evidence from Tell Abu Duwari apparently favours seeing it as lying north and east of the land of Larsa proper (see provisionally Stone 1990).

60 Kupper 1957, 197–244, still gives an excellent survey of the evidence for the ethnic composition of North Mesopotamia at this time (esp. 229–34).

61 For Assur at this time, see the authoritative work of Larsen 1976.

62 For indications that the events were yet more complex than this, with Yaggit-Lim's first palace being at Ṣuprum rather than Mari, see Durand 1985a, 164.

63 The impression that the Old Babylonian dialect of Akkadian was suddenly adopted across a wide stretch of the Near East may not be as misleading as one might suppose: see Durand 1985a, 160–1 for an abrupt switch from earlier script and dialect at Mari. There remains much that is enigmatic, though, since not all the dialectical and scribal peculiarities derive from earlier South Mesopotamian traditions.

64 The evidence is conveniently collected in Gasche 1989, 109–43.

65 Most of the evidence for the Kassite presence under the 1st Dynasty of Babylon was assembled in Landsberger 1954; a convenient survey is now given by Brinkman 1976–80; some additional references in de Smet 1990.

3 The written record

66 See Lieberman 1980, 347–8, on *maḫiṣtum*; the interpretation of this word rests on the resemblance between an abacus and a loom, a point of which Lieberman seems to be unaware.

67 For early clay tokens, see Schmandt-Besserat 1981, 1988 and Oates and Jasim 1986; for the Nuzi bulla now see Abusch 1981.

68 The credit for the reconstruction of these forerunners of writing belongs to P. Amiet, M. Brandes and D. Schmandt-Besserat. Among recent articles note Schmandt-Besserat 1981 and 1988, and Powell 1981 supporting her general position against the critique of Lieberman 1980. A comprehensive review of the tokens from Uruk itself is now given by Schmandt-Besserat 1988.

69 The repertoire of early signs is now presented in the massive work of Green and Nissen 1987; recent statements from the Berlin team on early cuneiform include Damerow, Englund and Nissen 1988, and Nissen, Damerow and Englund 1990.

70 For general Egyptological opinion on this point, see Ray 1986, 309.

71 BM 110116 illustrated in Walker 1987, 23; my thanks to Christopher Walker for weighing this tablet for me.

72 For wooden boards in the later second millennium, see Postgate 1986d, 22–3.

73 This is not without exceptions, as is shown for instance by belated entries on the 'round tablets' of the Ur III harvest estimates discussed most recently by Liverani 1990a, 155.

74 On Mesopotamian archives in general, see Weitemeyer 1955 (in Danish). For archives at Mari, see Sasson 1972, who also cites other general articles on the subject. Several pertinent specific studies will be found in Veenhof (ed.) 1986. For the Tello Ur III tablets, see Weitemeyer 1955, 24–7 (with references to and illustrations from De Sarzec's reports).

75 Thureau-Dangin 1939. For Ur III basket tags in general, see Schneider 1940. Early Dynastic examples are to be found in Allotte de la Fuÿe 1912, Nos 25–30; M. Lambert 1969 has a more complete list.

76 For the wording, see Edzard 1968, Nos 31–4; the form of the document is discussed by Cooper 1985, 107ff; see also Steinkeller 1991, No. 2.

77 Pinches 1908, Plate I; for other early sealed tablets, see Steinkeller 1977, 41.

78 See the passage translated in Cooper and Heimpel 1983, 77 (lines 53–6), with further comment by Alster 1987.

79 For sealed letters, see Kraus 1985; note that he also lists letters which have been sealed, without envelopes, where the sealing has an authenticating or acknowledging effect.

80 The genetic line comes through scrolls with clay tags, perhaps first attested in Crete (see Palaima 1988, 316), then through triangular labels inscribed in cuneiform or Aramaic in the first millennium BC and similar Elamite labels from Persepolis to the clay sealings of the Avroman papyri (cf. Postgate 1976, 5).

81 See Powell 1981, 424–31 for the issue and further literature.

82 Useful comments on early script are to be found in Civil and Biggs 1966, 12–16.

83 For this term, and similarities between the early Chinese and Mesopotamian writing systems, see Boltz 1986, 426; there are equally similarities in the development of Meso-American writing (see Justeson 1986).

84 For the third millennium lexical tradition, see Nissen 1981.

85 Early Sumerian incantations have been edited by Krebernik 1984; other 'literary' texts from Abu Salabikh include the Instructions of Šuruppak and the Keš Temple Hymn, which have

been the subject of much detailed study since their first recognition in Biggs 1974. For another such text, see now W. Lambert 1990.

86 See in general Kraus 1973, 18–21; Waetzoldt 1989. For field surveys with plans, see the comprehensive study of Liverani 1990a. For house plans, see Heinrich and Seidl 1967.

87 For some comments, see Kraus 1985, 137 n2; Sasson 1972, 57ff. For the occasional female scribes, see Waetzoldt 1988a, 31.

88 For tags for hired men (including a reed-worker and builder), see Weitemeyer 1962; brick-yard workers: Kohler and Ungnad 1909–23, Nos 1888–906 (also Donbaz and Yoffee 1986); harvesters: Kohler and Ungnad 1909–23, Nos 1325–6, 1333–6, 1373, 1787, 1789, 1822, and some of 1864–80; labels for animals: Kohler and Ungnad 1909–23, Nos 1907–23 (also Waetzoldt 1986b, 3–9); for dead sheep (and wool): see Goetze 1950, 85–94; Kraus 1984, 371–4. This is not an exhaustive list.

4 City and countryside

89 For the identity and nomenclature of the settlements at Sippar, see now Charpin 1988a.

90 A first report on the work at Tell Abu Duwari is given by Stone 1990. We should perhaps mention the methodical layout of an Old Babylonian settlement recovered at the site of ed-Diniyah, ancient Haradum, not far south-east of Mari on the Euphrates (plan in Kepinski and Lecomte 1985, 616), and indeed the walled city of Šaduppum, modern Tell Harmal, in the outskirts of Baghdad.

91 Personal observation, now sustained by the Warka surface survey (Finkbeiner 1991).

92 Cf. Postgate 1990a, 103–4.

93 Houses and building plots are often described in legal deeds as bordering on the square (*rebītum*: Schorr 1913, Nos 112 (Dilbat), 86, 92, 194, 202, 206, 278 (all Sippar)), and at least one document includes rights of access to the square (No. 86); square as a place for public disgrace (No. 229). At Terqa there was a *rebītum* called the 'Square of the land' (*mātim*) next to the palace, but this is of course in a north-western city which may well have had a different conformation from the typical southern city (No. 219).

94 References to various public and legal activities in the gates of temples or cities are to be found in the Chicago *Assyrian Dictionary* (CAD), vols A/i 83–8 (abullu) and B 19–22 (bābu A).

95 The evidence is dicussed in Renger 1984, 76–9; it remains possible to my mind that the *bīt mahīrim* was in fact a building to which people came to purchase items stored there, in other words, surely, a shop.

96 See Adams 1981, 84ff; and for another view, Sumner 1979.

97 For a prospective description of these procedures, which are in progress, see Matthews and Postgate 1987, 102–4; the potential of these techniques is now very much enhanced by research on the micromorphology of the deposits being undertaken by Wendy Matthews.

98 Kramer 1979, 155.

99 For Fara, see Martin 1988, 126–8; a similar picture is emerging at Abu Salabikh, where clearly public administrative documents have been found in what appears to be a large private residence (Postgate 1990a).

100 Jacobsen 1943; 1957, 99–109; both reprinted in Jacobsen 1970.

101 Larsen 1976, 161ff.

102 For the **maškim** in Neo-Sumerian texts, see A. Falkenstein 1956, and for the *mu'irrum*, see Walther 1917, with a more recent survey by Yoffee 1977, 81–142.

103 The only occurrence of **dag-gi.a** known to me in a third-millennium context is Steinkeller 1989a, No. 63:14, where some witnesses are called the 'neighbours of the ward', a situation exactly compatible with Old Babylonian usage; its rarity in our textual sources is a further indication of the way in which they reflect the activities of government at the expense of the private sector.

104 I cannot agree with Yoffee (in Donbaz and Yoffee 1986, 66–7) that the *bābtum* is likely to have been defined as a group of people, rather than a geographical unity. Proof is not to be had at present, but the parallelism with the village strongly suggests that the members of a *bābtum* are held together by their residential proximity. For a list of men by *bābtum* or *piqittum* (**si.lá**) at Mari, see Bottéro 1957, No. 180, with commentary on 226–7. Cf. also chapter 13 below, p. 244.

105 Stone 1987, 1–7 (with comment in Postgate 1990b).

106 References in Sjöberg 1967, 203.

107 Falkenstein 1956, II, 329–31.

108 TSŠ 245, as interpreted by Jacobsen 1957, 121 – surely correct despite the doubts of Sjöberg 1967, 208.

109 The best accounts are Walther 1917 and Klengel 1960.

110 The Kassites constitute an exception: of nomadic lifestyle, to judge from their encampments, tribally organized, and of eastern origin (cf. note 65 and Landsberger 1954).

111 As evidenced by references in historical inscriptions to excluding the feet of the Amorites from the land, and indeed by the building of the 'Fender off of Tidnum' and similar walls (cf. Wilcke 1969b, and pp. 42–3).

112 The protagonist of 'enclosed nomadism' was for years M.B. Rowton: see for instance Rowton 1973, and a list of other pertinent articles by him in Rowton 1976. A global account of nomadism is given by Khazanov 1984; the Mari texts continue to yield valuable new insights, and some useful detailed studies are contained in Silva Castillo 1981.

113 Amorite tribes keeping equids are mentioned in Ur III texts (Lieberman 1968–9, 53–9; mostly donkeys not onagers, although the text Legrain TRU 300 does associate Amorites with onagers). For further west, see Albright 1961; 1968, 62–4.

114 This was especially the case in the mid-second millennium, when the Sutians were involved in trade from the Middle Euphrates across the desert (the Amarna correspondence and Middle Assyrian texts from Assur, ed-Diniyah and Tell al-Rimah; see Heltzer 1981 for some of the evidence). See also Durand 1987a, 159–67 (our Text 13:7).

115 The Slubba have recently been studied in Betts 1989.

116 The principal evidence for the ancestral memories of the Amorites is the Assyrian King List, and the *kispum* text edited in Kraus 1965a as well as Finkelstein 1966b.

117 The text cited in Text 4:10 is explaining that, although the 'Northerners' and 'Southerners' do indeed retain their separate identities and live in separate villages, they are still of the same kind, like different coloured beads on a single necklace. In Near Eastern perceptions the north was on the left hand, the south on the right (see chapter 2 above, p. 38).

118 For the environment at El Kowm on the west of the Jebel Bishri, and early settlement there, see for instance Besançon *et al.* 1982.

119 Luke 1965, 26f. See also Heltzer 1981, 39. For the relations between nomads and settled in general, see Khazanov 1984, 69–84.

120 Landsberger 1954; see note 65 above.

53 Household and family

121 I choose this term in preference to 'extended family household' (e.g. Laslett 1972) to avoid the danger of confusion with the 'extended family'.

122 The houses at Fara (Šuruppak) were similar in layout and size to the Abu Salabikh houses, but those at Khafajah were generally smaller (though perhaps slightly earlier); see Matthews and Postgate 1987, 118–19.

123 Matthews and Postgate 1987, 102–4; see note 97 above.

124 See Leemans 1986, 20. The otherwise useful discussion of house size in Gelb 1976b, 197–8, is vitiated by his failure to realize that some 'house sales' are only compensating heirs for inequalities in spaces inherited; see Text 5:5.

125 Powell 1986, 11, cites the opinion of Nimkoff and Middleton that 'where agriculture and animal husbandry are co-dominant, one should also expect the extended family system to predominate'. It is not clear to me from Nimkoff 1965, 37f, whether this statement applies specifically to co-residence, or solely to the family as a social mechanism.

126 For the evidence there is, see Gelb 1979, 71ff.

127 On co-ownership of houses, see Gelb 1979, 77, with fn 142.

128 Summarized in Powell 1986, 10.

129 CH §§168–9; for inheritance by females, see Kraus 1969a, 13–17.

130 For the paternal estate, see Kraus 1969a in general, and the article 'bīt abim' in CAD, vol. A/i, 73–4.

131 For relatives as recipients of payments, see Krecher 1980, 493. For more than one seller (presumably some if not all related), see Edzard 1968, Nos 1, 2, 3, 4 etc. (ED III); Steinkeller 1989a, 121 (Ur III).

132 See Gelb 1979, 81ff.

133 For irrigation rights, see Nippur texts cited in Prang 1980.

134 Diakonoff 1985, 49;, see Renger 1987.

135 See Kraus 1951, 152ff, for these texts from the Ninlil-zimu archive, which has been discussed by Stone 1987, passim.

136 See Matouš 1949 for texts from Larsa; Prang 1980, II.B and II.C.1 for Nippur texts.

137 For other evidence for female inheritance, see Kraus 1969a, 13–17.

138 Leemans 1986; Kraus 1969a, 11–12; Klíma 1940, 27ff.

139 Stone 1987, 45.

140 See Barrelet 1980: but her scepticism about the intramural nature of the burials at Ur seems quite misplaced; field archaeologists will recognize that no report can convey all the indications observed on site which help to form the excavator's opinion, and that the views of an experienced excavator like Woolley cannot be responsibly overturned from the pages of a report. In favour of intramural burials, see Diakonoff 1985, 55, n22; and at Emar on the Euphrates in Syria, see Durand 1989.

141 For one exception, see Martin et al. 1985, 20–1.

142 Bayliss 1973, 118.

143 Sjöberg 1965.

144 Tsukimoto 1985; see e.g. Bayliss 1973, 120.

145 For passūr sakkim/banšur zag.gu.la (also zag.gar.ra), see Prang 1976, 16, 27; in one instance only this goes to a younger son. For a mention in the Epic of Gilgamesh, see Landsberger 1968, 83.

146 qadum zag.gar.ra TCL 11 174:14, see Matouš 1949, 168.

147 Ur: Woolley and Mallowan 1976, 29–30; T. as-Suleimeh: Rmaidh 1984, Figures 1 on p. 46 and 1–3 on p. 47; Tell Asmar: Delougaz, Hill and Lloyd 1967, 151 with Plate 72; Tell al-Dhiba'i: Mustafa 1949, 178 with Plate IIIA; Nippur: McCown and Haines 1967, 39–40.

148 In Old Assyrian texts, e.g. 'We are sacrificing one sheep to our god' (KTBl. 13, cf. Hirsch 1961, 35–40): Old Babylonian: 'They wrote to his brothers, his sons and the sons of the people of his god' (AbB 2, 88; cf. Renger 1973b, 103).

149 **udu níg.dé.a mí.ús.sá.e.ne** and **udu níg.dé.a.mí.e.ne**, see Wilcke 1985, 252f.

150 For the transfer of a *biblum* and *nudunnûm* on behalf of a priestess being dedicated, see PBS 8/ii, 183, edited in Harris 1964, 110–11, and Wilcke 1982, 440–50.

151 Ešnunna laws §§27–8: 'he has instituted a contract and feast for her father and her mother' (for legal niceties, see Yaron 1969); CH §128; the Ur III code appears to expect a written contract (**dub inim-kešda**) as evidence, but this relates to entitlement to divorce money, not directly to the legal status of the marriage (Finkelstein 1968–9, 69). See for the 'feast' especially Landsberger 1968.

152 Greengus 1969, 516.

153 Under the Akkad Dynasty, see Wilcke 1985, 252ff, on MAD 1, 169; see Landsberger 1968, 96 n4, for Ur III.

154 See Dalley 1980, 54; also Yaron 1965.

155 See CT 45, 86: 'shall a lady who is living in your paternal house, and whose married status is known to your city-ward, go away like that? Match (the payment to what she brought with her) as she came into you(r house)' (see Veenhof 1976, 154); also CH §141: 'If the wife of a man who is living in the man's house . . .', clearly implying that she need not have been co-resident.

156 For the payment of dowry only when she actually leaves her father's household: 'once half a mina of silver, her marriage payment (*terhas-sa*) had been tied into her hem and returned to her father-in-law, in future her sons are her heirs' (Wilcke 1982, 457, No. 5; with similar clauses e.g. p. 461, No. 7; for such texts, see also Harris 1974).

157 Thus CH §130: 'the wife (*aššat*) of a man, . . . who has not known a male' (i.e. a virgin).

158 To 'call on house of father-in-law': Yaron 1965; Greengus 1966, 66–70; Wilcke 1969a, 76–7; 1985, fn84.

159 Late Old Babylonian text from Tell Mohammed (Wilcke 1985, 291–2, also for the Ur III offerings for 'the setting up of the bed for the bride of the governor of Hamazi').

160 For the dress-pin, see Landsberger 1968, 104; for the witnesses in the case of Enlil-issu, Hallo 1964b, 97, on BE 6/ii, 58 (but Landsberger 1968, 91, n3).

161 See the dictionaries under *naṣārum*.

162 For incest, see simply Petschow 1976–80.

163 On divorce, see Koschaker 1951; Finkelstein 1976; see also the CAD, vol. S s.v. 'sissiktu'. Marvin Powell makes a plea that the considerable value of a mina of silver be made explicit: 'at least £10,000'.

164 Wilcke 1985, 261.

165 Divorce after bearing children is not mentioned by the Code of Hammurapi, but see Code of Ešnunna §59, which is unfortunately juristically very unclear (cf. Yaron 1969, 50). For divorce after the birth of children, see Koschaker 1951, 121–2, on Kish I, Plate 6 B.17; divorce before birth of children: CH §138 on return of *biblum* and *mala terhatim*. Formal dissolution of an engagement(?), see Edzard 1968, No. 85 (Akkad Dynasty, from Isin).

166 This certainly seems to follow from the office of prostitute (*harimūtum*) mentioned along with

other temple offices (*parṣum*) in the Old Babylonian text, Finkelstein 1968a, No. 45. See now Spaey 1990 with other literature.

167 Gelb 1979, 63–5.

168 Petschow 1976–80, 145b.

169 Leemans 1968, 181.

170 See Leemans 1968, 181–5; Finkelstein 1962.

171 On the freeing of slaves, see Falkenstein 1956, I, 92–5 (Ur III).

6 The temple

172 Eichmann 1989, 60–2.

173 The gift of a 'temple' by an individual is attested in CT 6 36a = VAB 5:220 (see Charpin 1986a, 269, fn2; Harris 1975, 187). For small chapels within the city at Ur, see Charpin 1986a, 268–9 (Hendursag) and 268, n1 (Ištaran).

174 Marvin Powell draws my attention to the fact that sheep-counts took place within the 'palace' and the é-mí at Pre-Sargonic Girsu, but there must have been many instances where there was no room for expansion. There are no dispassionate descriptions of temple establishments in the texts, but interesting details of the Ekur at Nippur, with dimensions, are given by a Kassite document (Kramer and Bernhardt 1975); see also the evidence assembled in Charpin 1986a, 325–42, for the establishments at Old Babylonian Ur.

175 See Harris 1955.

176 See Ellis 1983 and 1986a, b for the Ishchali archives.

177 Waetzoldt 1972, 91–9.

178 For the shrine in building plans, see King 1900, II, No. 107, and Thureau-Dangin 1903, No. 145: *papāhu* reached off the courtyard and leading into the shrine (ki-tuš).

179 For repeated 'mouth-opening' rituals in the Ur III period, see Civil 1967b, 211: flour and milk products for the ritual, which involved a reed hut.

180 See Seidl and Krecher 1957–71 and van Buren 1945.

181 The Qatna inventories are in Bottéro 1949; for other lists, including one unpublished from ed-Diniyah on the Euphrates, see the remarks accompanying the edition of a list from Me-Turnat on the Diyala, Black and al-Rawi 1983.

182 Libation practices are still in need of study (cf. Heimpel 1987). For Ur III references to kaš-dé-a rituals, see Schneider 1925(!), 55–7, No. 85; the term survives into the Old Babylonian texts (e.g. CBS 7522 in Robertson 1981; and see Krecher 1966, 40, n112, both references courtesy Tina Breckwoldt). While one can hardly doubt the literal meaning of the term as 'beer-pouring', in the texts it is mostly used in connection with animal sacrifice (cf. the Akkadian *nīqum* which often refers to sheep sacrifice but seems to derive from a verb meaning 'to pour a libation').

183 For aromatics, see e.g. Snell 1982; some of the archaeological evidence for Mesopotamia is to be found in Nielsen 1986. See also chapter 10 below, p. 202.

184 Sigrist 1984; for the 'fish-cake' utu₂ see Charpin 1986a, 314–15.

185 Old Babylonian: Figulla 1953; Ur III lists are not uniformly edited, but by way of illustration references to various texts listing fruit will be found in Postgate 1987, 115–27.

186 For offerings to locks, gates, drainpipes and other temple installations, see e.g. Levine and Hallo 1967; Kingsbury 1963; Sigrist 1984, 148–51; Charpin 1986a, 311–18.

187 Steinkeller 1987b, 27–30.

188 See e.g. Postgate 1986a, 170–71.

189 For the 'first-fruits', their boat and their standard (šu-nir), see Limet 1970, 68–9.

190 Sigrist 1977b.

191 For a recent survey of the *akītum* institution and its nature, see Black 1981.

192 For divine boat trips in general, see Sauren 1969 including the Pre-Sargonic evidence; other references in Ferrara 1973, 1. For a temple consecration at Girsu in the Ur III period, see Sauren 1969 under 1.5 (An, Enlil, and Ninhursag travelling to Girsu). For the Old Babylonian period: Finet 1981.

193 Harris 1967; van Lerberghe 1982.

194 Charpin 1986a, 322–5.

195 Kingsbury 1963.

196 Old Babylonian documents dealing with prebends are discussed in Cocquerillat 1955. The treatment of the system in Charpin 1986a, 260–9, represents a fundamental advance. Note that he observes the first signs of the 'commercialization' of the offices in the Ur III Dynasty (p. 261).

197 Sigrist 1984, 160; Charpin 1986a, 240ff (YOS 5 163).

196 See Charpin 1986a, 251, for this point.

199 Gelb 1976a.

200 Sauren 1970, 14.

201 Börker-Klähn 1975.

202 For Enheduana see Hallo and van Dijk 1968, 1–11; among many accounts of the priestesses in general, Sollberger 1954–6, 23–9, is still the most detailed.

203 See Weadock 1975; Enanedu quotations after Charpin 1986a, 200–1; see also the *gipārum* of Ningublaga in the inscription of Lipit-Ištar for his daughter En-nin-sun-zi, UET I 106:22 (Charpin 1986a, 220–3).

204 Weadock 1975, 101.

205 Harris 1975, and several articles there referred to; a convenient summary also in Jeyes 1983.

206 Dossin 1978, No. 38; see same phrase in Nos 36 and 37.

207 Stone 1982, 55–6.

208 Steinkeller 1981a, 81–2.

209 For the *nadītum* at Tell al-Rimah (Karana?), see Dalley 1984, 104ff.

210 See for example Stone 1982; Harris 1975, 305ff.

211 Charpin 1986a, 294; oxen (or bulls) are occasionally mentioned in the context of public sacrifices, and one is shown on the stele of Ur-Nammu, presumably as part of the rituals surrounding the building of the temple and ziggurat.

212 Compare also the letter of Zimri-Lim's daughter (quoted above, see note 206), and the Mari letter quoted Spycket 1968, 97. Also van Dijk 1967, 249, with n62. Some such statues were perhaps there as much or rather more as objects of worship and recipients of libations – the distinction may be blurred.

213 There is a considerable literature on this evidence;, see for example Moran 1969, 15–56; and a recent account in Malamat 1989, 79–96.

214 For the **arua** in Ur III texts, see Gelb 1972. For people as **arua** already in the early ED III period, see Edzard 1968, 20, on v.3.

215 See now van de Mieroop 1989.

216 By means of the *ikribum* institution, for which see for instance Garelli 1963, 252–5, and Larsen 1976, 149.

217 Harris 1955.

218 See most recently Charpin 1986a, 167–8; Harris 1967; van Lerberghe 1982.

7 The palace

219 The E-hursag at Ur, which in a sense is an Ur III palace, cannot have fulfilled all the functions of the main residence of the Ur III kings, which was 'unlikely to have been on the Temenos platform' (Woolley and Moorey 1982, 160–3).

220 The Mari archives in particular are replete with evidence for the exchange of gifts, a practice also very much in evidence in the world of the Amarna letters, in the fifteenth and fourteenth centuries BC (e.g. Liverani 1990b). For the role of gift exchange in society in the Old Babylonian period, see Zaccagnini 1983a. The Ur III texts also list gifts given to messengers, visiting dignitaries and others, especially rings of precious metal: Michalowski 1978; and Sigrist 1979. For gifts made and received by Zimri-Lim during a journey to the Mediterranean, see note 234 below.

221 See Malamat 1989, 20–2, for a short statement and Dalley 1984, 78–96 for a more general view of the contemporary culinary scene. As Charpin 1986a, 318, n3, points out, the Mari texts do not list complete menus, but are issues from the individual departments supplying foods of different kinds. For the ice, see Page(-Dalley) 1969; Charlier 1987.

222 Bottéro 1980–3.

223 For the Ur III messenger texts, see Jones and Snyder 1961, 280–310.

224 Whiting 1976.

225 See note 202.

226 For Taram-Uram, see Civil 1962; his interpretation of the name still seems probable to me, despite the doubts of Durand 1985a, 148, fn8.

227 Among several recent contributions on the ladies of the Ur III court, see e.g. Steinkeller 1981a; Michalowski 1982.

228 See the discussion in Gelb 1979, 65–8.

229 See the Middle Assyrian palace edicts making it clear that members of the harem accompanied the kings on journeys outside the city (Weidner 1956).

230 For the Mari harem, see Durand 1985b; for the role of 'singers' as royal concubines, see also Durand 1984, 128.

231 See Weidner 1956.

232 The study of the Ur III palace as an institution is in its infancy, although there is rich material available. Questions like the possible differentiation of the 'palace' as a government organization separate from the king's personal estate, or whether the frequent statements that an item 'entered' or 'left the palace' should be taken literally and physically, or understood as an administrative concept, still require examination. Perhaps the nearest approach at present is the article of Limet 1979. For workers physically in the palace, see the people 'inside the palace' (šà-é-gal-me) as opposed to 'present in the city' (lú ì-gál uru.ki-me) cited by Lafont 1990.

233 Frankena 1966, Nos 49–52.

234 This emerges from one of the most remarkable dossiers from the whole range of cuneiform documents, consisting of records of the elite gifts given and received during the trip to Ugarit, most of the tablets bearing their date and place of writing. See Villard 1986.

235 For the symbols and rituals associated with royalty, see chapter 14.

236 Zariqum, on whom see Hallo 1956; Kutscher 1979. For the Ur III provincial system in

general, see recently Steinkeller 1987b, 22–6, with notes on p. 24 on the question of hereditary governorships.

237 Three governors at least are royal princes: Šu-megri, king's son (Foster 1982, 22; Westenholz 1984, 80, n14); Nabi-ulmaš, son of Naram-Sin, governor of Tutu (Sollberger and Kupper 1971, 110); Lipit-ili, son of Naram-Sin, governor of Marada (Sollberger and Kupper 1971, 106).

238 The civilian:military duality is set out very clearly in Steinkeller 1987b.

239 The only major study of administrative procedures to be published remains that of Jones and Snyder 1961, although many detailed articles and American doctoral dissertations on aspects of Ur III administration have been written since then.

240 For the question of literacy among officials and others, see note 87. This book has not strayed into a detailed examination of the scribal world. An important general statement for the Old Babylonian period is that of Kraus 1973, 18–45. For Ur III times, see in particular the useful studies of Waetzoldt 1986a, 1988b and 1989. See also Sjöberg 1976; van Stiphout 1979; Civil 1985.

8 Crops and livestock

241 Two recent accounts of prehistoric Mesopotamia are Oates and Oates 1976 and Redman 1978.

242 For two instances of large quantities of fish-bone on Ubaid period sites, see Eridu (Safar *et al.* 1981, 101 and 107–10, with references to third-millennium fish-bones) and Oueili, where turtle bones are also recorded (Desse 1983; 1987).

243 For liquorice, see Townsend and Guest 1974, 445–9 and Chakravarty 1976, 259–61; for the roots of bulrush (*Typha domingensis*), see Townsend and Guest 1985, 213–16, also Postgate 1980a, 105–6 (mentioning 'sweet reed' in cuneiform texts); for sedge tubers (*Cyperus rotundus*; in Arabic *s'd*, a word probably already in Akkadian – see CAD, vol. S 338–99, s.v. 'suadu'), see Townsend and Guest 1985, 339–41 and Chakravarty 1976, 184–5.

244 The need to pasture sheep over a considerable distance from the southern plains during summer, indicated by the evidence cited by Kraus 1976b, can of course be avoided if the sheep are fed grain and other fodder over that period, and this option cannot be excluded.

245 These private contracts are described in Postgate and Payne 1975.

246 The exact anatomical identity of the **sa** (Akkadian *gīdum*, inter alia) remains uncertain. They can be weighed, and Neo-Babylonian contracts between shepherds and the Ebabbar at Sippar require the delivery of 2.5 shekels (i.e. about 20 g) of *gīdu* per animal; see Kraus 1966, 132. Traditionally the word has been understood as 'tendons', but Oppenheim 1948, 80–1, already expresses doubts. More recently Butz 1979, 349–50, has suggested 'intestines'.

247 See Oppenheim 1948, 16, n37, for the oath taken by the shepherd at the Nin-mar(ki) temple, and under B6 on the same page for a similar oath to prove that an ox died from disease, all at Ur III Girsu.

248 The basic work is Kraus 1966, esp. 56–8; the amounts of wool recovered from each animal come out at less than 1 kg on average. Since the wool yield of an animal could be checked, either at the time of shearing or with the presentation of the skin of the dead animal, it was not (necessarily or exclusively) the subject of a percentage agreement, and already in the Ur III period the liability of the shepherds seems to have been determined by records kept by the state's accountants (šatam, Gallery 1980); one stage of this process is represented by the dead animal tags authenticated by *šatammu*s from the reign of Sin-idinnam (Goetze 1950).

249 Biggs and Postgate 1978, 106–7, IAS 519. Note that 'shearing' is an inaccurate term, since at

this time the evidence indicates that sheep were only plucked (which meant that it had to be done in the spring when the wool was ready to be shed). For royal involvement in the annual shearing, see note 233 above; Charpin 1982b (including Hammurapi, AbB 2.25); Yoffee 1977, 13–20.

250 see CAD, vol. K 582b, s.v. 'kuruštû A'.

251 Maekawa 1983; Durand and Charpin 1980.

252 Steinkeller 1989b.

253 Hruška, 1988b; Ras al Amiya: Flannery and Cornwall in Hole *et al.* 1969, 435–8.

254 See G. Farber 1982.

255 Waetzoldt, in BSA 6 (forthcoming); see also Waetzoldt 1986b, 4–5, n6, for the use of brewing by-products.

256 Steinkeller 1987b, 30ff, on the animals deriving from the **gun mada** (which I prefer to translate as 'rental', not 'tax', 'of the land').

257 See Gomi 1980; Gelb 1969; Butz 1973–4; Kraus 1966.

258 Boehmer 1974.

259 Dyson 1960.

260 Postgate 1986.

261 Veenhof 1972, 1–2; also notes 113–14 above; for donkeys at Šuruppak, see Martin 1988, 89–90.

262 e.g. TR 3107 from Tell al-Rimah.

263 Grave 262, at or beyond the east side of the 6H82 house. For pork in OB times, cf. CAD N/ii, 232b.

264 The text has been translated by Kramer and by Aro (in Salonen 1968), but I have made use of Civil n.d. (an edition and translation of 'The Farmer's Instructions' for a meeting of the Sumerian Agriculture Group in Leiden, cited with permission of Miguel Civil; this edition is due for publication in the near future). For agricultural prayers, see Maeda 1979.

265 See for instance Powell 1984 on seeding procedures; and recently Maekawa 1990 for the animal management.

266 Issues usefully discussed in Halstead 1990.

267 There is a varied Ur III vocabulary for cutting, uprooting and harvesting reeds, thorn bushes and weeds, which remains to be studied in detail. Provisionally, see Oppenheim 1948, 46–7, with reference e.g. to YOS 4, No. 225; Civil 1987, 52.

268 See Petschow 1984, 188.

269 For interest rates in Old Babylonian texts, see Leemans 1950b; for a more recent account based on the texts from Kisurra, see Kienast 1978, I, 60–4.

270 Harris 1955.

271 Diakonoff 1965, 24–8 gives a compelling general account of the interacting forces underlying the economic polarization of Mesopotamian society.

272 The legumes and oil-plants are dealt with in several articles in BSA 2 (1985).

273 For modern interplanting, see for example Charles 1990; for textual references, see Postgate 1987, 122.

274 The arguments for considering *ašūhum* to be a pine, or at least a similar conifer, will be presented in BSA 6 (scheduled to appear in 1991).

275 For the sesame saga the articles of Waetzoldt and Bedigian in BSA 2 (1985) appear to be conclusive; since then sesame seeds have been identified among the contents of Tutankhamun's tomb.

276 The plant *duhnum* was originally identified as millet for etymological reasons, but although unproven there is no good reason to doubt it.

277 The fallow system in Early Dynastic times is examined exhaustively in LaPlaca and Powell 1990.

278 Marvin Powell reminds me that one of the principal weeds of South Mesopotamian fields in fallow is shoq (*Prosopis farcta*), which is itself a legume and probably an emergency food crop. It is said to confer various benefits, but I do not know if these include the fixation of nitrogen. For a possible rare, literary, mention of the use of manure, see Text 16:2.

9 Water and land

279 For the Euphrates' course in the Sippar region, see Gasche 1988; for its course more generally, see Adams 1981, chapter 1.

280 The standard modern work on soils is Buringh 1960; for a clear survey of the subject, see Charles 1988.

281 Gasche 1988; 1989.

282 Since hand-watering with buckets or shaduf requires no communal organization, it is inevitably under-represented in the administrative texts. Compare Yahdun-Lim's no doubt exaggerated claim 'I opened canals and abolished the irrigation-bucket in my land'! See for instance CAD, vol. D 56–7; Laessøe 1953; Salonen 1968, Tafel IV.4 for shaduf on a third millennium seal. For the suggestion that *zirīqum* in Ur III (e.g. Pettinato 1977), and indeed in Early Dynastic, texts refers to a shaduf, see Maekawa 1986, 119–21.

283 See note 133 above.

284 For a calendar of irrigation work throughout the year in Ur III times, see the fundamental article of Waetzoldt 1990; for mathematical exercises on irrigation works, see Powell 1988. An Old Babylonian archive to do with the administration of canal maintenance in the kingdom of Larsa is edited by Walters 1970a (with further analysis in Wright 1977).

285 On canal work by Pre-Sargonic rulers of Lagaš, see Hruška 1988a.

286 For the *gugallum* (Sumerian **gugal** or **kugal**), see Steinkeller 1988b, 87; 1989a, No. 56.

287 Waetzoldt 1990.

288 Cuneiformists fall into one of two camps on the subject of 'blind' workers, those who take the term literally, and those who find this implausible or distasteful, and try to explain it as 'unskilled' or in some such way. I fall into the first camp, for reasons set out in Gelb 1973, 87, and not to my mind contradicted by (e.g.) Garelli *et al.* 1982.

289 For salt areas, see Jacobsen 1982, 8–10. For the detailed critique of the 'salinity theory', see Powell 1985, who rightly stresses that no evidence exists which proves the long-term deterioration of land quality. This does not of course prove the opposite either, and we would have to know much more about the relationships between water supply and land used, the reversibility of salinity, and the social and technical feasibility of large-scale shifts in areas of cultivation to know if local salinity problems would have converged into a long-term deterioriation of the entire south. Note the account in Buringh 1960, 250, of plots in the south set aside as 'isolated salt areas' to which salts from surrounding fields can be leached.

290 See Adams 1981, 61–2; for ancient levées round Sippar, see n281.

291 Veenhof 1973.

292 Until recently the word for 'dyke' (**eg**) was regularly translated as 'canal', but it is certain that it is primarily a bank of earth (Pemberton *et al.* 1988, 212–17). Ur-Nammu's dyke measured '4 **danna** 260 **nindan**'.

293 See the statements of Diakonoff 1985, 49; Renger 1987.

294 This is the sense of Stone 1987, 17, citing Stone 1982; Stone 1982, 54, refers us to Stone 1977 in general. There the table on p. 279 demonstrated the frequency of transactions within the kin group, but I have not been able to find chapter and verse there to show that 'alienation of house and especially field property was apparently restricted to lineage members' (so 1982, 54), or even a clear negative statement as it is formulated in my text.

295 Diakonoff 1985.

296 Klengel 1976, using evidence differently interpreted by Renger 1987.

297 See Gelb 1979 on the Obelisk, and Foster 1985 (proposing Rimuš as the king responsible for the Girsu stele).

298 See Klengel 1976 in general, and p. 69 specifically for prices of land; in contrast to late second-millennium texts, pledge of land in Old Babylonian times is infrequent – see recently Kienast 1978, I, 66–103(and notes 304 and 324 below).

299 The quotation is from Diakonoff 1982, 44; in the second passage (Diakonoff 1974, 14, n12) his exact words are that 'the prices of land are governed by the average ratio of profit which in the Ancient East can for practical reasons be conventionally equated to the average interest on loans. Thus, an average profit of 33% means that the average price of land will not exceed the price of three yearly crops'. I am indebted to Marvin Powell for explaining this to me!

300 For this point, see Diakonoff 1982, 46; for the annulments, see Kraus 1984.

301 e.g. Klengel 1976, 80.

302 For land rental agreements, see Leemans 1975; 1976; Petschow 1984.

303 See Petschow 1984, 190–3.

304 See Steinkeller 1981b. That the economics of land use were integrated with the rest of the economy is clear from evidence that tenancy of a field (and/or house) might be considered as a substitute for interest on a silver loan, a situation which overlaps with antichretic pledge (Kienast 1978, I, 77–9, for Old Babylonian; see Steinkeller 1981b, 115–16, fn13, for Ur III).

305 For Lipit-Ištar, see Steele 1948, 14.

306 Petschow 1984, 185–6.

307 Petschow 1984, 188.

308 Harris 1967; van Lerberghe 1982.

309 The decisive shift in opinion stems from the work of I.M. Diakonoff, summarized in English in Diakonoff 1974. For the correct reading of the term for rented land (**apin-lá**), see Steinkeller 1981b, 114.

310 See Steinkeller 1987a, 20–3, for these early Ur references. For prebend fields at Abu Salabikh, see Biggs and Postgate 1978, 105, 115–16.

311 Land tenure conditions in the Old Babylonian period are complex and in need of further study, but on the *šukūšum* fields see for the present Ellis 1976, 12, etc.; as well as the references under *šukūšum* in the dictionaries.

312 For the lease of prebend land by a third party, see Kraus 1976a.

313 For lease of *ilkum* land, see Leemans 1976, 246.

314 See Postgate 1990c for a modern instance, van Driel 1988, 130–1, for Neo-Babylonian, and Liverani 1990a for Ur III.

315 See Gibson 1974. For another factor favouring tenants, see n542 below.

316 See Adams 1981, 20–1, for other considerations about the effects of private versus institutional land holding, and 14–19, 155, etc. for the shift in the Euphrates channel. On the Euphrates' courses, see also Gibson 1973.

10 The domestic economy

317 See Humphreys 1969 for a useful account of Polanyi's position; more recently the papers of a symposium 'Economic anthropology and history: the work of Karl Polanyi', *Research in economic anthropology* 4 (1981) 1–93. Terminology can vary: some 'redistributive' economies may usefully be thought of rather as 'exploitative'.

318 Surplus wealth was no doubt largely converted into precious metal, but more in the form of jewellery than as ready 'cash', but the claim in Diakonoff 1965, 24, that 'silver and jewelry might be hoarded in the household for prestige reasons but there was no money-market' seems to me to underrate the role of silver (see later in the chapter), at least in the Old Babylonian period.

319 For aromatics, see n183; early commodity values: Gelb *et al.* 1991, 291–8.

320 For small-scale commerce, see Landsberger 1967a and Renger 1984.

321 Leemans 1950a; for Ur III times, see Falkenstein 1956, I, 120; ZA 55.83 Nr 22; Old Assyrian: Veenhof 1988, 259–63.

322 The only Pre-Sargonic documents clearly recording loan transactions seem to be those edited by Bauer 1975, which are not legal instruments but administrative records. See Steinkeller 1981b, 141–2, who comments that similar texts are known from the Sargonic period, which 'also witnesses the appearance of the texts recording individual loans'.

323 In Old Babylonian times the term used for this, *šiprūtum*, was different from that used for real estate and (usually) persons – see Kienast 1978, I, 74, n319.

324 For a recent survey of pledge in the Old Babylonian period, see Kienast 1978, I, 66–80, with references to earlier literature. Important additional material: Kraus 1984, 264–84.

325 The best example of the effects of a military siege comes in fact from Neo-Babylonian Nippur – see Oppenheim 1955, who also discusses the social consequences of famine more generally. For the saline fields, see the Atrahasis passage cited in Jacobsen 1982, 11–12.

326 e.g. Diakonoff 1982, 53–6, perhaps rightly attributing the growth of this phenomenon, well attested later in North Mesopotamia, to the early second millennium in Babylonia.

327 For these lists, see most recently Hawkins 1988, bringing in later parallels from Anatolia.

328 The definitive source for royal edicts of this kind is at present (and likely to remain for some time) Kraus 1984, which conveys the wealth and complexity of the evidence. For comment on later and western parallels, see Lemche 1979.

329 The problems of this passage are fully treated in Larsen 1976, 63–80. Note the Neo-Sumerian texts apparently listing metal items affected by an **amargi**, discussed in Kraus 1970, 30–1, n94.

330 References in legal documents and letters are comprehensively collected in Kraus 1984.

331 The clearest accounts of these palace:merchant transactions are given in Charpin 1982b and Stol 1982, but many details remain to be established, and I am grateful to Tina Breckwoldt for discussing these with me, and in particular for her interpretation of the system of thirds adopted here.

332 YOS 12, No. 70; see Stol 1982, 145–8.

333 See Charpin 1982b, 42ff.

334 This usage has not always been correctly understood (e.g. Stol 1982, 145; Dalley 1984, 15), and its relationship to the prices used by the merchant texts remains to be determined.

335 See note 233 above.

336 The evidence is comprehensively presented in Snell 1982. Here too some of the details of the procedures have to be worked out, such as whether the silver equivalences are fixed or fluctuating, and, if the latter, at what stage in the procedure they were estimated. Snell's discussion of the different views as to the role of silver in these texts (pp. 58–9) does not

sufficiently allow for the probability that these texts do not offer a complete picture of the merchants' activities, but only an accountant's abstraction, balancing their two types of transaction with the palace against each other, transactions which do not necessarily have any direct connection.

337 A good example is Pinches 1908, No. 38; see also Neumann 1979, 44.

338 The evidence for the activities of the **damgar** in Pre-Sargonic Lagaš has not been fully treated. See M. Lambert 1981 on Ur-emuš and the texts naming him.

339 For Polanyi's views, see Humphreys 1969; the roles are not always defined in the same way, see 'a medium of exchange', 'a unit of account' and 'a standard of value' (Hallo and Curtis 1959).

340 There are various studies of particular aspects of the use of silver (and other metals) within the economy, but no comprehensive survey. Note the comments of Diakonoff 1982, 159; Lambert 1963; Kupper 1982. Recently, see Steinkeller 1989a, 133–8 for sale prices; for payment of hired workers, see Maekawa 1988, 65ff; Waetzoldt 1987, 118–20. See now the important article of Powell 1990.

341 Powell 1978a; Michalowksi 1978; Sigrist 1979.

342 The evidence for barley's role has not been systematically assembled. A detailed discussion of its relationship to metal as currency is in Powell 1990, 107. For one instance, see Text 10:2.

343 For gold at Amarna, see Edzard 1960; Leemans 1957–71. For ingots (*šibirtum*), see Neumann 1979, 40–1, also Text 10:3. The later second-millennium 'ox-hide' ingots of the Mediterranean and Levant are not attested in our period; for 'bun ingots', see Weisgerber *et al.* 1981, 208–9.

344 For the possibility of shells acting as currency in Egypt (as in Polynesia): Renger 1984, 56, citing Altenmuller; in China: Yang 1952, 12–14 (my thanks to Michael Loewe for this reference).

345 Veenhof 1977, 116 (cf. Dalley 1984, 65–9); see also in the dictionaries under *niggallum* (sickle), *pāšum* (axe) – see Oppenheim 1948, 138–9; for Mari: Bottéro 1957, 333 §111; for a Pre-Sargonic use of inscribed(?) hoes: Steinkeller 1991, Isin text No. 4; copper axes are also used for payment in the Obelisk of Maništušu. One should perhaps mention that the Sumerian for a shekel (**gín**) is written with the sign for an axe.

11 Foreign trade

346 On the obsidian trade, see Renfrew 1977.

347 Stol 1979, 83–100.

348 Dalley 1984, 170; for a whole dossier of 'laissez passers' for boats which had paid their customs dues, addressed to a harbour-master, see Burke 1964 (Nos 58–101).

349 For Godin Tepe: Weiss and Young 1975; for Habuba Kabira: Strommenger 1980.

350 For the sealings at Jebel Aruda: van Driel 1983.

351 Numerous articles by the excavators of Shahr-i Sokhta are to be found in the periodical *East and West* for the 1970s and 1980s. Shortughai: Francfort (ed.) 1989.

352 The chlorite (earlier usually described as steatite) bowls were studied in detail by P. Kohl 1975; Mesopotamian pottery is attested in the Gulf in the Ubaid period (Oates *et al.* 1977), Jemdet Nasr (Frifelt 1975) and third millennium.

353 Biggs 1966, 175–6.

354 For the **garaš** in Ur III, see Neumann 1979; for earlier, see Waetzoldt 1984, 415–16. Scholars still appear undecided whether the word is **garaš** or **gaeš**.

355 Garelli 1963; Veenhof 1972; Larsen 1967; 1976.

356 Tin sources reported in the Taurus: Yener and Özbal 1987.

357 Assyrians at Nuzi: Larsen 1976, 49; imports of tin through Shemshara: Larsen 1976, 88; Mari evidence for a connection with Elam: Dossin 1970.

358 Walker 1980.

359 For home production of textiles at Assur: Veenhof 1977, 114–15. For the details of packaging: Veenhof 1972, 28–45.

360 For the fragmentary *kārum* regulations and the *kārum*'s role in general, see Larsen 1976, 283ff.

361 For smuggling, see Veenhof 1972, 305–42.

362 The length of time that elapsed between the destruction of Level II and the Level IB occupation has been much discussed, and is now affected by new evidence for the eponym sequence from Mari: Birot 1985 and Veenhof 1985.

363 For these possible changes, see Larsen 1976, 220ff.

364 Veenhof 1977, 110–11.

365 For a recent collection of textual and archaeological data on Tilmun/Bahrain, see D. Potts (ed.) 1983. While Bahrain was certainly called Tilmun, the term may have included adjacent parts of the mainland as well.

366 See Muhly 1980–3.

367 The detailed evidence for exchange between the two areas is presented by Ratnagar 1981, 78–156.

368 The basic work is Leemans 1960; see also Ratnagar 1981; see Crawford 1973. On the tithes (**zag-10**) and ex voto offerings by merchants, see more recently Neumann 1979, 37; van de Mieroop 1989.

369 For these vessels, see Oppenheim 1954, 8, n8.

370 Some evidence for the commercial role of the Sutu is presented in Heltzer 1981.

371 Al-Adhami 1967, 159: 'enough carnelian for a necklace for the goddess Ningal'.

372 Leemans 1960, 106: letter from 'The Sippar *kārum* which is dwelling at Mari and Mišlan' (cf. p. 108, and Kraus 1982, 32); and note that the name Mišlan means 'two halves', surely emphasizing its role as a staging-post between Mari and Terqa (for the date of the letter, see Charpin 1989). Compare the caravansarai north-west of Najaf called 'Half-way khan' (an-Nuss).

373 Leemans 1960, 89–98.

374 That the Ur III merchants were entirely in palace employ is the view of Neumann 1979. For a state official in Pre-Sargonic Girsu known both as the '(chief) merchant of the goddess Bau' and as 'chief merchant' of the queen's estate (**é.mi**), whose sealing was found at Kish, see Lambert 1981.

375 For the *wakil tamkārī*, see Leemans 1950a, and for Sippar, Harris 1975, 74; Charpin 1982b, 61–4.

376 For the Old Babylonian *kārum* in general, see Kraus 1982, and for its assumption of legal, political and administrative roles in the wider community, see especially p. 29.

12 Craft and labour

377 See Ur III references to **gur$_{10}$** in Limet 1960, 293.

378 The **(giš).al** was a traditional agricultural tool which features in myths, and is often translated 'pick-axe'. According to M. Civil, an **al** is carried over his shoulder, together with the earth-

basket, by Ur-Nammu when participating in ziggurrat construction on the stele from Ur. Even if generally replaced by copper hoes, the wooden tool remained in use for specific purposes into Ur III times – see Maekawa 1990, 142, Table 8.

379 Loftus, cited in Moorey 1971, 61–2.

380 Limet 1960, 137–8.

381 For recent summaries of the position, see Muhly 1980–3; Moorey 1985.

382 e.g. the Bassetki statue of Naram-Sin (Ayish 1976, 64–5, with analysis of metal showing it to be almost pure copper, like the renowned cast copper Akkadian head – see Moorey 1985, 29–30).

383 The Uruk period installations excavated by Nissen at Warka (and described in Nissen 1988, 82) lack proof of their function; for institutional smiths at Girsu in the Ur III period, see Neumann 1987, 97–9.

384 Özgüç 1986, 39–51.

385 Al-Gailani 1965, 37–8; Davey 1979.

386 Temple craftsmen: Sigrist 1984, 160; for a Pre-Sargonic instance, see de Genouillac, TSA 20, col. v: smiths, carpenters, leather workers, reed-mat workers, textile workers, etc. (cited Limet 1988).

387 For the importation of goldsmiths from Larsa for a temple job at Ur, see Charpin 1986a, 324, who also mentions ad hoc payments to craftsmen from outside the temple at Nippur.

388 Goetze 1948; Fish 1953.

389 PG 958 in Woolley 1934, 206–7; see also Woolley 1955, 79; note that graves at Shahr-i Sokhta of about the same date often included a craftsman's tools.

390 e.g. Kulla, the brick-god, whose name was written with the logogram for a brick.

391 For the scant evidence of inherited trades, see Kraus 1969a, 10, n49.

392 Waetzoldt 1989, after Wilcke 1987, 104–6.

393 For timber production, see Neumann 1979, 60.

394 Glass-working manual: Oppenheim 1970; horse training: Ebeling 1951.

395 Craft jargon: Neumann 1987, 25, citing Sjöberg 1975.

396 Ur III field plans – and some from other periods – are comprehensively discussed in Liverani 1990a.

397 Note the miniature bricks found in Uruk levels at Tepe Gawra (Speiser 1935, 81); note also the sophistication involved in the exact construction of the Old Babylonian temple at Tell al-Rimah (D. Oates 1967, 79ff).

398 This archive is discussed in the doctoral dissertation of Loding 1974, and again by Neumann 1987. For the provenance of the archive, see Charpin 1986a, 153.

399 Hruška 1982, 113, with references; the operation seems to have been under the overall control of the high official called a **nu-banda**.

400 See Civil 1980, 231, on TCL 5.6036.

401 Oils: Waetzoldt 1985; pottery: Waetzoldt 1971. The debt of the Ur III bureaucracy to its Akkad Dynasty forerunners is emphasized once again by the texts listing pots recently edited as Steinkeller 1991, Texts 26 and 32.

402 The most recent studies of this archive are van de Mieroop 1987 and Ferwerda 1985; for leather-working in particular, see Stol 1983.

403 See chapter 11, note 359.

404 Waetzoldt 1972; for the numbers of workers, 97ff.

405 Maekawa 1980.

406 Ellis 1983; 1986a, b; for the Larsa text, see Lackenbacher 1982 (our Text 12:6).

407 The grinding of grain in a state establishment has long been known from the archive most recently treated in Uchitel 1984; pounding those grains, such as emmer, which need it was previously hard to illustrate (cf. Postgate 1984a, 107, and 110: 'no clear textual evidence for large-scale pounding'), is now attested in the form of work contracts from the Old Babylonian palace at Warka (Sanati-Müller 1988).

408 See chapter 3, n88.

409 Some herding contracts (see note 245 above) do include working conditions for the shepherds. Otherwise I have noted 'A contract for hoeing a field' (Stol 1977–8). Marvin Powell comments that Ur III contracts for harvesting and brickmaking are known.

410 Gelb 1965; Maekawa 1980; 1989; Waetzoldt, 1987; 1988a.

411 Maekawa 1980, 87ff.

412 Maekawa 1987; 1988; and, for workers borrowing barley from their state employees, 1976, 9–16.

413 There is general agreement that the **engar** was a full-time 'farm-manager' (Waetzoldt 1987, 120) with agricultural workers beneath him – see e.g. Liverani 1990a, 157, with n23.

414 Maekawa 1988, 62–71.

415 Uchitel 1984.

416 The nature of the *muškēnum* has exercised scholars ever since the publication of the Code of Hammurapi, and there is an enormous literature on the subject. The issue is dealt with in characteristically thorough fashion by Kraus 1973, 92ff.

417 Obligations to military and civilian service still need to be studied in detail. For 'corvée labour' – **(gi.)dusu**(wr. ÍL) – see for instance Hruška 1982, 109, n73; 111, n85; 114; Neumann 1987, 63, n296 (Ur III); Charpin 1986a, 156 (Samsu-iluna). For exemption, see the statue inscription edited by Sollberger 1956, 12, col. ii.

13 War and peace

418 Fara: Martin 1988, 98–9; Zabala: Powell 1978b, 18.

419 Lambert 1961; but the difficulties of operating with this prosopographical evidence are under-lined by Maekawa 1980, 87ff.

420 Sollberger and Kupper 1971, 99; the impression of accuracy given by the number 5400 is, however, spurious, since it represents 9 x 600, and is thus a fairly 'round' number in the sexagesimal system.

421 Ungnad 1938, 141, No. 37. Note that the Sumerian verb used is **KA . . . kéš**, which could suggest a contractual basis for the enlisting of these men (see note 429).

422 For Old Babylonian *ilkum*, see Ellis 1976, 12–25; neither this study nor those in CAD and RlA s.v. deal satisfactorily with the nature of *ilkum* duties, which beyond question could involve military service (although not, obviously, for priestesses, among others!). The evidence from Dilbat is considered in Klengel 1976, 104–10.

423 Steinkeller 1987b, 30ff. It is important to bear in mind that these payments were made to the state in respect of land allocated to the soldiers, and are hence a form of rental, rather than a 'tax', which would normally imply a payment made to the state qua government authority rather than landlord.

424 For the 'fisherman', see below, p. 245.

425 Wilcke 1983, 54–6.

426 For the Ubarrum archive, see Landsberger 1955; for the hiring contract from the first year of

Samsu-iluna: Kohler and Ungnad 1909–23, No. 551.

427 These Khafajah muster lists, mentioned by Jacobsen 1932, 57, are in Greengus 1979, Nos 305ff (my thanks to R.M. Whiting for telling me where to find them).

428 Kohler and Ungnad 1909–23, No. 1398, on which see Birot 1969, pp. 108–28.

429 Landsberger 1955, 128, with addendum in JCS 10 (1956) 39; note especially TCL 7 73 'he shall perform one campaign in the royal corps'. Usage makes it clear that the status of soldiers in the royal corps continued when they were not on campaign, and that they held real estate in connection with their service (e.g. 'an orchard of a soldier in the royal corps' BIN 2 77:4). For *kiṣrum* and its Sumerian equivalent, which may point to a contractual relationship (see note 421), see also Edzard 1957, 161, n861, and Wilcke 1969c, 195–7.

430 Lutz 1929, No. 22 (the edition is seriously out-dated).

431 Groneberg 1980, 15–16 s.v. 'Amurru(m)'; Klengel 1976, 101.

432 For the *bā'irum*, see CAD, vol. B 32–3 (not to be confused with *ba'rum* (ibid. 211) pace Charpin 1986a, 239).

433 Moorey 1986 gives a recent survey of horse and chariot in their early years. For chariots (with horses) in temple contexts see CAD A/i, 267 (Assur); Kingsbury 1963 (Larsa); Weidner 1952.

434 An early ED III deposit of copper weapons at Abu Salabikh included two adze heads weighing 1,264.4 g and 1,277.4 g, and a spearhead weighing 322.5 g.

435 For Šulgi, see note 421; for spearmen in Ur III administrative texts from Lagaš, Maekawa 1976, 17–18.

436 Even these earliest depictions seem to show a composite bow; see Moorey 1986, and for the details of bow construction Miller *et al.* 1986. For early weapons, see also Eichler 1983.

437 On the development of the sword, see Maxwell-Hyslop 1946; Yadin 1963, 60–1.

438 'The year Yahdun-Lim burned the harvest of the land of Samsi-Addu' (Dossin 1950b, 52; for 'maison' read 'moisson'!).

439 See Edzard 1976–80a.

440 Crown 1974; Dossin 1938b; note also the suggestion that the lifting of a torch to inaugurate an *andurārum* edict implies the rapid conveyance of the message by beacons (Finkelstein 1965, 236; see Kraus 1984, 70).

441 At Abu Salabikh, Uruk Mound (S. Pollock, personal communication).

442 Ebla battering rams: Steinkeller 1987c. For siege engines at Mari: Sasson 1969, 33–4.

443 Martin 1988, 98.

444 For plunder, see Sasson 1969, 47–8; Malamat 1989, 75–9.

445 T. Potts 1989.

446 For the Ur laments, see Kramer in Pritchard (ed.) 1969; and most recently Michalowski 1989. The Elamites were allied to the 'SU.A' people, who have recently been identified with the land of Šimaški (Steinkeller 1988c).

447 Gelb 1973, 71–2.

448 Westenholz 1970.

449 Gelb 1973, 87; one instance of the desire not to interpret the words for 'blind' in their literal sense is Garelli *et al.* 1982. The arguments cannot be rehearsed here in detail, but undoubtedly blinded individuals could remain productive members of society; see note 288. For blinding of prisoners Jerrold Cooper refers me to the Šu-Sin inscription in R. Kutscher, *The Brockmon Tablets at the University of Haifa: Royal Inscriptions* (Haifa 1989).

450 For slave marks, see Leemans 1968, 184–5; see also note 519 below.

451 See Civil 1967a, 36; Limet 1972b, 133–4, for the deportees from Simanum, somewhere in northern Mesopotamia.

452 Edzard 1957, 160–1; Leemans 1961; and, for the date of the texts and more recent literature, Ellis 1986c.

453 Doubtless in fact carrier pigeons (Cooper 1986, 33–9). Actual treaty texts are rare before the late second millennium, but state correspondence makes it clear that they did exist; one fragmentary Old Babylonian piece is Falkenstein 1963, 54–5 (with Kraus 1965b); a tablet from Susa is apparently a treaty in Elamite language between Naram-Sin of Akkad and an Elamite king (Hinz 1972, 75–7 and Plate 21). For the diplomatic scene in general, see Munn-Rankin 1956, updated – but not significantly invalidated – by many new passages, especially from Mari.

454 Villard 1986 (see note 234).

455 Whiting 1976; note that some of the VIPs referred to in the *asīrum* texts (note 452) had their own entourage (*ahītum*; cf. CAD, vol. A/i, 191b).

14 Religion and politics

456 Hallo 1957; Edzard 1974.

457 For this frequent topos, see e.g. Charpin 1986a, 275, lines 18–20: **aga** 'crown', **gu-za** 'throne', and **u₃-luh** 'staff' (of justice); Civil 1969, 140, lines 88–9.

458 Renger 1976; one prime example is the sacrifice of fattened oxen to different gods 'on the occasion of the king's going from Nippur to Uruk, when Ibbi-Sin received the crown' (Sollberger 1953, 48).

459 'In the temple the king of Kish put a stone bowl in place', Kesh Temple Hymn, line 107 (Biggs 1971, 202; the later version significantly omits 'of Kish'!).

460 For such names, see Edzard 1974.

461 Spycket 1968, 70.

462 van Dijk 1967, 233ff; 1973.

463 Falkenstein 1959; Black 1981. For the celebration in hymns of visits to Ur by kings based at Larsa or elsewhere, though not on the occasion of their coronation, see Charpin 1986a, 274 and 301–2.

464 Though note that at times the ritual seems to have taken place at Isin: Römer 1965, 143.

465 The evidence of the Middle Assyrian coronation ritual shows that such a ritual could be renewed annually, and was not necessarily only enacted once at the accession.

466 Renger 1975, 256b, citing TLB 2.2.

467 Renger 1975, on the **nu-gig**.

468 It should be mentioned that some scholars have suggested that the Ur royal cemetery represents some form of ritual sacrifice associated with an annual fertility rite. This seems to me to be improbable, and unsupported by convincing evidence (see for a recent confrontation with the issues Moorey 1984).

469 Frankfort *et al.* 1940.

470 Of several articles on offerings to royal statues, note recently Kutscher 1974; Michalowski 1977 (Ur III) and Bauer 1969 (Early Dynastic). For sheep offerings to the 'statue of the king' in the Ekur at Nippur, e.g. Charpin 1986a, 281.

471 Wilcke 1974, 180, with n56.

472 Wilcke 1974, 180, with nn52–4.

473 Jacobsen 1957, 127, n80.

474 Sjöberg 1972.

475 von Schuler 1967.

476 Wilcke 1974, 179; Jacobsen 1978–9; Farber 1983.

477 See, for this phrase, Wilcke 1974, 180; and for the king's relations to the assembly, p. 183.

478 Cooper 1986, 56, with n20.

479 For Mari year-names, see Dossin 1950b; for examples from the Ešnunna dynasties, see Greengus 1979, 23ff, Nos 41–2, 44.

480 Michalowski 1983 takes a cautious look at some of these concepts.

481 For the Assyrian King List passage, see Grayson 1981, 103. For the ancestral traditions of the Hammurapi and Samsi-Addu dynasties, see Kraus 1965a; Finkelstein 1966b.

482 See Birot 1980; Durand 1985a, 158–9.

483 Kupper 1961; now also S.N. Kramer, in J. Klein and A. Skaist (eds), *Bar-Ilan Studies in Assyriology dedicated to Pinhas Artzi* (Jerusalem 1990).

484 Note, though, the dual claims of the towns in the treaty quoted in Text 13:11 to a 'land' (*mātum*) and a 'pasture' (*nawûm*), and that even 'sedentary' communities like the city of Sippar had a pastureland (*nawûm*).

485 See Cooper 1983b, 11; note also how the territories of the different provinces of the Ur III kingdom are described as the 'field' (**a-šà**) or 'boundary' (**ki-sur-ra**) of the appropriate city god (Kraus 1955; Text 7:9).

486 For divine standards in battle: Charpin and Durand 1985, 317; as the identifying emblem of a unit: Greengus 1979, 71–4, No. 305:4.

487 Cooper 1986, 34–7.

488 For an offering to Enlil from Lagaš in Pre-Sargonic times, see Westenholz 1977; for the Ur III **bala** system, see most recently Steinkeller 1987b. Undoubtedly the same principles lie behind the system of contributions to the Assur Temple which is well attested in the eleventh century BC (see Postgate 1980b, 68–70; Pedersén 1985, 43–53).

489 Black 1988.

490 Full edition of the 'Curse of Akkad': Cooper 1983a; for the two Ur laments, see Kramer in Pritchard 1969; and Michalowksi 1989.

491 Some thoughts on this issue in Postgate forthcoming.

492 Note that it is shortly after this time that the kings of Aleppo strengthened their position, and became the first to use the formal title 'Great King', a well-recognized category in the subsequent Amarna period. Perhaps the texts from Tell Leilan will throw more light on the details of this.

493 See notes 327 and 328.

15 Laws and the law

494 There is more need to underline the distinction between laws and the law in English than in other languages, where different words are used: *diritto, droit, Recht*, 'the law' as opposed to *legge, loi, Gesetz*, 'law(s)'. There is an unspoken tendency to assume that law could not have existed before it was written, hence that the earliest 'codes' in some way coincide with the beginning of law; but for unwritten law, see the Catalonian water courts (see Postgate 1984b, 13).

495 See chapter 4, above; Klengel 1960.

496 CH §142.

497 Schorr 1913, No. 279 (VS 7 16:17–19; Dilbat).

498 Kohler and Ungnad 1909–23, No. 724 (BE 6/i.58); see also CAD, vol. B 10b for other instances.

499 Frankena 1974, No. 142.

500 CH §5; oaths prescribed by the Assembly certainly took place in a temple, but the parties 'go' to take them, and to my knowledge there is no explicit evidence for an Assembly meeting on temple premises. City gates were also places where judicial matters were transacted.

501 For Ur III panels of judges, see Falkenstein 1956, I, 32–47.

502 See principally Edzard 1968; Falkenstein 1956; Walther 1917.

503 For the Code of Hammurapi the principal English edition is Driver and Miles 1952; more recent translation into French: Finet 1973; for the other codes, see most conveniently Finkelstein 1968–9 with Yıldız 1981 (Ur-Nammu); Steele 1948 (Lipit-Ištar); Yaron 1969 (Ešnunna). Translations are in Pritchard 1969, with a more up-to-date German version and bibliography in Borger *et al.* 1982.

504 See e.g. Walther 1917, 100; as he comments on pp. 257–9, these may not strictly be 'appeals' in modern judicial terms.

505 Harris 1961. In Hammurapi's own reign we know that they were appointed by the king himself, and were associated with different cities: Babylon, Borsippa, Sippar, Dilbat, Larsa, Ur, Kish, and even Adab all have judges, and there must have been other towns as well.

506 Thureau-Dangin 1912b (translation needs slight emendation, see CAD, vol. E 302a).

507 Diamond 1971, 300, n2.

508 For oaths in Nin-mar(ki) temple, see n247 above.

509 Harris 1967; van Lerberghe 1982; Charpin 1986a, 167–8.

510 Edzard 1968, No. 99; for the river ordeal in general, see Bottéro 1981.

511 Falkenstein 1956, I, 47–54.

512 Walther 1917, 173–7. For another instance of the *rēdûm*, in the physical possession of a house, see Charpin 1986a, 73–4.

513 *gallābum*/**šu.i**: Walther 1917, 177–8; CAD, vol. G, 14–17; at Sippar, Harris 1975, 82–4.

514 *nāgirum*/**nimgir**: CAD, vol. N/i, 115–16; Ali 1964 for loss of seal; CH §16; for officiation in early real estate transactions, see the index in Edzard 1968, 217.

515 e.g. CH §37 (purchase deed to be broken); §39 (transferring ownership to female relative in writing); §48 (deletion or rather emendation ['wetting'] of debt tablet); etc.

516 For persistence of Mesopotamian legal traditions in the Aramaic law of Achaemenid Egypt, see Muffs 1969; see also n80.

517 See also chapter 5, p. 103; especially Greengus 1969 for the unwritten nature of the contract.

518 Falkenstein 1956, I, 99.

519 David 1927; CH §192–3. Many texts have been published since David's study, see for instance Boyer 1958, No. 1 (if the adopted son says 'you are not my father, you are not my mother,' they shall shave him and sell him for silver); for adoption see now E.C. Stone and D.I. Owen, *Adoption in Old Babylonian Nippur* (Winona Lake 1991).

520 On the meal (*kirrum*), see Landsberger 1968, 82ff.

521 For this practice, see now Krecher 1980, 494–5; note that the clause turns up in early Old Babylonian real estate sales from the north of Babylonia (San Nicolò 1922), but I take this to be a later corruption of the tradition. Also Bottéro 1971, 112.

522 See note 163. For symbolic actions in general, see e.g. Limet 1981; Charpin 1982a; Postgate 1984b; and a new comprehensive study: Malul 1988.

523 Postgate 1984b, 10–11.

524 By 'otherwise acknowledged' I am referring in particular to the impression of either a finger-nail, or the hem of a garment on the tablet. See e.g. Boyer 1939 for the finger-nail; CAD, vol. S, 322–5 for the hem; Liverani 1977 on both.

525 A major edition of the early land sale documents by I.J. Gelb and P. Steinkeller is now published: Gelb *et al.* 1991.

526 Edzard 1968; Krecher 1980.

527 These documents are edited in Edzard 1968, Nos 31–4; No. 32a is re-edited in Steinkeller 1991, with additional information on the impression of peg and string visible on the inside of the clay. Steinkeller 1977, 44, suggests that the seal on these pegs is that of the seller; although this cannot be disproved, the evidence from the Akkad period makes it likelier that it was an official's seal, and we know from the text that the herald officiated.

528 On the **burgul** seals, see Renger 1977, 77; Leemans 1982, 226–8.

529 For oaths in Sumerian: Edzard 1976; for their use in court: Walther 1917, 223ff; Falkenstein 1956, I, 62ff.

530 'His head will be smeared with hot bitumen' (Hana: CAD, vol. K 180a); 'they shall cut out his tongue and cut off his hand' (Susa; Ishchali: CAD, vol. L 210–11); divine vengeance e.g. Scheil 1930, No. 131.

531 See note 503 above.

532 Falkenstein 1956, II, No. 76, 6–7; many similar statements giving the reason for a verdict can be found by using Falkenstein's index under **mu** and **mu . . . še**.

533 Petschow 1984, 192–3.

534 The principal literature on *ṣimdatum* is Landsberger 1939; Ellis 1972 (in English, but overhauled by: Kraus 1979; 1984, 8–14).

16 Order and disorder

535 Nissen 1988, 140–1.

536 This is almost universal opinion at present (e.g. Charpin 1986a, 261: 'il ne fait pas de doute que la tendance au renforcement de l'économie privée au début de l'époque paléobabylonienne, . . .'); similar uncertainties surround possible shifts in property relations in northern Babylonia in the later years, with doubts being expressed about apparent changes in the pattern of land ownership at Dilbat (Renger 1987, 56–7, on Klengel 1976).

537 See chapter 12. p. 239.

538 Surveys round Tell al-Rimah in the 1960s and in the 'North Jazirah' in the 1980s show a clear break in occupation around 1000 BC, coinciding with the intrusion of the Aramaeans into Assyrian territory (see Postgate 1974). There is a contemporary break in the 'Hamrin basin' on the middle Diyala (see e.g. Postgate 1984c, 155).

539 See Postgate 1974.

540 chapter 9, p. 180.

541 Renger 1972; see also Bottéro 1980 for a survey of the *habiru* question.

542 For another advantage of being a tenant rather than a small land-owner, see Poyck 1962, 75: 'the remarkable fact that in this area the very heavy tenancy conditions are in fact the main reason that the tenants enjoy a better standard of living than the farmowners' (since they are forced to cultivate larger areas to pay their landlords, and hence dispose of more fallow on which more livestock can be fed). For the practice of increasing the sowing rate on less fertile land, see Poyck 1962, 50.

543 See Adams 1981, 167–8 and 177–8.

544 For claims by Old Babylonian kings to have restored 'the scattered population' to a settled life, see the passages cited by Edzard 1957, 116–17 and 175–6, and comments of Falkenstein

1963, 21. Edzard also cites Neo-Babylonian passages, and the resettlement of dispersed citizens is also a standard topos of Assyrian royal inscriptions. See also n554 below.

545 e.g. Groneberg 1980, 11ff, names beginning Āl-; 52ff, names beginning Dimat-; 108, Ili-idinnam, etc.; 115, names beginning Iškun-DN ('DN founded'); 147, Kuštārātum ('Tents'); 164ff, Maškan; 204, Sin-iqišam, Sin-išmeni; 218, Šamaš-nur-matim; etc. etc. For a general survey, see Leemans 1983; and pertinent comments in Diakonoff, 1985, citing the work of Kozyreva. Apart from the ubiquitous Amorites, we know that groups of Hurrians and Kassites were present in the south in the later Old Babylonian period (Yoffee 1989, 95–100; Klengel 1982, 143–8; Charpin 1977).

546 For a tentative move in this direction, see Postgate 1986c.

547 Kilmer 1972.

548 Adams 1981, 69–70; also Nissen 1988, 67–8. However, note the pertinent scepticisms of Weiss 1977 on the difficulties of population estimation from survey data.

549 'to live according to one opinion' (ana pîm ištēn wašābum – cf. AHw 873a).

550 On the other hand, an enigma is posed by the adoption of the Old Babylonian dialect and script throughout North Mesopotamia after the Ur III period (see note 63 above): at the time it reached Mari, the city was not under the control of a regional power.

551 See Na'aman 1984 for a recent study of these statements.

552 Charpin 1986a, 343–486.

553 Charpin 1986a, 222; 1988b; George 1985–6, 18–19. For Uruk cults moving to Kish: Stone 1987, 36, n18. For the abandonment of southern cities, see Gasche 1989.

554 Examples of institutional control of marginal lands: Ur III: Ur-Nammu's reclamation of marsh (see note 292 above); Old Babylonian: Charpin 1986a, 81–83 on Ki-abrig.

555 This seems to follow from Maekawa 1986 on the 'House of Namhani' which seems to have become the 'House of the (divine) Amar-Suen'. For palace involvement in temple activities, see also Falkenstein 1963, 50, on a long and formal inventory of the Nanâ Temple at Uruk (cited Charpin 1986a, 272, in the general context of palace interference). See also Hammurapi's letter to one of his Larsa administrators: 'don't give out any of the fields of the Sin Temple' Kraus 1968, No. 129.

556 Gallery 1980; Harris 1961.

557 See especially Kraus 1982 (cf. note 376). The kārum's role is not without parallel: compare the importance of merchant families in the politics of early medieval Italy.

558 e.g. Renfrew and Cherry (eds) 1986.

559 Wilhelm 1989, 7–9 and 70–1.

Bibliography

AfO	*Archiv für Orientforschung* (Graz)
AHw	W. von Soden, *Akkadisches Handwörterbuch* (Wiesbaden)
AJA	*American Journal of Archaeology* (Baltimore)
AOF	*Altorientalische Forschungen* (E. Berlin)
AS	*Assyriological Studies* (Chicago)
ASJ	*Acta Sumerologica* (Hiroshima)
BaghMit	*Baghdader Mitteilungen* (Berlin)
BASOR	*Bulletin of the American Schools of Oriental Research* (New Haven)
BiOr	*Bibliotheca Orientalis* (Leiden)
BSA	*Bulletin on Sumerian Agriculture* (Cambridge)
CAD	*The Assyrian Dictionary* (Chicago)
HUCA	*Hebrew Union College Annual* (Cincinnati)
Iraq	*Iraq* (London)
JAOS	*Journal of the American Oriental Society* (New York)
JCS	*Journal of Cuneiform Studies* (New Haven/Philadelphia)
JESHO	*Journal of the economic and social history of the Orient* (Leiden)
JNES	*Journal of Near Eastern Studies* (Chicago)
LSS	*Leipziger Semitistische Studien* (Leipzig)
MARI	*Mari: annales de recherches interdisciplinaires* (Paris)
NABU	*Nouvelles assyriologiques brèves et utilitaires* (Paris)
OIP	*Oriental Institute Publications* (Chicago)
OLZ	*Orientalistische Literaturzeitung* (Berlin)
OrNS	*Orientalia (Nova Series)* (Rome)
RA	*Revue d'Assyriologie et d'archéologie orientale* (Paris)
RlA	*Reallexikon der Assyriologie* (Berlin/New York)
Sumer	*Sumer* (Baghdad: Directorate General of Antiquities)
WA	*World Archaeology* (London)
WdO	*Die Welt des Orients* (Stuttgart)
ZA	*Zeitschrift für Assyriologie* (Berlin/New York)

Abusch, T. (1981) 'Notes on a matching pair of texts: a shepherd's bulla and an owner's receipt' in M.A. Morrison and D.I. Owen (eds), *Studies on the Civilization and Culture of Nuzi and the Hurrians in Honor of Ernest R. Lacheman on his 75th Birthday*, (Winona Lake, Indiana), 1–9.

Adams, R. McC. (1978) 'Strategies of maximization, stability, and resilience in Mesopotamian society, settlement and agriculture', *Proceedings of the American Philosophical Society* (Philadelphia) 122 (v), 329–35.

Adams, R. McC. (1981) *Heartland of Cities* (Chicago).

——and Nissen, H.J. (1972) *The Uruk Countryside* (Chicago).

Al-Adhami, K. (1967) 'Old Babylonian letters from ed-Der', *Sumer* 23, 151–65.

Albright, W.F. (1961) 'Abram the Hebrew: a new archaeological interpretation', *BASOR* 163, 36–54.

——(1968) *Yahweh and Gods of Canaan* (London).

Al-Gailani(-Werr), L. (1965) 'Tell edh-Dhiba'i', *Sumer* 21, 33–40.

——(1983) 'Cylinder seal discoveries in the Hamrin Basin', *Ur* (London, Iraqi Cultural Centre), 1983 (1), 47–50.

Algaze, G. (1989) 'The Uruk expansion', *Current Anthropology* (Chicago), 30, 571–608.

Ali, F.A. (1964) 'Blowing the horn for official announcement', *Sumer* 20, 66–8.

Allotte de la Fuÿe, F.-M. (1912) *Documents Présargoniques* (Paris).

Alster, B. (1987) 'A note on the Uriah letter in the Sumerian Sargon Legend', *ZA* 77, 169–73.

Ayish, A.-H. (1976) 'Bassetki statue with an Old Akkadian royal inscription of Naram-Sin of Agade', *Sumer* 32, 63–76.

Baines, J. (1989). 'Communication and display: the integration of early Egyptian art and writing', *Antiquity* (Cambridge), 63, 471–82.

Barrelet, M.-Th. (1980) 'Les Pratiques funéraires de l'Iraq ancien et l'archéologie: état de la question et essai de prospective', *Akkadica* (Brussels) 16, 2–27.

——(ed.) (1980) *L'Archéologie de l'Iraq du début de l'époque néolithique à 333 avant notre ère* (Paris).

Bauer, J. (1969) 'Zum Totenkult im altsumerischen Lagasch', *Zeitschrift der Deutschen Morgenländischen Gesellschaft*, Supplement 1 (i) (Wiesbaden), 107–14.

——(1975) 'Darlehensurkunden aus Girsu', *JESHO* 18, 189–218.

Bayliss, M. (1973) 'The cult of dead kin in Assyria and Babylonia', *Iraq* 35, 115–25.

Besançon, J., Copeland, L., Hours, F., Muhesen, S., and Sanlaville, P. (1982) 'Prospective géographique et préhistorique dans le bassin d'El Kowm (Syrie)', in J. Cauvin (ed.), *Cahiers de l'Euphrate* (Paris) 3, 9–26.

Betts, A. (1989) 'The Solubba: nonpastoral nomads in Arabia', *BASOR* 274, 61–9.

Biggs, R.D. (1966) 'Le Lapis Lazuli dans les textes sumériens archaiques', *RA* 60, 175–6.

——(1967) 'Semitic names in the Fara period', *OrNS* 36, 55–66.

——(1971) 'An archaic version of the Kesh Temple Hymn from Tell Abū Ṣalābīkh', *ZA* 61, 193–207.

——(1974) *Inscriptions from Tell Abū Ṣalābīkh* (Chicago: OIP 99).

——(1975) 'An Ur III agricultural account from Nippur', *Studia Orientalia* (Helsinki) 46, 21–30.

——(1976) *Inscriptions from Al-Hiba – Lagash: The First and Second Seasons* (Malibu: Bibliotheca Mesopotamica 3).

——(1981) 'Ebla and Abu Salabikh: the linguistic and literary aspects' in L. Cagni (ed.), *La lingua di Ebla* (Naples), 121–33.

——and Postgate, J.N. (1978) 'Inscriptions from Abu Salabikh, 1975', *Iraq* 40, 101–17.

Bintliff, J. and van Zeist, W. (eds) (1982) *Palaeoclimates, Palaeoenvironments and Human Communities in the Eastern Mediterranean Region in Later Prehistory* (Oxford: British Archaeological Reports, International Series, 133).

Birot, M. (1969) *Tablettes d'époque babylonienne ancienne* (Paris).

——(1980) 'Fragment de rituel de Mari relatif au *kispum*', in B. Alster (ed.), *Death in Mesopotamia* (Copenhagen: XXVIe Rencontre assyriologique internaionale), 139–50.

——(1985) 'Les Chroniques "assyriennes" de Mari', *MARI* 4, 219–42.

Black, J.A. (1981) 'The New Year ceremonies in ancient Babylon: "Taking the hand of Bel" and a cultic picnic', *Religion* (Newcastle-upon-Tyne) 11, 39–59.

——(1988) 'The slain heroes – some monsters of ancient Mesopotamia'', *Bulletin of the Society for Mesopotamian Studies* (Toronto), 15, 19–25.

Black, J.A. and al-Rawi, F. (1983) 'The jewels of Adad', *Sumer* 39, 137–143.

Blome, F. (1934) *Die Opfermaterie in Babylonien und Israel*, Teil I. (Rome: Sacra Scriptura Antiquitatibus Orientalibus Illustrata, 4).

Boehmer, R.-M. (1974) 'Das Auftreten des Wasserbüffels in Mesopotamien . . .', *ZA* 64, 1–19.

Böhl Festschrift (1973) Beek, M. A., Kampman, A.A., Nijland C. and Ryckmans, J. (eds), *Symbolae Biblicae et Mesopotamicae Francisco Mario Theodoro de Liagre Böhl dedicatae* (Leiden).

Boltz, W.G. (1986) 'Early Chinese writing' *WA* 17, 429–36.

Borger R., Römer, W.H.Ph., Lutzmann, H., von Schuler, E. (1982) *Rechtsbücher* (Texte aus der Umwelt des Alten Testaments I (i)).

Börker-Klähn, J. (1975) 'Šulgi badet', *ZA* 64, 235–40.

Bottéro, J. (1949) 'Les Inventaires de Qatna', *RA* 43, 1–40, 137–215.

——(1957) *Textes économiques et administratifs* (Archives Royales de Mari 7).

——(1971) 'Rapports sur les conférences: antiquités assyro-babyloniennes', in *Ecole Pratique des Hautes Etudes, IVe Section, Annuaire 1970/1971*, (Paris) 87–116.

——(1980) 'Entre nomades et sedentaires: les Habiru', *Centre de recherches d'histoire ancienne*, 38 (Besançon: Dialogues d'histoire ancienne 6), 201–13.

——(1980–3) 'Küche', *RlA* 6, 277–98.

——(1981) 'L'Ordalie en Mésopotamie ancienne', *Annali della Scuola Normale Superiore di Pisa* (Pisa/Bologna), III, 9 (iv), 1005–67.

——(1982) 'De l'aide-mémoire à l'écriture' in A.-M. Christin 13–37.

Boyer, G. (1939) 'Ṣupur X kima kunukkišu', in Koschaker Festschrift, 208–18.

——(1958) *Textes juridiques* (Paris: Archives Royales de Mari 8).

——(1965) 'La Preuve dans les anciens droits du Proche-Orient', *Mélanges d'histoire du droit oriental*, (Paris), 181–200.

Brandes, M. (1979) *Siegelabrollungen aus den archaischen Bauschichten in Uruk-Warka* (Wiesbaden: Freiburger Altorientalische Studien 3).

Brentjes, B. (ed.) (1987) *Das Grundeigentum in Mesopotamien* (E. Berlin: Jahrbuch für Wirtschaftsgeschichte, Sonderband).

Brinkman, J.A. (1976–80) 'Kassiten', in *RlA* 5, 464–73.

Brookes, I.A. (1982) 'Geomorphological evidence for climatic change in Iran during the last 20,000 years', in J. Bintliff and W. van Zeist (eds), 191–228.

Buccellati, G. (1966) *The Amorites of the Ur III Period* (Naples).

Buringh, P. (1960) *Soils and Soil Conditions in Iraq* (Baghdad).

Burke, M.L. (1964) 'Lettres de Numušda-nahrari . . .', in G. Dossin *et al.* *Textes Divers* (Archives Royales de Mari 13), nos 58–101.

Burrows, E. (1935) *Archaic Texts* (London/Philadelphia: Ur Excavations Texts 2).

Butz, K. (1973–4) 'Konzentrationen wirtschaftlicher Macht im Königreich Larsa: der Nanna-Ningal-Tempelkomplex in Ur', *Wiener Zeitschrift für die Kunde des Morgenlandes* (Vienna) 65/6, 1–58.

——(1979) 'Ur in altbabylonischer Zeit als Wirtschaftsfaktor', in Lipinski (ed.), I, 235–409.

Calvot, D. (1969) 'Deux documents inédits de Ṣelluš-Dagan', *RA* 63, 101–14.

Caplice, R. (1988) *Introduction to Akkadian* (3rd, rev. edn, Rome: Studia Pohl, Series Maior 9).

Carter, E. and Stolper, M.W. (1984) *Elam: Surveys of Political History and Archaeology* (Berkeley: Near Eastern Studies 25).

Cassin, E. (1955) 'Symboles de cession immobilière dans l'ancien droit mésopotamien', *L'année sociologique, IIIe sèrie* (1952) (Paris), 107–61.

Chakravarty, H.L. (1976) *Plant Wealth of Iraq*, vol. I (Baghdad).

Charles, M.P. (1988) 'Irrigation in lowland Mesopotamia', *BSA* 4, 1–39.

——(1990) 'Traditional crop husbandry in southern Iraq, 1900–1960 AD', *BSA* 5, 47–64.

Charlier, P. (1987) 'Les Glacières à Mari', *Akkadica* (Brussels) 54, 1–10.

Charpin, D. (1977) 'L'Onomastique hurrite à Dilbat et ses implications historiques', in M.-T. Barrelet (ed.), *Problèmes concernant les Hurrites*, (Paris), 51–70.

——(1980a) *Archives familiales et propriété privée en Babylonie ancienne: Etude des documents de 'Tell Sifr'* (Geneva).

——(1980b) 'A propos du *bît asîrî* sous Rîm-Anum', *RA* 74, 75–6.

——(1982a) 'Le Geste, la parole et l'écrit dans la vie juridique en Babylonie ancienne', in Christin, 65–73.

——(1982b) 'Marchands du palais et marchands du temple . . .', *Journal Asiatique* (Paris) 270, 25–65.

——(1986a) *Le Clergé d'Ur au siècle d'Hammurabi (XIXe–XVIIIe siècles av. J.-C.)*, (Geneva).

——(1986b) 'Les Elamites à Šubat-Enlil', in L. de Meyer, H. Gasche and F. Vallat (eds), *Fragmenta Historiae Elamicae* (Paris), 129–37.

——(1988a) 'Sippar: deux villes jumelées', *RA* 82, 13–32.

——(1988b) 'Le Repli des cultes sumériens en Babylonie du Nord', *NABU* 1988/2, 22.

——(1989) *NABU* 1989/4, 76–7.

——and Durand J.-M. (1985) 'La Prise du pouvoir par Zimri-Lim', *MARI* 4, 293–343.

Christin, A.-M. (1982) *Ecritures systèmes idéographiques et pratiques expressives* (Paris: Actes du colloque international de l'Université Paris VII, 22, 23 and 24 April 1980).

Civil, M. (1962) 'Un Nouveau Synchronisme Mari – IIIe dynastie d'Ur', *RA* 56, 213.

——(1967a) 'Šu-Sin's historical inscriptions: Collection B', *JCS* 21, 24–38.

——(1967b) 'Remarks on Sumerian and bilingual texts', *JNES* 26, 200–11.

——(1969) 'The Sumerian flood story', in W.G. Lambert and A.R. Millard, *Atra-ḫasīs: the Babylonian Story of the Flood*, (Oxford), 138–45, 167–72.

——(1980) 'Les Limites de l'information textuelle', in M.-Th. Barrelet (ed.) 225–32.

——(1985) 'Sur les "livres d'écolier" à l'époque paléo-babylonienne', in *Miscellanea Babylonica: mélanges offerts à Maurice Birot*, 67–78.

——(1987) 'Ur III bureaucracy: quantitative aspects', in McG. Gibson and R.D. Biggs (eds) 1987, 43–53.

——(n.d.) *The Farmer's Instructions* (cited from edition and translation contributed to meeting of Sumerian Agriculture Group, Leiden, 1987).

——and Biggs, R.D. (1966) 'Note sur les textes sumériens archaïques', *RA* 60, 1–16.

Cocquerillat, D. (1955) 'Les Prébendes patrimoniales dans les temples à l'époque de la Ire dynastie de Babylone', *Revue Internationale des Droits de l'Antiquité* (Brussels) 2(3), 39–106.

Cohen, S. (1973) 'Enmerkar and the Lord of Aratta' (University of Pennslyvania Ph.D; Ann Arbor, University Microfilms).

Collon, D. (1987) *First Impressions: Cylinder Seals in the Ancient Near East* (London).

Cooper, J.S. (1973) 'Sumerian and Akkadian in Sumer and Akkad', *OrNS* 42, 239–46.

——(1975) 'Heilige Hochzeit, B. Archäologisch', *RlA* 4, 259–70.

——(1978) *The Return of Ninurta to Nippur* (Rome: Analecta Orientalia 52).

——(1981) 'Gilgamesh and Agga: a review article', *JCS* 33, 224–41.

——(1982) 'Enanatum's colophon', *RA* 76, 191.

——(1983a) *The Curse of Agade* (Baltimore).

——(1983b) *Reconstructing History from Ancient Inscriptions: the Lagash–Umma Border Conflict* (Malibu: Sources from the Ancient Near East 2(i)).

——(1985) 'Medium and message: inscribed clay cones and vessels from presargonic Sumer', *RA* 79, 97–114.

——(1986) *Sumerian and Akkadian Royal Inscriptions, I: Presargonic Inscriptions* (New Haven: American Oriental Society).

——and Heimpel, W. (1983) 'The Sumerian Sargon legend', *JAOS* 103, 67–82.

Crawford, H.E.W. (1973) 'Mesopotamia's invisible exports in the third millennium B.C.', *WA* 5, 232–41.

Crown, A.D. (1974) 'Tidings and instructions: how news travelled in the Ancient Near East', *JESHO* 17, 244–71.

Dalley, S.M. (1980) 'Old Babylonian dowries', *Iraq* 42, 53–74.

——(1984) *Mari and Karana. Two Old Babylonian Cities* (London).

——(1989) *Myths from Mesopotamia* (Oxford).

Damerow, P. and Englund, R.K. (1987) 'Die Zahlzeichensysteme der archaischen Texte aus Uruk', in M.W. Green and H.J. Nissen, 117–57.

——, Englund, R.K. and Nissen, H.J. (1988) 'Die Entstehung der Schrift' and 'Die ersten Zahl-darstellungen und die Entwicklung des Zahlbegriffs', *Spektrum der Wissenschaft*, February 1988, 74–85 and March 1988, 46–55.

Davey, C.J. (1979) 'Some ancient Near Eastern pot-bellows', *Levant* 11, 101–11.

David, M. (1927) *Die Adoption im altbabylonischen Recht* (Leipziger: Leipziger rechts-wissenschaftliche Studien 23).

Davies, D.H. (1957) 'Observations on land use in Iraq', *Economic Geography* (Worcester, Mass.) 33, 122–34.

Delougaz, P. (1940) *The Temple Oval at Khafajah* (Chicago: OIP 53).

——and Lloyd, S. (1942) *Presargonic Temples in the Diyala Region* (Chicago: OIP 58).

—— Hill, H.D. and Lloyd, S. (1967) *Private Houses and Graves in the Diyala Region* (Chicago: OIP 88).

de Meyer, L. (1982) 'Deux prières *ikribu* du temps d'Ammi-ṣaduqa', in Kraus Festschrift, 271–8.

de Sarzec, E. (1884–1912) *Découvertes en Chaldée* (Paris).

de Smet, W. (1990) 'Kashshû in Old-Babylonian documents', *Akkadica* (Brussels) 68, 1–19.

Desse, J. (1983) 'Les Faunes du gisement obeidien final de Tell el 'Oueili', in J.-L. Huot (ed.), *Larsa et 'Oueili – Travaux de 1978–1981* (Paris: Editions Recherches sur les Civilisations, Mémoire 26), 193–200.

——(1987) 'Analyse des ossements …', in J.-L. Huot (ed.), *Larsa et 'Oueili* (Paris: Editions Recherches sur les Civilisations, Mémoire 73), 159–60.

Diakonoff, I.M. (1965) 'Main features of the economy in the monarchies of ancient Western Asia', *Troisième Conférence Internationale d'histoire économique* (The Hague), 1–32.

——(1974) *Structure of Society and State in Early Dynastic Sumer* (Malibu: Monographs of the Ancient Near East 1(3)).

——(1982) 'The structure of Near Eastern society before the middle of the 2nd millennium BC', *Oikumene* (Budapest) 3, 7–100.

——(1985) 'Extended families in Old Babylonian Ur', *ZA* 75, 47–65.

Diamond, A.S. (1971) *Primitive Law Past and Present* (London).

Donbaz, V. and Yoffee, N. (1986) *Old Babylonian Texts from Kish Conserved in the Istanbul Archaeological Museums* (Malibu: Bibliotheca Mesopotamica 17).

Dorrell, P. (1972) 'A note on the geomorphology of the country near Umm Dabaghiyah', *Iraq* 34, 69–72.

Dossin, G. (1938a) 'Les Archives épistolaires du palais de Mari', *Syria* (Paris) 19, 105–26.

——(1938b) 'Signaux lumineux au pays de Mari', *RA* 35, 174–86.

——(1939) 'Une Mention de Hattuša dans une lettre de Mari', *Revue Hittite et Asianique* (Paris) 5, 70–6.

——(1950a) *Correspondance de Šamši-Addu* (Paris: Archives Royales de Mari 1).

——(1950b) 'Les Noms d'années et d'éponymes dans les archives de Mari', in A. Parrot (ed.), *Studia Mariana* Leiden, 51–61.

——(1952) *Correspondance de Iasmah-Addu* (Paris: Archives Royales de Mari 5).

——(1955) 'L'Inscription de fondation de Iahdun-Lim, roi de Mari', *Syria* (Paris) 32, 1–28.

——(1956) 'Une Lettre de Iarim-Lim, roi d'Alep, à Iasub-Iahad, roi de Dir', *Syria* (Paris) 33, 63–9.

——(1970) 'La Route de l'étain en Mésopotamie au temps de Zimri-Lim', *RA* 64, 97–106.

——(1972) 'Le Madarum dans les "Archives Royales de Mari"', in D.O. Edzard (ed.), 53–63.

——(1978) *Correspondance féminine* (Paris: Archives Royales de Mari 10).

Driver, G.R. and Miles, J.C. (1952) *The Babylonian Laws*, volume I (Oxford).

——(1955) *The Babylonian Laws*, volume II (Oxford).

Durand, J.-M. (1982) 'Espace et écriture en cunéiforme', in A.-M. Christin, 51–64.

——(1984) 'Trois études sur Mari', *MARI* 3, 127–80.

——(1985a) 'La Situation historique des Šakkanakku', *MARI* 4, 147–72.

——(1985b) 'Les Dames du palais de Mari à l'époque du royaume de Haute-Mésopotamie', *MARI* 4, 385–436.

——(1986) 'Fragments rejoints pour une histoire élamite' in L. de Meyer, H. Gasche and F. Vallat (eds), *Fragmenta Historiae Elamicae* (Paris), 111–128.

——(1987a) 'Documents pour l'histoire du royaume de Haute-Mésopotamie, I', *MARI* 5, 155–98.

——(1987b) 'Villes fantômes de Syrie et autres lieux', *MARI* 5, 199–234.

——(1989) *NABU*, 85–8 no. 112.

——(1991) 'Fourmis blanches et fourmis noires', *Mélanges Jean Perrot, I*, (Paris).

Durand, J.-M., and Charpin, D. (1980) 'Remarques sur l'élevage intensif dans l'Iraq ancien', in M.-Th. Barrelet (ed.), 131–56.

Dyson, R.H. (1960) 'A note on Queen Shub-ad's "onagers"', *Iraq* 22, 102–4.

Ebeling, E. (1951) *Bruchstücke einer mittelassyrischen Vorschriftensammlung für die Akklimatisierung und Trainierung von Wagenpferden* (E. Berlin).

Edmonds, C.J. (1957) *Kurds, Turks and Arabs: Politics, Travel and Research in North-eastern Iraq 1919–1925* (London).

Edzard, D.O. (1957) *Die 'Zweite Zwischenzeit' Babyloniens.* (Wiesbaden).

——(1959) 'Enmebaragesi von Kiš', *ZA* 53, 9–26.

——(1960) 'Die Beziehungen Babyloniens und Ägyptens in der mittelbabylonischen Zeit und das Gold', *JESHO* 3, 38–55.

——(1968) *Sumerische Rechtsurkunden des III. Jahrtausends aus der Zeit vor der III. Dynastie von Ur* (Munich).

——(1974) 'La Royauté dans la période présargonique', in P. Garelli (ed.), 141–9.

——(1976) 'Zum sumerischen Eid', in Jacobsen Festschrift 63–98.

——(1976–80a) 'Itinerare', *RlA* 5, 216–20.

——(1976–80b) 'Keilschrift', *RlA* 5, 544–68.

——(1981) 'Königslisten und Chroniken: A. Sumerisch', in *RlA* 6, 77–86.

——(ed.) (1972) *Gesellschaftsklassen im Alten Zweistromland und in den angrenzenden Gebieten* . . . (Munich: XVIII Rencontre Assyriologique Internationale).

Eichler, B.L. (1983) 'Of slings and shields, throw-sticks and javelins', *JAOS* 103, 95–102.

Eichmann, R. (1989) *Uruk: die Stratigraphie* (Ausgrabungen in Uruk-Warka Endberichte 3).

Ellis, M. de J. (1972) 'Simdatu in the Old Babylonian sources,' *JCS* 24, 74–82.

——(1976) *Agriculture and the State in Ancient Mesopotamia* (Philadelphia: Occasional Publications of the Babylonian Fund, 1).

——(1983) 'Correlation of archaeological and written evidence for the study of Mesopotamian institutions and chronology', *AJA* 87, 503–7.

——(1986a) 'Delivery records from the archive of the Kititum temple at Ishchali', in K.R. Veenhof (ed.), 112–20.

——(1986b) 'The archive of the Old Babylonian Kititum Temple and other texts from Ishchali', *JAOS* 106, 757–86.

——(1986c) 'The chronological placement of King Rim-Anum', *RA* 80, 65–72.

Englund, R.K., Grégoire, J.-P., and Matthews, R.J. (forthcoming) *The Proto-Cuneiform Texts from Jemdet Nasr, II* (Berlin).

Falkenstein, A. (1956) *Die Neusumerischen Gerichtsurkunden* (Munich).

——(1959) 'Akiti-Fest und Akiti-Festhaus', in *Festschrift Johannes Friedrich zum 65. Geburtstag*, 147–82.

——(1963) 'Zu den Inschriftenfunden der Grabung in Uruk-Warka 1960–1961', BaghMit 2, 1–82.

Falkenstein Festschrift (1967) *Heidelberger Studien zum Alten Orient: Adam Falkenstein zum 17. September 1966*, ed. D.O. Edzard (Heidelberg).

Farber, G. (1982) 'Rinder mit Namen', in Kraus Festschrift, 34–6.

Farber, W. (1983) 'Die Vergöttlichung Naram-Sins', *OrNS* 52, 67–72.

Faust, D.E. (1941) *Contracts from Larsa dated in the reign of Rîm-Sin* (Yale Oriental Series: Babylonian Texts, vol. VIII).

Ferrara, A.J. (1973) *Nanna-Suen's Journey to Nippur* (Rome: Studia Pohl Series Maior 2).

Ferwerda, G.Th. (1985) *A Contribution to the Early Isin Craft Archive* (Leiden: Nederlands Instituut voor het Nabije Oosten: *TLB/SLB* 5).

Figulla, H.H. (1953) 'Accounts concerning allocations of provisions . . .', *Iraq* 15, 88–122 and 171–92.

Finet, A. (1973) *Le Code de Hammurapi* (Paris).

——(1981) 'Les Dieux voyageurs en Mésopotamie', *Akkadica* (Brussels) 21, 1–13.

——(1985) 'Mari dans son contexte géographique', *MARI* 4, 41–4.

——(ed.) (1970) *Le Temple et le culte* (Ham-sur-Heure: Actes de la XVIIe Rencontre Assyriologique Internationale).

Finkbeiner, U. (ed.) (1991) *Uruk: Kampagne 35–37 (1982–1984). Die archäologische Oberflächenuntersuchung (Survey)* (Mainz: Ausgrabungen in Uruk-Warka, Endberichte 4).

Finkelstein, J.J. (1962) 'Mesopotamia', *JNES* 21, 73–92.

——(1965) 'Some new *misharum* material and its implications', in Landsberger Festschrift, 233–46.

——(1966a) 'Sex offenses in Sumerian laws', *JAOS* 86, 355–72.

——(1966b) 'The genealogy of the Hammurapi Dynasty', *JCS* 20, 95–118.

——(1968a) *Old Babylonian Legal Documents* (London: Cuneiform texts from Babylonian tablets in the British Museum 48).

Finkelstein, J.J. (1968b) 'An Old Babylonian herding contract and Genesis 31:38f.', *JAOS* 88, 30–6.

——(1968–9) 'The laws of Ur-Nammu', *JCS* 22, 66–82.

——(1976) 'Cutting the *sissiktu* in divorce proceedings', *WdO* 8, 236ff.

Fish, T. (1953) 'Texts from Umma about reeds', *Manchester Cuneiform Studies* (Manchester) 3, 42–5.

Foster, B.R. (1982) *Administration and Use of Institutional Land in Sargonic Sumer* (Copenhagen: Mesopotamia 9).

——(1985) 'The Sargonic victory stele from Telloh', *Iraq* 47, 15–30.

Francfort, H.-P. (1989) *Fouilles de Shortughai: Recherches sur l'Asie Centrale protohistorique* (Paris).

Frankena, R. (1966) *Briefe aus dem British Museum* (Leiden: Altbabylonische Briefe 2).

——(1968) *Briefe aus der Leidener Sammlung (TLB IV)* (Leiden: Altbabylonische Briefe 3).

——(1974) *Briefe aus dem Berliner Museum* (Leiden: Altbabylonische Briefe 6).

Frankfort, H.A. (1939) *Sculptures of the Third Millennium B.C. from Tell Asmar and Khafajah* (Chicago: OIP 44).

——(1948) *Kingship and the Gods. A Study of Ancient Near Eastern Religion as the Integration of Society and Nature* (Chicago).

——(1954) *The Art and Architecture of the Ancient Orient* (Harmondsworth).

Frankfort H.A., Jacobsen, T., *et al.* (1940) *The Gimil-Sin Temple and the Palace of the Rulers at Tell Asmar* (Chicago: OIP 43).

Frifelt, K. (1975) 'A possible link between the Jemdet Nasr and the Umm an-Nar graves of Oman', *Journal of Oman Studies* (Muscat) 1, 57–80.

Gadd, C.J. (1948) *Ideas of Divine Rule in the Ancient East*.

Gallery, M. (1980) 'The office of the *šatammu* in the Old Babylonian period', *AfO* 27, 1–36.

Gallery Kovacs, M. (1989) *The Epic of Gilgamesh* (Stanford).

Garelli, P. (1963) *Les Assyriens en Cappadoce* (Paris).

——(1966) 'Tablettes cappadociennes de collections diverses', *RA* 60, 93–152.

——(ed.) (1974) *Le Palais et la royauté* (Paris: Compte Rendu, XIXe Rencontre Assyriologique Internationale).

——, Charpin, D., and Durand, J.-M. (1982) 'Role des prisonniers et des déportés à l'époque médio-assyrienne', in H. Klengel (ed.), *Gesellschaft und Kultur im alten Vorderasien* (E. Berlin: Schriften zur Geschichte und Kultur des alten Orients 15), 69–75.

Gasche, H. (1988) 'Le Système fluviatile au sud-ouest de Baghdad', *BSA* 4, 41–8.

——(1989) *La Babylonie au 17e siècle avant notre ère* (Ghent: Mesopotamian History and Environment, Series II. Memoirs, I).

Gelb, I.J. (1965) 'The ancient Mesopotamian ration system', *JNES* 24, 230–43.

——(1968) 'An Old Babylonian list of Amorites', *JAOS* 88, 39–46.

——(1969) 'Growth of a herd of cattle in ten years', *JCS* 21, 64–9.

——(1972) 'The Arua institution', *RA* 66, 1–32.

——(1973) 'Prisoners of war in early Mesopotamia', *JNES* 32, 70–98.

——(1976a) 'Homo ludens in early Mesopotamia', *Studia Orientalia* (Helsinki) 46, 43–76.

——(1976b) 'Quantitative evaluation of slavery and serfdom', in B.L. Eichler *et al.* (eds), *Kramer Anniversary Volume* (Neukirchen-Vluyn: Alter Orient und Altes Testament 25), 195–207.

——(1977) 'Thoughts about Ibla: a preliminary evaluation, March 1977', *Syro-Mesopotamian Studies* (Malibu) 1, 3–30.

——(1979) 'Household and family in early Mesopotamia', in E. Lipinski (ed.), I, 1–97.

——(1981) 'Ebla and the Kish civilization', in L. Cagni (ed.), *La lingua di Ebla* (Naples), 9–73.

——, Steinkeller, P., and Whiting, R.M. (1991) *Earliest Land Tenure Systems in the Near East* (Chicago: OIP 104).

George, A.R. (1985–6) 'The topography of Babylon reconsidered', *Sumer* 44, 7–24.

Gibson, McG. (1973) 'Population shift and the rise of Mesopotamian civilisation', in A.C. Renfrew (ed.), *The Explanation of Culture Change: Models in Prehistory* (London), 445–63.

——(1974) 'Violation of fallow and engineered disaster in Mesopotamian civilization', in T.E. Downing and McG. Gibson (eds), *Irrigation's Impact on Society* (Tucson), 7–20.

—— and Biggs, R.D. (eds) (1977) *Seals and Sealing in the Ancient Near East* (Malibu: Bibliotheca Mesopotamica 6).

——(1987) *The Organization of Power: Aspects of Bureaucracy in the Ancient Near East* (Chicago: Studies in Ancient Oriental Civilization no. 46).

Goetze, A. (1948) 'Umma texts concerning reed mats', *JCS* 2, 165–202.

——(1950) 'Sin-iddinam of Larsa. New tablets from his reign', *JCS* 4, 83–118.

Gomi, T. (1976) 'Shulgi-Simti and her libation place', *Orient* (Hamburg) 12, 1–14.

——(1980) 'On dairy productivity at Ur . . .', *JESHO* 23, 1–42.

——(1984) 'On the critical economic situation at Ur early in the reign of Ibbi-Sin', *JCS* 36, 211–42.

Grayson, A.K. (1981) 'Königslisten und Chroniken', *RlA* 6, 77–135.

Green, M.W. and Nissen, H.J. (1987) *Zeichenliste der archaischen Texte aus Uruk* (Berlin: Ausgrabungen der Deutschen Forschungsgemeinschaft in Uruk-Warka, 11: Archaische Texte aus Uruk, Band 2).

Greengus, S. (1966) 'Old Babylonian marriage ceremonies and rites', *JCS* 20, 55–72.

——(1969) 'The Old Babylonian marriage contract', *JAOS* 89, 505–32.

——(1979) *Old Babylonian Tablets from Ishchali and Vicinity* (Nederlands Instituut voor het Nabije Oosten).

Groneberg, B. (1980) *Die Orts- und Gewässernamen der altbabylonischen Zeit* (Wiesbaden: Répertoire Géographique des Textes Cunéiformes 3).

Guest, E. (1966) *Flora of Iraq, I: Introduction* (Baghdad).

Gurney, O.R. (1956) 'The tale of the Poor Man of Nippur', *Anatolian Studies* 6, 145ff.

Hallo, W.W. (1956) 'Zariqum', *JNES* 15, 220–5.

——(1957) *Early Mesopotamian Royal Titles: A Philologic and Historical Analysis* (New Haven: American Oriental Series 43).

——(1964a) 'The road to Emar', *JCS* 18, 57–88.

——(1964b) 'The slandered bride', in *Studies presented to A. Leo Oppenheim, June 7, 1964*, 95–105.

——(1977) 'Seals lost and found', in McG. Gibson and R.D. Biggs (eds), 55–60.

——and Curtis, J.B. (1959) 'Money and merchants in Ur III', *HUCA* 30, 103–39.

——and van Dijk, J.J.A. (1968) *The Exaltation of Inanna* (New Haven).

Halstead, P. (1990) 'Quantifying Sumerian agriculture – some seeds of doubt and hope', *BSA* 5, 187–95.

Harris, R. (1955) 'The archive of the Sin Temple in Khafajah', *JCS* 9, 31–120.

——(1961) 'On the process of secularization under Hammurapi' *JCS* 15, 117–24.

——(1963) 'The organization and administration of the cloister in ancient Babylonia', *JESHO* 6, 121–57.

——(1964) 'The nadītu woman', in *Studies Presented to A. Leo Oppenheim, June 7, 1964* (Chicago), 106–35.

Harris, R. (1967) 'The journey of the divine weapon', in Landsberger Festschrift, 217–24.

——(1969) 'Notes on the Babylonian cloister and hearth', OrNS 38, 133–45.

——(1974) 'The case of three Old Babylonian marriage contracts', JNES 33, 363–9.

——(1975) Ancient Sippar (Istanbul/Leiden).

Hawkins, J.D. (1988) 'Royal statements of ideal prices: Assyrian, Babylonian, and Hittite', in J.V. Canby et al. (eds), Ancient Anatolia: Aspects of Change and Cultural Development (Essays in honor of Machteld J. Mellink) (Madison), 93–102.

Heimpel, W. (1987) 'Libation', RlA 7, 1–5.

Heinrich, E. and Seidl, U. (1967) 'Grundrisszeichnungen aus dem alten Orient', Mitteilungen der Deutschen Orient-Gesellschaft (Berlin) 98, 24–45.

——(1982) Die Tempel und Heiligtümer im alten Mesopotamien (Berlin).

Heltzer, M. (1981) The Suteans (Naples: Istituto Universitario Orientale).

Henrickson, E. (1981) 'Non-religious residential settlement patterning in the late Early Dynastic of the Diyala region', Mesopotamia (Turin), 16, 43–133.

Hinz, W. (1972) The Lost World of Elam: Recreation of a Vanished Civilization (London).

Hirsch, H. (1961) Untersuchungen zur altassyrischen Religion (AfO Beiheft 13/14).

Hole, F., Flannery, K.V. and Neely, J.A. (1969) Prehistory and Human Ecology of the Deh Luran Plain (Ann Arbor).

Hruška, B. (1982) 'Zur Verwaltung der Handwerker in der frühdynastischen Zeit', in H. Klengel (ed.), Gesellschaft und Kultur im alten Vorderasien (E. Berlin: Schriften zur Geschichte und Kultur des alten Orients, 15), 99–115.

——(1988a) 'Die Bewässerungsanlagen in den altsumerischen Königsinschriften von Lagaš', BSA 4, 61–72.

——(1988b) 'Überlegungen zum Pflug und Ackerbau in der altsumerischen Zeit', Archiv Orientalni (Prague) 56, 137–58.

——(1990) 'Das landwirtschaftliche Jahr im alten Sumer', BSA 5, 105–14.

Humphreys, S. (1969) 'History, economics and anthropology', History and Theory (Gravenhage) 8, 165–212.

Huot, J.-L. (ed.) (1987) La Préhistoire de la Mésopotamie (Paris).

Jacobsen, Th. (1932) in H. Frankfort, Th. Jacobsen and C. Preusser, Tell Asmar and Khafaje: The First Season's Work in Eshunna 1930/31 (Chicago: Oriental Institute Communication 13).

——(1939) The Sumerian Kinglist (Chicago: AS 11).

——(1943) 'Primitive democracy in ancient Mesopotamia', JNES 2, 159–72.

——(1946) 'Mesopotamia', in H. Frankfort et al., The Intellectual Adventure of Ancient Man (Chicago: also published as Before Philosophy, Harmondsworth, 1949).

——(1953) 'The reign of Ibbi-Suen', JCS 7, 36–47.

——(1957) 'Early political development in Mesopotamia', ZA 52, 91–140.

——(1959) 'An ancient Mesopotamian trial for homicide', Studia Biblica et Orientalia III: Oriens Antiquus (Rome: Analecta Biblica 12), 130–50.

——(1970) Toward the Image of Tammuz (Cambridge, Mass.).

——(1976) The Treasures of Darkness (New Haven/London).

——(1978–9) 'Iphur-Kishi and his times', AfO 26, 1–14.

——(1982) Salinity and Irrigation Agriculture in Antiquity (Malibu: Bibliotheca Mesopotamica 14).

——(1987) The Harps That Once . . .: Sumerian Poetry in Translation (New Haven/London).

Jacobsen Festschrift (1975) Sumerological Studies in Honor of Thorkild Jacobsen, ed. S.J. Lieberman (Chicago: AS 20).

Jean, C.-F. (1931) *Larsa d'après les textes cunéiformes . . .* (Paris).

Jeyes, U. (1983) 'The nadītu women of Sippar', in A. Cameron and A. Kuhrt (eds), *Images of Women in Antiquity* (London/Canberra), 260–72.

——(1989) *Old Babylonian Extispicy: Omen Texts in the British Museum* (Istanbul/Leiden).

Jones, T.B. (1969) *The Sumerian Problem* (New York).

—— and J.W. Snyder (1961) *Sumerian Economic Texts from the Third Ur Dynasty* (Minneapolis).

Justeson, J.S. (1986) 'The origin of writing systems: Preclassic Mesoamerica', *WA* 17, 437–58.

Kamp, K.A. and Yoffee, N. (1980) 'Ethnicity in ancient Western Asia during the early second millennium B.C.; archaeological assessments and ethnoarchaeological prospectives', *BASOR* 237, 85–104.

Kepinski, C. and Lecomte, O. (1985) 'Mari et Haradum', *MARI* 4, 615–21.

Khazanov, A.M. (1984) *Nomads and the Outside World* (Cambridge: Cambridge University Press).

Kienast, B. (1960) *Die altassyrischen Texte des Orientalischen Seminars der Universität Heidelberg und der Sammlung Erlenmeyer-Basel* (Berlin).

——(1978) *Die altbabylonischen Briefe und Urkunden aus Kisurra* (Wiesbaden: Freiburger Altorientalische Studien 2).

Kilmer, A.D. (1972) 'The Mesopotamian concept of overpopulation and its solution as reflected in the mythology', *OrNS* 41, 160–77.

King, L.W. (1900) *The Letters and Inscriptions of Hammurabi* (London).

Kingsbury, E.C. (1963) 'A seven day ritual in the Old Babylonian cult at Larsa', *HUCA* 34, 1–34.

Klengel, H. (1960) 'Zu den šibūtum in altbabylonischer Zeit', *OrNS* 29, 357–75.

——(1976) 'Untersuchungen zu den sozialen Verhältnissen im altbabylonischen Dilbat', *AOF* 4, 63–110.

——(1982) ' "Fremde" im Herrschaftsbereich des Samsuditana von Babylon', *Gesellschaft und Kultur im alten Vorderasien* (Berlin), 143–8.

——(1987) 'Non-slave labour in the Old Babylonian period: the basic outlines', in M.A. Powell (ed.), 159–66.

Klíma, J. (1940) *Untersuchungen zum altbabylonischen Erbrecht* (Prague).

Kohl, P. (1975) 'Carved chlorite vessels: a trade in finished commodities in the mid-third millennium B.C.' *Expedition* 18 (i), 18–31.

——(1978) 'The balance of trade in Southwestern Asia in the mid-third millennium B.C.', *Current Anthropology* (Chicago) 19, 463–92.

Kohler, J. and Ungnad, A. (1909–23) *Hammurabi's Gesetz* (Leipzig) III–VI (vol. VI is by Koschaker and Ungnad).

Komoróczy, G. (1975) 'Zur Aetiologie der Schrifterfindung im Enmerkar-Epos', *AOF* 3, 19–24.

Koschaker Festschrift (1939), Friedrich, J., Lautner, J.G., and Miles, J.C. (eds) *Symbolae ad iura orientis antiqui pertinentes Paulo Koschaker dedicatae* (Leiden: Studia et Documenta ad iura orientis antiqui pertinentia 2).

Koschaker, P. (1940) 'Kleidersymbolik in Keilschrifttexten', *Actes du 20e Congrès International des Orientalistes, Bruxelles 1938*, 117–19.

——(1951) 'Zur Interpretation des Art. 59 des Codex Bilalama', *JCS* 5, 104–22.

Kramer, C. (1979) 'An archaeologist's view of a contemporary Kurdish village: domestic architecture, household size, and wealth', in C. Kramer (ed.), *Ethnoarchaeology: Implications of Ethnography for Archaeology* (New York), 139–63.

Kramer, S.N. and Bernhardt, I. (1975) 'Die Tempel und Götterschreine von Nippur', *OrNS* 44, 96–102.

Kraus, F.R. (1951) 'Nippur und Isin nach altbabylonischen Rechtsurkunden', *JCS* 3.

——(1955) 'Provinzen des neusumerischen Reiches von Ur', *ZA* 51, 45–75.

——(1958) *Ein Edikt des Königs Ammi-ṣaduqa von Babylon* (Leiden).

——(1964) *Briefe aus dem British Museum* (CT 43 and 44) (Leiden: Altbabylonische Briefe 1).

——(1965a) *Könige, die in Zelten wohnten* (Amsterdam).

——(1965b) Review of BaghMit 2, *BiOr* 22, 289–90.

——(1966) *Staatliche Viehhaltung im altbabylonischen Lande Larsa* (Amsterdam).

——(1968) *Briefe aus dem Archive des Šamaš-ḫazir* ... (Leiden: Altbabylonische Briefe 4).

——(1969a) 'Von altmesopotamischen Erbrecht', in J. Brugman *et al.*, *Essays on Oriental Laws of Succession* (Leiden), 1–17.

——(1969b) 'Erbrechtliche Terminologie im Alten Mesopotamien', in J. Brugman *et al.* (eds), *Essays on Oriental Laws of Succession* (Leiden), 18–57.

——(1970) *Sumerer und Akkader, ein Problem der altmesopotamischen Geschichte* (Amsterdam).

——(1973) *Vom mesopotamischen Menschen der altbabylonischen Zeit und seiner Welt* (Amsterdam).

——(1976a) 'Feldpachtverträge aus der Zeit der III. Dynastie von Ur', *WdO* 8, 185–205.

——(1976b) 'Akkadische Wörter und Ausdrücke: nawûm', *RA* 70, 172–9.

——(1979) 'ṣimdatum/ṣimdat šarrim', *RA* 73, 51–62.

——(1982) '"Karum", ein Organ staedtischer Selbstverwaltung der altbabylonischen Zeit', in A. Finet (ed.), *Les Pouvoirs locaux en Mésopotamie et dans les régions adjacentes* (Brussels), 29–42.

——(1984) *Königliche Verfügungen in altbabylonischer Zeit* (Leiden).

——(1985) 'Altbabylonische Briefe mit Siegelabrollungen', in *Miscellanea Babyloniaca* (Birot Festschrift), 137–45.

Kraus Festschrift (1982) G. van Driel, Th.J.H. Krispijn, M. Stol and K.R. Veenhof (eds), *Zikir šumim: Assyriological Studies Presented to F.R. Kraus on the Occasion of his Seventieth Birthday* (Leiden).

Krebernik, M. (1984) *Die Beschwörungen aus Fara und Ebla* (Hildesheim/Zurich/New York).

Krecher, J. (1966) *Sumerische Kultlyrik* (Wiesbaden).

——(1980) 'Kauf. A.1', *RlA* 5, 490–8.

Kühne, H. (1983) 'Tall Malḥat eḏ-Ḏerū. Eine Station auf dem Wege nach Kappadokien?', in R.M. Boehmer and H. Hauptmann (eds), *Beiträge zur Altertumskunde Kleinasiens, Festschrift für Kurt Bittel* (Mainz), 299–308.

Kupper, J.-R. (1954) *Correspondance de Bahdi-Lim* (Paris: Archives Royales de Mari 6).

——(1957) *Les Nomades en Mésopotamie au temps des rois de Mari* (Paris).

——(1961) *L'Iconographie du dieu Amurru* (Brussels).

——(1982) 'L'Usage de l'argent à Mari', in Kraus Festschrift, 163–72.

Kutscher, R. (1974) 'An offering to the statue of Šulgi', *Tel-Aviv* (Tel Aviv) 1, 55–9.

——(1979) 'A note on the early careers of Zariqum and Šamši-illat', *RA* 73, 81–2.

——(1983) 'A torchlight festival in Lagaš', *ASJ* 5, 59–66.

Lackenbacher, S. (1982) 'Un Texte vieux-babylonien sur la finition des textiles', *Syria* (Paris) 59, 129–49.

Laessøe, J. (1953) 'Reflexions on modern and ancient Oriental water works', *JCS* 7, 5–26.

——(1963) *People of ancient Assyria: their inscriptions and correspondence* (London).

Lafont, B. (1990) *NABU*, 13, no. 17.

Lambert, M. (1953) 'Textes commerciaux de Lagash', *RA* 47, 57–69 and 105–20.

——(1954) 'La Période présargonique: la vie économique à Shuruppak (II)', *Sumer* 10, 150–90.

——(1961) 'Recherches sur la vie ouvrière: les ateliers de tissage de Lagash au temps de Lugalanda et d'Urukagina', *Archiv Orientalni* (Prague) 29, 422–43.

——(1963) 'L'Usage de l'argent-métal à Lagash au temps de la IIIe Dynastie d'Ur', *RA* 57, 79–92 and 193–200.

——(1968) (C. Virolleaud), *Tablettes économiques de Lagash (Epoque de la IIIe Dynastie d'Ur)* (Paris: Cahiers de la Société Asiatique 19).

——(1969) 'Deux étiquettes de panier', *RA* 63, 97–100.

——(1981) 'Ur-Emush "Grand-marchand" de Lagash', *Oriens Antiquus* (Rome) 20, 175–85.

Lambert, W.G. (1968–9) 'A new source for the reign of Nabonidus', *AfO* 22, 1–8.

——(1990) 'Notes on a work of the most ancient Semitic literature', *JCS* 41, 1–33.

Landsberger, B. (1915) *Der kultische Kalender der Babylonier und Assyrer* (LSS 6 (i–ii)).

——(1939) 'Die babylonischen Termini für Gesetz und Recht', in Koschaker Festschrift, 219–34.

——(1954) 'Assyrische Königsliste und "Dunkles Zeitalter"', *JCS* 8, 31–45, 47–73 and 106–33.

——(1955) 'Remarks on the archive of the soldier Ubarum', *JCS* 9, 121–31, with addenda in *JCS* 10 (1956), 39.

——(1967a) 'Akkadisch-hebräische Wortgleichungen', in *Hebraische Wortforschung* (Leiden: Supplement to Vetus Testamentum 16), 176–204.

——(1967b) *The Date Palm and its By-products According to the Cuneiform Sources* (AfO Beiheft 17).

——(1968) 'Jungfräulichkeit: ein Beitrag zum Thema "Beilager und Eheschliessung"', in J.A. Ankum, R. Feenstra and W.F. Leemans (eds), *Symbolae iuridicae et historicae Martino David dedicatae, II, Iura orientis antiqui* (Leiden), 41–105.

Landsberger Festschrift (1965) *Studies in Honor of Benno Landsberger* (Chicago: AS 16).

LaPlaca, P.J. and Powell, M.A. (1990) 'The agricultural cycle and the calendar at pre-Sargonic Girsu', *BSA* 5, 75–104.

Larsen, M.T. (1967) *Old Assyrian Caravan Procedures* (Istanbul/Leiden).

——(1976) *The Old Assyrian City-state and its Colonies* (Copenhagen: Mesopotamia 4).

——(1977) 'Partnerships in the Old Assyrian trade', *Iraq* 39, 119–45.

——(1982) 'Your money or your life! A portrait of an Assyrian businessman', in M. Dandamayev et al. (eds), *Societies and Languages of the Ancient Near East: Studies in Honour of I.M. Diakonoff*, 214–45.

——(1987) 'Commercial networks in the ancient Near East', in M. Rowlands, M. Larsen and K. Kristiansen (eds), *Centre and Periphery in the Ancient World* (Cambridge), 47–56.

——(1989) 'What they wrote on clay', in K. Schousboe and M. T. Larsen (eds), *Literacy and Society* (Copenhagen), 121–48.

Laslett, P. (1972) 'Introduction' in P. Laslett and R. Wall (eds), *Household and Family in Past Time* (Cambridge), 1–89.

Lautner, J.G. (1936) *Altbabylonische Personenmiete und Erntearbeiterverträge* (Leiden).

Layard, A.H. (1853) *Discoveries in the Ruins of Nineveh and Babylon* (London).

——(1854) *Nineveh and its Remains* (London 6th edn).

Leemans, W.F. (1950a) *The Old Babylonian Merchant, his Business and his Social Position* (Leiden: Studia et documenta ad iura Orientis Antiqui pertinentia III).

——(1950b) 'The rate of interest in Old Babylonian times', *Revue internationale des droits de l'antiquité* (Brussels) 5, 7–34.

——(1952) *Ishtar of Lagaba and her Dress* (Leiden).

——(1957–71) 'Gold', *RlA* 3, 505–15.

Leemans, W.F. (1960) *Foreign Trade in the Old Babylonian Period as Revealed by Texts from Southern Mesopotamia* (Leiden: Studia et documenta ad iura orientis antiqui pertinentia VI).

——(1961) 'The asīru', *RA* 55, 57–76.

——(1968) 'Old Babylonian letters and economic history . . .', *JESHO* 11, 171–226.

——(1975) 'The role of landlease in Mesopotamia in the early second millennium BC', *JESHO* 18, 134–45.

——(1976) 'Die Arten der Zuverfügungstellung von Boden für Landwirtschaftliche Zwecke in der altbabylonischen Zeit', *WdO* 8, 241–53.

——(1982) 'La Fonction des sceaux, apposés à des contrats vieux-babyloniens', in Kraus Festschrift, 219–44.

——(1983) 'Trouve-t-on des "communautés rurales" dans l'ancienne Mésopotamie?', in *Les communautés rurales, II: Antiquité* (Brussels: Recueils de la Société Jean Bodin, XLI), 43–106 (written 1976).

——(1986) 'The family in the economic life of the Old Babylonian period', *Oikumene* (Budapest) 5, 15–22.

Lees, G.M. and Falcon, N.L. (1952) 'The geographical history of the Mesopotamian plains', *Geographical Journal* (London) 118, 24–39.

Legrain, L. (1936) *Archaic Seal-Impressions* (London/Philadelphia: Ur Excavations 3).

——(1937) *Business Documents of the Third Dynasty of Ur* (London/Philadelphia: Ur Excavations Texts 3).

Leichty, E. (1989) 'Feet of clay', in Sjöberg Festschrift, 349–56.

Lemche, N. (1979) 'Andurārum and Mīšarum: comments on the problem of social edicts and their application in the ancient Near East', *JNES* 38, 11–22.

Lenzen, H. (1966) *22. Vorläufiger Bericht über die . . . in Uruk-Warka unternommenen Ausgrabungen* (Berlin).

Levine, B.A. and Hallo, W.W. (1967) 'Offerings to the temple gates at Ur', *HUCA* 38, 17–58.

Levine L.D. and Young, T.C. (eds) (1977) *Mountains and Lowlands: Essays in the Archaeology of Greater Mesopotamia* (Malibu: Bibliotheca Mesopotamica 7).

Lieberman, S.J. (1968–9) 'An Ur III text from Drehem recording "Booty from the land of Mardu"', *JCS* 22, 53–62.

——(1980) 'Of clay pebbles, hollow clay balls, and writing: A Sumerian view', *AJA* 84, 340–58.

Limet, H. (1960) *Le Travail du métal au pays de Sumer au temps de la IIIe Dynastie d'Ur* (Paris).

——(1970) 'L'Organisation de quelques fêtes mensuelles à l'époque néo-sumérienne', in A. Finet (ed.), 59–74.

——(1972a) 'Les Métaux à l'époque d'Agadé', *JESHO* 15, 3–34.

——(1972b) 'L'Etranger dans la société sumérienne', in D.O. Edzard (ed.), 123–38.

——(1978) 'Etude sémantique de ma-da, kur, kalam', *RA* 72, 1–12.

——(1979) 'Le Rôle du palais dans l'économie néo-sumérienne', in E. Lipinski (ed.), I, 235–48.

——(1981) 'Rationalité et religion dans le droit sumérien', *Akkadica* (Brussels) 22, 15–32.

——(1988) Review of Neumann 1987, *OLZ* 83, 667–9.

Lipinski, E. (ed.) (1979) *State and Temple Economy in the Ancient Near East* I–II (Louvain: Orientalia Lovaniensia Analecta 5–6).

Liverani, M. (1977) 'Segni arcaici di individuazione personale', *Rivista di filologia e di istruzione classica* (Turin) 105, 106–18.

——(1990a) 'The shape of Neo-Sumerian fields', *BSA* 5, 147–86.

——(1990b) *Prestige and Interest: International Relations in the Near East ca. 1600–1100 B.C.* (Padua).

Lloyd, S. and Safar, F. (1943) 'Tell Uqair: excavations by the Iraq Government Directorate of Antiquities in 1940 and 1941', *JNES* 2, 131–58.

Loding, D. (1974) 'A craft archive from Ur' (Ph.D. Dissertation, University of Pennsylvania: Ann Arbor, University Microfilms).

——(1981) 'Lapidaries in the Ur III period. Written sources concerning stoneworkers (ca. 2000 BC)', *Expedition* (Philadelphia) 23 (iv), 6–14.

Luke, J.T. (1965) 'Pastoralism and politics in the Mari period' (Ph.D. Dissertation University of Michigan: Ann Arbor).

Lutz, H.F. (1929) 'Old Babylonian letters', *University of California Publications in Semitic Philology* (Berkeley) 9, 279–365.

McCown, D.E. and Haines, R.C. (1967) *Nippur I: Temple of Enlil, Scribal Quarter, and Soundings* (Chicago: OIP 78).

McFadyen, W.A. and Vita Finzi, C. (1978) 'Mesopotamia: The Tigris–Euphrates delta and its Holocene Hammar fauna', *Geological Magazine* (London) 115, 287–300.

Maeda, T. (1979) 'On the agricultural festivals in Sumer', *ASJ* 1, 19–33.

Maekawa, K. (1976) 'The erín-people in Lagash of Ur III times', *RA* 70, 9–44.

——(1980) 'Female weavers and their children in Lagash', *ASJ* 2, 81–125.

——(1983) 'The management of fatted sheep ... in Ur III Girsu/Lagash', *ASJ* 5, 81–111.

——(1986) 'The agricultural texts of Ur III Lagash of the British Museum (IV)', *Zinbun: Memoirs of the Research Institute for Humanistic Studies, Kyoto University* (Kyoto) 21, 91–157.

——(1987) 'Collective labor service in Girsu-Lagash: The pre-Sargonic and Ur III periods', in M.A. Powell 1987, 49–71.

——(1988) 'New texts on the collective labor service of the erin-people of Ur III Girsu', *ASJ* 10, 37–94.

——(1989) 'Rations, wages and economic trends in the Ur III period', *AOF* 16, 42–50.

——(1990) 'Cultivation methods in the Ur III period', *BSA* 5, 115–45.

Malamat, A. (1989) *Mari and the Early Israelite Experience* (Oxford).

Malul, M. (1988) *Studies in Mesopotamian Legal Symbolism* (Neukirchen-Vluyn: Alter Orient und Altes Testament 221).

Mann, M. (1986) *The Sources of Social Power, I: A History of Power from the Beginning to AD 1760* (Cambridge).

Martin, H.P. (1988) *Fara: A Reconstruction of the Ancient Mesopotamian City of Shuruppak* (Birmingham).

——, Moon, J., and Postgate, J.N. (1985) *Graves 1–99* (London: Abu Salabikh Excavations, 2).

Mason, K. (ed.) (1944) *Iraq and the Persian Gulf* (British Admiralty, Naval Intelligence Division, Geographical Handbook Series).

Matouš, L. (1949) 'Les Contrats de partage à Larsa', *Archiv Orientalni* (Prague) 17 (ii), 142–73.

Matthews, R.J. and Postgate, J.N. (1987) 'Excavations at Abu Salabikh, 1985–86', *Iraq* 49, 91–119.

Maxwell-Hyslop, R. (1946) 'Daggers and swords in Western Asia', *Iraq* 8, 1–65.

Messerschmidt, L. (1906) 'Zur Technik des Tontafel-Schreibens', *OLZ* 9, 185–96, 304–12, 372–80.

Michalowski, P. (1978) 'The Neo-Sumerian silver ring texts', *Syro-Mesopotamian Studies* (Malibu) 2 (iii), 43–58.

——(1977) 'The death of Šulgi', *OrNS* 46, 220–25.

——(1982) 'Royal women of the Ur III period – Part III', *ASJ* 4, 129–42.

——(1983) 'History as charter: some observations on the Sumerian King List', *JAOS* 103, 237–48.

Michalowski, P. (1989) *The Lamentation over the Destruction of Sumer and Ur* (Winona Lake, Indiana).

Miglus, P. (1982) 'Die Stadttore in Assur – das Problem der Identifizierung', *ZA* 72, 266ff.

Millard, A.R. (1973) 'Cypriot copper in Babylonia, c. 1745 B.C.', *JCS* 25, 211–14.

——(1987) 'Cartography in the ancient Near East', in J.B. Harley and D. Woodward (eds), *Cartography in Prehistoric, Ancient, and Medieval Europe and the Mediterranean* (Chicago), 107–16.

Miller, R., McEwen, E., and Bergman, C. (1986) 'Experimental approaches to Near Eastern archery', *WA* 18, 178–95.

Moorey, P.R.S. (1971) 'The Loftus hoard of Old Babylonian tools from Tell Sifr in Iraq', *Iraq* 33, 61–86.

——(1978) *Kish Excavations 1923–1933* (Oxford).

——(1984) 'Where did they bury the kings of the IIIrd Dynasty of Ur?', *Iraq* 46, 1–18.

——(1985) *Metals and Metalwork, Glazed Materials and Glass* (Oxford: British Archaeological Reports, International Series 237).

——(1986) 'The emergence of the light, horse-drawn chariot in the Near East, c. 2000–1500 B.C.', *WA* 18, 196–215.

Moran, W.L. (1969) 'New evidence from Mari on the history of prophecy' *Biblica* (Rome) 50, 15–56.

Muffs, Y. (1969) *Studies in the Aramaic Legal Papyri from Elephantine* (Leiden).

Muhly, J. (1980–3) 'Kupfer B. Archäologisch', *RlA* 6, 348–64.

Munn-Rankin, J.M. (1956) 'Diplomacy in western Asia in the early second millennium B.C.', *Iraq* 18, 68–110.

Mustafa, M.A. (1949) 'Soundings at Tell al Dhiba'i', *Sumer* 5, 173–86.

Na'aman, N. (1984) 'Statements of time-spans by Babylonian and Assyrian kings and Mesopotamian chronology', *Iraq* 46, 115–23.

Neumann, H. (1979) 'Handel und Händler in der Zeit der III. Dynastie von Ur', *AOF* 6, 15–67.

——(1987) *Handwerk in Mesopotamien: Untersuchungen zu seiner Organisation in der Zeit der III. Dynastie von Ur* (E. Berlin: Schriften zur Geschichte und Kultur des alten Orients 19); cf. Limet 1988.

Nielsen, K. (1986) *Incense in Ancient Israel*. (Leiden: Supplement to Vetus Testamentum 38).

Nimkoff, M.F. (1965) *Comparative Family Systems* (Boston).

Nissen, H.J. (1975) 'Geographie', in Jacobsen Festschrift, 9–40.

——(1981) 'Bemerkungen zur Listenliteratur Vorderasiens im 3. Jahrtausend', in L. Cagni (ed.), *La lingua di Ebla* (Naples), 99–108.

——(1983) *Grundzüge einer Geschichte der Frühzeit des Vorderen Orients* (Darmstadt).

——(1988) *The Early History of the Ancient Near East, 9000–2000 B.C.* (Chicago/London: revised and translated version of Nissen 1983).

Nissen. H.J., Damerow, P. and Englund, R.K. (1990) *Frühe Schrift und Techniken der Wirtschaftsverwaltung im alten Vorderen Orient* (Berlin).

Nougayrol, J. (1959) 'Une Forme rare de "L'hommage au roi déifié"', *Analecta Biblica* (Rome) 12, 276–81.

Nützel, W. (1976) 'The climatic changes of Mesopotamia and bordering areas', *Sumer* 32, 11–24.

Oates, D. (1967) 'The excavations at Tell al Rimah, 1966', *Iraq* 29, 70–95.

——(1968) *Studies in the Ancient History of Northern Iraq* (London).

——(1985) 'Walled cities in Mesopotamia in the Mari period', *MARI* 4, 585–94.

——and Oates J. (1976) *The Rise of Civilization* (Oxford).

Oates, J. and Jasim, S.A. (1986) 'Early tokens and tablets in Mesopotamia: new information from Tell Abada and Tell Brak', *WA* 17, 348–62.

——, Davidson, T.E., Kamilli, D., and McKerrell, H. (1977) 'Seafaring merchants of Ur?', *Antiquity* 51, 221–34.

Oppenheim, A.L. (1948) *Catalogue of the Cuneiform Tablets of the Wilberforce Eames Babylonian Collection in the New York Public Library, Tablets of the Time of the Third Dynasty of Ur* (New Haven: American Oriental Series 62).

——(1954) 'The seafaring merchants of Ur', *JAOS* 74, 6–17.

——(1955) 'Siege-documents from Nippur', *Iraq* 17, 69–89.

——(1970) 'The cuneiform texts', in A.L. Oppenheim, R.H. Brill, D. Barag and A. von Saldern, *Glass and Glassmaking in Ancient Mesopotamia* (Corning: reprinted 1988), 4–101.

Owen, D.I. (1981) 'Of birds, eggs and turtles', *ZA* 71, 29–47.

Özgüç, T. (1986) *Kültepe-Kaniš II* (Ankara).

Page(-Dalley), S.M. (1970) 'Ice, offerings and deities in Old Babylonian Rimah', in A. Finet (ed.), 181–3.

Palaima, Th.G. (1988) 'The development of the Mycenaean writing system', in J.-P. Olivier and Th.G. Palaima (eds), *Texts, Tablets and Scribes: Studies in Mycenaean Epigraphy and Economy offered to Emmett L. Bennett, Jr.* (Salamanca), 269–342.

Parpola, S. (1988) 'Proto-Assyrian', in H. Hauptmann and H. Waetzoldt (eds.), *Wirtschaft und Gesellschaft von Ebla* (Heidelberg), 293–8.

Parrot, A. (1948) *Tello. Vingt campagnes de fouilles (1877–1933)* (Paris).

Pedersén, O. (1985) *Archives and Libraries in the City of Assur, I* (Uppsala).

Pemberton, W., Postgate, J.N., and Smyth, R.F. (1988) 'Canals and bunds, ancient and modern', *BSA* 4, 207–21.

Petschow, H.P.H. (1956) *Neubabylonisches Pfandrecht* (Berlin).

——(1976–80) 'Inzest', in *RlA* 5, 144–50.

——(1984) 'Die §§45 und 46 des Codex Hammurapi. Ein Beitrag zum altbabylonischen Bodenpachtrecht und zum Problem: Was ist der Codex Hammurapi?', *ZA* 74, 181–212.

Pettinato, G. (1972) 'Il commercio con l'estero della Mesopotamia meridionale nel 3 millennio av. Cr. alla luce dei fonti letterarie e lessicali sumeriche', *Mesopotamia* (Turin) 7, 43–166.

——(1977) 'Due testi inediti di agrimensura neosumerici e il problema delle qualità del suolo agricolo', *Rendiconti della Classe di Scienze morali, storichi e filologiche* (Rome: Accademia Nazionale dei Lincei) Serie VIII, vol. 32, 63–95.

Pettinato, G. with Grégoire, J.-P., Owen, D.I. and Waetzoldt, H. (1985) *Studi per il vocabolario sumerico 1/i: G. Reisner, Tempelurkunden aus Telloh* (Rome).

Pinches, T.G. (1908) *The Amherst Tablets* (London).

Postgate, J.N. (1974) 'Some remarks on conditions in the Assyrian countryside', *JESHO* 17, 225–43.

——(1976) *Fifty Neo-Assyrian Legal Documents* (Warminster).

——(1980a) 'Palm-trees, reeds and rushes in Iraq ancient and modern', in M.-Th. Barrelet (ed.), 99–109.

——(1980b) Review of H. Freydank (Vorderasiatische Schriftdenkmäler 21), *BiOr* 37, 67–70.

——(1983) *The West Mound Surface Clearance* (London: Abu Salabikh Excavations, vol. 1).

——(1984a) 'Processing of cereals in the cuneiform record', *BSA* 1, 103–13.

——(1984b) 'Cuneiform catalysis: the first information revolution', *Archaeological Review from Cambridge* 3, 4–18.

Postgate, J.N. (1984c) 'The historical geography of the Hamrin basin', *Sumer* 40, 149–59.

——(1986a) 'Administrative archives from the city of Assur in the Middle Assyrian period', in K.R. Veenhof (ed.), 168–83.

——(1986b) 'The equids of Sumer, again', in R.H. Meadow and H.-P. Uerpmann (eds), *Equids in the Ancient World* (Wiesbaden), 194–206.

——(1986c) 'The transition from Uruk to Early Dynastic: continuities and discontinuities in the record of settlement', in U. Finkbeiner and W. Röllig (eds), *Ğamdat Naṣr: Period or Regional Style?* (Wiesbaden).

——(1986d) 'Middle Assyrian tablets: the instruments of bureaucracy', *AOF* 13, 10–39.

——(1987) 'Notes on fruit in the cuneiform sources', *BSA* 3, 115–44.

——(1989) 'The ownership and exploitation of land in Assyria in the 1st millennium B.C.', in M. Lebeau and P. Talon (eds), *Reflets des deux fleuves: volume de mélanges offerts à André Finet* (Leuven), 141–52.

——(1990a) 'Excavations at Abu Salabikh, 1988–89', *Iraq* 52, 95–106.

——(1990b) 'Archaeology and the texts – bridging the gap', *ZA* 80, 228–40.

——(1990c) 'A Middle Tigris village', *BSA* 5, 65–4.

——(forthcoming) 'In search of the first empires', *BASOR* 1993/4.

——and Payne S. (1975) 'Some Old Babylonian shepherds and their flocks', *Journal of Semitic Studies* (Manchester) 20, 1–21.

Potts, D. T. (1984) 'On salt and salt gathering in ancient Mesopotamia', *JESHO* 27, 225–71.

Potts, D.T. (ed.) (1983) *Dilmun: New Studies in the Archaeology and Early History of Bahrain* (Berlin: Berliner Beiträge zum Vorderen Orient 2).

Potts, T.F. (1989) 'Foreign stone vessels of the late third millennium B.C. . . . .' *Iraq* 51, 123–64.

Powell, M.A. (1976) 'Evidence for local cults at presargonic Zabala', *OrNS* 45, 100–4.

——(1978a) 'A contribution to the history of money in Mesopotamia prior to the invention of coinage', in B. Hruška and G. Komoróczy (eds), *Festschrift Lubor Matouš* (Budapest; appeared 1981), 211–43.

——(1978b) 'Texts from the time of Lugalzagesi: problems and perspectives in their interpretation', *HUCA* 49, 1–58.

——(1981) 'Three problems in the history of cuneiform writing: origins, direction of script, literacy', *Visible Language* (Cleveland) 15 (iv), 419–40.

——(1984) 'Late Babylonian surface mensuration', *AfO* 31, 32–66.

——(1985) 'Salt, seed, and yields in Sumerian agriculture. A critique of the theory of progressive salinization', *ZA* 75, 7–38.

——(1986) 'The economy of the extended family according to Sumerian sources', *Oikumene* (Budapest) 5, 9–14.

—— (ed.) (1987) *Labor in the Ancient Near East* (New Haven: American Oriental Series 68).

——(1988) 'Evidence for agriculture and waterworks in Babylonian mathematical texts', *BSA* 4, 161–72.

——(1989) 'Masse und Gewichte', *RlA* 7, 457ff.

——(1990) 'Identification and interpretation of long term price fluctuations in Babylonia: more on the history of money in Mesopotamia', *AOF* 17, 95–118

Poyck, A.P.G. (1962) 'Farm studies in Iraq', *Mededelingen van de Landbouwhogeschool te Wageningen, Nederland* (Wageningen) 62, 1–99.

Prang, E. (1976) 'Das Archiv von Imgua', *ZA* 66, 1–44.

——(1980) 'Sonderbestimmungen in altbabylonischen Erbteilungsurkunden aus Nippur', *ZA* 70, 36–51.

Pritchard, J.B. (ed.) (1969) *Ancient Near Eastern Texts relating to the Old Testament* (3rd edn: Princeton).

Ratnagar, S. (1981) *Encounters: The Westerly Trade of the Harappa Civilization* (Delhi/Oxford).

Ray, J.D. (1986) 'The emergence of writing in Egypt', *WA* 17, 307–16.

Redman, C.L. (1978) *The Rise of Civilization* (San Francisco).

Reiner, E. (1966) *A linguistic analysis of Akkadian* (The Hague).

——(1986) 'Why do you cuss me?', *Proceedings of the American Philosophical Society* 130, 1–6.

Reisman, D. (1973) 'Iddin-Dagan's sacred marriage hymn', *JCS* 25, 185–202.

Reiter, K. (1989) *NABU* 4, no. 107.

Renfrew, A.C. (1977) in F. Hole, *Studies in the Archaeological History of the Deh Luran Plain* (Ann Arbor), 289–311.

——and Cherry, J.F. (eds.) (1986) *Peer Polity Interaction and Socio-political Change* (Cambridge).

Renger, J. (1967) 'Untersuchungen zum Priestertum in der altbabylonischen Zeit, 1. Teil', *ZA* 58, 110–88.

——(1969) 'Untersuchungen zum Priestertum der altbabylonischen Zeit, 2. Teil', *ZA* 59, 104–230.

——(1972) 'Flucht als soziales Problem in der altbabylonischen Gesellschaft', in D.O. Edzard (ed.), 167–82.

——(1973a) 'Who are all those people?', *OrNS* 42, 259–73.

——(1973b) '*mārat ilim*: Exogamie bei den semitischen Nomaden des 2. Jahrtausends', *AfO* 24, 103–7.

——(1975) 'Heilige Hochzeit, A. Philologisch', *RlA* 4, 251–9.

——(1976) 'Inthronisation', in *RlA* 5, 127–36.

——(1977) 'Legal aspects of sealing in ancient Mesopotamia', in McG. Gibson and R.D. Biggs (eds), 75–88.

——(1984) 'Patterns of non-institutional trade . . .', in A. Archi (ed.), *Circulation of Goods in a Non-palatial Context in the Ancient Near East* (Incunabula Graeca 82), 31–123

——(1987) 'Das Privateigentum an der Feldflur in der altbabylonischen Zeit', in B. Brentjes (ed.) 1987, 49–67.

——(1990) 'Report on the implications of employing draught animals', *BSA* 5, 267–79.

Rmaidh, S.S. (1984) 'Tell es-Sleimeh', *Sumer* 40, 43–54 (Arabic) and 57–8 (English).

Robertson, J.F. (1981) 'Redistributive economies in Ancient Mesopotamian society: a case study from Isin-Larsa period Nippur' (Ph.D. Dissertation, University of Pennsylvania: Ann Arbor, University Microfilms).

Röllig, W. (1975–6) 'Der altmesopotamische Markt', *WdO* 8, 286–95.

Römer, W.H.Ph. (1965) *Sumerische Königshymnen der Isin-Zeit* (Leiden).

——(1970) 'Königshymnen der Isinzeit und Königsinvestitur', *Zeitschrift der Deutschen Morgenländischen Gesellschaft, Supplement 1* (Wiesbaden), 130ff.

Rouault, O. (1977) *Mukannišum. L'administration et l'économie palatiales à Mari* (Paris: Archives Royales de Mari 18).

Rowton, M.B. (1973) 'Autonomy and nomadism in Western Asia', *OrNS* 42, 247–58.

——(1976) 'Dimorphic structure and topology', *Oriens Antiquus* (Rome) 15, 17–31.

——(1982) 'Sumer's strategic periphery in topological perspective', in Kraus Festschrift, 318–25.

Safar, F., Mustafa, M.A., and Lloyd, S. (1981) *Eridu* (Baghdad).

Salim, S.M. (1962) *Marsh Dwellers of the Euphrates Delta* (London: Monographs on Social Anthropology 23).

Salonen, A. (1968) *Agricultura Mesopotamica* (Helsinki).

Sanati-Müller, S. (1988) 'Texte aus dem Sinkašid-Palast. Erster Teil: Gerstenwerkverträge und Mehllieferungsurkunden', BaghMit 19, 471–538.

Sanlaville, P. (1985) 'L'Espace géographique de Mari', *MARI* 4, 15–25.

San Nicolò, M. (1922) *Die Schlussklauseln der altbabylonische Kauf- und Tauschverträge* (Munich: Münchener Beiträge zur Papyrusforschung 4).

——(1948) 'Haben die Babylonier Wachstafeln als Schriftträger gekannt?', OrNS 17, 59–70.

Sasson, J.M. (1969) *The Military Establishments at Mari* (Rome: Studia Pohl 3).

——(1972) 'Some comments on archive keeping at Mari', *Iraq* 34, 55–67.

——(1977) 'Treatment of criminals at Mari', *JESHO* 20, 90–113.

——(1987) *NABU* 1987/4, 63–4.

Sauren, H. (1969) 'Besuchsfahrten der Götter in Sumer', OrNS 38, 214–36.

——(1970) 'Les Fêtes néo-sumériens et leur périodicité', in A. Finet (ed.) 11–29.

Scheil, V. (1900) *Textes élamites-sémitiques, Première Série* (Paris: MDP 2).

——(1930) *Actes juridiques susiens* (Paris: Mémoires de la Mission Archéologique en Perse 22).

Schmandt-Besserat, D. (1981) 'From tokens to tablets', *Visible Language* (Cleveland) 15, 321–44.

——(1988) 'Tokens at Uruk', BaghMit 19, 1–175.

Schneider, A. (1920) *Die Anfänge der Kulturwirtschaft: Die sumerische Tempelstadt* (Essen).

Schneider, N. (1925) 'Der Götterkult 1. Teil', *Orientalia* (Series Prior) 18, 1–101.

——(1940) 'Die Urkundenbehälter von Ur III und ihre archivalische Systematik', OrNS 9, 1–16.

Schorr, M. (1913) *Urkunden des altbabylonischen Zivil- und Prozessrechts* (Leipzig: Vorderasiatische Bibliothek 5).

Seidl, U. and Krecher, J. (1957–71) 'Göttersymbole', RlA 3, 483–98.

Sigrist, M. (1977a) 'Offrandes dans le Temple de Nusku à Nippur', JCS 29, 169–83.

——(1977b) 'Les Fêtes eš-èš à l'époque néo-sumérienne', *Revue Biblique* (Paris) 84, 375–92.

——(1979) 'Le Trésor de Dréhem', OrNS 48, 26–53.

——(1984) *Les* sattukku *dans l'Ešumeša durant la période d'Isin et Larsa* (Malibu: Bibliotheca Mesopotamica 11).

Silva Castillo, J. (ed.) (1981) *Nomads and Sedentary Peoples* (30th International Congress of Human Sciences in Asia and North Africa).

Sjöberg, A.W. (1965) 'Beiträge zum sumerischen Wörterbuch', in Landsberger Festschrift, 63–70.

——(1967) 'Zu einigen Verwandtschaftsbezeichnungen im sumerischen', in Falkenstein Festschrift, 201–31.

——(1972) 'Die göttliche Abstammung der sumerisch-babylonischen Herrscher', *Orientalia Suecana* (Uppsala) 21, 87–112.

——(1975) 'Der Examenstext A', ZA 64, 137–76.

——(1976) 'The Old Babylonian Eduba', in Jacobsen Festschrift, 159–79.

Sjöberg Festschrift (1989) H. Behrens, D. Loding and M.T.Roth (eds) *DUMU-E₂-DUB-BA-A: Studies in Honor of Åke W. Sjöberg* (Philadelphia).

Sjöberg, A.W. and Bergmann, E. (1969) *The Collection of the Sumerian Temple Hymns* (New York: Texts from Cuneiform Sources 3).

Snell, D.C. (1982) *Ledgers and Prices: Early Mesopotamian Merchant Accounts* (New Haven/London: Yale Near Eastern Researches 8).

Sollberger, E. (1953) 'Remarks on Ibbi-Sin's reign', JCS 7, 48–50.

——(1954–6) 'Sur la chronologie des rois d'Ur et quelques problèmes connexes', *AfO* 17, 10–48.

——(1956) 'Selected texts from American collections', *JCS* 10, 11–31.

——(1957–8) 'A propos des échanges de cadeaux', *AfO* 18, 51.

——(1965) *Royal Inscriptions, Part II* (London/Philadelphia: Ur Excavations Texts 8).

——and Kupper, J.-R. (1971) *Inscriptions royales sumériennes et akkadiennes* (Paris).

Spaey, J. (1990) 'Some notes on KÙ.BABBAR/Nēbih Kezēr(t)i(m)', *Akkadica* (Brussels), 67, 1–9.

Speiser, E.A. (1935) *Excavations at Tepe Gawra, I: Levels I–VIII* (Philadelphia).

Spycket, A. (1968) *Les Statues de culte dans les textes mésopotamiens des origines à la 1re Dynastie de Babylone* (Paris).

Steele, F.R. (1948) 'The code of Lipit-Ishtar', *AJA* 52, 3–28.

Steinkeller, P. (1977) 'Seal practice in the Ur III period', in McG. Gibson and R.D. Biggs (eds) 1977, 41–53.

——(1981a) 'More on the Ur III royal wives', *ASJ* 3, 77–92.

——(1981b) 'The renting of fields in early Mesopotamia and the development of the concept of "interest" in Sumerian', *JESHO* 24, 113–45.

——(1982) 'The question of Marhaši . . .', *ZA* 72, 237–65.

——(1987a) 'Grundeigentum in Babylonien von Uruk IV bis zur früh-dynastischen Periode II', in B. Brentjes (ed.), 11–27.

——(1987b) 'The administrative and economic organization of the Ur III state: the core and the periphery', in R.D. Biggs and McG. Gibson (eds), *The Organization of Power: Aspects of Bureaucracy in the Ancient Near East* (Chicago: Studies in Ancient Oriental Civilization, 46), 19–42.

——(1987c) 'Battering rams and siege engines at Ebla' *NABU* 14.

——(1988a) 'The date of Gudea and his dynasty', *JCS* 40, 47–53.

——(1988b) 'Notes on the irrigation system in third millennium southern Babylonia', *BSA* 4, 73–92.

——(1988c) 'On the identity of the toponym LÚ.SU(.A)', *JAOS* 108, 197–202.

——(1989a) 'Sale Documents of the Ur III Period' (Wiesbaden: Freiburger Altorientalische Studien 17).

——(1989b) 'Studies in third millennium palaeography 3: sign DARA₄', *Studi epigrafici e linguistici* (Rome) 6, 3–7.

——(1991) *Third Millennium Legal and Administrative Texts in the Iraq Museum, Baghdad* (Winona Lake, Indiana: forthcoming).

Stol, M. (1976) *Studies in Old Babylonian History* (Istanbul/Leiden).

——(1977–8) 'A contract for hoeing a field', *Jaarbericht Ex Oriente Lux* (Leiden) 25, 50–5.

——(1979) *On Trees, Mountains and Millstones in the Ancient Near East* (Leiden).

——(1981) *Letters from Yale* (Leiden: Altbabylonische Briefe 9).

——(1982) 'State and private business in the land of Larsa', *JCS* 34, 127–230.

——(1983) 'Leder(industrie)', *RlA* 6, 527–43.

Stone, E.C. (1977) 'Economic crisis and social upheaval in Old Babylonian Nippur', in Levine and Young (eds) 1977, 267–89.

——(1982) 'The social role of the nadītu woman in Old Babylonian Nippur', *JESHO* 25, 50–70.

——(1987) *Nippur Neighborhoods* (Chicago: Studies in Ancient Oriental Civilization 44).

——(1990) 'The Tell Abu Duwari project, Iraq, 1987', *Journal of Field Archaeology* 17, 141–62.

Stone, E.C. and Zimansky, P. (1989) 'Maškan-šāpir identified', in *Mār Šipri: Newsletter of the Committee on Mesopotamian Civilization* 2 (Boston), 1–2.

Strommenger, E. (1980) *Habuba Kabira: eine Stadt vor 5000 Jahren* (Mainz).

Strommenger, E. and Hirmer, M. (1964) *The Art of Mesopotamia* (London).

Sumner, W. (1979) 'Estimating population by analogy: an example', in C. Kramer (ed.), *Ethnoarchaeology: Implications of Ethnography for Archaeology*, 164–74.

Thureau-Dangin, F. (1903) *Recueil de tablettes chaldéennes* (Paris).

——(1912a) *Une Relation de la huitième campagne de Sargon (714 av. J.-C.)* (Paris: Textes cunéiformes du Louvre 3).

——(1912b) 'Notes assyriologiques: XVI. Un jugement sous le règne de Samsu-iluna', RA 9, 21–4.

——(1932) 'La Ville ennemie de Marduk', *RA* 29, 109–19.

——(1939) 'Sur des étiquettes de paniers à tablettes provenant de Mari', in Koschaker Festschrift, 119–20.

Townsend, C.C. and Guest, E. (1974) *Flora of Iraq, Vol. 3: Leguminales* (Baghdad).

——(1985) *Flora of Iraq, Vol. 8: Monocotyledones* (Baghdad).

Tsukimoto, A. (1985) *Untersuchungen zur Totenpflege (kispum) im alten Mesopotamien* (Neukirchen-Vluyn: Alter Orient und Altes Testament 216).

Uchitel, A. (1984) 'Daily work at the Sagdana millhouse', *ASJ* 6, 75–98.

Ungnad, A. (1938) 'Datenlisten', *RlA* 2, 131–95.

——(1939) 'Die Formulare für die altbabylonische Personenmiete', Koschaker Festschrift, 96–101.

van Buren, E.D. (1945) *Symbols of the Gods in Mesopotamian Art* (Rome: Analecta Orientalia 23).

van de Mieroop, M. (1987) *Crafts in the Early Isin Period* (Leuven).

——(1989) 'Gifts and tithes to the temples in Ur', Sjöberg Festschrift, 397–401.

van Dijk, J.J. (1967) 'VAT 8382: ein zweisprächiges Königsritual', in Falkenstein Festschrift, 233–68.

——(1973) 'Un Rituel de purification des armes et de l'armée', in Böhl Festschrift, 107–17.

——(1978) 'Isbi'erra, Kindattu, l'homme d'Elam, et la chute de la ville d'Ur', JCS 30, 189–208.

van Driel, G. (1983) 'Seals and sealings from Jebel Aruda 1974–1978', *Akkadica* 33, 34–62.

——(1988) 'Neo-Babylonian agriculture', *BSA* 5, 121–59.

van Lerberghe, K. (1982) 'L'arrachement de l'emblème *šurinnum*', in Kraus Festschrift, 245–57.

van Stiphout, H.L.J. (1979) 'How did they learn Sumerian?', *JCS* 31, 118–26.

van Zeist, W. and Bottema, S. (1982) 'Vegetational history of the Eastern Mediterranean and the Near East during the last 20,000 years', in Bintliff and van Zeist, 277–322.

Veenhof, K.R. (1972) *Aspects of Old Assyrian Trade and its Terminology* (Leiden).

——(1973) 'An Old Babylonian purchase of land . . .', in Böhl Festschrift, 359–79.

——(1976) 'The dissolution of an Old Babylonian marriage according to CT 45, 86', *RA* 70, 153–64.

——(1977) 'Some social effects of Old Assyrian trade', *Iraq* 39, 109–18.

——(1985) 'Eponyms of the 'Later Old Assyrian period' and Mari chronology', *MARI* 4, 191–218.

——(1988) 'Prices and trade: the Old Assyrian evidence', *AOF* 15, 243–63.

——(ed.) (1986) *Cuneiform Archives and Libraries*: (Leiden: XXXe Rencontre Assyriologique Internationale).

Villard, P. (1986) 'Un Roi de Mari à Ugarit', *Ugaritforschungen* (Neukirchen-Vluyn) 18, 387–412.

Vogel, K. (1959) *Vorgriechische Mathematik, Teil II* (Paderborn: Mathematische Studienhefte, Heft 2).

von Schuler, E. (1967) 'Eine neue Inschrift Šulgis', *Berliner Jahrbuch für Vorgeschichte* (Berlin) 7, 293–5.

Waetzoldt, H. (1971) 'Zwei unveröffentlichte Ur-III-Texte über die Herstellung von Tongefässen', *WdO* 6, 7–41.

——(1972) *Untersuchungen zur neusumerischen Textilindustrie* (Rome).

——(1980–3) 'Leinen. (Flachs)', *RlA* 6, 583–94.

——(1981a) 'Zur Terminologie der Metalle in den Texten aus Ebla', in L. Cagni (ed.), *La lingua di Ebla* (Naples), 363–78.

——(1981b) 'Zu den Strandverschiebungen am Persischen Golf und den Bezeichnungen der Ḫors', in J. Schäfer and W. Simon (eds), *Strandverschiebungen in ihrer Bedeutung für Geowissenschaften und Archäologie*, 159–84.

——(1984) ' "Diplomaten", Boten, Kaufleute und Verwandtes in Ebla', in L. Cagni (ed.), *Il bilinguismo a Ebla* (Naples), 405–37.

——(1985) 'Ölpflanzen und Pflanzenöle im 3. Jahrtausend', *BSA* 2, 77–96.

——(1986a) 'Keilschrift und Schulen in Mesopotamien und Ebla', in L. Kriss-Rettenbeck and M. Liedtke (eds), *Erziehungs- und Unterrichtsmethoden im historischen Wandel* (Bad Heilbrunn), 36–50.

——(1986b) 'Ein altbabylonischer Schultext und zwei Wirtschaftstexte aus dem Vorderasiatischen Museum', *AOF* 13, 3–9.

——(1987) 'Compensation of craft workers and officials in the Ur III period', in M.A. Powell (ed.), 117–41.

——(1988a) 'Die Situation der Frauen und Kinder anhand ihrer Einkommensverhaltnisse zur Zeit der III. Dynastie von Ur', *AOF* 15, 30–44.

——(1988b) 'Die Entwicklung der Naturwissenschaften und des Naturwissenschaftlichen Unterrichts in Mesopotamien', in J.G. Prinz von Hohenzollern and M. Liedtke (eds), *Naturwissenschaftlicher Unterricht und Wissenskumulation*, 31–49.

——(1989) 'Der Schreiber als Lehrer in Mesopotamien', in J.G. Prinz von Hohenzollern and M. Liedtke (eds), *Schreiber, Magister, Lehrer: zur Geschichte und Funktion eines Berufstandes* (Bad Heilbrunn), 33–50.

——(1990) 'Zu den Bewässerungseinrichtungen in der Provinz Umma', *BSA* 5, 1–29.

Walker, C.B.F. (1980) 'Some Assyrians at Sippar in the Old Babylonian period', *Anatolian Studies* (London) 30, 15–22.

——(1987) *Cuneiform* (London).

Walters, S.D. (1970a) *Water for Larsa: an Old Babylonian Archive Dealing with Irrigation* (New Haven: Yale Near Eastern Researches, 4).

——(1970b) 'The sorceress and her apprentice', *JCS* 23, 27–38.

Walther, A. (1917) *Das altbabylonische Gerichtswesen* (LSS 6 (iv–vi)).

Weadock, P.N. (1975) 'The *giparu* at Ur', *Iraq* 37, 101–28.

Weidner, E.F. (1952) 'Weisse Pferde im alten Orient', *BiOr* 9, 157–9.

——(1956) 'Hof- und Harem-Erlasse assyrischer Könige aus dem 2. Jahrtausend v.Chr.', *AfO* 17, 257–93.

Weisgerber, G. (ed.) (1981) 'Mehr als Kupfer in Oman: Ergebnisse der Expedition 1981', *Der Anschnitt: Zeitschrift für Kunst und Kultur im Bergbau* (Essen) 5–6, 174–263.

Weiss, H.P. (1977) 'Periodization, population and early state formation in Khuzistan', in L.D. Levine and T.C. Young, 347–69.

——(1986) 'The origins of Tell Leilan and the conquest of space in third millennium Mesopotamia', in H. Weiss (ed.), *The Origins of Cities in Dry-Farming Syria and Mesopotamia in the Third Millennium BC* (Guilford, Connecticut), 71–108.

——and Young, T.C. (1975) 'The merchants of Susa', *Iran* 13, 1–17.

Weitemeyer, M. (1955) *Babylonske og assyriske arkiver og biblioteker* (Copenhagen).

——(1962) *Some Aspects of the Hiring of Workers in the Sippar Region at the Time of Hammurabi* (Copenhagen).

354 EARLY MESOPOTAMIA

Westenholz, A. (1970) '*berūtum, damtum*, and Old Akkadian KI.GAL: burial of dead enemies in Ancient Mesopotamia', *AfO* 23, 27–31.

——(1975) *Literary and Lexical Texts and the Earliest Administrative Documents from Nippur* (Malibu: Bibliotheca Mesopotamica 1).

——(1977) 'Diplomatic and commercial aspects of temple offerings ...', *Iraq* 39, 19–21.

——(1979) 'The Old Akkadian empire in contemporary opinion', in M.T. Larsen (ed.) *Power and Propaganda: A Symposium on Ancient Empires* (Copenhagen: Mesopotamia 7), 107–23.

——(1984) review in *AfO* 31, 80 n. 14.

——(1987) *Old Sumerian and Old Akkadian texts in Philadelphia, Pt. 2: The 'Akkadian' Texts, the Enlilemaba Texts, and the Onion Archive* (Copenhagen: Carsten Niebuhr Institute Publication 3).

Whiting, R. (1976) 'Tiš-atal of Nineveh and Babati, uncle of Šu-Sin', *JCS* 28, 173–82.

——(1987) *Old Babylonian Letters from Tell Asmar* (Chicago: AS 22).

Wilcke, C. (1969a) 'ku-li', *ZA* 59, 65–99.

——(1969b) 'Zur Geschichte der Amurriter in der Ur-III-Zeit', *WdO* 5, 1–31.

——(1969c) *Das Lugalbandaepos* (Wiesbaden).

——(1972) 'Der aktuelle Bezug der Sammlung der sumerischen Tempelhymnen und ein Fragment eines Klageliedes', *ZA* 62, 35–61.

——(1973) 'Politische Opposition nach sumerischen Quellen: ...', in A. Finet (ed.), *La voix de l'opposition en Mésopotamie* (Brussels: Institut des Hautes Etudes), 37–65.

——(1974) 'Zum Königtum in der Ur III-Zeit', in P. Garelli (ed.), 177–232.

——(1982) 'Exkurs A: nudunnûm und nišītum', in Kraus Festschrift, 440–50.

——(1983) 'Ein Gebet an den Mondgott vom 3. IV. des Jahres Ammiditana 33', *ZA* 73, 49–54, and 'Ein Vertrag über Personenmiete', ibid. 54–6.

——(1985) 'Familiengründung im alten Babylonien', in E.W. Müller (ed.), *Geschlechtsreife und Legitimation zur Zeugung*, 213–317.

——(1987) 'Die Inschriften der 7. und 8. Kampagnen (1983 und 1984)', in B. Hrouda (ed.), *Isin-Išān Bahriyāt III* (Munich), 83–120.

Wilhelm, G. (1989) *The Hurrians* (with a chapter by Diana L. Stein) (Warminster).

Wirth, E. (1971) *Syrien: eine geographische Landeskunde* (Darmstadt).

Woolley, C.L. (1934) *The Royal Cemetery* (London/Philadelphia: Ur Excavations, 2).

——(1955) *The Early Periods* (London/Philadelphia: Ur Excavations, 4).

——and Mallowan, M.E.L. (1976) *The Old Babylonian Period* (London/Philadelphia: Ur Excavations, 7).

——and Moorey, P.R.S. (1982) *Ur 'of the Chaldees'* (rev. edn: London).

Wright, H.T. (1969) *The Administration of Rural Production in an Early Mesopotamian Town* (Ann Arbor: University of Michigan Museum of Anthropology, Anthropological Papers no. 38).

——(1977) 'Recent research on the origin of the state', *American Review of Anthroplogy* 6, 379–97.

Yadin, Y. (1963) *The Art of Warfare in Biblical Lands* (London).

Yang, Lien-sheng (1952) *Money and Credit in China: A Short History* (Cambridge, Mass.).

Yaron, R. (1965) 'The rejected bridegroom', *OrNS* 34, 23–9.

——(1969) *The Laws of Eshunna* (Jerusalem).

Yener, A. and Özbal, H. (1987) 'Tin in the Turkish mountains: the Bolkardağ mining district', *Antiquity* 61, 220–6.

Yıldız, F. (1981) 'A tablet of Codex Ur-Nammu from Sippar', *OrNS* 50, 87–97.

Yoffee, N. (1977) *The Economic Role of the Crown in the Old Babylonian Period* (Malibu: Bibliotheca Mesopotamica 5).

——(1989) ' "Outsiders" in Mesopotamia' (in Russian), *Vestnik Drevnii Istorii* (Moscow) ii, 95–100.

Zaccagnini, C. (1983a) 'On gift exchange in the Old Babylonian period', in O. Carruba *et al.* (eds), *Studi orientalistici in ricordo di Franco Pintore*, (Pavia), 189–253.

——(1983b) 'Patterns of mobility among ancient Near Eastern craftsmen', *JNES* 42, 245–64.

Zhi, Yang (1989) 'The excavation of Adab', *Journal of Ancient Civilizations* (Northeast Normal University, Changchun), 3, 1–21.

Index

Note: Figures in bold refer to the principal passage relating to the entry, or, for toponyms, to a map or, for rulers, to a chronological table. Names of deities are preceded by an asterisk (*). See pages 365–7 for indexes of Sumerian and Akkadian words.

Sumerian words